HER WORSHIP:
HAZEL MCCALLION AND THE
DEVELOPMENT OF MISSISSAUGA

Mississauga is Canada's sixth largest city and its largest suburban municipality. Toronto's upstart western neighbour – with its multicultural population of more than 700,000 – is a place not only of endless subdivisions and monotonous industrial-commercial parks, wide thoroughfares, and even wider expressways, but also of some distinctive older communities, notable lakefront and riverside parks, and occasionally bold architecture. Hazel McCallion, Mississauga's octogenarian mayor, is a national celebrity and a municipal icon. Head of the city council since 1978, she holds a position with limited formal authority but remains the virtually undisputed – and often feared – leader of this sprawling city.

The first full-length study of McCallion's politics and the development of Mississauga, *Her Worship* examines the mayor's shrewd pragmatism and calculated populism. Tom Urbaniak argues that McCallion's executive skills and dynamic personality only partially explain her dominant and pre-emptive political position. He points also to key historical and geographical factors that contributed to a kind of civic stability – but also to curtailed public engagement and missed opportunities – in a place that had once been fraught with political rivalry and heated conflicts over future growth. A fascinating account both of a remarkable public figure and of an area that is emblematic of 'edge city' development in North America, *Her Worship* is a fresh look at municipal governance and politics in rapidly growing communities.

TOM URBANIAK is a political scientist at Cape Breton University.

TOM URBANIAK

Her Worship

Hazel McCallion and the Development of Mississauga

UNIVERSITY OF TORONTO PRESS
Toronto Buffalo London

© University of Toronto Press Incorporated 2009
Toronto Buffalo London
www.utppublishing.com
Printed in Canada

ISBN 978-0-8020-9902-0 (cloth)
ISBN 978-0-8020-9602-9 (paper)

Printed on acid-free paper

Library and Archives Canada Cataloguing in Publication

Urbaniak, Tom, 1976–
Her Worship : Hazel McCallion and the development of
Mississauga / Tom Urbaniak.

Includes bibliographical references and index.
ISBN 978-0-8020-9902-0 (bound). – ISBN 978-0-8020-9602-9 (pbk.)

1. McCallion, Hazel, 1921–.   2. Misissauga (Ont.) – Politics and
government.   3. Mississauga (Ont.) – History.   4. Mayors – Ontario –
Mississauga – Biography.   5. Mississauga (Ont.) – Biography.   I. Title.

FC3099.M57Z49 2008   971.3'535   C2008-906270-1

University of Toronto Press acknowledges the financial assistance to its
publishing program of the Canada Council for the Arts and the Ontario
Arts Council.

University of Toronto Press acknowledges the financial support for its
publishing activities of the Government of Canada through the Book
Publishing Industry Development Program (BPIDP).

Contents

HER WORSHIP:
HAZEL MCCALLION AND THE
DEVELOPMENT OF MISSISSAUGA

Introduction

'The pick-up truck is still in for repairs!'

So exclaimed Hazel McCallion as the meeting of the Mississauga city council was called to order on 19 February 2003.[1] Four days earlier, the then eighty-two-year-old McCallion, mayor of the sprawling municipality that she has come to personify, had been knocked to the ground by a turning vehicle while crossing at an intersection in her home neighbourhood of Streetsville. But after only two days in hospital, surrounded by cards and flowers from adoring constituents, the bandaged leader was back to her full schedule. In returning to service, she had bested the errant pick-up truck and its no doubt shocked and remorseful driver.

The Toronto media, usually strangers to in-depth coverage of Mississauga politics but often happy to seek out the eminently quotable and feisty mayor, ate up the story. So did the public. 'Hurricane Hazel,' the 'force of nature,' the 'mayor for life,' the 'people's mayor,' had done it again. It was another distinction for the reputedly fearless leader, who is often credited with building, almost literally from the ground up, an effectively run modern city while keeping spending in check, commanding obedience from municipal councillors, employees, and civic organizations, and instilling fear and respect in provincial and federal politicians.

Her critics – for most of her political career a small and hushed minority, but numbering among them residents who have been more active than most in the civic and non-profit sectors – have painted a more troubling picture. They have seen a 'take-no-prisoners' local dictator, an opportunistic populist, a Canadian Huey Long who has stifled legitimate and open debate, who ridicules the activists and 'special interests' who bother to surface, and who refuses to tolerate open criticism of her leadership. Although prepared to acknowledge McCallion's political savvy and her remarkable knowledge of detail, they have criticized her lack of compassion and her anti-intellectual rhetoric. Her very practicality and rather austere demeanour may, in their view, have sapped the energy from, or pre-empted, cultural initiatives and efforts to make the city's neighbourhoods, and especially its vast commercial districts, less repetitive and sterile. She has been unable, they claim, to fully come to terms with Mississauga's growing cultural diversity.

She is an enigmatic character. It is a cliché to say that about politicians, but in McCallion's case it is certainly true. She is regarded as fanatical about frugality – 'I spend the taxpayers' money the way I spend my own, which is seldom.' After yet another minor car accident, this one in April 2006 (and this one finally reported by the media), she at last agreed to accept a taxpayer-funded chauffeur – although she is often seen driving without one. (Nor is she hard to spot; her licence plate still says 'Mayor1.') She had previously insisted that a driver would be a waste of money. But she has been for some time the highest-paid mayor in Canada (making more even than her counterparts in Toronto and Montreal), a fact that has occasioned no controversy within the city. She admits to having 'no artistic bone in my body,'[2] but she has built great landmarks that have garnered national attention. Some of the new parks and trails in her city would surely have met with the approval of a Burnham or an Olmsted.

She has spared few efforts to recruit seasoned top bureaucrats, sometimes even poaching respected senior provincial public servants. (Without fail, they call her 'Madam Mayor,' even when referring to her in the third person. To everyone else, she is simply 'Hazel.') She has been extremely demanding of them, yet seldom has she challenged the elected members of her councils to perform their roles with much more than plodding, make-no-waves mediocrity. And those councillors have been consistently re-elected – even though most of them have indeed not made waves or laboured as ceaselessly as the tireless mayor. Being seen as a member of the McCallion team has had its benefits.

To what extent, then, has Hazel McCallion wielded the power and influence her boosters and critics have ascribed to her? And what personal characteristics have animated her? Should we focus only on personal characteristics? Is there something about the kind of city Mississauga is, and its stages or phases of physical development and political maturation, that have made it ripe for a leader like McCallion? What difference has McCallion's leadership made to the character and politics of Mississauga? What can other growing communities learn from the Mississauga experience? This book tries to answer these questions.

McCallion, a Gaspé native who is descended from Scots and from French Huguenots and who came of age during the Great Depression, has been mayor of Mississauga since 1978. She has held one municipal public office or another continuously since 1968. She was the mayor of the Town of Streetsville when that small municipality was forced in 1973 to merge into Mississauga, a merger she opposed for all to hear. The former newspaper editor and business manager for the engineering firm Canadian Kellogg has been acclaimed, or opposed only by fringe candidates, in all but one of her ten bids for re-election as Mississauga's mayor. Even in 1982, when former mayor Ronald Searle emerged to oppose her after the Divisional Court found that she had controlled a debate despite a conflict of interest, McCallion took 71 per cent of the vote. Since then she has released no campaign platform, and since 1991 she has mounted no campaign whatsoever. 'Her Town, Her Rules' is the title of one magazine article about McCallion;[3] it summarizes well the prevailing perception in Mississauga. And not just Mississauga: 'The truth is she's the only person in the province that scares the bejesus out of me,' mused former premier David Peterson.[4] He has not been alone.

'Her Town' is now Canada's sixth-largest city and the country's largest suburban municipality, population seven hundred thousand. Since World War II it has gone from being primarily rural and pastoral, Anglo and white, to being mostly built out, physically and architecturally sterile in many places but also multicultural and multiracial and, although relatively affluent in the aggregate, by no means socio-economically monolithic. An 'edge city' rather than a suburb in the old sense,[5] Mississauga is not a bedroom residential enclave, although it has countless single-use subdivisions with their crescents, cul-de-sacs, and protruding garages. The dramatic demographic and landscape changes have also been characterized by extensive, although relatively low-density, industrial and commercial development.

Has all this land development contributed in some way to the McCallion phenomenon or propped up the diminutive leader? Stop a Mississaugan in a parking lot – the typical one will not know much about local politics, will probably not have voted in the last local elections, but will grin at the mention of 'Hazel' and will even claim to have run into her at the hockey arena or the grocery store (she shops at a different one each week in order to meet her people). Our average citizen will attribute the Hazel magic to Hazel herself: she's a scrapper, as comfortable in the Legion hall as she is in the premier's office. She's outspoken. She's everywhere. She takes no nonsense. And as one of her idealistic but soon-to-be-disappointed young opponents said during the 1985 mayoral race, there may be some invisible psychological barrier to challenging her: 'She's like everybody's favourite grandmother.'[6]

This is true as far as it goes. But our parking-lot correspondent, if more reflective, might add that McCallion's popularity has been self-reinforcing, especially in an environment with weak local media. It's a paradigm, really. After her decisive and high-profile handling of the mass evacuation of Mississauga in November 1979 following the spectacular derailment of a chemical-filled Canadian Pacific train, the notion became as solid as concrete: Hazel is a leader who can scarcely do wrong.

Alas, the personality explanation seems incomplete. The Hazel fans who declare that she ought to have been prime minister or premier should stop to think about how she would have fared under endless scrutiny – in Question Period, in a scrum, with a steady stream of revelations of some scandal in government, with complex economic problems of global proportions, with entrenched interest groups. There would also probably have to be an entourage, a security detail, chauffeurs. There would be no more walking down the street unaccompanied ('our Hazel' – beholden to no one) in every parade.

And it is not just the qualitative difference between federal and provincial politics on the one hand and city politics on the other that is germane here. Would McCallion have lasted this long as mayor of Toronto – with its large council, its socialist wing, its incurable grandstanders, its big media, and its big unions? Would she or would she not have decided to march in the Gay Pride parade? On many issues, she would have made enemies.

Even a small town might have been more difficult to dominate. McCallion's own political c.v. offers some indication of this. Between 1970 and 1973 she was the popular mayor of Streetsville, but she was not the personification of Streetsville or even its single dominant force. The town of seven thousand was a mature little polity – people knew each other. (They also knew the other local politicians or political aspirants, so McCallion did not have a huge head start on name and face recognition.) They had an entrenched habit of actually turning out to vote in large numbers. They also had a habit of showing up at public meetings. They volunteered, and they served on the town's elaborate network of boards and committees. There were even recognized and persistent activists – environmentalists, preservationists, an effective organization representing the town's large Portuguese minority. As we shall see, McCallion thus had to accommodate herself to the middle-class progressives who were the power in Streetsville. True, she was still at an early stage in her political career and may therefore have simply lacked the craftiness to overshadow the others. But the evidence will show that she was already confident, feisty, and calculating. And she calculated that Streetsville was to be governed as a partnership; it could not be a sole proprietorship.

The Stars Align in Mississauga

Even Mississauga – or the Township of Toronto, as it was known before 1968 – had not always been ripe for pre-emptive, overriding leadership. Enter Mary Fix. In 1952 she was swept into office (first as deputy reeve, becoming the reeve two years later) at the head of an angry, almost spontaneous reform movement. Taxes had skyrocketed in large part because of scattered, poorly planned subdivisions and almost no industrial and commercial development to offset the residential.

Fix, whom we shall meet again in chapter 3, seemed to be the right person to fix things. She had been Ottawa's first woman lawyer. She had been a columnist for *Chatelaine*. She had been an executive with the T. Eaton Company. She was urbane, spoke French almost as well as English, and, as reeve, she would be asked to serve in prominent executive positions for national and provincial organizations that were representing municipalities.

True, there was some resistance to a strong woman in politics. This was the 1950s, after all. Fix herself, however, was convinced that most of her troubles were actually caused by vested interests that had serious problems with her development policies.

Fix managed to lower taxes, to restructure the administration of the municipality, to bring in – for the first time – seasoned professionals, some of them with national reputations. She travelled the world courting industrial development. Whether because of her efforts or not, there was major industrial development – by 1959 industrial/commercial had come to account for almost half of the local assessment, a figure not attained before or since.

But Mary Fix was never electorally secure. She was to sit on the sidelines in 1956 when Tom Jackson defeated her. She returned to her post the following year (terms were then for one year), but she faced strong challenges after that. She was finally defeated for good in late 1959.

The old guard, you see, was still breathing. Fix had little tolerance for the old families who had run the township since time immemorial, but those families could still command some loyalty. Even worse for her, perhaps, was her insistence on antagonizing the residential developers. She slapped unprecedented lot levies on them and declared that it would be many years before subdivisions ought even to be considered in huge swaths of the township. The developers ran crying to the province, and when they appeared to be close to convincing the minister of municipal affairs to overrule Fix, and when they launched lawsuits to recover the money that the township (and other municipalities that had imitated the township) had been collecting, she summoned them all to a meeting, slammed the door shut, and said, with all the gravity she could muster, that she would put a stop to all residential development if they refused to play her game. Grudgingly, they backed down – and bided their time until the next election.

Developers with bowler hats are not necessarily crowd favourites at election time, but Mary Fix was also making her own political base uneasy. She had stopped the tax increases, but she was in addition bringing some order to development. That meant that infrastructure could not be extended to the middle of nowhere to accommodate a subdivision or factory: development would have to be infill and contiguous. Any good planner or economist would tell you that. The only problem is that middle-class homeowners do not like development in their backyards. Mary Fix's opponents had something to go on.

They also had someone to go with. Lakeview merchant Robert Speck seemed affable and respectable. He was already on council and seemed capable of holding his own. And when he defeated Fix he would hold his own, but not as a lone crusader. Reeve Speck and his allies on council wanted to make some deals, especially with the bigger developers. Bring on the 'new towns' in the country. Get the developers to agree to install some of the infrastructure, and the municipality would get help from its friends in the provincial government. Taxes could be kept under control, most of the development could be 'greenfield' (meaning not in people's backyards), and the developers would not be trying to defeat the council.

This development regime lasted into the 1970s, but its stalwarts failed to notice that the population was again growing restless. 'Reform' was again in the air. Anti-developer activists were being elected in Toronto, and some of the ferment spilled across the border. Moreover, growth pressure in Mississauga was so intense that slapdash developments were again popping up in established areas. It was now noticed that the politicians were remarkably chummy with the big developers. 'How much is [Bruce] McLaughlin giving you?' a crusading young doctor demanded of Mayor Chic Murray, who had taken the helm following Speck's death in 1972.[7]

That young physician was Martin Dobkin. He came almost from nowhere to win the 1973 election for mayor. He had nothing that could be considered a well-organized coalition, but he ended up coming to office with a few friends: six of the ten members of the first council for the new *City* of Mississauga were labelled slow-growth 'reformists.'

As is often the case with inexperienced reformists, this new mayor lasted only one term. He had succeeded in discrediting the developer-friendly old guard – he even launched a judicial inquiry to expose the dirt he thought was there, only to have that inquiry shut down by the courts – but he could not withstand the backlash from the developers and the old-guard politicians. The poor neophyte was blamed for everything from high taxes to the endless conflict and shouting matches that now characterized the council meetings. 'It was like big city politics, it really was,' one former reporter told me.[8]

The reporters loved it, but enough of the public did not. Dobkin was replaced in 1976 by old-guard councillor Ron Searle, who made the mistake of interpreting his victory as a mandate for the resurrection of the old regime. That attempt only further discredited his kind. With the old guard and the reformers lying gravely wounded, a leadership vacuum had arisen. Into it stepped Hazel McCallion.

What a time it was to step in. The city-wide interest groups were weak. The developers were discredited. The public was yearning for stability. And most of the municipality was serviced (with water and sewer) for development. The local leaders need not be beholden to anyone.

Instead of trying to stop or radically slow development, why not allow the municipality to profit from it and keep the taxpayers happy? After all, the developers were vulnerable. They were vulnerable especially to the mayor's steep and precedent-setting development charges. When these took effect in 1982 they exceeded the city's authority under provincial legislation, but they were accepted (very reluctantly) by the developers. With virtually the whole land mass of the city serviced with the basic infrastructure, no developer or small groups of developers held monopolies or privileged positions with respect to land. The development charges were used to cover the capital costs for almost all new amenities, including 'soft' services such as recreation and libraries, and to create a formidable capital reserve.

The revenue growth and development-charges policies, in turn, resulted in acceptable tax increases (and sometimes decreases), a reputation for good fiscal management, and a steady supply of new amenities, thereby contributing to ratepayers' resounding satisfaction with their mayor. The mayor then used this popular support as a political resource to establish and fortify her pre-emptive position and to deflect, diffuse, or scatter any civic organizations or interest groups that had the potential to become politically threatening. We shall see this taking place across policy sectors – land-use planning, the arts, heritage, the environment, transportation – and in defining the agenda for relations with other governments.

The Coming Changes

It is possible now to predict that a sea change in Mississauga politics will soon occur, even if McCallion remains in office. The era of major 'greenfield' development is now nearly at an end; the 'suburban canvas' is almost exhausted. And a new reform/neighbourhood movement appears to be gaining momentum in many parts of the Greater Toronto Area, although it is still in its formative stages in Mississauga, likely because of overriding, pre-emptive mayoral leadership. But the dominant-individual type of mayoral leadership will soon be impossible. A close working alliance with residents' groups – what some social scientists call a 'middle-class progressive regime' – or with the business elite – a 'development regime' – may become a precondition for stable municipal governance.[9]

It is also therefore likely that were McCallion suddenly to leave the political scene a period of political conflict and instability – what political scientist Douglas Yates calls 'street-fighting pluralism' – would ensue.[10] Owing in part to the mayor's long-standing pre-emptive, overriding leadership, few established and effective interest groups would be available to mediate the various demands and pressures that might arise from those detecting an opportunity to make their issues and concerns, or their personal ambitions, a prominent part of some new agenda.

Thus this book will explore new frontiers in the study of Canadian politics: the effects of suburban planning and development on municipal leadership, and vice versa; the impact of rapid population growth on local democratic institutions; and the nature and durability of suburban reform movements. And of course we will dig below the surface of one of the country's best-known and longest-serving mayors.

We shall turn first to Hazel McCallion's road to the mayor's office.

1 The Road to 327 Queen

It would be impossible to find two places in Canada that stand in sharper contrast: upstart, teeming, young, fast-paced but aesthetically challenged Mississauga and the quiet, old, breathtakingly scenic, economically struggling hometown of Hazel McCallion. And yet the *ville natale* gave her some initial and valuable training.

On the south shore of the Gaspé Peninsula, on the Baie des Chaleurs, where the waters have already opened up to appear as a vast, endless ocean, sits the community of Port-Daniel – or rather the communities of Port-Daniel, for contiguous but distinctive settlements come into view here. There is Port-Daniel-Est, dominated by the spire of an impressive, stone Catholic church. This settlement has one of the few railway tunnels in Eastern Canada and the neoclassical LeGrand Hotel, now the headquarters of the town of Port-Daniel-Gascons. Here you'll find two pleasant sandy beaches and you will see a large cross commemorating the assumed landfall of Jacques Cartier in 1534.

On the largely Anglo western side of the harbour – the side young Hazel would come to know best – no spire dominates. Instead one finds some small fish plants, including the *poissonnerie* still run by Hazel's relatives, elegant Gothic Revival homes, and summer cottages along the Point Road leading to the now-deteriorating Port-Daniel lighthouse.

It is candy for the eyes, and it appeared that way to earlier eyes as well. One retired Ontario school principal who in the 1930s spent the summers of his youth in Port-Daniel wrote in his memoirs that he saw it as a magical place.[1] In 1940 the celebrated novelist Gabrielle Roy stumbled upon Port-Daniel, decided to board with a kindly older couple, and, despite her chronic loneliness, would for years find there the inspiration for her writing.[2]

Although the physical layout of these coastal settlements has not changed much in decades, and although the population remains stagnant at about eighteen hundred, the linguistic reality has changed. Walk into the town hall or a local store, and the language of communication is exclusively French. It was not always so. One, two, three generations ago, there were many more English speakers. Most of the businesses were run by the English. Their main church, St James Anglican, was well attended. It was common for people from the west side to speak no French. Now, the anglophones who remain – on increasingly marginal farms, in the economically precarious but still functioning fishery, in tourism, or the come-from-away retirees – almost all speak the language of common usage, the local version of the *langue de Molière*.

Despite the linguistic and religious divisions that were once so prevalent, the residents – French and English – refer to a 'Gaspésian character.' They speak of a strong sense of place, a phenomenon that is perhaps common in relatively isolated or detached coastal societies – Newfoundland, Cape Breton, Prince Edward Island, the Gaspé. The Gaspésian qualities are described as hardiness and independence. Internal conflicts and petty rivalries may be common, but the locals will express stubborn collective pride and stand as one against threats from the outside. Those who have left often long to be back, especially in old age. Hazel McCallion's own visits have been more frequent these last few years, as evidenced by the little guest register at the back of the sanctuary of St James.

From time to time she is joined by most of the Journeaux clan – from Ontario, Alberta, New Brunswick, Yukon, and elsewhere. In 2006, when I sat in on a gathering of twenty-five of them, I could not help but notice certain common physical features – especially the tightly constructed lips around which most of the facial wrinkles tend to be concentrated. Unlike others in the area, the Journeaux do not come across as melancholic. There is not a tendency to be almost forlorn in viewing the world. They seem outspoken but not brash, confident but not jovial.

When they visit St James, the Journeaux walk through the old cemetery. There lies the heritage of most of anglophone Port-Daniel – the Beebs, the Dows, the Joneses, and those members of the Journeaux clan (the majority) who dropped the 'x,' or had it dropped for them through continuous misspelling, in the nineteenth century after the first had emigrated from Jersey Island. The most recently erected monument in that cemetery – obviously a replacement for an older one – commemorates Herbert and Amanda Maud Journeaux (née Travers), Hazel's parents.

Amanda Maud, who was of Scottish lineage, had grown up a little west of Port-Daniel in the largely Anglo-Protestant community of Shigawake. Her father, James Urias, was listed variously as a mill owner and farmer. There may have been some concern that Amanda Maud would not survive more than a few days. Her birth and baptism, fifteen years into her parents' marriage, are not recorded in the parish register until two decades later, when a sworn statement was made saying that she had been born in New Carlisle (about thirty kilometres away) and baptized a few days later in that larger town.[3] In such instances it is reasonable to surmise that there had been complications with the pregnancy. Amanda Maud was the fifth child in her family. Mother Margaret McRae would have one more, Basil Claude, but she would not survive to see her grandchildren. She died in 1886, before Amanda Maud's tenth birthday, and just ten days after the death of her oldest and already-married daughter, Vienna.[4]

Herbert, son of John Francis Journeaux and Mary Dow, was the grandson of a Jersey Island émigré. As with many of the early Huguenots in the Gaspé, John Francis's father would likely have sojourned in the area for only a few months of each year, during fishing expeditions, before settling down permanently. Anglican clergy, including the famous George Jehosaphat Mountain, a future bishop, often found it necessary to preach to that generation in French. And even as they became anglicized, the readings would have initially been a problem for many. When one of John Francis's brothers was married in 1859, we learn that the mother, Elizabeth Ann neé Hall, could not sign as a witness because she did not write.[5] But all the children of the area were by then spending some time in school, and illiteracy would soon be rare in these parts.

As with most of his male fellow parishioners, John Francis would be described as a farmer. But he almost certainly would have been doing other trades as well. The town had a bustling port at the time. Its limestone was being shipped to the Prince Edward Island kilns of the Wheatley River Lime Company (by the time Hazel was born, the limestone was going mostly to the Chicoutimi Pulp Company).[6] And most of the people could count on a balanced diet. One itinerant church minister recorded in his diary in 1869 that 'in addition to the fishing, which is good, agriculture supplies the inhabitants with abundant produce and in Port Daniel there are several rich farmers.'[7]

Despite the losses in Amanda Maud's family, one notices in the registers that very few young children were dying in the nineteenth century. Were many deaths going unrecorded? Not likely, assures the Anglican diocesan archivist.[8] More than a few of the deceased were in their eighties. James Urias Travers died in 1923, in his ninetieth year. Could it have been the 'abundant produce'? Could it have had something to do with the climate? Conditions were variable, to be sure, but Port-Daniel was often blessed with glorious and comfortable summers. The St James Centennial Committee dug up an old Canadian Weather Office bulletin from 1869: 'The climate is so pure and healthy that disease is almost unknown, to such an extent even that the four or five physicians scattered amongst the 35,593 people who inhabit the counties of Gaspé and Bonaventure have great difficulty in living very quietly on the practice of their profession.'[9]

Herbert and Amanda Maud were married in 1906,[10] at a relatively old age by the standards of the time: he was twenty-seven and she was thirty, of exactly the same vintage that Hazel and her husband would be at their wedding.

Hazel Mary Muriel Journeaux was born on Valentine's Day, 1921. She would be the last of Herbert's and Amanda Maud's five offspring and the only one actually born in Port-Daniel West, in the home her parents had purchased a few years earlier. Two brothers and two sisters awaited her.

The family was by no means destitute, but an ethic of frugality dominated. They all congregated in that one-and-a-half-storey frame house, elegant yet unpretentious. Despite occasional shortages of certain provisions, the family always had enough food, much of it from the small farm that surrounded the house. Indeed, the dwelling itself was almost dwarfed by a huge barn. They certainly benefited from all that 'abundant produce.' There were plenty of vegetables, and there was fish, milk, and poultry. Hazel McCallion, the octogenarian mayor, speculates that her health and strong constitution may be attributed in part to a healthy childhood. 'There was no junk food.'

Hazel's mother was a talented piano player and a fixture at St James Anglican, the now sparsely attended place of worship. (Hazel is helping to sustain financially this little landmark, justly described as 'pretty and creditable' when it was erected in 1907.)[11] Amanda Maud Travers was one of the first trained nurses in Port-Daniel, having graduated in 1901. But the young Hazel, who in old age still reminisces fondly about her mother's beautiful voice, tended to gravitate more to her entrepreneurial father than to her arts-loving mother. The Depression forced Herb Journeaux to turn to his own family to keep the enterprise afloat. So Hazel, at age eleven or twelve, already found herself handling payroll, making disbursements from petty cash, and studying the books.

The family was churchgoing and active in the parish, but not profoundly religious. The mother was more devout than the father. There may have been prayers before bedtime, but no Bible readings or involved theological discussions. Both mother and father were on the Vestry of St James, and when special appeals were made the records show that the Journeaux were almost inevitably among the contributors.

Recreation was of the simple variety. Years later, Hazel McCallion would claim she had only two toys, one of which was a doll. Hazel would look back on her childhood and consider herself a 'tomboy.'[12] The youngsters with whom she associated – most of whom attended the same two-room school as Hazel – would frolic along the rugged coast. Sometimes they would give themselves shivers by pointing to the steep, hellishly named Cap à l'Enfer, where the limestone quarries were. They would tell stories of ghosts rising up from the shipwrecks in the Baie, especially the wreck of the *Colbourne*, which went down one terrible October night in 1838, claiming thirty-eight lives. They knew that some of the British barque's furniture and its sea chests had been retrieved to become local heirlooms,[13] and they would have wondered where other buried or sunken riches could be found. They would watch the waves crash near the little lighthouse.[14] It was not uncommon to run into strangers. Even before Hazel was born the place was being described as 'a charming summer resort.'[15] And locals and visitors alike loved one of the family dogs, the one belonging to sister Gwen. 'Byng' had even been trained to retrieve the mail.

The winters could be harsh – the old-timers swear the drifts and blizzards were much worse than they have been in recent years. But for many of the youngsters there was a beloved winter pastime: when she was just five years old, Hazel was taught how to skate. Her instructor was brother Lockhart, with whom she was always close while remaining aloof from the rivalries among the older siblings – and those siblings were at odds often, some locals remember. In fact, a few old neighbours recall (or recall second-hand) that the brothers fought constantly, more than would be normal, and continued to fight – even physically – into adulthood, an adulthood cut short for both of them because of separate car accidents. 'The Journeaux were rough and ready,' one childhood acquaintance remembers. 'But they were all characters.'[16]

Hazel eventually helped to organize a girls' hockey team, assigning to herself the role of tough and scrappy forward. Later, as a young adult living in Montreal, she would play 'professionally,' earning five dollars a game for the Montreal Kik Cola women's hockey team. She grew to stand not even five feet high, but she was fast and agile, and she found in the sport a certain gritty satisfaction.

Politics was a favourite topic of conversation around the Journeaux kitchen table. Father, brother Lockhart, and daughter Hazel dominated these conversations. The family was staunchly Conservative. Lockhart would go on to become the mayor of Port-Daniel West in 1945, serving with one interruption until 1955, and then briefly from 1963 until his sudden death in a car accident near Quebec City in 1964. He was on hand to inaugurate telephone service in 1947 and managed to extract other infrastructure benefits from Premier Maurice Duplessis by threatening to run provincially as an independent – and printing up signs to prove it. 'Hazel and Lockhart had the brains in the family,' eldest sister Linda recalled in 2001. 'And so it didn't surprise us when Hazel went into politics.'[17]

Port-Daniel had no high school. Many of those wishing to pursue an education beyond grade nine went to Quebec City. At age sixteen, therefore, Hazel Journeaux left home, briefly to St John's outside Montreal and then to Commissioner's High School in Quebec City. With the exception of vacations, she would never return to live in the Gaspé. It was a difficult adjustment. A friend remembered Hazel as 'one of the shyest girls I had ever met.'[18]

Hazel would complete her junior matriculation (grade eleven) in Quebec City before moving on to Montreal. Her father had hoped she would pursue a degree in economics and return to run the family business, but money remained scarce. So Hazel enrolled in the Congregation of Notre Dame's secretarial college, in the old Mother House, now the site of Dawson College. She studied business-letter writing, office organization, clear communication, and some of the principles of management. Some of her surviving correspondence from young adulthood shows the crisp, pithy, logically sequenced, generally grammatically sound but by no means elegant style of writing that would be her hallmark as a politician.[19]

The head of the school was extremely strict, but she was also a tough negotiator on behalf of her students, not hesitating to speak with anger to senior men of business. She made sure her charges received good placements and good working conditions.

An initial placement for Hazel did not work. Signed on to help run an office for the Quebec North Shore Paper Company, she could not stand the loneliness and remoteness of a tough industry town. 'That was no place for a young woman.' She returned to the frown and sympathy of Sister St Catherine of Palma.[20]

Finding new employment was relatively easy. Many of the men were off to war, the Depression was over, and there suddenly was an urgent need to develop Canada's industrial capacity. Canadian Kellogg was an engineering company focused on designing and building industrial facilities. Hazel Journeaux was sent to be the office manager in downtown Toronto. It was an early taste of power. Her nominal superiors were usually too busy to micro-manage her – and, besides, she quickly won their trust as someone who did the work without complaining and who would try to resolve problems on her own rather than running up the ladder. With the war still on, the company – often in the person of the young Hazel Journeaux – was given quasi-public authority to commandeer plants for public service. Hazel was often sent to New York to negotiate with head office on behalf of the Canadian branch. She recalls trying to enlist in the 'Wrens' (Women's Royal Canadian Naval Service), but says her superiors had the offer rescinded. She was needed for 'essential' wartime work at Kellogg.

Before long, Hazel was helping to coordinate Kellogg's significant part in the design and construction of Canada's first synthetic petroleum-based rubber factory. The Crown-owned Polymer Corporation was pressed into service in Sarnia, fed by a pipeline from Alberta, to compensate for the near collapse of Asian sources resulting from World War II. And compensate it did; by the end of the war this marvel of engineering – a project that took shape in only two years, while keeping C.D. Howe awake at night – was producing 90 per cent of Canada's supply. The urgency with which Kellogg's work had to be completed is apparent in the contracts. 'Canadian Kellogg agrees to do all things necessary to procure and deliver ...' 'Canadian Kellogg shall perform or cause to be performed all services necessary (including the preparation and filing of all necessary governmental forms) to expedite the shipment of such materials and equipment ...' 'Canadian Kellogg agrees that it will with all reasonable speed and dispatch prepare purchase requisitions and place purchase orders for the materials and equipment ...'[21]

There was enough here also to keep the young Hazel Journeaux awake at night. Many of those requisitions, many of those purchase orders, and the need for urgency became her direct concern.

The Sarnia operations 'kept Canada in the war,' one historian has concluded.[22] Journeaux's experience there would lead to other big projects. In the 1950s, she would even play a critical role in developing the 'Four Sisters' generating station in Lakeview. (A half-century later, as mayor of Mississauga, she would preside at the demolition of the

four huge stacks that had dominated the skyline of southeast Mississauga.)

The Anglican Young People's Association

While in her twenties, Hazel Journeaux devoted most of her non-remu-
nerated hours to the Anglican Young People's Association. Before she
moved from Montreal, her contacts had helped find for her a sturdy
home on Toronto's Oakwood Avenue, where she could board with an
empty-nest couple who became like second parents. Straddling Toronto's boundary with the Borough of York, the community of Wych-
wood-Oakwood would then have been called a suburb; most of its
construction had taken place within the previous thirty years. But it was
a streetcar suburb, where shops jostled with homes and apartments,
and where the middle class and the working class lived in close proximity.

Journeaux started attending St Michael and All Angels Anglican
Church. It was then a large and growing parish, with eleven hundred
families. The dynamic minister, George Boyd Snell, who would go on
to serve as the eighth bishop of Toronto (1966–72), was then in his mid-
thirties, a scholar and an extrovert. His very personal, hands-on style of
leadership was plain for all to see. He was known for refusing to let go
of a problem until it was solved. On Maudy Thursday in 1945 he
declared that he would sit in the church all day waiting for the faithful
to show up with funds. The Building Fund had been running short –
the rationing and distraction of wartime must have had something to
do with it – but no matter: the money must be raised.[23]

Hazel's host couple, although members of the United Church,
encouraged her to join her new parish's AYPA branch. She had not previously heard of the organization, but it provided her with new friendships – and also with tremendous opportunities for leadership in an
environment that tended to be accommodating of her ambitions. The
organization, whose four pillars were 'worship, work, fellowship, and
edification,' also happened to be well connected to people of importance in the church and society.[24]

Fellow AYPA members were quick to notice Hazel Journeaux's 'magnetic personality.' This reputed young dynamo was never reluctant to
assume any new position of responsibility. Within a year of becoming
active in the local branch, she was on the provincial council. In 1945 she
became its president. She organized a major convention in Toronto; it

was attended by a record-setting three thousand young people and was described as 'a milestone in the history of the A.Y.P.A.' These efforts won her a lifetime membership, despite the reservations of some of the members of the awards committee, who were reluctant to bestow such a high honour on someone who had been involved with the AYPA for so short a time. We know that Hazel Journeaux herself had done nothing to posture for the award – as her nominators went through some effort to ensure that its presentation would be 'a surprise.'[25]

Also in 1945, after only two years with the movement, Hazel Journeaux became a member of the national council as Ontario representative. During the war, the dominion council had come to be composed primarily of women, and although a gender balance would be struck in the ensuing years, the men would never again be as dominant as they had been.

Colleagues, male and female, immediately noticed that there was something different about the perky Hazel Journeaux. They wondered in jest whether she was an 'inhuman automaton,' managing to run a growing office for Canadian Kellogg while seemingly not turning down any responsibility for the AYPA. They speculated that Journeaux's religious faith must have something to do with her fortitude.[26]

Becoming dominion vice-president in 1947, Journeaux that year embraced with vigour an even greater opportunity – to be one of the Canadian Anglican delegates to the Second World Conference of Christian Youth in Oslo, Norway. Held as Europe lay still in ruins following the horror that had befallen it, the conference was hailed as a watershed event, bringing together many Protestant and Orthodox (but not Catholic) young people who had participated in Christian anti-Nazi resistance movements and many who would become renowned theologians and public officials.

Seventy countries were represented by the twelve hundred delegates. Out of the pangs of conscience, there arose a consensus that Christian churches had forfeited their role as social critics. This must change, the delegates believed. The conference even produced stinging critiques of classical liberalism, nationalism, communism, and capitalism, all of which, in their excess, were deemed soulless and dehumanizing.[27] The conference has likewise been credited with contributing to the revival of ecumenism. Indeed, many of the Anglicans – it is not clear whether Journeaux was among them – openly defied a bishop's injunction not to take communion at High Mass because of the sectarian division with the Norwegian church.[28]

Journeaux herself saw this as an occasion to raise sensitive political issues. Two months before the conference, she had written to William Lyon Mackenzie King – it was probably her first letter to a prime minister – reminding him of a resolution of AYPA's provincial council calling for just compensation to Japanese Canadians who had been subject to internment during World War II, and for a full investigation of the matter: 'I trust that I will be able to advise the Conference Delegates of the fair treatment accorded to Japanese Canadians by the Government of Canada.'[29]

We do not know if she said anything in Oslo about Japanese Canadians, but it seemed from subsequent correspondence to have been the whirlwind European tour that excited her most, with its Scottish mist or just missing the young Princess Elizabeth at the Canterbury conference or riding the Copenhagen trolleys and sampling French cuisine. On 15 July she was sent off like a departing general, complete with confetti and streamers, from Toronto's Union Station. In Montreal, she boarded a Trans Canada Airlines plane for Scotland, her memorable first flight by air. 'Just get that hungry look and they rush to you with scrumptious eats,' she later wrote. 'Yawn, and you are tucked in with a cosy blanket by the pretty air hostess. No they don't supply a handsome man to hold your hand.'[30] Even when asked now to reflect on the conference, Hazel McCallion gives a vivid account of the sites and sights, but not the theology.[31]

Although Journeaux did launch a Bible study group at her parish immediately after returning from Oslo,[32] it is noteworthy that what was probably the only detailed written account this Canadian delegate produced for the consumption of the general AYPA membership was a light and dreamy travelogue. The exuberant reflections, even if omitting the more profound and intellectually challenging aspects of the conference, were not unusual for Hazel Journeaux. AYPA colleagues noted her 'sunny smile.' A very happy, pleasant expression is evident in the pictures from that period. Some of her notes to AYPA fellow executives even contained touches of warm informality. 'Lucky girl,' she once wrote to a colleague about to embark on a holiday in Texas. 'Watch out for those handsome-looking Texans. It will be okay if you bring a dozen or more back with you.'[33]

Although she concedes now that politics has hardened her, even in her AYPA days Hazel could be stern and hectoring. Put in charge of a national used-clothing drive, she admonished the branch presidents: 'Attached to this letter is a calendar of the weeks each council is required to supply workers. This is your guide. Will it be necessary for your [diocesan] Council Presidents to phone and request volunteers from the Branches, or will the Branches answer to the call by phoning in the name of volunteers?'[34]

Hazel Journeaux's appointment as dominion president in 1949 only whetted her appetite for leadership, along with the whirlwind schedules and opportunities to deal decisively with what sometimes seemed an endless succession of issues. She threw herself into the organization's work more than ever. She claimed the association's principles 'to be my way of life.'[35] Highly driven, she wrote that 'our lives can be wasted so easily if we allow ourselves to drift through life without an aim or purpose. We become as drifting boats without helmsmen and there is every possibility that we will end up as driftwood on the shores of life's stream.'[36]

Some of the executive members had been concerned that there was a disconnect between the work of the local branches, where total membership numbered at least eight thousand, and the dominion leadership. Journeaux decided to meet this problem by making herself highly visible. She toured eastern Canada, and the expedition won rave reviews. '[I]t is impossible for me to try to put in words the results of your visit,' exclaimed AYPA's Nova Scotia provincial president, 'but I can say the results will show in the branches, local and diocesan councils, that we are now more aware of our responsibilities "To Christ and His Church" and that from now on more co-operation may be expected from this Diocese.'[37]

She kept up a steady stream of correspondence, never forgetting promises made to her and persisting with her colleagues if their project or reporting deadlines had come and gone. She put into place an apparatus to plan celebrations for the AYPA's golden jubilee in 1952. The commemorative book that year featured a president's message from Journeaux, not her successor who at the time of publication was the actual president. On many issues, she showed some impatience with slow progress. Her articles in the organization's magazine, the *AYPA Monthly*, focused only briefly on theological themes and much more on good organization, leadership, and professional dedication. Sometimes she lectured; sometimes she would 'speak frankly'; and she did both much more than her predecessors had done. She maintained a dizzying pace, remarking that without her car she would not have been able to manage.

But for all her exuberance and visibility, Journeaux was a cautious reformer. She saw organizational problems as being essentially leadership problems rather than problems of institutional design or attributable to other systemic ailments. 'There isn't anything wrong with the A.Y.P.A. as there is with those in the A.Y.P.A.,' she opined in a reply to the restless president of the organization's Montreal diocesan council.

> In my travels I find that few leaders really know what the A.Y.P.A. is all about. They do not put into the A.Y.P.A. the same amount of thought, effort, etc. as they would put into a job for which they were receiving money. The A.Y.P.A. will run most effectively when it is lead [sic] by a person or persons who really know their job, are enthused about it and are ready to give the great amount of time it takes to make a success of it. That applies right from the Dominion Council down.

She added that it was incumbent on would-be reformers to work within the system. 'I have very little use for those who complain about a situation but are not willing to do anything about it. For instance those outside the Church who cannot think of anything good to say about the Church. I always say to them if the Church is as bad as you say it is why don't you join and see how you can bring about a change.'[38] And although she professed concern that too many of the branches were really 'social clubs' that ought to be taking on more meaningful and onerous issues, her accounts of her travels continued to be social accounts rather than more reflective observations on the state of the church.[39] She did, however, let on that 'I think we have to admit that evil is on the increase in our communities. Too often we say our present system has failed. A new "system" will never remedy the situation. It requires the active interest of Christians in the life of the community. Too few Christians are willing to take public office and adhere to their Christian principles.'[40] One of her twenty magazine articles as president mentioned the need to combat 'racial discrimination, unemployment, poverty, slums and sickness,'[41] and she warned elsewhere that young people who lead lives without purpose risk being engulfed by 'this materialistic world.'[42] But the social justice work was to be done through the 'Church and other reliable organizations in the community.'[43]

During this period she also appeared to be diplomatic, even deferential, towards those in authority. In January 1950 she received a condescending letter from Calgary bishop Richard Ragg, objecting to the diocesan AYPA's request for the names of outlying members (those not affiliated with any branch). '[Q]uite obviously, the Dominion Council A.Y.P.A. has not the very least idea of distances and the fewness of the

Clergy covering these distances in Western Canada.... I can assure you that we are very alive to our rural problems in this Diocese, there are, however, certain things which can be done and certain things which are utterly impossible of accomplishment.'[44]

Journeaux sat on the letter for a whole month. She finally replied defending the dominion secretary, who was specifically criticized by the bishop, but also tried gently to deflect blame to the AYPA Western Canada delegates themselves: 'As the request for this set-up came from the Western delegates, I do not feel that the Dominion Council Executive can assume responsibility for this provision in the A.Y.P.A. set-up. It is always our wish to comply with the requests of the delegates who are chosen as the representatives of the Dioceses across Canada.'[45]

As much as she relished her work as president, it would appear that a little more than a year into her two-year term the budding leader and already seasoned manager was becoming exhausted. In August and September 1950 colleagues referred to an 'illness' and Journeaux herself was commenting that her doctor was telling her to take a vacation.

There were some personal satisfactions, however. A bond had developed between Journeaux and the chair of the literature committee, the committee in charge of organizing resources for use by branches and for putting out promotional and instructional material. Samuel Robert McCallion was from the nearby Church of the Good Shepherd in the working-class – and sometimes noisy and grimy – suburb of Mount Dennis. The family was seen as stable and sturdy, and the parents were active in the church, where a pew plaque was put in to recognize their sponsorship. The organizations at Good Shepherd, including the AYPA, often interacted with their counterparts in Hazel Journeaux's more affluent parish.[46]

Sam McCallion had some of Hazel's qualities of eagerness and ambition. The tall, lanky young man – three years Journeaux's junior – had always been regarded as a serious fellow. His high school colleagues remembered him dressing more formally than many of the other students. Like Journeaux, he had been an average student, but hard-working. He excelled at photography and it would remain a passion all his life. Their 'romance' was well known to AYPA people,[47] and Sam accompanied Hazel on some of her trips.[48]

Sam McCallion's committee reports were always comprehensive. He spoke frequently at the dominion council meetings, and his name appears more often than any of the others as the mover or seconder of motions. Well before the end of Journeaux's term as president in June 1951, the couple was engaged – and Journeaux, commenting favourably on the intensive preparations of the annual national conference, joked that she would convert the conference-planning committee into the committee to plan her and Sam's September wedding.[49] Although there is no evidence she used such coercion, AYPA members were treated like extended family at the ceremony. One of those who attended described it as a 'huge wedding' with a 'nice, informal air.' It was topped off memorably by a choir of fifty AYPA members.[50]

Heading West

The newly married Hazel and Sam McCallion promptly showed up in what was then the Township of Toronto. They were part of the first major suburban wave. The rural backwater was now suddenly finding itself close to a rapidly expanding city. 'The sixty year doldrums,' as one municipal leader was to call the old times, were over.[51]

The World War II victory parties had barely dispersed when people started arriving in great numbers – returning veterans, young families from the city, even some immigrants from abroad. Their motorcars loaded beyond capacity, they cruised west along the Queen Elizabeth Way, modern and sleek with its arches, boulevards, and distinctive green 'ER' lampposts, the mother of future Canadian expressways and still a worthy tribute to the future Queen Mother who had inaugurated it during that glorious royal visit of 1939.

The city limits then still seemed like the city limits. However, the outlines of the old 'streetcar suburbs' were visible from the highway – off in the distance in the south – strung out along that great-grandmother of provincial highways, Number 2, the Lakeshore Highway, one day to be quaintly dubbed 'the Heritage Highway.' Mimico, New Toronto, Long Branch, and even Port Credit had their chemical and starch factories and smokestacks, their working-class neighbourhoods, their clanging rail yards.[52]

Of course, heading west to their new home in 1951, the newlywed McCallions could still see old Ontario. Here a snake fence, there an apple orchard, and beyond that a Gothic Revival or neoclassical abode presiding proudly over what even a middling farmer could persuade himself was a very fine property indeed.[53]

But they also could see the new crops of settlement. The old patterns of human residency – along those rail lines, at crossroads, later along trolley lines[54] – were becoming unhinged. And although many of the riverside mill towns lived on in their scenic settings (indeed, some of these mills continued to produce and even expand), their locations were now historical holdovers. Even the old-timers could but vaguely remember their parents' tales about the days when industry came to power rather than power to industry.

These new homesteads, turning up here and there in little clusters amid the gentle countryside, and usually built by upstart (but still small relative to what they would become) companies using repetitive plans, seemed to have only passing regard for the old places. Their residents did not need the land for cultivation, but neither did they need to be in town. Their automobiles could have them in the city in minutes should they need to stock up or experience the company of strangers – or work in a city office, as Hazel McCallion would continue to do. Town and country: they could enjoy both while not quite living in either. They could *commute*, and they would, even though offices and industries themselves were soon to be drawn to the cheaper suburban land, space for car parking, opportunities to build anew, and, from time to time, the wooing of feisty local politicians.

Crossing the Etobicoke Creek, some eight miles beyond the Humber, they would have come across even denser orchards, for they were now below the ancient Iroquois Ridge where the microclimate was relatively temperate. And they were now finally in the Township of Toronto, population in 1951 not even 35,000. But no sign proclaimed it, notwithstanding the locals' boast that the name belonged rightfully to the township and had actually been stolen by the city. No chamber of commerce or service club or boosterist local reeve had yet erected one. The township that in 1968 would become a town of more than 125,000 people, and that six years after that would absorb the small municipalities of Streetsville and Port Credit to become the city of Mississauga, with a population surpassing 200,000, was a place of scattered communities.

Almost all of these hamlets and villages had their roots in the nineteenth century, before 1850 actually, when settlers rushed to take up lands purchased by the Crown from the Mississauga First Nation in 1805, 1818, and 1820. The Mississaugas themselves started a company to cash in on the rush, laying out the future Port Credit and establishing its first harbour. But disease and the self-dealing and prejudice of the colonial officials were hard obstacles to overcome. By 1847 most of the Mississaugas decided to relocate from their village along the Credit to the southwest, to the Grand River Valley.[55]

Although many of the nineteenth-century settlers were to fail or move on, their times seemed full of promise, the land bountiful. Many only barely noticed that much of the terrain was tied up in clergy reserves and in special grants to some of the most illustrious members of the colonial establishment, the same group that the firebrand rebel William Lyon Mackenzie, a frequent rabble-rouser in these parts, had dubbed the 'Family Compact.' Some of these magnates were not-quite-absentee landlords. Chief Justice John Beverley Robinson built for himself an elegant retreat house – in the very British Regency style, of course – and was seen often where the Dundas Highway crossed the Credit River. He was seen there often, that is, until 'The Grange,' as he called it, became too much of a financial burden even by his bountiful standards.[56]

That stalwart Tory would not be the only one to move on. In the 1860s the township of golden opportunity seemed to fall into a long, quiet repose. The land was almost all settled now; many of the younger generation were leaving for the west, western Ontario at first and western Canada later, or the cities or the United States. There were only so many ways a one- or two-hundred-acre farm could be sliced up for the descendants. Indeed, consolidation, not atomization, was to become the order of the day.[57]

Then there were those railways, and the dreams they brought of new commerce and new frontiers, but also the prospect of heartbreak and decline. Only some villages would reap the rewards of a line and a station, as furiously as their rustic little politicians or denizens might try to bribe the big promoters.[58] It is no wonder, therefore, that the artists who came for inspiration to places like Meadowvale, Streetsville, and Erindale would label their surroundings as idyllic or sleepy or peaceful. For by the early twentieth century, they seemed endearingly static, stagnant, and frozen in time.

Some of the big city's urban gentry noticed what the artistic bohemians were noticing. For some, 'cottage country' was the new enclave of Lorne Park, west of Port Credit, where prominent Toronto architects like Langley and Burke were happy to divert some of their professional energies to the more leisurely work of designing retreats in the woods. One early-twentieth-century refugee even waxed poetic: 'The peace and quiet rests o'er all / The breeze that cools my brow / The simple things the country gives / They meant contentment now.'[59]

Or it was the outskirts of Clarkson, further to the west but still in the township, where by the 1920s Mazo de la Roche – in the shadow of Captain Harris's Georgian estate, vast and elegant but without modern conveniences, on orders of the squire, who preferred to live in the past – was gathering ideas for her internationally celebrated *Jalna* series of novels.[60]

Not all who spilled over from the city before the big suburban onslaught were well heeled or artistically cultivated in the middle-class sort of way. In the far northeast of the township, site of the Malton Airport, opened in 1939 and initially using a brick house as its 'terminal,' things had stirred early. No one called for A.J. Casson or George Chavignaud, both of whom had spent considerable time painting and living in the township.[61] Hands, many hands, were needed, and perhaps the occasional brain to build the wartime Lancaster bombers and other fighting machines. The government-constructed workers' houses, sprinkled along streets with triumphant names like 'Victory' and 'Churchill,' were far less triumphant, being at most glorified shacks. At least they were better than the makeshift 'slums' that authorities for the city of Toronto, starting after World War I, were dumping onto Lakeview, in the extreme southeast of the township.

Yet these were but signs and foreshadowings. The McCallions would still find a township largely rural in its geography and traditional in its politics. When they exited the Queen Elizabeth Way at Centre Road (Hurontario Street) and headed north to the Dundas Highway, they would have come upon Cooksville, the seat of the township. Once home to Canada's first commercial winery and even an oil refinery, it now was anchored by its brick factory and surrounding farms. It had the usual school and churches. The Cooksville crossroads – Toronto Township's main 'Four Corners' – still had a hotel, two old banks, and a general store (once owned by the enterprising Jacob Cook himself), which twenty years earlier had been picked up and moved with everything still inside to accommodate a petrol station and a minor widening of the intersection. Nearby, various little shops and restaurants enlivened the place, some of them catering to Italian and Croatian immigrants, many of whom trudged every day to work at the vast and somewhat bleak Cooksville brickyards on the western outskirts of the village. Indeed, parts of the brickyards might well have been mistaken for the moon. Fortunately, the popular fairgrounds provided fun and relief. The annual and always anticipated Toronto Township Agricultural Fair would be held for a few more years yet.[62]

Most of the fair-goers and brickyard workers would have barely noticed the red-bricked, gabled, century-old township hall – and perhaps they did not need to. The 'governance' and 'administration' of this municipality were slapdash affairs. Planners and professional assessors were nowhere in sight. And yes, most of the politicians smoked cigars, especially in the comfortable backrooms where many of the decisions were made.

The 'Dixie boys' tended to dominate here. The settlement of Dixie, just east of Cooksville along the Dundas Highway, was an unlikely place for the township's political notables. Largely agricultural, it had managed to cultivate some proud and stable families over several generations. They even had their implied hierarchies. Years later Grant Clarkson, the last of the Dixie old-timers, would recall the understood formula for problem solving. 'When the Guthries had a problem, they took it to the Stanfields. When the Stanfields couldn't solve it, they went to the Palletts. And the Palletts couldn't solve the problem, so they went to the Clarksons. The Clarksons couldn't solve the problem, so they went to the Watsons. And the Watsons couldn't solve it, so they went to God.'[63]

Maybe instead of God, Clarkson should have said 'Tom Kennedy.' Himself a Dixie fruit-grower, this walking local institution had seamlessly, perhaps even unintentionally, made himself the undisputed patriarch of Peel County. Skinny and soft spoken, with a perpetual frown caused by a First World War facial injury, 'the Colonel' lacked both charisma in the conventional sense and a temper. He spoke slowly and with hesitation, but when he did speak it seemed to be from the heart. His constituents were sure that the Honourable Thomas Laird Kennedy cared.

How did they know it? Well, as Ontario's minister of agriculture for more than twenty years, and even as interim premier in 1948–9, after George Drew left to lead the federal Conservatives, Kennedy always found time for the little things – the unrushed conversations in his own county's back concessions, the personal attention to the ill and the dispossessed, the invitations to the lowly and the little to share tea with him in his kitchen on a Sunday afternoon.

Certainly, Kennedy could be as shrewd a politician as the rest of them. The personal touch and the patronage back home were never far from the minds of any of the honourable members. But Kennedy seemed different from the rabidly partisan machine operatives. Even in the assembly he could have a soothing effect: 'I wasn't in favour of turning the other cheek, but I always felt that a man who is reasonable with his language and his arguments will come out far ahead of one who lets fly with hot words.'[64]

The colonel's reputation was unassailable, but when it came to any profound analysis of growth management and dealing with development, Kennedy had little to offer to the men who sat around the council table and hung on the patriarch's every word. To be sure, he had a connection to the land – an almost spiritual one, in fact. 'The love of the soil is firmly implanted in my heart,' he told Premier Leslie Frost when finally stepping down from the cabinet in 1952.[65] But this rural romanticism actually led to an uncritical attitude about the subdivisions that were now popping up. He was happy to greet those hopeful travellers as they exited the Queen Elizabeth Way and rolled into his bailiwick. As Kennedy saw it, suburban development was a laudable desire 'of thousands of our people to forsake the crowded life of the cities and find more healthful and congenial surroundings in the open country. This is a good sign from the standpoint of the future of our Province.'[66]

The arriving McCallions passed Cooksville and headed north, beyond the Burnhamthorpe Sideroad, beyond the Base Line, to the Britannia Sideroad. Heading west on this dirt road, they stopped on the outskirts of Streetsville. There was still less evidence here of the suburban boom. Indeed, the couple's relatives had cautioned them against moving to such a far-off locale. But even in this place, in the township's northwest, the old era was passing. With few difficulties a local farmer had subdivided part of his property into several five-acre parcels. The McCallions bought one, and Hazel, the self-described country-girl, thought that it reminded her of home.

Making Streetsville Home

It was December 1951 when the couple settled near Streetsville. A year later, Peter, the first of their three children, was born. It was a pleasant setting in which to raise a family. In the days before the subdivisions stretched to the horizons, many had described the Streetsville area as picturesque. 'Is it any wonder that I love Streetsville,' retired schoolteacher Millie Lundy wrote at the time, 'and that when I look around and see the beauty of hills and valley, river and creek and sky, I know it is the finest spot in the world in which to live.'[67]

This idyllic place, with its volunteer fire department, one-man hydro operation, frozen skating ponds, and river swimming hole, had its widely known stories and legends – the large sleigh that local pranksters stole from a farm one Halloween night and placed atop the Odd Fellows Hall, or the 'Streetsville Ghouls Scare' of 1937 when the press descended in hordes after grave robbers apparently demanded ransom for the return of the body of a young cancer victim. The corpse was found, despite non-payment.[68]

For the newcomer McCallions, the 1950s were occupied by the demands of a young family, Hazel's continuing full-time schedule with Canadian Kellogg, but also a growing number of entrepreneurial endeavours. The couple started a dry-cleaning company, Elite Cleaners, in town in Streetsville. Sam continued with some freelance photography. He got an old Heidelberg press and started a printing company, which, like the cleaners, was given a name (Unique) to denote distinction. Within a few years, the press was moved to a small industrial building on Falconer Drive in the north end of Streetsville, and the *Plaza News* (later the *Streetsville Shopping News*) was started. It contained advertisements and advertorials profiling Streetsville merchants.

This penchant for business, however, soon brought to the fore another old love, politics. During the 1940s, Hazel Journeaux had been actively volunteering with the federal and provincial Conservative party in her York South constituency. Her AYPA friends had remarked that Hazel had taken a strong interest in local campaigns, eagerly volunteering where she could. Now, as she made her rounds to secure advertisements for her monthly publication – remarkably, for more than twenty years into her Mississauga mayoralty, she would continue to insist on helping to solicit advertisements, saying she enjoyed the great feeling of success derived from each sale – she heard about local problems.

These were Streetsville problems, for although the family actually resided on the outskirts, in Toronto Township, most of the McCallions' business and social activities were in town. The local politicians were well-meaning but overwhelmed old-timers. They were not like the old intellectuals and professionals, the literate gentry, that had once dominated Streetsville's local politics. They were people like small-time developer and entrepreneur Bill ('Danny') Arch, a village council fixture in the 1950s and briefly the Peel County warden. Decisions were made on an ad hoc basis. The municipality's 'official plan' was simply a patchwork summary of the hodgepodge of recent zoning decisions that had come before it. Residents chuckled as they told of infrastructure projects that seemed to take no account of what was town property and what was private property. Securing the appropriate easements, expropriations, and permissions seemed to be just a strange annoyance. The Planning Board saw its role as a simple one – to 'do everything possible for industry'[69] – and in 1962 it found itself in an 'embarrassing position' when its five thousand dollars of expenditures on routine activities exceeded the measly council apportionment by two thousand dollars.[70]

McCallion decided that she could do more than chuckle at these ·seemingly legitimate complaints. Already active with the Chamber of Commerce for several years, she decided in 1963 to express her interest in the presidency. She secured it easily, and it gave her a new pulpit.

John Fulton, a well-educated business executive, had been hearing similar murmurings from local businesspeople and middle-class families who had settled in the Streetsville subdivisions after World War II. In 1964 Fulton captured the mayoralty from old-timer Marshall Adamson, who himself had succeeded lifelong resident Frank Dowling, whose father and grandfather had been in local politics. The political veterans were, it is true, concerned about excesses – Dowling and Adamson had opposed the construction of Centre Plaza, which to this day stands out as a rude intrusion into the historic streetscape. They were more successful in opposing the demolition of the elegant, Italianate, 1870s-vintage Streetsville Grammar School at 327 Queen Street South, which in 1966 would become the town hall and police station. But they had seldom become tough or animated, nor had they regarded the job as more than a leisurely civic service for which, after all, the remuneration was negligible.

Fulton was different. He would lead the municipality in a business-like way and not in the friends-and-neighbours style. Streetsville was no longer a rural backwater where things seldom changed. Exhibit A: The growth! The population had increased to six thousand from barely more than six hundred at the end of World War II.

Fulton tried to get like-minded colleagues onto the municipality's boards and commissions, and to Hazel McCallion he offered the important volunteer post of member of the Planning Board. Barely in her seat, McCallion criticized the board for having no strategic approach to decision-making and for lacking a clear plan. She read the material thoroughly, often requested more, and posed sharp and relevant questions to development applicants. Within a year, she was chair of the board.[71]

Despite the demands of a young family, and despite the birth in 1964 of her third child, Paul, McCallion's Chamber of Commerce presidency was marked by assertion. Most prominently, she called for a plebiscite to relax the town's fifty-year-old prohibition on the sale of alcoholic beverages. The results of the popular vote decisively supported McCallion's position.[72]

By the fall of 1965, McCallion was enjoying a high profile in Streetsville. The Chamber of Commerce was more active than ever. Its trade fair had been a resounding success. As editor and business manager of the *Streetsville Booster*, the monthly tabloid newspaper that in September 1964 had replaced the *Streetsville Shopping News*, and which was commenting extensively on local politics, McCallion provided a platform for reform talk in the municipality.

So when she threw herself into the race for deputy reeve, many had high expectations, even though a woman had never previously been elected in Streetsville. But it was a nasty election, complete with stolen signs and all manner of innuendo. McCallion considered herself a victim of dirty tricks.[73]

Her bitterness was exacerbated by her loss, by more than two hundred votes, to an old-timer, George Parker, then a manager at the long-standing Reid flour-milling factory. By this time, however, the reformers were a reasonably cohesive group. Several of their candidates had gone down to defeat with McCallion, but they began to coalesce around the one who had been elected, Jack Graham, and for the next two years *The Booster*, unlike the more staid and long-established weekly *Streetsville Review*, gave the council, especially Mayor Bill Tolton, decidedly negative coverage on everything from the politicians' salaries, to the supply of water, to apartment buildings, to planning. Jack Graham's analyses were always quoted at length, even when he had not been at the meeting.

Tolton's profile was not that of an old-school personage. He had studied urban planning, was familiar with case studies from around the world, and was well ahead of his time in warning of the social and environmental costs of urban sprawl. With a degree in agricultural science from the University of Guelph, he had published in Streetsville the *Canadian Florist* magazine and *Canadian Bee Journal*. But as a politician Tolton could appear indecisive, and the more he was criticized the more he seemed to recoil and retreat behind closed doors. This of course made him even more vulnerable to attack. And in Hazel McCallion he had found an opponent who could smell weakness and vulnerability, and would exploit it.

The completion and opening, in November 1967, of Streetsville's modern Centennial Library should have been a major accomplishment for Mayor Tolton. He had invested considerable time, even some of his own money. In a plebiscite, the voters had supported a new library.

All seemed well in hand, until the pesky local lawn bowlers complained. They were using the green adjacent to the old building; they had been since 1890, in fact. The town found a new place for them in Memorial Park, but then the separate school board expropriated that site. The lawn bowlers now suddenly remembered that the library lands had been deeded years earlier to the municipality by the Cunningham family on the condition that the green be retained.

Frustrated, Mayor Tolton searched for a new site. He secured a good deal from the Graydon family, which owned land a few blocks north of the old library. It was well situated, right beside Centre Plaza and its big parking lot. Counting the purchase price of the land, the new library came in over budget – $130,000 rather than $95,000 – but over-budget public projects were nothing out of the ordinary.

Yet the critics of the mayor, McCallion prominent among them, had a field day. Tolton was violating the results of the plebiscite by moving the library! The town's purchase of the new lands involved 'land swapping,' a practice that was promptly cast in the most suspicious terms. Everything was being done in secret! The new design was deemed atrocious. And on it went. Of course the critics did not mention that the lawn bowlers would still be left with their facility, and the old library (a century-old former tinsmith shop that is now a historic landmark) would be retained and used for public meetings and receptions.[74] As for the secrecy, municipal property transactions are routinely decided *in camera* (that is, behind closed doors), and this would be no different with McCallion at the helm.

Although McCallion had resigned her Chamber of Commerce position when she had declared for council, she had retained her Planning Board platform. 'Chairman' McCallion now used that position to full effect, which usually meant rattling Mayor Tolton. She pointed out to her colleagues the section of the Planning Act that empowered the board to consult directly with the public. And in discussing the nature of modern planning, she cautioned the other board members that it was not their job to be experts, but to retain the services of experts. She proposed to bring on such persons to help with the development of a new, comprehensive official plan and to hold a series of public meetings to get feedback.[75]

Here we see germinating an approach to leadership that years later would characterize McCallion's Mississauga mayoralty – reliance on a strong technocratic base and outreach to a mass public. This actually put her in a pre-eminent position. She would be the interface, the public face of the administration and the one who would interpret to the technocrats the public, democratic will. At the same time, she could hold at bay her colleagues (board or council members) by leaning on the wisdom of experts. And where expedient, the expert advice could deflect public input that seemed inconvenient and unreasonable. Whereas in Streetsville she would find a public organized into long-standing and vibrant organizations, in Mississauga she would not. Her frequent public meetings and personal appearances, her very accessibility, her populist style, would actually stymie their development.

Under McCallion's leadership, the Streetsville Planning Board did indeed draft a comprehensive official plan, reducing densities in most places, proposing a development freeze (interim control bylaw) for the downtown, and designating new parks and amenities. It was generally well received and got through council, despite the hard feelings McCallion had stirred up at some of the public meetings, where it was common for her to publicly interrogate Mayor Tolton.[76]

In the municipal election campaign of December 1967, McCallion was ready to try again for deputy reeve. She remained allied with Jack Graham, who had made a name for himself not only as a reformer on the Streetsville council but as the county warden for Peel in 1966. 'Wherever you saw one's sign on a pole, you saw the other's on a pole,' former reeve Don Hewson remembered many years later. This time, McCallion was victorious, with a margin of nearly two hundred votes over her new opponent, Councillor Ross Machin. And her friend Graham was the new mayor.[77]

Six months later, McCallion would be luckier still. Reeve Hewson, a patent lawyer, resigned because of his busy schedule at work. Although he was relatively new to town, having moved there only in 1965, he had not been part of the coalition that had included McCallion. During his short political sojourn, he had not been immune to the intra-council sniping.

For the first few months of 1968, the McCallion-Graham political partnership held. A spate of reforms was pushed through council, including a sweeping protocol governing how development applications were to be scrutinized. It would now be required that the police department, the fire department, the parks board, the recreation committee, and the school boards submit a formal appraisal of any application prior to council's debate. Respected professionals in the community were appointed to the committees, boards, and commissions suited to their areas of expertise.

But it did not take long for Graham and McCallion to split. Who provided the spark? Those lawn bowlers, of course. This time they got involved in a dispute with the neighbouring homeowner over property lines. Graham thought he could arbitrate it himself, which only made things worse. McCallion pounced on an opportunity, and now began to publicly criticize Graham. The mayor, stubborn in his own right, shot back with his own accusations about McCallion's supposedly inadequate leadership in chairing one of council's committees.[78]

It was the issue of Streetsville's municipal status, however, that proved to be Graham's political undoing. Going into the 1968–9 term, he and McCallion had still been singing from the same hymnbook. By this time, the provincially commissioned report on municipal restructuring west of Toronto, the Plunkett Report, by commissioner Thomas J. Plunkett – recommending a one-tier 'urban county of Mississauga' covering all of southern Peel and Halton – had been roundly rejected. Even the minister of municipal affairs had declared that Thomas Plunkett 'isn't Moses leading the Israelites and he isn't God.'[79]

But Graham and McCallion were still praising the report at county council, the only municipal politicians anywhere to do so. In fact, that was the problem, McCallion had claimed. The report was being rejected more by politicians than by the public.[80]

However, McCallion soon began to realize that, although the Streetsville public and its strong civic organizations had been concerned with the supposedly haphazard, ad hoc leadership of the Tolton council, the citizens did not seem prepared to sacrifice their town on the altar of some impersonal 'business' principles. 'Rational' planning be damned; there was an emotional attachment, a community spirit. The surrounding Township of Toronto had become the Town of Mississauga, and its civic leaders were perceived to be in bed with developers. Streetsville wanted none of that.

McCallion did not stand down immediately. Instead, she rather innocuously called for a consultants' report to examine the town's boundaries. The consultants ended up rejecting amalgamation but proposing a much-enlarged Streetsville, one that could control the development of its hinterland and have some room for new industries.

This was it! Here was a scheme to reconcile rational planning with the community's heritage and identity. Some of the inconvenient details of the report did not have to be harped on – such as the recommendation that the downtown be eventually moved to a large, new site. At its core, this was a plan for the retention and expansion of Streetsville; it offered something to address concerns about future economic development, but most important, something for the community-minded and those concerned about controlling the almost-imminent development around Streetsville.[81]

McCallion took the initiative now. First she berated Graham for dragging his feet on releasing the report. When it finally was unveiled at a packed public meeting, she effectively isolated him. The mayor wanted to follow a different direction than that advocated by 'experts' and the community.[82]

By the end of 1968, the *Mississauga Times* was observing that, for all their smarts, McCallion and Graham could not co-exist. One of them would have to go.

Jack Graham blinked first. It was now October 1969. Business-like but stubborn, he remained convinced that the dissolution of Streetsville as a municipal entity was inevitable. But it won him few friends among the local organizations and in the local grocery stores and restaurants. Even his seven-year-old daughter was being teased at school over her father's growing political alienation.[83] Although he claimed at the time to be stepping aside voluntarily, Graham would be much more candid years later. 'I wouldn't be elected as dogcatcher. There wouldn't have been two votes! Not even my wife would have voted for me!'[84]

So when the new year dawned, Streetsville had a new mayor. Neither she nor the denizens would have allowed themselves to predict that this mayor would be the town's last.

2 'A Public – Not a Mass'

Hazel McCallion had learned some valuable lessons about Streetsville. She had learned not only that there was considerable disaffection with the local politicians but that the public expected them to be more than businesspeople. In the mid-1960s her *Booster* editorials were still complaining about town council holding up development.[1] But in late 1969 when she ran to succeed the retiring Jack Graham as mayor, beating back a challenge from former mayor Bill Tolton, she was demanding less development. She called her platform 'Planning for People.' It was enough to earn her 120 more votes than Tolton. It was not an overwhelming victory. Already another former mayor, George Wilson, was waiting in the wings to challenge her the next time. She would have to be attentive.

She realized that neighbourhood activism – and indeed an emotional attachment to the community – were embedded within the political culture of Streetsville and that this local political culture was being legitimated as part of a larger societal reappraisal. One town councillor, Fred Kingsford, put it eloquently:

> Today we live in a world where more and more people are questioning our value system. There is a strong need by many to take a close look at some of the values which we have tossed aside in the name of progress. People are in search of personal identification, and, in ever increasing numbers, they are looking towards the neighbourhood and the community for answers for that ongoing search. Only a few years ago, it would have been unheard of for residents of a community to stop a highway expressway from coming through their neighbourhood or prevent their municipal government from forsaking an older area of a community or town.[2]

Elizabeth Hoople, a retired high-school teacher who would become a feisty activist in her old age, had moved to Streetsville in the early 1930s. Forty years later she would explain why she immediately became attached to the town: 'It was a small village but it didn't take me long to realize that there was something special and different about it. It was the collective spirit of the place.'[3]

Streetsville had grown more than tenfold since Hoople had moved there. There were almost seven thousand people when McCallion ran for mayor. But it was still a 'collective' – a compact community with a single downtown where people knew each other. And any development issue became an issue for the whole municipality. The good citizens could see beyond their laundry lines.

The activism no doubt had much to do with the heady 1960s. But there were local historical reasons as well. It was a place where Tories and radicals had long assembled – and where they had perhaps morphed and melded into what the Toronto history professor and reform councillor William Kilbourn called 'Tory radicalism.'[4]

In the 1820s and 1830s, the place had been William Lyon Mackenzie's base of operations and the headquarters of some of his most virile opponents. Streetsville's famous 'Battle of Mother Hyde's Hostelry' was not an isolated incident. This 1832 riot pitted a Tory/Orange gang, the Town Line Blazers, against the village's leading reformers, just as the latter were sitting down to a dinner to celebrate Mackenzie's latest victory. It was not uncommon for brawls to break out during the frequent speeches delivered in the area by Mackenzie and his collaborator Samuel Lount.[5]

Mackenzie's routine expulsions from the assembly necessitated frequent elections – and therefore political conflict in Streetsville. After the 1837 rebellion, the fleeing Mackenzie took shelter briefly with friends in Streetsville but wrote later that 'some who saw me at Comfort's Mill went and told the armed Tories of Streetsville.' He was on his way before these 'most violent partisans' crashed into William Comfort's home.[6]

A reputation for strident political expression would persist. The most active and outspoken were the local intellectuals, who were usually given senior civic offices. Take the famous Anglican churchman Rev. Robert Jackson Macgeorge, a writer of some renown in both Canada and Britain. He was based at Streetsville's Trinity Anglican Church. In the 1840s, he found some spare time for editing the popular weekly

Streetsville Review. 'His virile helmsmanship put the little village sheet in the forefront of Canada West's newspapers,' writes William Perkins Bull in his 1937 history of the Anglican Church in Canada. 'Among the things he abhorred were toll gates, rabid teetotallers and prohibitionists, railroads, mud, muddled militia, and stupidity in general.'[7]

Many long-time reeves and county wardens, including Orange Church, who was not as strident a Protestant as his name implied, and physician John Barnhart, had also established reputations for themselves as provocative editors and essayists. Dr G.A. Montemurro, reeve during the 1940s, was a well-known physician. Rev. Frank Vipond, a prominent military chaplain, was an energetic community organizer in Streetsville between the world wars. Among the many projects he championed was the construction of the village's elegant and very distinctive brick cenotaph, which sits on a pedestrian square right in the middle of Main Street.[8]

In the early twentieth century, the area's natural beauty and proximity to Toronto attracted many artists and intellectuals. Several academics who used the area as a retreat formed a vibrant literary association in nearby Meadowvale Village. Major General François-Louis Lessard, the highest-ranking French Canadian officer during World War I, settled there after the war.[9]

After the commencement of the post–World War II suburban expansion, many highly educated professionals moved to Streetsville. They were urged to be active in civic affairs, in keeping with the local ethos of civic engagement and meritocracy. Dr Robert Blackburn chaired the Streetsville Public Library Board in the 1950s and 1960s while also heading the University of Toronto's library system. He was succeeded by Erindale Secondary School principal Ian Ferguson. Artists like Ted Ledsham and Wilfred Gelder, as well as art professor John Emerson, were involved extensively on the town committees. Architect Vic Dale chaired the Planning Board after McCallion's election to council.

Hazel McCallion, as the new mayor, adjusted herself very nicely to the political reality of Streetsville. She did not try to streamline the many volunteer committees that were reporting to council (as she would later do as Mississauga's mayor). She expanded them. She reached out to the Portuguese community. Some of her election literature was printed in that language, and she supported the library's efforts to acquire at public expense holdings in Portuguese. She supported the establishment of a promotions committee of council and gave it unqualified support to organize a major festival, the Streetsville Founders' Bread and Honey Festival, dedicated to the history and traditions of the town.

She did not fret too much that Streetsville's per capita assessment was but eighth in the county or that industrial/commercial assessment had fallen from 27.5 per cent to 23.6 per cent of overall assessment between 1968 and 1969.[10] That ratio would continue to fall as small old-economy plants like Derby Pet Foods and Quaker Oats continued to close. When the Town of Mississauga approved a huge Chrysler Canada plant just outside Streetsville's boundaries McCallion certainly did not celebrate the anticipated influx of jobs. 'The town of Mississauga,' she scoffed instead, 'has the responsibility for putting [industry] there, and Streetsville has the responsibility for solving the problems.'[11] When the politically retired Jack Graham somewhat simplistically blamed the industrial decline on the 'council of Streetsville' because 'they don't get public support from the merchants – they get it from the subdivisions,' McCallion barely flinched.[12]

'It has been the record of this community to support plans which put people first and development second'[13] is what she preferred to say. The developers sensed it too. The development that was happening in Streetsville was subject to the highest public-amenity charges in the county, $1,100 per home and $475 per apartment.[14]

McCallion could point with pride to the fact that taxes were holding stable in Streetsville. And she did, but she put her emphasis on a quality-of-life agenda. In 1972 she released an eleven–point program based on consultation with civic and non-profit groups. Except for a reference to 'a more dynamic commercial core,' none of the objectives alludes to the economy, taxes, and fiscal prosperity. Instead, there is talk of the municipality acquiring natural areas, building riverfront walkways, preparing itself for ultra-modern transit (magnetic levitation!), keeping densities in check, building a curling arena, restoring certain 'pioneer traditions,' and preserving historic structures.[15]

As for that 'dynamic commercial core,' McCallion and her council colleagues bypassed the mayor's old outfit, the Streetsville and District Chamber of Commerce. Instead, they put a team of four University of Waterloo planning students in charge. The leader of the group, Doug Flowers, was a local boy – and proud of it. The civic committees and commissions were asked to cooperate with the students, who were coordinating things from their own office downtown. Actual work was done. New lamp posts and benches were installed. Streetsville became the first town in Canada to have interlocking brick sidewalks. The *Mis-*

sissauga Times called the plans 'attractive and realistic' and compared them favourably to the province's cold, rationalist 'rule by flow chart.'[16]

The Fight to Save Streetsville

McCallion was indeed presenting herself as a critic of the authors of those flow charts. As mayor she pledged her fierce and undying support to the anti-amalgamation movement. It would be a disaster, she asserted, if the province were to force Streetsville to be swallowed up by what had been the Township of Toronto and was now the rapidly sprawling Town of Mississauga. That sprawl was expected soon to reach the frontiers of Streetsville itself.

First on the agenda, therefore, was to persuade the provincial government to abandon municipal affairs minister Darcy McKeough's latest proposal – to create a Halton-Peel Region with Streetsville submerged into Mississauga. The scheme was favoured by Mississauga but opposed by the other nine Peel County municipalities. As late as 3 December 1969 McKeough was telling the Mississauga council that 'I will attempt to have the discussions on regional government brought to a successful conclusion during 1970.'[17] He objected strongly to a county-council motion calling for a Peel-only region, emphasizing that he was 'deeply troubled by the limited scope and attitude evident in the resolution.'[18]

Internal correspondence, now at the Ontario Archives, makes clear that the developers were telling the government they favoured the absorption of Streetsville. But Peel North MPP Bill Davis, still then the minister of education, was worried. The fear seemed to be connected to local public opinion in Streetsville (which was part of his riding) and elsewhere. Even former premier Leslie Frost was privately warning his successor, John Robarts, to proceed more slowly.[19] Soon, McKeough also was publicly conceding that he had to pay heed to the lack of local support. He tried to save face, saying he had determined it would make more sense first to bring in an overall development plan for south-central Ontario.

Just hours after McKeough shelved the Halton-Peel proposal – on 18 March 1970 – Streetsville council seized the initiative. It passed a resolution to apply to the Ontario Municipal Board to annex almost ten thousand acres (seven thousand from Mississauga and three thousand from Oakville), a measure consistent with the much-touted *Boundary Study*.[20] McCallion insisted the move was not farfetched. Regional boards were running the schools, and the province was taking care of most of the cost of the South Peel Water and Sewage System. Although rapid growth was imminent, the area surrounding Streetsville was still sparsely populated and would immediately add just a few thousand residents to the town. A furious Mississauga responded promptly with an application to annex all of Streetsville.[21]

Could an objective observer have concluded that there was any chance of an independent Greater Streetsville? Maybe. Two months after shelving the Halton-Peel proposal, McKeough released his promised development concept for the city-region. The maps accompanying *Design for Development: The Toronto Centred Region* (*TCR*) showed Streetsville as a 'service centre' apart from Mississuaga. It would be surrounded by parkway belts, corridors for transportation, infrastructure, and green space. Some media outlets interpreted the plan as favouring a distinct 'city' for the Streetsville area. It likewise was noted that Streetsville's *Boundary Study* was remarkably consistent with the new provincial announcement.[22] Not surprisingly, a town-council resolution quickly affirmed 'the whole-hearted support of the Town of Streetsville in implementing the plan.'[23]

But the *TCR* plan was one of the slew of schemes in this period, all apparently so promising and so grounded in expert analysis – and so destined to conflict with the reality on the ground or to be vague enough to have little meaning. Indeed, McKeough was signalling that he had not changed his mind about Streetsville at all. Within a week of *TCR*'s release, Mississauga's planning commissioner was boasting to the press that the minister had assured him there would be no annexation of Mississauga lands by Streetsville.[24] A draft letter from McKeough to McCallion contained a paragraph, taken out at the last minute, asserting 'that Streetsville as we know it will disappear as major local government reforms are established in this area.'[25] McCallion, for her part, said she was worried that pressure from developers would force the province to sideline Streetsville, and she raised the alarm when plans for the Erin Mills 'new town' were being approved despite the apparent contradiction with the *TCR* plan.

With the Halton-Peel plan scuttled and nothing yet proposed to take its place, and impatient as ever for something to happen to break the stalemate, McKeough actually considered letting the OMB decide between Streetsville and Mississauga. Ministry staff talked him out of it, however, persuading him to hold out for a comprehensive policy.[26]

In February 1971 McKeough was shuffled out of Municipal Affairs when Davis became premier. The new minister, Dalton Bales, seemed to share the premier's caution and ambivalence on the Peel dossier. Very little was now being said by the province, although Bales professed continued commitment to restructuring.

Most of the local leaders were sure the reprieve was only temporary. Some restructuring would happen. But what? Could they take the initiative and propose something palatable? By late 1971 the county's Municipal Organization Committee was seriously at work drawing and redrawing innumerable maps. McCallion, who was on the committee, favoured 'Plan F,' a Peel-only region with an enlarged Streetsville.

The more they thought of it, the more the Streetsville leaders sensed that the odds at the county were against it. There was, of course, no hope of Mississauga being on Streetsville's side. And although Streetsville cultivated alliances with some of the other Peel municipalities, the town was worried that an undesirable deal could be hatched among the majority of county councillors should Mississauga agree to a minority of seats on a Peel-only regional council (which would allow central and northern Peel to retain their influence) in exchange for the absorption of Streetsville and Port Credit. McCallion now started calling for Queen's Park to come forward with its own plan without waiting for county council.

When the Municipal Organization Committee decided in the early spring of 1972 to focus its research on 'Plan C' – which included only three lower-tier municipalities, with Streetsville to be swallowed by Mississauga – many Streetsvillites began pushing for a dramatic display of public opinion. The result was the Streetsville Citizens' Organization for Retention and Expansion, better known as SCORE – hardly anyone remembers what the acronym stood for. It was chaired by Blake Goodings, who also headed the South Peel chapter of the Association of Professional Engineers of Ontario. SCORE's pro-Streetsville petition managed to collect 3,147 signatures, the majority of adult residents in Streetsville and the immediately surrounding area. The petition was translated into Portuguese, signs were printed, an essay contest was organized in local schools (the theme was 'Streetsville – A Place to Stand, A Place to Grow,' an expression taken from an upbeat song about Ontario often used on the Tory hustings), motivational speakers such as Colin Vaughan of 'Stop Spadina' fame met with residents, and a centrally located 'drop-in centre' was opened.

The SCORE executive managed a ninety-minute meeting with Premier Davis. Goodings came away from that encounter encouraged; he believed Davis would not act in Peel unless there was some consensus from county council, which was not yet forthcoming. But after conferring with McCallion and others, Goodings had reason to rethink his optimism. In a letter to town council a few days later, SCORE – no doubt realizing the dangers of relying too heavily on county council – maintained that the province should make a decision soon about Streetsville's never-abandoned application to annex lands from Mississauga and Oakville.[27]

That summer the province was indeed signalling that time was running out on the status quo. And now the unsympathetic Darcy McKeough was back in charge of Municipal Affairs as part of a larger super-ministry, and he was speaking with confidence: 'the province recognizes now that it is perhaps too much to ask of municipal politicians to be the authors of what is ultimately and properly municipal policy.'[28] (Publicly ambivalent as ever, the premier was still telling a local radio station that the province would wait for 'a degree of consensus' to emerge among local leaders.)[29]

It seems the province had calculated that there could be both a provincial initiative and a degree of local consensus. In late June McKeough asked ministry bureaucrats to present to him some alternatives. Of the three that came back, one was congruent with the Peel-only, three-municipality model (sans Streetsville), but the other two were Halton-Peel schemes that included an expanded 'Streetsville,' which would take in all the Mississauga lands north of Eglinton Avenue, including even the airport. The ministry bureaucrats had long been in favour of a Halton-Peel Region but opposed to a separate Streetsville, while they knew Davis had been affected by the great consternation over the previous Halton-Peel scheme. They seemed to have now assumed that a Halton-Peel Region could garner support from at least some of the local politicians (namely Streetsville's) within the premier's own constituency.[30]

At some point between early July and 16 August 1972, the Streetsville option was dropped. Because the original options were prepared for McKeough, it is likely the decision was his – although he almost certainly would have consulted with, if not taken direction from, Bill Davis. On 16 August the cabinet's Policy and Priorities Board was presented with a Halton-Peel option as a well as a Peel-only model with three lower-tier municipalities. Neither contained a Streetsville. The Peel-only alternative was selected for further consideration, despite the public servants' cautionary note about the 'serious political imbalance that the present proposed two-tier structure would impose in Peel,'[31] as most of the population was concentrated in Mississauga.

It was time now for Louis H. Parsons to do his handiwork. The smooth young operator and diehard Tory was second-in-command on the Mississauga council and a staunch Davis loyalist. Known affectionately as 'Lou' to the local old guard and to the provincial Conservative bigwigs, he was that year the county warden. He suddenly prepared a report and used his influence among reluctant county politicians to move forward the county-council deliberations that had stalled after the Municipal Organization Committee had reported. Thus, at the beginning of September 'Plan C' (Peel-only region with three municipalities, with Streetsville absorbed by Mississauga) was pushed through county council by a 12-to-10 vote and a 26-to-18 weighted majority. The key – and still curious – swing vote was Nance Horwood's. The Brampton reeve broke with her colleagues from that municipality to support the Parsons recommendation.[32]

The way was clear for the cabinet, in December 1972, to quietly endorse a Peel-only region.

If she now knew what was in store for her municipality, McCallion was not showing it. Just before Christmas she told the *Globe and Mail* that she had no doubt her town would be saved. Her less feisty Port Credit counterpart could manage only a shrug and an 'I don't know.'[33] And in late January 1973, when the province finally made public its plans, McCallion still seemed undaunted. She rushed to the media microphones and, with the sweep of an arm, pronounced the whole business a 'can of worms' that had to be squashed.[34]

With local newspapers again reporting that the town was mobilizing for action, McCallion and her councillors heeded a call from SCORE to set up a new anti-amalgamation campaign dedicated specifically to refuting the provincial proposal. This would include a consultant's report assessing the feasibility of Streetsville's absorbing its hinterland and a plebiscite on the town's future. McCallion moved her office, by now a command post, to a storefront 'information centre,' and the final battle to save Streetsville commenced.

A new movement, calling itself SPUR (Streetsville's Place Under Regionalism), promptly put out a statement. This was a battle not only for a municipal body corporate but for a town that seemed to have a distinctive character and values:

Our influence, our say as to what we want as a way of life will be lost. As the matter now stands, and which would continue under an expanded Streetsville Area Municipality, we have the ear of our representatives and can usually get things done in our best interest because Council knows we won't for long tolerate it otherwise. Under a government with jurisdiction over all of South Peel, our representation and thus control over our own destiny, will be assimilated and decided by politicians who cannot identify with our collective philosophies.[35]

Streetsville could simply not be persuaded otherwise. MPP Arthur Meen, the provincial point person on the file, showed up in Streetsville to try to convince the politicians and public that amalgamation would result in better services. But he tripped and stumbled when he tried to get specific. Which services would improve? He turned to the accompanying bureaucrats to furnish some evidence. That was hard to do. 'I started into some bafflegab,' recalls Ron Farrow, who was heading the province's Local Government Organization Branch. 'It was the worst meeting of my career!'[36]

As mayor of Mississauga, McCallion has consistently opposed holding plebiscites on any subject. But in her final year as mayor of Streetsville she set to work trying to persuade the Ontario Municipal Board for permission to hold one on Streetsville's future. This of course was resisted fiercely by Mississauga, whose mayor, Chic Murray, was enthralled with the provincial proposal. 'If we'd written it ourselves we couldn't have done it better,' he chimed as he left the January provincial announcement, seeming to forget that Mississauga, with two-thirds of Peel's population, would get fewer than half the seats on the new regional council.[37] Mississauga's solicitor, Len Stewart, dismissed the Streetsville plebiscite attempt as 'an unnecessary, pointless, pernicious practice.'[38]

The plebiscite request was denied by the OMB and denied on appeal to the provincial cabinet. McCallion did, however, personally hand in Streetsville's lengthy brief just hours before the 31 March deadline for submissions. The town hunkered down to see what legislation would be introduced.

McCallion knew that John White, the new minister responsible for municipal affairs, was sympathetic to Streetsville. Internal documents confirm that this 'red Tory' was suspicious of developers and their friends.[39] But White's sympathy would do little for Streetsville. The whole matter was actually up to Bill Davis. The premier was receiving aggressive counterbriefs from Mississauga dismissing Streetsville's arguments as 'a lot of nonsense.'[40] Such rhetoric was not in the lexicon of 'Bland Bill,' but some of his media interviews were now not sounding too encouraging.

'After very careful consideration, the views put forward by the Town of Streetsville to establish a separate municipality could not be accepted,' White's parliamentary assistant, Arthur Meen, finally announced to the legislative assembly on 28 May. 'It is the government of Ontario's view that the best interests of the people of Streetsville, and indeed of Port Credit also, will be served if those areas are combined with Mississauga. This will form a municipality that can bring a cohesive and skilled full-time administrative presence to bear upon the complex problems of urban growth.'[41]

But town council would not acquiesce to what seemed like the final nail in the coffin of the municipality of Streetsville. It reacted with a lengthy motion decrying the announcement, criticizing Meen for being so ill informed during his visit to Streetsville and, most important, blasting its MPP (the premier) for not meeting with the people of Streetsville to justify the province's intentions. The motion renewed council's call for Davis to appear in town, and it went so far as to demand his resignation as MPP for Peel North should he fail to show.

The day after that resolution was passed, McCallion wrote to White. She did not mince words. 'It is unfortunate that our Member of Parliament has forced us to pass such a resolution, as we had great confidence and faith in him – a faith which has been completely shaken.'[42]

Outspoken NDP MPP Michael Cassidy described Streetsville's resolution as being 'without precedent' for an Ontario municipality. This might have been an overstatement, but it did reach its intended target, the Honourable Mr Davis. The premier agreed to come to Streetsville on 14 June. McCallion promptly booked the largest venue possible. Those who showed up would not soon forget the great confrontation.

When Davis arrived at the community hall in the arena building on that oppressively hot Thursday evening, the town was ready for him. Someone had even posted a few of the premier's old election posters below the 'Welcome to Streetsville' signs. Affixed across Davis's smiling image was a big sticker with the word 'SOLD!' Inside the mercifully air-conditioned hall, the premier found about five hundred residents (plus a few opposition MPPs, who could not resist an invitation to such an entertaining spectacle), most of them in a foul mood. When the guest of honour was introduced, a few scattered supporters rose to clap, but they were drowned out by loud 'boos' and catcalls.

No doubt relieved when the crowd fell silent, Davis was in for another treat. The next stage guest to be introduced was Hazel McCallion, who was greeted by raucous – and seemingly endless – cheers. Davis applauded politely.

No amount of smooth talking or calm reasoning could reassure this audience. Although most now were resigned to Streetsville's fate – an advertisement in the *Streetsville Review* three weeks earlier had even called on people to wear black arm bands to the first annual Streetsville Founders' Bread and Honey Festival – they were not going to let Davis get away with it. And the opposition would have plenty of fodder for the debate in the assembly.

'I am not saying for a moment there isn't some logic to the arguments of the town of Streetsville and the citizens there, heaven knows,' Davis would concede in that debate. Then, with typical ambiguity mixed with an attempt to convey moderation and objectivity, he added: 'It is just as difficult for us to make a determination that does upset a number of people in Streetsville as it would be to accede to their request, believing it, perhaps, in the long run not to be in the interest of the total community.'[43]

And the mail would continue to come in. It came from the young Doug Flowers:

This town is a public, not a mass, it is aware and concerned, its citizens participate because they have an identity and a sense of community ... [R]elationships develop quickly in this town and consequently there is a high degree of social stability ... I am honestly overwhelmed by the high degree of social concern and commitment to people that the leaders of Streetsville exhibit. It is my personal belief that should Streetsville be expanded [as opposed to amalgamated with Mississauga], the future residents of the new community will benefit not only from a high degree of people-oriented planning but also from a rare community spirit which emanates from the town.[44]

It came from the older Elizabeth Colley:

I come originally from Alberta, but have lived in five provinces of Canada and in Great Britain. And never have I experienced a sense of true neighbourhoodness and community spirit such as I have found in Streetsville.

Although writing as a private citizen and one who voted you into office, I find my position [as librarian] in Streetsville gives me a unique opportu-

nity to talk with all manner of citizens. I can assure you that my dismay at
the threatened takeover is shared not only by those born here and living
here all their lives but perhaps even more by those of us who have deliberately chosen to settle here because we value the quality of life in Streetsville.[45]

It came from genteel folks who had become irreverent. Local historian Mary Manning told the premier that her ancestors would have
voted Tory at a time when the Liberals were guaranteed to win even if
they had fielded a dog as a candidate. 'Let us hope the Conservatives
have not become the "dog,"' she wrote.[46]

Erindale College history professor Desmond Morton, a Streetsville
resident, took to writing not to Davis directly, but for public consumption. The town was 'neither rich nor exclusive,' he insisted in the *Mississauga Times*. It was fighting the province 'because it has the kind of
sense of community that Tory politicians often talk about in speeches.'
Hazel McCallion had realized it. 'Once a pillar of Progressive Conser-
vatism, [she] is now anathema to the provincial politicians and their
local allies.'[47]

But ultimately it was to no avail. On 29 June 1973, it was all but over.
The bill received royal assent. Only six months remained in Streetsville's life as a municipality. Amalgamation was pushed through, but
the wound would linger. In the 1975 provincial election, most of the
Streetsville polls, once so solidly Tory, would go to the NDP.

Saying Farewell

Streetsville-the-municipality went out in style. The last week of October
and the first week of November in 1973 were 'Streetsville Days,' when
most of the local organizations put on almost continuous celebrations
and family activities. On 30 November a banquet in the community centre brought together all who had volunteered on the town's many
boards and commissions. There were 'eight men with white gloves
doing nothing but serving wine,' the town treasurer recalled. But
perhaps the highlight of the evening was the presentation to each of
the volunteers of a silver plate with the town crest engraved in the
middle.[48]

The new head of regional council announced that the new Region of
Peel would not be launched with any New Year's fanfare because 'people are simply too busy New Year's Eve to take time off for something

as minor as the start of a new region.' Lou Parsons added that when the Township of Toronto became the Town of Mississauga on 1 January 1968, the only people who showed up to usher out the old municipality and welcome the new one were councillors, department heads, and those staff members who had to be there.[49]

In Streetsville, it was a different story. Many residents put their parties on hold to bid farewell to their town. There was not even standing room in the modest council chamber as the town council held its final meeting. It took place at almost the last possible moment – 7 p.m. on New Year's Eve. As the evening drew to a close, the mayor's chain of office was given for safekeeping to the Streetsville Historical Society.

And McCallion, forced to retire at age fifty-two as Streetsville's mayor but about to embark on a political career in a new forum, as councillor for the Streetsville ward, recited a poem composed by deputy reeve Jim Graham. The verses reflected on a town whose identity and sense of community could transcend even a high-profile politician:

A town, its people, their laughter and tears,
Their labour and leisure, their hopes and their fears,

A place to share this gift of living,
To become involved through an act of giving.

In a town, in a meeting, in a friendship, in a care,
Tonight we give thanks for the blessings we share.[50]

Hazel McCallion had learned from small-town politics the importance of being accessible and visible. She would not forget that. But it could be argued that in taking a seat on Mississauga city council she would be leaving 'a public' and joining 'a mass.' It was an unstable, disorganized mass that would soon be eager for some stability – for some sure-footed leadership.

3 Growing Pains

All was not well on Hazel McCallion's new political turf. The Town of Mississauga, formerly the Township of Toronto and soon to be the City of Mississauga, with the addition of little Streetsville and little Port Credit, had become polarized over the politics of growth. The suburban scuffling had started more than twenty years before the shotgun arrangement that turned the town into a city.

It took but a few weeks in 1952 for the grumble to become a murmur, thence a tremor, and finally (or so it would have seemed to the trembling local notables) a deafening roar. The correspondence had seemed innocuous at first – the envelope with the local tax bill. Many no doubt left it unopened in a corner of the kitchen counter. The deadline for payments was weeks away; it could wait while some of the more immediate needs of a young family were attended to.

When the contents of those envelopes finally were examined, faces turned red, residential blocks suddenly became political hornets' nests, unease and even anger became palpable. Fifty per cent tax increases? Two hundred per cent tax increases? All this unruly new development must have something to do with it. Who was making the expenditure decisions? And could the township really afford those huge water and sewer lines from the lake to distant Malton?

Suddenly, being a township councillor, or being the township clerk, did not feel so satisfying. For the incumbents craved the honour and respect that seemed to come with their offices. Always appearing folksy and 'down-to-earth,' for pretension was frowned upon in these parts, the local politicians could not help but appreciate the nods, the handshakes, the introductions and respectful applause at local events. They could remain close to home, still have a family life, but feel like a somebody. It was all rather comfortable. In fact, a few years earlier the reeve had thought nothing of urging that the whole township council be acclaimed to office. 'I am only making this appeal to the people feeling that I should try to save the taxpayers the unnecessary expense.'[1]

Now, however, these gentlemen, usually so calm and content, were hearing few kind words. Angry housewives were calling them at home late into the evenings. The callers were not taking kindly to assurances. Probably for the first time in the councillors' political 'career' (if it could be called that, for was it really supposed to be that much different from being president of a local service club?) they were having to insist on ending a telephone conversation. Their commitments to their day jobs – and their sensitivities – could not allow what had once been occasional and friendly repartee to become much less friendly.

They would never previously have heard from some of these people; these were new folks in town. Yet surely they were still friends and neighbours. Could not the problem be resolved in the time-honoured friends-and-neighbours tradition, over a cup of tea and a handshake? Of course, the guests would not fit into the home of Reeve Sid Smith. His electrical business was doing well, but his was no mansion. Maybe even the council chambers would be too small. No matter, the township could borrow the gymnasium at the Port Credit High School. Somehow, things would be worked out and all could enjoy a relaxing summer.

It did not go as planned. Even William Lyon Mackenzie could not have provoked such wrath in the township. A crowd of nine hundred or more had gathered. A neutral observer would not help but feel sorry for the men on the stage: the reeve, the councillors, and the target of the most criticism, township clerk J. Herbert Pinchin, in whom resided the institutional memory of the township. Still the owner of a turkey farm and orchard on the Streetsville Road, along with a gravel pit, this soft-spoken sixty-nine-year-old *éminence gris* had himself been the reeve in the 1920s. Now he was the municipal man with many hats, though he never sought a pay increase. And he had many extracurricular activities. He remained treasurer of the Clarkson-Dixie Fruit Growers' Association, in which capacity he was in frequent contact with the old Dixie families – in other words, the local notables. The tax assessment, the contracts, the subdivision plans, most ended up on his desk in one form or another.[2]

With such an informal way of conducting business, there was no capacity for damage control, no ability to react to complaints in a collected and confident manner. One of the stunned old-guard councillors could only observe meekly that the council's public relations had been 'practically nil.' The *Toronto Daily Star* told it like it was: this was 'a revolt.'[3]

At least they could hope that a revolt without a leader might peter out. The meeting would end and the people would scatter.

But they would not scatter before the protest movement found a committed spokes*woman*. Some in the audience might have recognized the fifty-six-year-old widow with a strong, intelligent voice. She had been volunteering here and there on civic committees. A resident of the township since 1939, in a small but elegant Cape Cod–style house on the Centre Road (Hurontario Street) just south of the Queen Elizabeth Way, she seemed urbane. She was fluently bilingual and had been Ottawa's first woman lawyer. A sometime columnist for *Chatelaine* magazine, she had even tried her hand at fiction writing. She had worked in New York and Paris as the chief purchaser for the T. Eaton Company. Even Mary Fix's surname seemed appropriate for the task that she was now to embrace.

Years later, longtime residents would observe many similarities between Fix and Hazel McCallion. They both would bring to their political work an extraordinary amount of personal energy, devoting almost all their waking hours to their communities. Both became fixtures, recognized by everyone. Both would seem to be savvy, no-nonsense, business-like administrators, unafraid to be outspoken.[4] Both would receive almost uniformly positive press.

But now, with a few sharp and articulate words at a township meeting such as had never before been witnessed, Mary McNulty Fix was to become the unofficial head of a protest movement. She was to be charged with somehow mending what she would later call 'the 120 square miles of trouble known as the Township of Toronto.'[5] She could spot the problem right away. The council was simply overwhelmed. It could not run a large business, as the township had become. The reeve and councillors could not plan ahead, for it had never really been necessary to do so in the past. 'They are doing petty jobs,' Fix complained. 'While they argued about $2 boots for firemen, they had not time to look at the $3,000,000 debenture debt they were piling behind them.'[6]

Fix's resolution calling for a provincial investigation was passed unanimously by the residents at that meeting, and later she presented a 950–signature petition to this effect to municipal affairs minister George Dunbar.[7] She even wrote to Peel's federal member of Parliament, senior Conservative Gordon Graydon, who as House Leader had bravely held the Tory opposition fort in Ottawa through the second half of World War II while the inept John Bracken dilly-dallied about securing a seat for himself in the Commons. Now, Fix had no apprehension about tracking Graydon down in New York, where he was attending United Nations meetings as part of a Canadian delegation. The world could wait. The Township of Toronto was on fire![8]

The resulting provincially commissioned report, by the consulting firm Entwistle and Co., confirmed many of the residents' charges.[9] 'All the legal requirements surrounding some of the issues have not yet been entirely fulfilled,' the report stated diplomatically. This was in reference to the municipality's failure to seek Ontario Municipal Board approval for bond issues. Other examples of the municipality's failure to implement professional best practices included haphazard assessment practices resulting in an unwarranted shift from industrial to residential assessment and from farm to residential assessment. There was also the burden placed on the southern water consumers as a result of connecting the A.V. Roe plant in Malton. The latter local outlay had been justified on the dubious grounds that the municipality had already been planning to extend the line to the village of Burnham-thorpe, in the east-central part of the township.

Added to all this was the failure to pursue long-overdue federal payments-in-lieu-of-taxation, for both the Avro site and the Long Branch Rifle Ranges; the need to be bailed out by 'patient' bankers to the tune of seven hundred thousand dollars; and the failure to give much responsibility to the treasurer, the one person in the municipality who had significant financial and accounting qualifications.[10]

Even the normally docile local newspaper could not help but take notice. 'In our opinion, township council must bear some of the responsibility, inasmuch at [sic] it has not kept the people informed on what has been transpiring; it has not made subdividers pay substantially enough for services.'[11]

The anger carried over into the 1953 municipal elections, in which most incumbents were swept aside. Fix took office initially as deputy reeve. The new head of council was Professor Anthony Adamson, already a renowned planner-architect and the brains behind the launch of urban-planning studies at the University of Toronto. He was just back from a study leave in Europe, sponsored by the United Nations. His task had been to document how various countries dealt with growth management.[12] But the professorial Adamson, who was born in the township but who spoke with a distinctly aristocratic British accent thanks to his childhood overseas, was laid back and philosophical about local small-mindedness.[13] It fell to Fix to be the determined fixer, leaving Adamson puzzled with her voracious passion for results. She was, by most accounts, the dominant member of the 1953–4 council, chairing the all-important Water Committee, the body charged with sorting out the financial mess caused by the ill-timed and ill-planned water line to Malton. This was done, and Fix was credited with putting the financing of basic infrastructure on a more business-like footing. She made amends with the Ontario Municipal Board, whose approval had not been sought by the previous council for debentures required for an expansion of the township hall.

In 1954 Fix became acting reeve for several months while the professor was bedridden with pneumonia – he had fallen into icy water while supervising flood relief in the little village of Churchville, an old, sleepy, picturesque Credit River mill town near the township's northern border. Illness was nothing new for Adamson. He had barely survived tuberculosis as a young adult, and this had left him paralysed for several years while he recovered in Arizona.[13] (But what had not killed him obviously made him stronger – he would die peacefully in 2002, at the age of ninety-six.) Adamson did not run for re-election, and Fix was acclaimed the new reeve on 1 January 1955.

By the time she took the helm, the municipality's population had reached approximately fifty thousand, more than double what it had been ten years earlier. About two-thirds of the people resided in suburban subdivisions, although rural lands still covered more than two-thirds of the township. Voter turnout in the rural areas continued to be about twice what it was in the subdivisions. This mixture of suburban and rural, and the need to juggle or somehow strategically direct and accommodate the pressures of development, would animate and bedevil Fix's leadership.

The Tribulations of Mary Fix

In unpublished reflections written in her retirement, Fix directed some remarks to women aspiring to go into politics. She did not consider the general population, or any major segments within it, averse to her because she was a woman. In her first campaign brochure in 1952 she did, however, include a special appeal to women. 'You are the first ones hit by excessive taxes,' she warned. 'You are the guardians of the family budget.'[14]

Inge and Bill Cumberland are among the few people still living who knew Fix well. They recall that it was in their basement in 1952 that Fix finally decided to go into politics, citing the tax-increase crisis and the mismanagement. Having worked actively on Fix's campaigns, the Cumberlands insist that there was absolutely no overt hostility in the suburban neighbourhoods to Fix as a woman in politics. However, they speculate that there may have been some suspicion or resentment among the farmers, whom they regarded as 'very conservative.'

Fix's Catholicism appears not to have been a factor, says Bill Cumberland: 'She never advertised her religion.'[15] Those of Fix's records that have survived contain very few references to religion. In her draft, partial memoirs, she mentions her faith not at all. However, a relative of a municipal official who served prior to the Fix era, and who resided in the rural north, where the Orange Lodge had enjoyed a long presence, told me that there was a somewhat resentful perception among his neighbours because, during Fix's reeveship, there was a proliferation of Catholic churches and schools.[16] Some people apparently believed that Fix, and not the changing demographic make-up of the community, was somehow responsible.

Her religious and moral compass, whatever it was, obviously was compatible with industrial development. Under Fix, residential building was curtailed severely while the reeve travelled across Canada and beyond in an effort to attract industrial enterprises, and thus to ease the burden on the existing residential taxpayers. Predicting that her municipality would be Canada's future 'Ruhr Valley,' Fix was given de facto 'carte blanche authority' to work out deals for the budding industrial areas.[17] By 1958 the value of industrial building permits totalled more than fifteen million dollars, outstripping residential development.[18] Even the federal government's 1959 termination of the Avro Arrow program, resulting in massive layoffs, including thousands in the township, was not enough ultimately to dampen progress on local industrial expansion. In 1951 industrial assessment had amounted to 23.2 per cent of the total and commercial assessment stood at just 7.1 per cent. By 1959 the combined industrial-commercial assessment stood at almost 50 per cent.[19]

Fix was unyielding in her attempt to secure the old 'Rifle Ranges' (126 barren acres on the lakefront) from the federal government in order to make more room for industrial development and to create a better balance between the industrial-commercial and residential assessment bases. The note she scribbled on a map that she kept with her records suggests how important this issue was to her: 'Rifle Range property: I bought the 35 acres for sewage plant in 1955 & after much manoeuvring acquired all the rest in 1958. I contacted politicians, military authorities, C.D. Howe and finally got everything through "War Assets Disposal," but the story would make a book.'[20]

Fix's industrial-development strategy ran the risk of alienating not only the homebuilders and developers but other businesspeople as well. The old rural council had set up an industrial commission, consisting primarily of small but well-known and politically influential businessmen. Fix became frustrated with their inertia and had them all dismissed.

> They apparently talked solemnly about how vitally necessary it was to get Industry into the Township and how strange it was that we were not getting any. As far as any help or practical suggestions were concerned, the gentlemen might just as well have been playing poker in there behind the closed doors. Maybe they were. I only hope they were enjoying their meetings more than we enjoyed ours. I had difficulty in bearing with this frustrating nonsense which indeed had a comic-opera aspect.[21]

Even before she graduated from deputy reeve to reeve, Fix was well aware that, for another reason, easing the tax burden by situating more industry in the township would be politically perilous. She knew that 'residents of the various communities always object strenuously to industry in their midst.'[22] But it was a policy she regarded as the most rational and the most necessary. She was also determined to eliminate scattered development, so as to minimize the expense and strain on the municipality's already burdened physical infrastructure. As far as Fix was concerned, good management meant channelling development to but a few viable areas.

The comprehensive *Industrial Development Study*, prepared in 1958 by the Township of Toronto Planning Board, sheds light on the dynamics of development in the township. Despite its large land mass (approximately sixty thousand acres), the municipality had very limited options for where to situate industrial development or, for that matter, any major development. After examining the whole township, the study rejected most of the northern half, and even significant parts of the southern half, for consideration for industrial development in the foreseeable future, largely on the grounds that servicing was many years away.

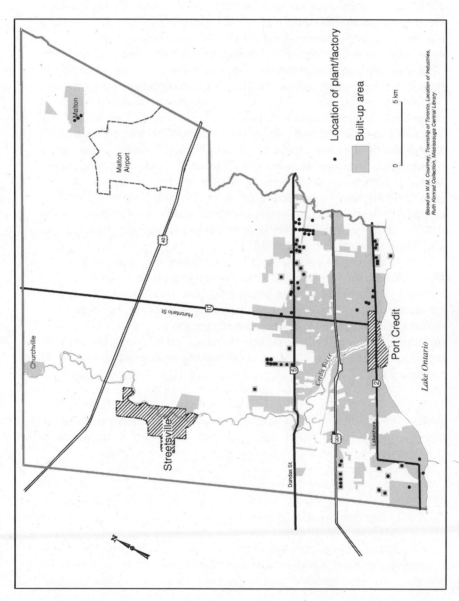

Map 3.1. Industrial Enterprises, Toronto Township, 1959

Location of plant/factory

Built-up area

0 ___ 5 km

Based on W.M. Courtney, Township of Toronto, Location of Industries,
Ruth Konrad Collection, Mississauga Central Library.

Malton

Malton
Airport

Churchville

Streetsville

Dundas St

Huronto St

Credit River

Port Credit

Lakeshore

Lake Ontario

N

In the end, the board settled on Clarkson (especially the area around the intersection of what are now Southdown Road and Royal Windsor Drive) and South Dixie, both of which were contiguous with existing residential areas. In the case of South Dixie, the board acknowledged expansion even that far north (along Dixie Road between the Queen Elizabeth Way and Highway 5) to be a concern: 'The relation to the neighbouring residential area is not ideal because the leeward situation of built up and future residential areas necessitates the exclusion of obnoxious industries from the area.'[23]

Fix secured the help of nationally renowned planning experts like Max Bacon and Eugene Faludi. The subdividers were now made to contribute to the construction of infrastructure in the new neighbourhoods and were required even to assist with the cost of some of the basic servicing for the industrial parks. As Fix put it, 'As far as I am concerned, the welcome sign on the doormat of this township should be upside down for chisellers looking for favours which will burden farms and homes with an extra tax load.'[24]

Fix's subdivision charges netted four million dollars between 1955 and 1959. She forced residential developers to include plans for industry in their subdivisions or to pay more to her subdividers' fund.[25] As president of the Urban-Rural Municipal Association, she vigorously opposed attempts by developers to have these charges eliminated or to have the Planning Act amended to give the authority only to the province. The irate reeve was convinced that the province was beholden to the developers.[26]

> The control of housing development is ... vital and it involves dealing with one of the most powerful, sometimes one of the most sinister groups on this continent. The builders and developers, with their enormous and wealthy organization, are a pressure group able to make most Governments and Government-sponsored Housing Authorities or Mortgage Corporations cringe before their might and before their singular ability to reach into very high places to obtain the 'go-ahead' for more and more housing, whether or not it is needed.[27]

She counselled her successors not to get 'emotionally involved' with the developers and builders. Fix was convinced that these corporate interests were the main obstacle to her remaining in power. 'You will recall that, in 1955, we had declared a period of freezing for subdividers. This proved a very unpopular move for one, and I had an enforced holiday for the year 1956 – a consequence which did not surprise me at all.' She likewise surmised that 'the builders were so fed up with people like me who insisted on economic balance and proper building conditions that they decided to take the bit into their collective teeth and to show all the Ontario municipalities who was boss.'

In 1959 four developers selected by the Urban Development Institute, including one in the Township of Toronto, launched lawsuits against their respective municipalities to recover all added charges that were being imposed on them. Fix immediately summoned to the township hall the twenty-two developers who had interests in the municipality ('they had never been told off en masse before') and declared that all subdivisions would be halted until the suits were dropped. Although the developers complied, Fix mused later that 'incidentally, this was my last year in politics. Mere coincidence? Who can tell?'[28]

Fix knew that it would be difficult to cultivate a strong, animated power base to counter the opposition machinations: 'When everybody is moderately happy, a great many will not even bother to vote. This leaves to small, well-organized minorities to get in their fine work ... I could feel the builders getting their knives sharpened for me.'[29] Bill Cumberland recalls that Fix would say that she felt very lonely shortly after each election. Although she could count on a fairly solid group of campaign volunteers (but not in the rural areas, where she seldom campaigned), they promptly dispersed after election day. She was left with organized opponents but unorganized proponents.

Dealing with confident and organized opponents proved to be a constant difficulty in the management of council. Despite attempting to take control of the municipality from an old guard, Mary Fix found that the formal transparency with which council operated had to be compromised rather than augmented, in order not to reveal the apparent weaknesses and divisions on council to its circling enemies.

Predictably, breaches in transparency became an easy rallying cry for opponents. In 1957 a 'Citizens' Committee for Good Government' was formed to discredit Fix and to urge, explicitly, that former reeve Tom Jackson be returned. The signatories asked the readers, 'Are you satisfied with government-by-secret-meeting, closed to press and public ... [and] "Council-controlled censorship?"'

The missive did contain a few appeals to Fix's traditional base of support in the southern part of the township, especially the Clarkson and Credit Reserve neighbourhoods. But consider the anti-Fix group's main accusations:

- 'If you live in the north are you happy about paying higher Hydro rates than in the south?'
- 'What do you think of the delays in sewer connections for homes, business and industry?'
- The correspondents urged a vote for Jackson 'so that Toronto Township may once again return to good government and sound administration.'[30]

The writers were thus appealing to the more rural and established elements in the township, among whom Fix's support had never been strong. The township's former zoning director remembers how difficult it was to face, even with Fix and planner Max Bacon in attendance, hostile rural crowds fearing higher taxes because of the relief Fix sought to provide to the *suburban* ratepayers. These constituents were also deeply suspicious of anything other than a *laissez-faire* approach to planning.[31]

In reply to all this, the best that Fix could do was to insist that 'we cannot extend immediately the vast network of services required, but the feeder watermains and the sewage collector mains of the distant future are now on the drawing boards of our consulting engineers as a guide to the day when Toronto Township will probably be the teeming City of South Peel.'[32] She also attempted to show that Jackson's platform was folly and that it appealed to special interests. She accused him of trying 'to make millionaires of a handful of Dixie landowners' by having sought to proceed with a gargantuan industrial scheme in an area where water and sewer services were still years away.

> My modest 1955 zoning plan for Dixie, endorsed by Council, October 17, 1955, with my deputy-reeve, Mr. Jackson, signing the council policy resolution, was PROMPTLY SCRAPPED by him the instant he got elected. The above super-colossal scheme was substituted. He has plagued planning board staff while both in and out of council ever since.
>
> ... I believe DEVELOPMENT SHOULD MOVE IN CONCENTRIC CIRCLES FROM LAKESIDE SERVICING BASES, PACING SEWER AND WATER MAINS. ANYTHING ELSE IS FINANCIAL SUICIDE....
>
> ALSO: Two subdividers in the northern area are moving Heaven and Earth to get under way with 3700 lots for homes, none of which would pay their way in school taxes.[33]

Fix survived that election, but not by much. And she did not have to wait long for the next big challenge. In December 1958 her opponents put up another well-known candidate, Dixie's Leslie Hughes. A worried Fix fended him off by producing deeds and mortgage instruments showing that Hughes and his wife had mortgaged their sixty acres to Applewood-Dundas Ltd. (then the township's largest homebuilder, run by Gordon and Harold Shipp) and that Applewood had agreed to pay thirty-five hundred dollars per acre at such time as servicing was available.

Applewood had written to the township asking to be relieved of most subdivision charges and servicing requirements, a request that Fix had dismissed out of hand. Fix now charged that Hughes would either be forced to deal with issues in which he had a personal interest, or else he would be completely ineffective on council, given the significance of the issue.[34] Although she managed to damage Hughes' credibility and to win that election, the old guard and the developers would surely have regarded this as another provocation from the outspoken reeve.

This provocation, as with most such challenges in politics, would not be forgotten.

The Development Regime

Waiting in the wings was Robert Speck – smart, personable, a fruit-market owner but vaguely urbane in his loose-fitting suits. He was forty-four years old in 1959 and had served two terms on the council, most recently as deputy reeve. He seemed fit and healthy; few would have suspected that within a decade his heart condition would become the subject of local conversation, not to mention the object of daring medical interventions.

And Robert Speck was not Mary Fix. Granted, the first female reeve had a passion that everyone took to be genuine. She seemed to be everywhere. One month she would be in Europe stubbornly recruiting corporate investors and their industrial property taxes. Then she would turn up in Toronto or Montreal, imparting her wisdom, in French and English, to intrigued fellow municipal leaders who could be forgiven for assuming that Ottawa's Charlotte Whitton, the outspoken first Canadian woman mayor, had moved to *a township*. She thought nothing of imposing a litany of financial and infrastructural obligations on builders who had hitherto faced few questions and even fewer restrictions. They could now count themselves fortunate if the iron-fisted reeve supported their projects at all, based on her preference for orderly, contiguous development. Moreover, if she thought any of her council colleagues was an amateur, she did not hesitate to say so. Her reforming zeal prompted grins of admiration.

Yet it all now seemed passé. The crisis had subsided. The wildy unscientific assessment system had been reformed. The ratepayers in the suburban neighbourhoods were not seeing the staggering tax increases that had helped to put Fix into office. They were seeing industry and planning, and a township on the move.

On the move where? On the move, it seems, to becoming the 'teeming city of South Peel.' It would get there, Fix had insisted, through rational planning. That meant putting an end to scattered development, and thus antagonizing the builders, developers, and speculators. That also meant putting industry close to residential areas, thus antagonizing many residents in Fix's core political base, the suburban subdivisions. And that meant delaying urban services and thus perhaps eliminating the retirement windfalls of the rural north's residents and farmers, including many of the old, stalwart families.

Who said that rational economic planning was shrewd politics? Robert Speck had not said it. To be sure, this practical man also spoke of the great City On The Lake, of expansion and of economic development. But he spoke to his would-be constituents from across the picket fence, rather than the podium, his boots firmly on the ground. No economics lectures here! He could vary his accent, so to speak, when he moved from the middle-class suburbanite with an eye to nature to the working-class bungalow owner with an eye to moving up one day, or the farmer with an eye to his nest eggs.

When he could not convey the message in person, he could do so through advertising. Because the freedom to communicate and persuade seems to exist in abundance for those who can pay for it, and only in theory for those without means, Robert Speck's campaign needed money – and it found it, from somewhere.

A whiff of Liberalism might have hung over him, and his familial connections to that party helped him to seem at arm's length from the local Tories, but most of his friends and campaign workers were undoubtedly good and stalwart Tories – loyal friends like Chic Murray, who would become his deputy reeve; Ron Searle, a councillor; and, let it not be forgotten, Brampton's Billy Davis, for whom the insiders at Queen's Park were expecting great things now that the legendary Tom Kennedy was in repose at the Dixie Union Cemetery.

And then there were the developers – a new generation of young, ambitious businesspeople. There was the dapper S.B. 'Bruce' McLaughlin, the 'young man in a hurry,' who saw Hurontario Street as a future Yonge Street and began buying up farms in the 1950s. By the early 1960s, he had obtained a law degree (after which he would consider himself an intellectual and not merely a wealthy entrepreneur). More importantly, he now controlled four thousand acres around the geographical centre of the township.

A little to the west of the McLaughlin lands, almost six thousand acres were owned by the legendary E.P. Taylor, a brewing magnate who had almost tripped over the land development business when he began working on Don Mills and quickly realized that spectacular profits could be made. Only slightly less impressive were the thirty-five hundred acres in northwest Mississauga collected by Markborough Developments, a company controlled by several large financial interests but whose main interest now lay in the township.

These were the so-called Big Three. But there were a few other notables – local families in fact who tended to function as both developers and builders (it has long been common for large development companies across North America to get the necessary approvals and concept plans but then to sell lots to large building companies). Noteworthy among them was Harold Shipp, remarkably soft spoken for a developer and even prone to sentimental emotion, especially when talking about Canada. He spoke with a gentle stutter and had a reputation for being rather cautious. He had begun building in Toronto Township in 1950, and it became the focus of his operations. By that time, he was already the driving force behind his father's company, G.S. Shipp and Son Ltd. The Shipps' Applewood development in the township was one of Canada's largest suburban residential developments, although father and son also built shopping plazas and car dealerships. (Sometimes they would visually link these business interests, as when they advertised suburban homes with cars parked on the roof.) He was active in industry associations, and in the early 1970s he would serve as president of the Housing and Urban Development Association of Canada.[35]

Iggy Kaneff arrived in Canada from Bulgaria in 1951 – with 'five dollars in my pocket,' as he likes to tell it. He immediately began working for the Shipps, but in 1957 he started his own company, bearing his name. This short, impeccably tailored gentleman – not flamboyant like McLaughlin but with a strong hint of European elegance and courtliness – always heeded his father's advice that he should keep his investments close to home. And home for him was the township. 'I feel very, very proud [of Kaneff's success],' Harold Shipp would tell a reporter. 'Here is a guy who made it.'[36]

Speck and his fellow local politicians adopted a much warmer approach to these men and their ilk than had Mary Fix. It had some of the appearance of Harvey Molotch's classic 'growth machine'[37] or of Clarence Stone's 'development regime.'[38] The developers had resources the township did not have. Indeed, before the end of the first month of Robert Speck's first term as reeve, the senior staff of the municipality had submitted a comprehensive report on development. Although noting that 'the Township of Toronto has one of the best overall assessment ratios in the Province of Ontario [47.07 per cent industrial–commercial],'[39] the managers suggested that future growth, even industrial growth, would require comprehensive arrangements with the developers. 'While superficially it may be suggested that the number of housing units released should be directly related to the increase in industrial assessment in the Township, we feel that such an approach has some serious shortcomings.'[40]

Thus, the municipality needed large, affluent developers with large holdings prepared to undertake major projects and to contribute to the cost of public infrastructure, while the developers needed a well-connected and savvy political leadership prepared to advocate with the province for major infrastructure projects. Those projects would have to be big indeed. By 1963 the water-works capacity had been earmarked to be quintupled over the next twenty-five years. The funds would come to the municipality from the developers and from special arrangements to be negotiated with the Ontario Water Resources Commission and with senior provincial politicians.[41] The biggest coup would be the province's eighty-eight-million-dollar South Peel Water and Sewage System, inaugurated in 1968.

So comprehensive agreements were negotiated after round-table discussions with the Big Three developers. These agreements, which were so wide ranging that municipal solicitor Basil Clark warned councillors they probably would not withstand a legal challenge if one were ever launched, provided for, among other things, the purchase of land for a postal facility at below-market rates, the advance payment of agreed-upon levies, an ecumenical centre in the future Square One Shopping Centre, and eight day-care centres.[42]

The close working relationship had become the norm. One group of consultants would observe after several years of this that it 'may be that

Mississauga is the only municipality using [this] type of [comprehensive development] agreement.' And such agreements are

> to some extent an expression of good faith, giving the developer a commitment on the part of the municipality that, having assembled large tracts of land and set up a development team, the developer will be allowed to carry out his project subject to certain requirements.
>
> For the municipality, the agreement provides assurance that the developer will phase his development in such a way as to maintain a balanced overall assessment, and agree to such things as the provision of school sites at a set price, and the construction of community facilities.[43]

In 1969 it was decided to move the whole town administration from the Four Corners in Cooksville (then the principal intersection in Mississauga) several kilometres north to a new office building in a still virtually empty tract of land owned by S.B. McLaughlin Associates.[44] Limiting the town's future options was a provision in the contract with McLaughlin stating that the new building 'cannot be leased, sold, or sublet for other than municipal purposes.'[45] In other words, the deal gave the impression of corporate advantage sanctioned by a public body in possible contradiction to the public interest.

But it was not strictly a one-way street. Town council agreed only after a fire destroyed part of the town's old Cooksville (Four Corners) building; the cause is undetermined to this day. Even then, the politicians did not merely submit. McLaughlin ended up providing the new building in exchange for the much-less-valuable, fire-damaged Cooksville headquarters. At this point the plan was sold enthusiastically to the community as 'an attractive proposal' and as an 'offer too good to turn down.'[46]

Even so, McLaughlin had to sweeten his offer just hours before the town-council meeting that was scheduled to reach a decision on the matter. He promised to give Mississauga a new fifteen-acre site with fifteen thousand square feet of office space in return for the town's current buildings (which were much smaller) and eight-acre site at Confederation Square. Town manager Dean Henderson was now able to point out that the land being offered by McLaughlin was worth $1,306,800, with the fifty-one-thousand-square-foot building valued at $1,275,000. The present seven acres were valued at $1.082 million and the partially burned town hall at only $500,000.[47]

As reeve, Speck enjoyed popularity and job security. He easily beat back Mary Fix in her attempted comeback at the end of 1961 and faced no serious opponent after that, acclamations being the norm. In 1968, when the Township of Toronto became the Town of Mississauga, it seemed obvious that the distinction of being the first mayor should go to Robert Speck.

His heart attacks, becoming an almost regular occurrence now, only modestly whittled away at his schedule and did nothing to diminish his popularity. But finally, in December 1971 his political colleagues waited nervously as he became Canada's seventeenth heart-transplant patient (the donor, a young Toronto subway accident victim, was to be immortalized in the lush Richard's Memorial Park on the Mississauga lakefront). Robert Speck was never to be defeated by the electors of his municipality, but one hundred days after the risky operation, he was recalled by the Great Elector. He was succeeded immediately after the funeral by his trusted lieutenant, Chic Murray – the *ill-fated* Chic Murray.

The seeds of regime collapse had been sown even before the more dour fifty-seven-year-old Murray took the helm. In 1971, recognizing growing public concern about the way the municipality was being developed (a few anti-developer candidates had done remarkably well in the 1970 municipal elections), council finally established a citizens' committee to make recommendations on the plans for the lands owned by the Big 3 (Markborough, Erin Mills, and McLaughlin). But the committee's work proceeded in a rather lacklustre manner.[48] Council did not fully appreciate the urgency.

Smelling blood, the provincial opposition parties were starting to accuse the Mississauga politicians of being agents for the developers and members of the Tory Big Blue Machine. NDP member Michael Cassidy called Mayor Murray a 'bagman' for both the Conservatives and the big corporations. Cassidy also claimed, with some cause, that following Speck's death in April 1972 and Murray's elevation to the mayor's office, Councillor Lou Parsons had been appointed 'the reeve over the then deputy reeve [Grant Clarkson] because the then deputy reeve was a bit uncomfortable with the powers that be.'[49]* Although

---

* In 1968, when the Township of Toronto became the Town of Mississauga, the office of mayor was created. The offices of reeve and deputy reeve remained in place, however, functioning in effect as first deputy mayor and second deputy mayor, respectively. All three positions were elected at large.

he seldom engaged in any public recrimination with his council colleagues, Clarkson, a member of one of the old local families, had come
to embrace various environmental and conservation causes.[50]

The developers did not always help themselves by being so outspoken on a wide range of public affairs. Each of the major developers,
took up, for example, the cause of annexing Port Credit and Streetsville,
even before the latter municipality elected a reform council that was
sometimes overtly hostile to the developers. In a 1972 interview, Bruce
McLaughlin explained why he favoured amalgamation: 'We need all
the strength we can possibly get here in South Peel in order to resist the
impact of Toronto on us. We want to do our own thing. We can't do it
unless we're united, unless we're strong enough and efficient enough
to prove to the provincial government that we're a viable unit.'[51] When
the provincial politicians went ahead with amalgamation, with Mississauga's politicians cheerleading, it looked to many like Big Money had
won out again.

It certainly looked that way in 1973 to a young political novice running for mayor on a slow-growth platform. But he was certain that he
could come from nowhere to stun the establishment.

4 'Big City Politics'

At some point during the winter of 1972–3, an unusual visitor appeared before Hazel McCallion in the Streetsville town hall. He was a thirty-one-year-old fresh-faced family physician, and it was his first time in the building. The mayor of the little town may have recognized him as the county coroner, called in when his services were needed. But that happened only occasionally, and he usually was back at his private office attending to sentient patients. He had virtually no public profile.

No stench of death hung over Martin Dobkin on this occasion. This brash, inexperienced youngster was proposing to run for mayor of Mississauga! What was said next remains in dispute. Dobkin remembers McCallion being taken aback, not because of his inexperience but because *she* had intended to run for the post. But McCallion does not recall that she was seriously considering contesting the top job, although there was speculation to this effect in the local press. Besides, there was another battle to wage. Streetsville's last great effort to avoid being taken over had yet to begin.

If McCallion's initial reaction to Dobkin is in dispute, her parting words are not. The Streetsville politician bestowed her blessing on the upstart. 'Well, you'd better win, then!' she boomed as the unexpected visitor turned to leave.[1]

Could such an outcome be imagined? Here was a man with no political machine, no money behind him, and no prospect of raking in significant campaign contributions, considering his anti-developer sentiments. Incumbent Chic Murray, Robert Speck's erstwhile protégé and successor, had, it seemed, as much money as he would need for signs, telemarketers, slick advertising, motivational receptions and celebrations, all the paraphernalia of a sophisticated campaign. He had been in local politics for a decade and a half. The developers backed him.

But therein lay Murray's problem. Dobkin would not have to be brilliant or wealthy or famous or articulate; he just had to pin any suspicion, distrust, dislike, or annoyance over development onto the incumbent. 'How much is [Bruce] McLaughlin giving you?' he would thunder at Murray during all-candidates' meetings.[2] The bold challenger, encouraged by the 1972 Toronto elections in which much of the old guard was forced to retire, underwrote his $4,000 campaign with his own money, a far cry from the $18,500 to $60,000 (depending on whose estimate you believe) Murray had collected in donations.[3]

The contrast between the candidates was stark. Dobkin turned Murray's experience and resources into assets – for the underdog. 'If I had the 15 years of experience the mayor says he has in his literature, I would be ashamed to put such experience in my literature – I wouldn't want anyone to know about it.'[4] The slicker and more expensive Murray's campaign became, the more this appeared to the voters to confirm Dobkin's message that Murray was too close to the 'fast-back' developers.

Dobkin's youth and lack of political baggage proved appealing to many voters, though most would have caught a glimpse of him only in newspaper photographs, not in person. 'Have you ever seen a picture of him?' Bob Keeping, who helped Dobkin, would ask years later. 'He looked so innocent. He was like the boy next door!'[5]

At first, the confident Murray thought little of Dobkin. 'My father had not the slightest idea that he was going to lose,' Jim Murray would reminisce almost thirty years after that watershed election. 'However, during the election [campaign], it became obvious that there was a significant anti-development mood in some pockets. Did he think there was [such a mood] prior to that? No. When Martin Dobkin was nominated he thought he was a nuisance candidate.'

But the younger Murray conceded that his father should have seen the writing on the wall. Dobkin 'was in the right place at the right time … It could have been … open the phone book and write the guy's name down and he would have won the election in all probability. The mood of the public was that there's too much development, it's going too fast, and we need to stop and have a second look and say "slow down."'[6]

Indeed, by the late 1960s population pressure and demand for suburban housing were becoming especially acute. Mississauga's population grew by an annual rate of 10 per cent in 1972 and 1973.[7] Small infill developers were deluging the municipality with proposals. Comprehensive development agreements (such as those requiring the provision of amenities) had been negotiated with the large developers, especially the Big Three, and some modest subdividers' fees were expected from everyone else, but there were no across-the-board 'prices of admission' for the smaller developers. There were no across-the-board parkland-dedication standards. Precious neighbourhood green spaces, such as the Rattray Marsh on the Lake Ontario shoreline, seemed on the verge of being lost.[8]

When residents saw new projects being slapped together, some of which reportedly did not even meet basic building-code requirements, they began to notice that the local politicians had been having very cordial relations with the large developers.[9] After all, the council had even relocated the town hall to make a developer happy! The very large developers might not have been the ones proposing the project that most offended any given resident, but few residents would have made fine distinctions among developers and among builders. The rhetoric employed by the reformist challengers in the 1973 municipal election suggested that a direct connection was now being drawn between localized land-use-related, aesthetic, and amenity-related grievances, and a growing perception that the well-established municipal politicians were in an unhealthy alliance with unscrupulous large developers.

Although the development regime had succeeded in opening up vast new greenfield sites, non-contiguous with most of the existing residential areas, to serviced development, and although basic infrastructure had been installed with the province's assistance, making most of the municipality available for development, the implementation of the comprehensive plans drawn up in collaboration with the large developers might actually, in one sense, have been moving too slowly. The huge Erin Mills and Meadowvale 'new towns' had been designed on paper to the last detail, but they were still in their early phases. As all the major parties were still scrambling to marshal their resources to meet growing demand, large tracts of land were, in effect, tied up. This was forcing more growth into the established neighbourhoods. As the municipal elections approached, malcontents and reformers were coming out of the woodwork.

In affluent Ward 2, arguably vying with Streetsville for the epicentre of reform, it was almost as if Mary Helen Spence had tripped on a cord. In late 1971, concerned about a proposed development close to her home on Bexhill Road, she started going door to door. She began to hear things – about other developments, about Councillor Lou Parsons, about the old guard. But the grumbling had hitherto been scattered and disorganized. People were now finally talking to each other. Soon the core of concerned residents heard that Rattray Marsh was about to be bulldozed. They helped to breath new life into a long-standing but small and exhausted citizens' group. Clarkson Road was to be widened for no apparent reason, taking out dozens of Mississauga's most majestic trees. Like wildfire, word spread to other blocks and neighbourhoods. The Council of South Mississauga Community Associations was formed. News spread outside the ward, and the Save Our Trees and Streams Society (SOTAS) was born, counting among its founding members the world-renowned planner Macklin Hancock, a Cooksville resident.

Back in Ward 2, the concerned residents quickly wrote off the councillor and, indeed, the whole council. Middle-class and upper-middle-class women, most of whom were well-educated stay-at-home parents, and some of whom were committed environmentalists, were the core of the movement. It was a movement that now figured it would need to claim a share of power. It set its sights on the next election and recruited thirty-one-year-old Spence.

By late summer 1973 McCallion, too, was on the election hustings, running not for mayor but for councillor for the Streetsville ward, that town's demise as a municipality having by then been confirmed. She was easily fending off her challenger, Grant Clarkson, Mississauga's reeve (in effect deputy mayor). By his own admission, Clarkson had found no place else to run when the amalgamation caused a redistribution of wards. He did live close to Streetsville, had long been active in town, and was an acknowledged supporter of natural conservation projects. But he was associated with the Mississauga old guard and had called the popular McCallion a 'political warmonger.'[10] These were serious liabilities for Clarkson. On election day, he would capture only 24 per cent of the vote.

Dobkin, Spence, and McCallion joined the other reform candidates in criticizing the 'old guard' for being close to the developers and for ignoring the aspirations of residents and their neighbourhoods. Although these candidates had not organized themselves into an electoral association, there were common proposals in their platforms. They demanded a strong official plan, slower development, a large central park and generally more park space, stringent restrictions on high-density development (including an end to high-rise construction), formal and extensive participation for community groups in planning and development issues, a relocation of the civic centre back to the Four Corners in Cooksville, major improvements to public transit, and that serious consideration be given to merging the community's beleaguered transit system (which was contracted out at the time to Charterways Bus Lines) with the Toronto Transit Commission.[11]

These candidates and their supporters would have endorsed the *Globe and Mail*'s unflattering description of the municipality: 'An aggressively bland community of two-car garages, hamburger stands, windy plazas, tacky acres of new townhouses and bulky apartments ... Don Mills revisited.'[12] Not to be outdone by dramatic rhetoric, candidate Dobkin had referred to Hurontario Street, Mississauga's main north-south thoroughfare, as 'the worst abortion in planning and development in Peel County ... a gallery of cars shooting in and out of the high rises and strip plazas.' His slogan was 'Make Mississauga Liveable.'[13]

On the fateful first day of October, three full months before the new city would officially come into existence, the candidates gathered at T.L. Kennedy Secondary School, the traditional election-night place of congregation. It quickly became apparent that six of the ten victorious candidates were reformers. Martin Dobkin was among them. This was a startling upset, but it also demonstrated that the anxiety in the municipality was not distributed uniformly. Map 4.1 shows the active subdivision applications in 1972 superimposed on the ward boundaries for the 1973 municipal election. Although we do not have data on the precise location and extent of subdivision applications in the still-independent municipalities of Streetsville and Port Credit (which became Mississauga's Wards 8 and 9 for the 1973 election, adding about 10 per cent to Mississauga's population), we do know from news reports and archival records that several development projects within Port Credit were causing considerable angst.[14] We also see that Streetsville was almost surrounded by Mississauga subdivision applications.

The reformers were elected in Wards 2, 4, 6, 8, and 9. These happen to be the areas of the most intensive development activity, including development close to established areas. Wards 1 and 7, which returned members of the old guard, were relatively quiet from a development perspective. Although Ward 3 was busy, almost all the existing built-up areas north of Dundas Street were in fact industrial, meaning that new development was not contiguous with existing residential areas. The south side of Dundas Street was industrial/commercial. A utility green

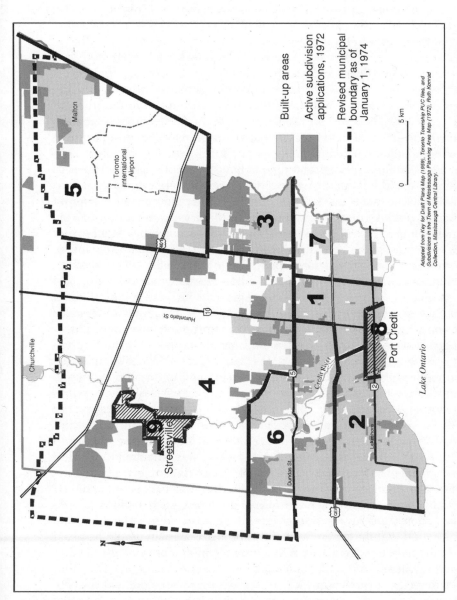

Map 4.1. Active Subdivision Applications, Town of Mississauga, 1972, with Overlay of Ward Boundaries, 1973 Elections

Built-up areas

Active subdivision applications, 1972

Revised municipal boundary as of January 1, 1974

0   5 km

Adapted from Key for Draft Plans Map (1959), Toronto Township PUC files, and Subdivisions in the Town of Mississauga Planning Area Map (1972), Ruth Konrad Collection, Mississauga Central Library.

Malton

Toronto International Airport

Churchville

Hurontario St

Streetville

Dundas St

Credit River

Lakeshore

Port Credit

Lake Ontario

N

belt (and the Queensway, a four-lane thoroughfare) separated those areas from the Applewood residential district to the south.

The Reformers in Power

They were outsiders, essentially. Three of the six reformist politicians were women. Dobkin was Jewish in a municipality with a very small Jewish community. Only Hazel McCallion and the Ward 4 councillor, Caye Killaby, had any previous experience in elected office. Although the reformers had railed against the status quo, for the most part they were an unknown quantity.

Early on the developers seemed to have been optimistic that a *modus vivendi* could be found. A few olive branches were extended. Harold Shipp wrote to the new Ward 2 councillor, Mary Helen Spence, offering to pick up the cost of a new song about Mississauga by country music star Tommy Hunter, a resident of Spence's ward.[15] Bruce McLaughlin was pledging to be a big supporter of community festivals – and he was offering to make his planners available to help create a 'new, system-planned city.'

Could the reformers be co-opted? Dobkin gave no such indication. In the weeks preceding the official swearing in, he continued to lob criticisms against the developers and even against the municipality's planners. He was extending no olive branches of his own.

And once the reformers had their hands on the levers of authority, other things started to happen. Yes, the economic uncertainty had a role in taking care of seemingly out-of-control development. Annual population growth rates sank well below the double digits (to 5.6 per cent in 1975).[16] But the reformist politicians were an active bunch, at least initially. The lot levies were increased tenfold to more than three thousand dollars in most cases. A huge public process was launched to develop an official plan for the city (the official plan of the former Town of Mississauga had been merely a hodge-podge that had been amended countless times). For the first time before or since, a staffed Public Participation Office was set up to encourage broad input. The reformers promised that the centrepiece of this new official plan would be phasing – gradual, incremental development contiguous with the already built-up areas.

Council also moved quickly to secure for future generations the ecologically precious Rattray Marsh in southwest Mississauga. Its fate had been a source of simmering controversy for more than a decade. (Hazel

McCallion still constantly brings up the marsh acquisition to underscore her own environmental credentials.) More public money was expended to expropriate the beautiful lakefront Adamson estate, saving it from becoming a condominium development. Dobkin was even now musing about land-banking – buying up or expropriating vacant land and releasing it for development gradually at uninflated prices.

Such actions signalled a sea change. A 1974 management review by Stevenson and Kellogg Consulting noted:

> What might be described as a fundamental shift in emphasis in Mississauga planning has taken place over the past year. This shift is from a less demanding control on development to exceedingly tight control. This is exemplified by the 50 or so conditions attached to an application now in process from Markborough Properties.[17]

Obviously, then, this 'fundamental shift' was not only rhetorical. By the fall of 1974 municipal observers were even treated to the spectacle of Bruce McLaughlin publicly begging the council for a ninety-minute meeting.[18] 'We don't know what's going on,' he complained.[19]

But the reformers' opponents were also capable of offering stiff resistance, and this they did – leading one reporter to opine that the ensuing altercations were representative of 'big-city politics' in its dramatic, chaotic splendour.[20] One of the old-guard councillors – Malton's Frank McKechnie, who had been serving since 1958, when he squeaked into office at age twenty seven – often took to supporting the reformers. But the others – Ron Searle, Harold Kennedy, and Milton (Bud) Gregory – remained firmly in the old-guard camp. They launched spirited attacks against 'all this idealistic planning.' They poked and prodded the neophyte mayor at every opportunity. And they could often exploit his lack of acumen. After all, this was a mayor who had admitted that 'I'm not really a socializing type.'[21] Dobkin worked hard as mayor, to be sure. But he also insisted on carrying on part time with his medical practice. It's hard to leave a battlefield and hope that the enemy will simply await your return.

The enemy's forces were of mixed quality. They ranged from the awkward – like the slow-talking Harold Kennedy, who appeared to genuinely believe that people were picking on McLaughlin because he was a 'local boy who became successful'[22] – to the much more sophisticated, like McLaughlin himself, who continued to try to seize the initiative by publishing grand, futuristic plans for the city centre.

The old guard was helped by circumstances. Someone had to pay to run the local government – and costs were escalating rapidly throughout the public sector. In 1974 it proved to be a struggle even to hold the mill-rate increases to 17 per cent.[23] The reformers blamed it on the province, citing among other things the costs of setting up the new Region of Peel. The old guard insisted that the 'idealistic planning' was culpable.

The reformers were also being undermined from within. In the year following the election seventy four Mississauga staff members resigned. Among them were most of the senior managers: city manager Dean Henderson, works commissioner William Anderson, clerk John Corney, industrial commissioner Kenneth Rowe, and solicitor Len Stewart. Only some left because the services had migrated to the region. Others were offered jobs at the region anyway, where Tory stalwart and former Mississauga councillor Lou Parsons was holding forth as the provincially appointed chairman. And still others were being offered jobs by the developers.

The old guard tried to make a public incident of each resignation. The provincial government also gravely weighed in with expressions of concern that Mississauga was on the verge of collapse. 'I am concerned about the number of senior staff who have left,' said senior minister John White. 'I am following the matter closely, in the hope that the new Council can settle in and do the job that the people elected it to do, without undue abrasiveness, without too ambitious an expenditure program and such like.'[24]

The resignations did leave Dobkin and his allies with some room to manoeuvre because the vacancies could be filled with loyal people – former Streetsville administrators, for example, some of whom did indeed receive promotions. But there was no way to deny that the administration was reeling. By the end of 1974 Dobkin took his case to the press. His columns did not mince words: The deserters were trying to sabotage the council. He charged that former mayor Murray, as well as the former town manager and former deputy town manager, had not offered him 'any welcome or any assistance.' The other senior officials were supposedly not much better. 'When I first came over to City Hall, the reaction of senior staff varied from indifference and non-cooperation, to hostility.' Dobkin even claimed that a former senior member of the engineering department had confided that he was resigning 'to get away from the public.' Another former senior staffer was supposedly encouraging his erstwhile subordinates to leave the employ of the city. The mayor commented gravely: 'I do not need to point out how this situation would have been handled in a private corporation – with an immediate firing and/or lawsuit.'[25]

Dobkin was utterly beside himself at the press coverage the deserters were managing to garner:

On November 6, 1974, a photograph appeared in The Mississauga News with former City Engineer, Mr. Ernie Bodnar (another member of senior staff who went to work for a developer – the McLaughlin Group) holding up a sweater with the number 69 on it. A party was thrown for Mr. Bodnar by some of his friends where Mr. Bodnar was feted as some sort of a martyr-hero. Mr. Bodnar seemed to be quite proud of the fact that he was the 69th person to leave.[26]

Regional chairman Parsons dismissed Dobkin's accusations. Any problems were simply indicative of the incompetence of Mississauga reformers. Parsons was not just any critic. He had control of some important institutional levers, and he used them to thwart the reformers. He cancelled some meetings of the Regional Planning Committee, chaired by Councillor McCallion (the Mississauga mayor and councillors were also all regional councillors, holding ten of the twenty one seats at the upper-tier level). He conducted much of his correspondence with the province out of radar range. He managed to get provincial grants for Mississauga's downtown planning funnelled to the region instead of to the city.[27]

By early 1975 it looked as if the reformers had stalled. It even looked as if the old guard was starting to clamber back. But then Dobkin dropped a bombshell. He called for a judicial inquiry.

The allegations were never disclosed publicly. There had long been rumours of impropriety swirling around some of the former Mississauga officials. The largely speechless councillors – it does not appear that Dobkin had briefed them in advance of his proposal, with the possible exception of Hazel McCallion – agreed unanimously to the inquiry. But the old-guard councillors soon had second thoughts. Was this a desperate fishing expedition? Was this all being done for political reasons? How much would it cost? When council named the presiding judge, Ray Stortini, some critics claimed that he had an association with the Liberal party, the party of choice for Dobkin and some of the reformers. The province also called the whole exercise into question and refused to give the inquiry powers of search and seizure.

Dobkin had not guessed that the sharpest challenge would come

from Dr Gordon Watt, who had been the mayor's brilliant young executive assistant. Watt, a medical doctor and a lawyer, not to mention a
friend of Dobkin's, had been hired in late 1973. At the time the old
guard had charged that the mayor was wasting money. Why would the
mayor require a full-time executive assistant? Why was the job going to
Dobkin's university buddy?

When Watt resigned at the end of April 1975 no one thought much of
it. It seemed amicable enough. The ambitious young man was moving
on. Dobkin showed up at the retirement reception with nothing but
kind words. Watt's involvement with city politics was over.

Or was it? In September, just as Stortini's hearings were about to get
underway, Parsons stood up at a regional council meeting to make a
surprise announcement of his own. Watt had sworn an affidavit asserting that the judicial inquiry was indeed nothing more than a cynical
political fishing expedition.[28]

Dobkin's own credibility was now being called into question, but he
still seemed unfazed – apparently confident that the inquiry would
turn up dirt. The provincial Liberals, for their part, were keeping up the
pressure in the legislature, asserting that the province should be supporting this investigation. During the inquiry kerfuffle, and after, they
kept a running file on 'Mississauga.' They wondered why a developer
who was being touted as a possible inquiry witness, one who would
make revelations, had been able to get an Ontario Municipal Board
hearing sped up following the intervention of the minister. The party's
research director, who had been doing some digging, advised leader
Stuart Smith that 'the Big Blue Machine [was] in action' on the Mississauga controversy.[29]

Some of the old guard turned to the courts to have the inquiry
quashed. The Mississauga Hydro Commission, as well as Chic and Jim
Murray, argued that the inquiry had no right to investigate other 'corporations' – including the hydro commission and, even more problem-
atically, the former Town of Mississauga. This argument succeeded and
succeeded again on appeal.[30] All told, the bill to the city would run to
more than three hundred thousand dollars, although only a few days of
hearings would ever be held and no report would be issued.

The Murrays were not finished. They launched lawsuits with claims
totalling nine hundred thousand dollars against Dobkin, McCallion,
lawyer Joseph Pomerant (who had apparently given advice to the
mayor), and inquiry counsel Noel Bates. When Judge Stortini, in wrap-
ping up his work, reported that the matters merited further investigation, the old guard insisted that, by so declaring, he was in contempt.

The lawsuits all eventually failed or were withdrawn, but the whole experience plunged local politics into further disarray. Legal costs associated with the affair continued to mount while suspicion persisted that some of the old guard actually had been engaged in funny business. No one came out of this with reputation intact.[31]

Could the reformers have done better? To do so they would have had to build a solid community/neighbourhood coalition. And they might have had some resources with which to work. The civic groups during this period, although inexperienced and largely independent of each other, were not as passive as they would be during McCallion's years as mayor. One of the weekly local newspapers, the pro-reform *Mississauga Times*, was recognized by the Canadian Community Newspapers Association as 'the best all-round large circulation' local newspaper.[32] Recall that in Streetsville (McCallion's ward, with the same boundaries as the town where she had been mayor from 1970 to 1973) the voter turnout in local elections was typically between 50 and 60 per cent, which was considered high in relative terms. The community had two of its own newspapers, including one owned by the McCallions. There were articulate conservation groups, such as Streetsville Against a Vanishing Environment (SAVE), and a full range of service clubs that took an active interest in local affairs. Even the Streetsville Chamber of Commerce was a pro-reform organization, consisting largely of resident small-business owners and middle-class professional practitioners. There had been widespread support for the Streetsville mayor's much-publicized policy statement of December 1972, which contained planks similar to those espoused by the Mississauga reformers a year later in the city council elections. That statement had been made town policy by a unanimous vote of the Streetsville council.[33]

Ward 2's Councillor Spence (nicknamed 'Mary Helen Spends' by her opponents) could benefit from the articulate and active support of SOTAS and of the Council of South Mississauga Community Associations, of which she had been a leader and which she continued to cultivate while on council. The latter group was remarkably active, often took a city-wide perspective,[34] and prepared by far the most detailed submission (fifty pages) of any citizens' group in response to the 1975 Official Plan Review.[35] In fact, it was the residents' federation (CSMCA) that had urged Spence to run. Well organized, they had some clout against the developers. They were able to get five major developers to amend significantly their plans for southwestern Mississauga, and they were able to retain expert witnesses to go before the Ontario Municipal Board to present a strong case.[36] Many of the SOTAS members, mean-

while, were genuine environmentalists or conservationists, some of
whom had been involved in the long and successful battle in the 1960s
and early 1970s to save the Rattray Marsh, which was in Ward 2. Spence
created – and remained in contact with – neighbourhood advisory committees. Although these entities were not all highly active or outspoken,
they probably did help to keep some of Spence's political supporters
interested and informed.

All said, however, it would have taken tremendous work for the
reformers to reap bountiful harvests. Some of the nascent residents'
groups were even subject to direct attacks from developers. Save Our
Trees and Streams was the target of what may have been the first
SLAPP (strategic lawsuit against public participation) in Canada. It had
not incorporated, and its core members were sued individually. For two
years it could focus on almost nothing but fighting a small-time developer complaining that a project had been held up because the group
had successfully urged council to demand tough environmental standards. The case was eventually thrown out, but by then the members
were too tired to continue with their other work.

Although the press in Mississauga was robust at the time relative to
other suburban communities (and even included some publications
that were sympathetic to the reform movement) the newspapers were
weeklies, not dailies. There was only limited Mississauga news coverage or commentary on radio or television. A report prepared for the city
on public participation in the official plan review process lamented
'the lack of major media sources' and expressed concern about 'the
public's general lack of information about the City, its workings and its
composition.'[37]

In the 1973 election campaign, several neighbourhood associations
had shown support for Dobkin and his reformist colleagues. However,
most of these groups were very new, having been formed within the
previous two years to protest road widenings, high rises, strip malls,
and other projects deemed undesirable. Although some of the neighbourhood groups did contribute to the official plan review process,
their comments were often parochial and reactionary. They supported
some of the reform principles, such as better transit, a pedestrian-ori-
ented city centre, and new recreational facilities – provided these did
not intrude on their immediate areas. The Credit Reserve Association (a
residents' group in south-central Mississauga) commented, for example, that 'light rail transit facilities should be encouraged as long as they
do not run on streets.'[38] A few kilometres away, the Credit Woodlands

Residents' Association was also supporting reforms in principle but resisting them in practice: 'We believe that the proposed Go [sic] system on the C.P.R. is a desirable feature and a valuable asset to our community, however, the planning of a station at Burnhamthorpe is incompatible with our recommendations as to expansion of the artery [which it opposed].'[39] The city's Public Participation Office, which had been set up by the new council to generate and organize the responses, observed wryly that 'residents want the LRT to pass through areas other than their own.'[40]

The large suburban canvas, with its disparate and scattered neighbourhoods, was an obstacle to the reform-movement-in-power. The residents who spoke in the localized flare-ups sometimes figured a problem would be solved if the trouble were to gravitate to some distant neighbourhood, or, better yet, to vacant land. In a conflict over whether a bridge should be built in a south Mississauga neighbourhood one woman declared: 'I don't really care what happens elsewhere – I just don't want that damn bridge going in.' Another resident referred to the 'hole in the doughnut,' the undeveloped north-central Mississauga. 'It should be developed and other areas left alone.'[41] For the most part, this actually is what would transpire later, during the McCallion mayoralty.

'He did a lot of good,' says Hazel McCallion, referring to Dobkin's mayoralty and especially his environmentalism and determination to rein in the developers.[42] But he was hounded by opponents on and off council every time he tried to do anything. She concurs with the suggestion that had she been mayor in 1974 she would have had much more daunting political prospects than those she faced later. Dobkin's obstacles would have challenged even a more seasoned politician.

And by 1976, after three years of turmoil, many constituents, it seemed, were yearning for stability.

Ron Searle Becomes Mayor

'We the people of Mississauga have paid a high price for radical rhetoric,' charged Ron Searle as he launched his campaign for mayor of Mississauga. 'The time has come to begin again in working together to build a Mississauga in which we can be proud and where our children can live secure in the knowledge that we in the new council have as our major objective a city that provides affordable houses and employment opportunities.'[43]

Begin again. Affordable houses. Employment opportunities. Keen observers would have seen these as code words for the return of the *ancien régime* of the Speck-Murray era, when local politics was not conflict ridden, when development was seen as inherently good. The reformist years, Searle charged, had made municipal politics 'sheer, unadulterated hell.'[44]

But the old guard had been bruised and scattered. Now, it is true that by 1976 many Mississaugans did not have a first-hand memory of pre-1974 administrations. In 1977 the city's Policy Planning Unit would estimate that only 24.6 per cent of heads of households had lived in Mississauga for more than ten years.[45] But the spectre of the old guard had been kept alive by the reformers – in the fireworks on council, in the aborted judicial inquiry. And although Dobkin and the reformers had failed to establish a stable regime of their own, the reformist policies and rhetoric had led to recriminations among some of the old stalwarts. Former mayor Chic Murray and some of his associates in the business community were not actually supporting Searle now. It appears that they turned on the council stalwart after he panicked and initially backed Dobkin's stunning motion to set up the wide-ranging judicial inquiry.

Worse for Searle, some of the old-guard malcontents were putting their support behind another candidate. Accountant and local business executive Gerry Townsend emerged from his elegant house on Mississauga Road – the 1850s estate of the proprietors of the once bustling Barber Woollen Mills – to announce that he was running for mayor. He would reportedly manage to spend on his campaign the impressive sum of sixty thousand dollars. (Ever the pauper, incumbent Dobkin announced that he would not accept donations in excess of five hundred dollars 'and no funds from anyone who does any building or developing in Mississauga.') Townsend criticized the whole council and adopted as his motto 'Common Sense and Leadership.' He pledged to 'mend relations with the staff, the Region, the Provincial Government, developers, and citizens' groups to get Mississauga going.' He asked, for example: 'Where was the "common sense" when the Council *unanimously* [emphasis added] resolved to proceed with a judicial inquiry without adequate information? The Council and the Mayor should be held accountable for this tremendous cost and lost hours.'[46]

Townsend had already been campaigning for three months when Searle finally declared his own candidacy. But despite the late start Councillor Searle's profile far exceeded Townsend's, and when Townsend criticized Dobkin it only seemed to help Searle, who after all had been fighting the good doctor in the trenches for three years. To improve his chances, Townsend would have had to implicate Searle more directly – which he did not. And now Dobkin's foes, including the *Mississauga News*, were starting to worry that Searle and Townsend would split the anti-Dobkin vote and allow the young incumbent to come up the middle. The opposition must unite behind Searle! This was now a message being heard repeatedly. The result was a great relief to those who wanted the doctor out of city hall. Searle polled 15,405 votes, Dobkin came in with 11,731, and Townsend was a close third with 11,340.[47]

It was November 1976, and the reform movement had waned. But four reformers would still take their seats around the council table. There was the passionate and outspoken Mary Helen Spence. The young NDPer Larry Taylor had replaced the retiring Caye Killaby. And veteran local politician Frank McKechnie (Ward 5 councillor, but henceforth better known as 'the mayor of Malton') was now being identified with the reform camp.

And then there was Hazel McCallion. In fact, she was returned by acclamation in Streetsville, the town that had so recently been a political hothouse. It was now sinking into a quiet repose. Amalgamation had cut away its civic institutions and municipal committees, and the people felt assured that a very outspoken councillor was representing them at Mississauga city hall.

There would have been reasons to be optimistic about Searle's prospects. Yes, he had been identified with the old guard. But those who knew him then – and those who know him now – speak of a compassionate and honourable person, a World War II veteran, a gentle man and a gentleman. Some of the reformers who to this day can barely bring themselves to utter the names of their adversaries speak kindly of Searle. 'He was, at least in some ways, a *progressive* conservative,' says Larry Taylor, referring to Searle's philosophy and party affiliation.[48] 'I respected him,' says Mary Helen Spence.[49]

But a certain stubbornness and sensitivity, a thin skin, may have hurt Searle. Sometimes he may have been too proud. 'He was very much taken with the majesty of the office,' recalls Taylor. He found it difficult to brush aside criticism.

Searle chose to interpret his victory as a complete repudiation of the reform movement. As one of his senior campaigners says, looking back, the mayor remained 'very closely aligned' with the provincial Big Blue

Machine. Local journalist John Stewart wrote a tongue-in-cheek poem referring to Searle as 'an unofficial spokesman' for UDI.[50] That would be the Urban Development Institute. The pro-Dobkin *Mississauga Times* tried in vain to remind the young doctor's successor that the old days, meaning the development-regime days, were over. 'Searle must realize that the city cannot go back and relive the past. We must look forward.'[51]

But Searle was not to be fazed. In fact, he was not shy about trying to resurrect the reputation of the hitherto-maligned developer Bruce McLaughlin. He was asked about this in a 1997 oral-history interview with the Mississauga Heritage Foundation:

> *Question*: A lot of the photographs you see in the newspapers back in that era, lots of them involved you in situations where you were being photographed with developers or in new developments and that sort of thing. If I was somebody reading the paper back then, it would seem to me that you were chummy with developers, with McLaughlin.

> *Response*: Should I not be chummy with developers? I mean, who has done more for this City than Bruce McLaughlin? I mean, a man who had foresight that no other person has ever had ... A man who, I believe, never sacrificed personal integrity for profit. I mean he's gone through some hard times, but he's the man who had the foresight to see where the centre of this City should be.[52]

Looking back, and still defiant and perhaps in some ways romantically optimistic about human nature, Searle has faulted his predecessors for not appreciating Mississauga's leading developers, 'who had the interest of the City at heart. Sure, they wanted to make a buck, but they were going to do it honestly.'[53]

Although the city's tree committee was dissolved,[54] Searle was hard pressed to tamper with structures that were holdovers from the previous administrations. This gave opponents and malcontents many access points. Reporting to council was a planning and development committee, half of whom were citizen appointees; a recreation-service advisory committee; a transit committee; an architectural advisory committee; and an environmental advisory board. The members of these committees did express displeasure when their prerogatives were challenged.[55]

But the elephant in the room was the new official plan. Favoured by the reformist majority on the previous council, but still unapproved at the time of Searle's election, the document had advocated phasing, that is, designating only a few areas for development (generally those contiguous with the existing neighbourhoods), and allowing additional development only after the designated areas had been largely built out. Searle had declared his steadfast opposition to any predetermined phasing program, insisting it would give power to bureaucrats and not the elected people.[56] Councillor Fred Hooper, a Searle ally, remarked that 'whether the first, second or all 10 go at once doesn't make any difference to me.' He was rebuked, however, by planning commissioner Russell Edmunds: 'I thought there was some sort of lesson in this year's capital budget discussions that you can't have 10 areas developing at once.'[57] By June 1977, commenting again on the official plan, a frustrated Edmunds was admitting that 'we're a little farther ahead [a year after the scheduled adoption] but not much.'[58]

The reformers were likewise able to score numerous political points by decrying Searle's reluctance to take assertive action with regard to the imposition of lot levies and development charges. 'We've been merrily going along with development along the Cooksville Creek,' McCallion protested. 'At present the major watercourse levy is not covering the projected costs ... Until we pass that levy, every new approval in the Cooksville Creek is money down the drain.'[59]

Reluctantly, Searle allowed the press into the city's negotiations with the developers over lot levies. In so doing, the mayor nevertheless protested that the previous reform administration had conducted such negotiations behind closed doors in the mayor's office. He now argued, to no avail, that the Big Three developers (Markborough, McLaughlin, Erin Mills) would be put at a serious disadvantage if forced to disclose their business strategies in public.[60] Yet Searle's critics charged that the decision to open the doors did not go far enough – that the public, not only the press, should be allowed to hear such negotiations.[61]

Although the city was able to settle the 'John Doe' developer levies (the levies imposed on the smaller developers), it was not able to come to an arrangement with the Big Three. Lengthy negotiations ensued,[62] but the protests and revelations of the council opposition kept stalling any progress.[63] Any questionable agreements quickly became public knowledge – such as the two-thousand-dollar-per-month maintenance fee to be paid by the city to Markborough properties for maintaining an artificial lake in its Meadowvale community.[64]

Ever the entrepreneur, developer Bruce McLaughlin brought forth yet another proposal for what he termed affordable housing in the city centre area, but the company wanted to be immunized from increasing levies. Searle chastised some of his fellow councillors for their probing questions directed at McLaughlin – but, try as he might, the exasper-ated mayor did not have the strong political backing that would have been required to suppress the spectacle.

In the midst of all this, Hazel McCallion was able to reinforce her opposition to Searle while gaining the support of at least one developer, Longmoor, which promised to pay the full levies, although the company wanted to develop in an area that, based on the draft phasing guidelines, would not have been released for development until after 1980.[65] McCallion also shrewdly raised concerns that the business inter-ests outside the city centre would suffer because of Searle's policies. She was thus able to portray herself as taking a hard line with developer McLaughlin while not being anti-business.[66]

Determined as always, McLaughlin continued to insist that the key to his entire scheme was a quick decision.[67] A core plan was, indeed, approved two weeks later, but not without continued bickering and recriminations. 'Bruce McLaughlin had a vision and we just confirmed it,' scoffed McCallion.[68] Opposition in the community also rose to the surface. 'Many people think a downtown must be more than a bevy of architecturally magnificent buildings huddled around a giant shopping complex,' wrote John Stewart. 'Many people think Bruce McLaughlin's singularly unimaginative track record hardly qualifies him to attempt a project of such stature.'[69]

Reports from the finance commissioner that new growth would pre-cipitate consistent increases to property taxes allowed the reformers yet again to portray themselves as champions of fiscal discipline. McCal-lion began expressing concern about the *financial* consequences of con-tinued growth, emphasizing that growth must pay its own way.[70] In so doing, she was able to appeal both to the anxiety caused by the old guard's pro-developer image and to the concerns about the reformers' fiscal management.[71] Even the pro-Searle and pro-developer *Missis-sauga News* sympathized with Hazel McCallion's lament that the city manager was taking until April to table the draft budget.[72]

McCallion was also cool to many public amenities, citing fiscal disci-pline. For example, she voted with Searle to curtail the city's summer playground program from fifty full-day sessions to forty two half-day sessions. The future mayor was, perhaps once again, reading the under-lying public mood perceptively. She seemed to concur with Searle that the fear of tax increases was so strong 'you can cut it with a knife.'[73] McCallion was now even calling for the abolition of municipal grants to civic groups. Councillors 'were not elected to give out donations,' she charged.[74]

Even on the all-important phasing issue there was room for the reformers to equivocate. Planning staff continued to contend that phasing was essential and that council should not be swayed by developers who promise 'affordable' housing. The staff argued instead that council could facilitate affordable housing by allowing smaller units.[75] This rebuke from the professional staff undermined Searle's opposition to phasing. But the prospect of small units in already built-up areas would provide an opening for McCallion later to abandon phasing on the basis that *abandonment* would protect existing neighbourhoods – and allow the city to finance amenities through steep development charges.[76]

With respect to any relationships or rapport with the developers, McCallion continued to emphasize reformist values. 'I'm not a pro-developer,' she told the Erindale Women's Institute in March 1978.

> Development is not absolutely essential. When we have thousands of acres of land, not suitable for farming but great for building on, why should we waste forests and precious farmlands? Some day, we'll regret it. I have five acres of good agricultural land in Streetsville, and I could make a killing if it were developed, but I can't take the money with me and there comes a time when we have to contribute to the future. We can't be completely selfish.[77]

That land would be sold off in future years. But for now it helped to bolster McCallion's reputation as a green councillor. And to prove it, she joined her fellow reformist holdovers in outspoken but unsuccessful attempts to prevent the Region of Peel from putting a sewer pipe through the ecologically sensitive Roy Ivor Bird Sanctuary near Erindale.[78]

Searle's own equivocations, however, made him look weak. Faced with a hall full of angry residents protesting a possible bridge over the Credit River to extend the Queensway, a major thoroughfare, Searle suddenly reversed his earlier support for the project and tried now to appeal to the audience by opposing the project. As one newspaper columnist put it, even Searle's old friends were beginning to find him unreliable. 'Searle's position with the Big Blue Machine had been a little shaky of late, and it's no secret that some establishment types would prefer to see a mayor at city hall who comes across with the goods.'[79]

Searle then reverted to his old position and promptly endorsed a staff study calling for the Queensway bridge and other road widenings, such as those affecting east–west thoroughfares Lakeshore Road and Dundas Street. The mayor argued that Toronto had major traffic problems because of 'political' decisions, such as cancelling the Spadina Expressway, but he himself found it difficult to maintain a constant stance.[80] On several issues, recalls Willson McTavish, a Searle confidant, McCallion was able to point to Searle and say, 'Mr. Mayor, make a decision! Any decision!'[81]

The increasingly embattled Mayor Searle was soon also arguing publicly with the city's planning commissioner over whether yet another staff report on the long-term development in fact called for backing away from phasing (Searle claimed inaccurately that it did).[82] This allowed McCallion, although voting for phasing (a principle she would later repudiate),[83] to focus her complaints instead on Searle's alleged ambiguity, misrepresentation, and mismanagement.[84]

Searle faced other difficulties. There continued to persist strong perceptions that the pre-1974 *ancien régime* had been corrupt or at least too eager to compromise the public interest. Indeed, the ghost of the aborted judicial inquiry kept resurfacing during the Searle mayoralty. Whenever it did, the mayor invariably restated his old-guard credentials.

Reformist councillor Larry Taylor proposed to recruit an independent person to review the inquiry files and make a recommendation as to their disposition.[85] Searle replied with an emotional and forceful address to council: 'Even though they [former politicians] have been found not guilty of the charges, they have been subjected to harassment over the past weeks. These innocent people have been defiled and reviled – their jobs have been threatened; they've been held up to ridicule and their financial security has been harmed.' Searle charged that the defamation and conspiracy suit against several co-defendants, including former mayor Dobkin and Councillor McCallion, contained far more serious allegations. 'These people who started this thing have been completely untouched for the last two and one half years while those totally and absolutely innocent have had rumors bandied about and have had their names muddied in the press.'[86]

With these hard feelings, even the scheduling of meetings came to be hampered, and basic business was sometimes conducted only with great difficulty. The lack of quorum at some meetings was often caused by intentional absences meant to stall the proceedings.

A Littered Battlefield

The mayoralty of Ron Searle demonstrates how difficult it can be to re-establish a governing coalition after it has been subjected to sustained attack from a reform-movement-in-office. Searle tried in vain to recreate the development coalition. He failed because it had been discredited, notwithstanding the damage the reformers had sustained to their own credibility.

It would be too simplistic to attribute Searle's woes exclusively to McCallion's effective political manoeuvring and her undoubted ability to appeal to often disparate opposition impulses. Indeed, McCallion herself attributes her eventual victory over Searle, and the fact that 'people came out of the woodwork' to support her, not to her own effective opposition but to Searle's faltering and the perception that 'it was still the old regime.'[87] The circumstances had combined to make it opportune for a skilled politician like McCallion to outflank an old-guard-oriented mayor by appealing to both quality-of-life and fiscal issues. McCallion perceived that the public had grown tired of politics dominated by developers as well as the instability, confrontation, and perceived lack of fiscal discipline ascribed to the reformers.

What the electorate craved was a leader who could be seen as independent of the big-developer interests but who could also ensure stability, modest or no tax increases, and major assessment growth but no major encroachments on the neighbourhoods. The conditions were ripe for such a leader. Hazel McCallion recalls that she had determined, prior to announcing her candidacy for mayor in the 1978 elections, that 'it was time to either go up or go out.'[88]

She chose well.

5 'My People ... Their Leader'

Everyone was anticipating a great skirmish. The 1978 race for mayor of Mississauga was to have been like its predecessor contests – marked by hot words and a sharp ideological clash between the front-running candidates. The incumbent, Ron Searle, believed the predictions and wasted no time mounting an offensive. He charged that his challenger, Councillor Hazel McCallion, the *de facto* leader of the opposition, had been the 'power behind the throne' in the ill-fated mayoralty of the upstart, neophyte, anti-developer mayor Martin Dobkin, whom the then-councillor Searle had soundly defeated after one term. She had supported Dobkin's 'witch hunt' – the judicial inquiry, eventually shut down by the courts, to investigate alleged malfeasance among some of the pre-reformist politicians and administrators. Searle reminded his audiences that McCallion had fought ferociously to keep Streetsville out of Mississauga. She had denounced the latter as a monstrous creature. And now she was pledging to that creature her undying loyalty!

Searle claimed that he would have had even more to say if not for his challenger's gender. 'My instinct is to hammer the hell out of her, but I can't really do it. I'm really intimidated by the fact that she's a woman.'[1] With comments like that one, the incumbent was attracting the wrong kind of attention to himself. He was also showing that this might actually have been a very good time for a strong woman to be running for mayor. The people of Mississauga were very young. A significant majority of the eligible voting population was under thirty five.[2] Old prejudices against women in politics would certainly have been less prevalent among young adults. But among the old-guard politicians and businesspeople, McCallion might indeed have benefited from a certain old-school reticence: one had to appear to be a gentleman when dealing with a woman.

McCallion, the reputed street fighter running on a much smaller budget than the mayor, merely shrugged off most of Searle's comments. It was as if she was somehow aware that she had an appointment with her destiny. She did note that Searle had been a member of the largely discredited pro-developer 'old guard,' but she figured that most people knew this anyway. Besides, if the voters remembered anything about her association with Dr Dobkin, it was the fact that both he and she could not possibly be accused of being in bed with the developers – those developers who had taken the area from largely rural to largely suburban, quintupling the population in less than a generation. And she had spoken enough about fiscal responsibility and economic development to convince people she could be a competent administrator. She could even point to her Streetsville days to prove it.

Pundits judged that McCallion's speeches were duller than Searle's. By late in the campaign she had even dispensed with her attempts at humour. She had been fond of telling the story of how she and Searle were forced to climb a ladder to heaven, writing on the way up their broken promises. 'When I was on the fifth rung, my hand was stepped on,' McCallion said. 'It was my opponent coming down for another box of chalk.'[3]

But now, it seemed, she wanted to appear mayoral.

Searle unveiled a simple campaign slogan to emphasize the practical, decent man he considered himself to be. He was 'A Good Mayor.' Two weeks before voting day, he was one-upped by McCallion. She would be 'A Better Mayor.'

She also proved to be the better campaigner. On the night of 13 November 1978, at T.L. Kennedy Secondary School, then still Mississauga's traditional election-night gathering place, the changing numerical wall signs came to a rest at 28,005 votes for McCallion, almost 3,000 more than for the incumbent. Husband Sam pulled out a marker and altered one of the mayor-elect's campaign signs. 'Hazel McCallion for Mayor' became 'Hazel McCallion IS Mayor.'

She moved quickly to consolidate her authority, giving a feisty inaugural speech in which she pointed fingers at assembled federal and provincial dignitaries for not treating Mississauga fairly. In showing who was boss, she could be direct, abrasive, and determined to be visible. She immediately claimed to have discovered some correspondence that Searle had kept from council; the latter complained that his successor had been deliberately digging through files to discredit him.[4]

On a more trivial note, she even ordered a new council portrait session scheduled because she had not worn her chain of office the first time. The local press had reported that a psychic was predicting only one term for McCallion. Perhaps even the confident new mayor was assuming there would not be many more opportunities for official photographs. Or perhaps she simply liked that trapping of authority – despite a folksy personal style that caused her in other respects to be not at all remote from her public. 'There's no truth to the rumour that she wears her chain of office 24 hours a day,' a future regional chairman would feel compelled to quip.[5]

But in setting the new tone, McCallion also proved that she could be subtle. She decided that councillors should take their oath of office individually, instead of collectively, because they are 'as important as the mayor.' She favoured having a deputy mayor, but suggested that the position be rotated from month to month. This would stroke the egos of the councillors but of course make it more difficult for any one of them to rise above the rest.[6]

Relentlessly, she preached economy and frugality. She gave what she called 'a seminar' on cutting red tape, and, in place of the old Administration Task Force, she put two councillors in charge of a committee to find savings.[7] The committee never reported formally, but the staff was put on notice – it was being watched. She resisted library funding increases, quipping that 'this isn't the year of the child; it's the year of the budget.'[8] She sensed that the political climate lent itself to fiscal savings, and she voted against 22 per cent salary increases for the politicians, although she did not actually push for a salary freeze in advance of the vote, a vote she lost. 'I'm a little tired of hearing [McCallion] telling people that she pleaded with us not to do it,' one councillor muttered. 'She never even discussed it with me.'[9]

The budget process itself was rather messy that first year. There were conflicting amendments at one point, but new expenditures were held to an absolute minimum as McCallion had wanted – so much so that when it was revealed a month after approval that there had actually been a surplus of more than one million dollars the previous year, one of the councillors exclaimed that he felt duped. 'It makes me wonder what the hell we're doing going over the budgets and nitpicking over $200 items.'[10]

At the regional council, McCallion was just as forthright. She moved successful amendments to reduce salary expenditures by more than half a million dollars. She insisted that the police could use an auxiliary force to mitigate the need to always hire new, fully trained constables. She opposed an increase to the health board's budget.[11]

And she continued to oppose Lou Parsons. He was back for another term as chair, despite her objections. But he suddenly announced his resignation in April 1979, simply citing the 'pressures of political life.'[12] It was assumed widely that he meant the 'pressures of Hazel McCallion.' A month later it was announced that he would head Traders Associates, a development company in which Bruce McLaughlin had the largest stake.

It was apparent that McCallion seemed to lack any consistent or stable circle of advisers or confidants. Even husband Sam admitted early in the new term that, 'we'll discuss politics on occasion, but she doesn't come to me for advice ... I'll offer it every once in a while. Whether or not she takes it is a different matter.'[13] And at city hall, the seats available to private citizens on standing committees were disappearing. The Environmental Advisory Board was not reconstituted in the new term. The Human Relations Committee (dealing with multiculturalism) would not last the full term. Private citizens would no longer be eligible to chair most committees. Citizens, along with school board representatives, would be taken off the Planning Committee. In the ensuing years, its potential to serve as a base of opposition to the mayor would be weakened further, with its chairship rotating from month to month.[14]

No councillor was made budget chief; McCallion herself would take the chair of the Budget Committee. The budget is a matter for the whole council, not for a select group of councillors, she insisted. And Mississauga would never have those fancy titles given to councillors – like 'children's advocate' or 'homelessness advocate' – that one finds in the City of Toronto. The more the supposed collegiality, the more formidable would become the position of mayor.

In fact, McCallion brought into being a new creature, one that she would use frequently in the years to follow – mayoral committees. She established a mayor's task force on representation to examine governance issues, but little was done on its key recommendations, including more secretarial support for councillors. She launched the Mississauga Clean City Campaign, appointed citizens to it, and used the stature of her office to challenge corporations to do more to address the litter problem.

The bureaucracies at the city and the region were not intransigent old cadres. They were being populated with seasoned professionals, of course, but most of these were relatively new. Hazel McCallion herself had more institutional memory than most of the administrators, even the senior ones. As we have seen, there was tremendous turnover during the reform period. And this was a growing community. The public administration was in flux; there was simply not to be a crusty and cynical Sir Humphrey Appleby leveraging his role at the head of an entrenched civil service in order to protect 'our chaps.'[15] More typical was someone like Richard L. Frost. Born in 1947, he started his career in Burlington as assistant clerk in 1972. He moved to the Region of Peel in 1975 to be appointed clerk and became chief administrative officer in 1979. Shortly after taking office as CAO, Frost gave a presentation to an urban planning class at Queen's University. Unlike the Toronto bureaucrats, it is simply not our approach to devote time ahead of a debate to lobby politicians, Frost said. (As he was preparing to step down from that post in 1989 to become city manager of Winnipeg, someone gave him a copy of Peter Rossi's and David Boesel's edited collection *Cities under Siege*.[16] It was about the chaotic urban ghetto realities that he would not have been encountering in Peel.)

But all would not be peace and tranquility. McCallion would praise staff in public, but behind the scenes she kept them on the defensive. It was something she would do throughout her mayoralty. The 'girls who answer the phone' cannot always say who is in charge in a department when the head is out of the office, she complained in an early mayoral memo to the city manager and the regional CAO.[17] The problem will be fixed immediately, the top regional bureaucrat promised. He seemed to be more bothered – 'it has been eating away at the back of my mind' – by 'an unsigned letter from the Mayor of Mississauga' to the regional chair complaining of staff coffee breaks that were too long, overuse of 'flex time,' water meter readers who are too sluggish, and other pet peeves.[18] This sniping with respect to small issues did have the effect of keeping the staff on edge.

And so did the possibility of reorganization. Constant growth offers a certain assurance of continuous employment, but not immunization against reorganization. In fact, it is easier to throw things into flux. Why should Mississauga, already one of Ontario's largest cities, rely on the region for 'industrial promotion?' Bring that down to the city level, McCallion proposed. But we are doing a fine job here, the regional bureaucrats believed. No matter: the motion passed regional council, and the province quickly complied by bringing amendments to the Regional Municipality of Peel Act. The affected employees were given a few weeks' verbal warning, and a formal letter of lay off only thirteen days before termination. Even that letter had to say that, actually, the bill had not yet been given royal assent. But by then there would probably be no lead time at all. Although they did eventually land jobs with Mississauga and Brampton, their soft landing was never assured.[19]

Any close observers would have noticed something intriguing about this whole debate. Municipal affairs minister Tom Wells advised the legislature that McCallion had told him Mississauga did not want the power to hold industrial land, a power that some municipalities already had. The reformers on the 1974–6 council might well have asked for such authority. After all, they had been touting the virtues of land-banking as a way to exercise more leverage over development.

But the reformers had faded. When NDP MPP Colin Isaacs insisted during the same debate that 'an official [land-use] plan is needed for Ontario' (a position that McCallion would promote strongly two decades later, when green politics again took centre stage),[20] not many people seemed to take him seriously. Wells dismissed the claim as 'hogwash.' Mississauga East MPP Bud Gregory, a former councillor who had not been aligned with the reformers, was even more blunt: 'Even in the Region of Peel – Tory Peel – there is the odd New Democrat. They are hard to find. We try to jail them when we find them.'[21]

It was a joke, of course, albeit an awkward one. After all, those jails would have been overflowing a few years earlier, when the NDP came close to winning in Mississauga North. Many disgruntled residents, disgruntled especially with development politics, had at the time parked their protest votes with the left-wing party.

But that had been a passing phase, and McCallion knew it.

Decisiveness and stability were the order of the day now. Even those who had stood with the reformists were willing to tolerate the new approach. The *Mississauga Times*, which had been critical in the past of secrecy at city hall, observed that McCallion was sequestering her council for too many closed-door sessions. But the same editorial then quickly reproached itself for 'just nitpicking.' The writer was even willing to forgive altogether the lack of transparency: 'The closed door meetings may be a major contributor to effective and efficient management at City Hall.'[22]

'She's a brawler – but an indiscriminate brawler,' the new regional chairman, Frank Bean, would remark. 'She fights everybody – prime ministers, premiers, cabinet ministers, politicians and civil servants at all levels.'[23]

And she quickly showed herself willing to confront developers, while sending a strong message that there would be fiscal discipline. She made her stand on an unlikely issue, moving to rein in the flamboyant Harold Shipp in his most prominent community role: chairman of the Mississauga Community Festival, popularly known as 'Fritterfest.' City hall had launched this event in 1974 and had subsidized it in annual amounts ranging from $10,000 to $85,000. By most accounts, the 1978 festival had been a big success. Attendance was estimated at sixty thousand, its highest yet. There were 188 sponsors, contributing a total of $87,350, the most ever.

But the deficit stood at $43,000. Despite reports from the city manager that the festival was functioning effectively, and that staff logistical support was nothing out of the ordinary for a major community event, McCallion made clear that the city would not cover the deficit.[24] She was not swayed by an editorial in the *Mississauga Times* that called on the city to continue to subsidize 'Mississauga's coming-out party.'[25] Instead, the mayor appeared at the meeting of the festival's board on 8 January 1979. After some of the members waxed eloquent about the festival's role in enhancing community spirit and the city's profile, 'Mayor McCallion suggested,' the minutes say,

> that the financial success is the most important aspect of the project, regardless of any apparent success it had in promoting the City. She suggested that the executive should be much more businesslike in their organizing efforts. There are other successful Festivals in Mississauga, and City Council's assumption of the debt would establish an undesirable precedent. Municipalities throughout Canada are experiencing growing financial crises, and Mississauga is no exception. A hard line must be adopted. Mayor McCallion then left for another engagement.[26]

Taken aback, Shipp himself wrote a cheque for the $43,000. He also resigned as president, recommending that the mayor's husband, Sam McCallion, who had not been a member of the board, be the new president.[27] Shipp's executive vice-chairman agreed that the mayor's husband would give the Mississauga festival the one thing it so badly needed – the sympathy of the mayor: 'I heartily endorse Mr. Harold Shipp's recommendation and know of no other person in the Mississauga area who would be able to have freedom of access and at the same time the support of our Mayor. It would seem to me that Mr. McCallion is the obvious choice.'[28]

Sam McCallion did not take the position. Another chair was eventually found: Hyl Chappell, the former Liberal MP. He promised to run a lean festival, on a $23,000 budget, relying on sponsorship.[29] The 1979

Fritterfest would be characterized by the local papers as a success, and it was on budget. But the volunteer effort was difficult to sustain. The diminished festival lasted two more years before incurring another large deficit, resulting in internal recriminations. It was then closed down for good.

The Derailment

But the most dramatic proof that there was a new regime in town was played out in front of an international audience.

Canadian Pacific train 54, originating in Ohio, crossed into Canada at Sarnia. There and at Chatham, new cars were added, including a tanker filled with deadly chlorine. Other cars were loaded with butane, propane, toluene, styrene, and other flammable substances. 'This train with a cargo of dangerous goods, with some tank cars having plain bearings, with some tank cars not having completed or not being subject to a retrofit programme, with no hotbox detectors en route, proceeded through one of Canada's most populous urban areas,' Mr. Justice Samuel Grange would write after the fact. 'There is even some doubt that the whole of the train could be seen from one end to the other. To me, to proceed in such circumstances at 50 miles per hour could not be justified.'[30]

Could it be real? A mushroom cloud over Mississauga? The quiet night of Saturday, 10 November 1979, was shattered by a spectacular conflagration. Twenty-four cars ended up off the track. It was reported that the fireball was visible from as far away as St Catharines and Kingston.[31] The train had derailed at the Mavis Road crossing. Exploding debris had landed in some cases hundreds of metres from the track. Flames shot into the air as bewildered emergency personnel sprang into action. The propane explosions were not the main problem, however. It was the chlorine that was escaping into the air.

In the weeks preceding the emergency, senior staff at the region had been worrying about their capacity to handle disasters. In a 16 August internal memo, the CAO expressed angst about the lack of clarity in the role of emergency measures officer, which had been assigned as an adjunct function to an employee with other duties: 'I don't think we can assume in Peel that we are isolated from the possibility of having a major peacetime emergency situation.' He met with the chief of police on 11 September, but there were more questions than answers. On 30 October, less than two weeks before the derailment, the problems perceived by the CAO had still not been resolved:

At this point in time I am not exactly sure about the direction this program should move except to say that lines of communication must be firmed up and people's perception of their responsibility must be clarified so that if an emergency occurs, I have the certain knowledge that the right people are getting the necessary information when they need it.[32]

But the local police and fire services had actually become more seasoned thanks to some major previous incidents. The year before, three thousand people had been evacuated because of an oil refinery fire in Port Credit. The same year there had been a fatal airplane crash at the airport. And in 1975 Brampton had been the site of a school shooting that had left two dead and fourteen injured. 'Peel always gets the big ones – hijacking, air crashes, high school shooting, bizarre murders, refinery fires, and now a major derailment,' one radio journalist mused.[33]

This now was a dangerous fire. If the main tankers were breached, which seemed possible, much of the city could resemble a battlefield straight out of World War I. The gas would kill. Brakeman Larry Krepa had managed to close some key valves, but still there was cause to be very nervous. Police Chief Doug Burrows soon started ordering evacuations – first of six thousand, then of fifteen thousand residents.

One of Burrows' early acts was to request that the mayor be informed. But she was not – at least not at first. She got word from citizens, however, and had one of her sons climb onto the roof of the family home, from which he could see the spectacular fire. McCallion got the police chief on the line at 1:30 a.m. and was told of the potential seriousness of this event. She started making other calls to ensure that there would be places for evacuees. At 7:30 a.m., she was at the makeshift command post, which itself had already been moved because of shifting winds.

Square One Shopping Centre was opened up to house residents, as was the International Centre in Malton, and then Streetsville Secondary School. As reports came in of clouds of smoke spreading, more neighbourhoods were evacuated. Within twenty four hours, most of Mississauga's population – about 220,000 people in all, almost everyone in Mississauga (and small parts of Oakville and Etobicoke) south of Burnhamthorpe Road – had been told to be on the move. Even one of the initial evacuation centres, at Square One, had to be vacated. Mississauga 'is closed until further notice,' McCallion declared. Those at the scene would remember that one of the most difficult decisions was the one to evacuate Mississauga Hospital and several long-term care facilities.

Without a moment's rest, McCallion continued to work the phones furiously. There must be adequate room for the evacuees. There must be supplies. There must be medical personnel. There must be a system to help reunite family members split up in the rush. Bring in all available experts and helping hands, wherever in the province they could be found. The evacuation of Mississauga Hospital must be seamless. City hall would be open twenty four hours a day. Hotlines would be in constant operation.

And she was happy to speak with the media, as they began showing up from all over, more than 250 reporters and camera people – from so far away, in fact, that some had trouble spelling or saying 'Mississauga.' (Toronto-area reporters placed bets among themselves about whether CBS anchor Walter Cronkite would pronounce Mississauga correctly. He did not.) The evacuation was proceeding like clockwork, she assured them, but the federal government would have to supply answers. Why were there such lax regulations governing the movement of hazardous goods? She dutifully produced copies of old city council resolutions that had demanded more stringent standards well before this disaster occurred. Yet more fortuitously, in the two weeks before the disaster she had been railing against PCB burning at a Mississauga factory.[34] She could even demonstrate that as recently as a few days before the accident she had been pushing federal transport minister Don Mazankowski to enhance rail safety.[35] She claimed not to be intimidated by technical and engineering jargon, recalling her management experience at Canadian Kellogg.

Other important people were soon there too, including Ontario solicitor general (and attorney general) Roy McMurtry, the provincial minister responsible for emergency planning. He was the chair of meetings of the central control group. The public saw some of McMurtry, but it saw McCallion more. On one level, this was to be expected. When a crisis is centred on one city, the political head of that city is called into prominence. But McCallion did not hesitate to seize opportunities to take charge, and to be seen doing it. She knew better than to meddle in technical or specialized decision-making, remembers then fire chief Gord Bentley. But when it came to articulating the interests of the city, she was front and centre. Once, after conferencing with various senior officials in a trailer, McCallion had apparently seated herself closest to the door. Following the conference she stepped out to address the waiting media hordes. But she stepped out only a little. The other bigwigs had to remain half inside, peering over the mayor's shoulder.[36]

We know that the Mississauga councillors were satisfied that their input was not needed at the command post. On Monday, most of them showed up there 'and agreed that the mayor was the only person needed at the command post representing city interests.'[37]

Eight firefighters were hospitalized briefly for fear that they had inhaled highly toxic substances. There was actually one visible casualty as a result of all this – McCallion herself. She badly twisted an ankle running into one of the evacuation centres. The little mayor had to be carried into press conferences by Ontario Provincial Police deputy commissioner Jim Erskine. This was vintage Hazel, determined to be with her people no matter what.

On the third day, as the burning continued but the main tankers held, some evacuees were allowed to return, following an agonizing four-hour meeting of the control group. (McCallion became frustrated with that meeting, and as a result all future meetings contained a much smaller group of officals, with others brought in as needed.) Gradually, the subdivisions were repopulated. The city that had become a ghost town was coming back to life. By Saturday, six days after the disaster, almost everyone was home.

Luck had been on the city's side, McCallion conceded. It was the mayor who coined the term 'The Mississauga Miracle.' Had the derailment happened a kilometre east or west of where it did, the boxcars would have gone crashing into homes. And thank goodness the tankers remained intact! Meteorological conditions (not too much wind) were favourable for the whole week. Was it also not a miracle that most people left without a fuss? Only about two per cent disobeyed orders to leave. And although after the second day the mayor had to work hard to assuage grumpy evacuees, all told they did not complain too bitterly as they passed sleepless nights in the shelters or with family and friends outside the city. There was only very minor looting. Police records show seventy seven house break-and-enters for 11–16 November 1979, compared with eighteen the week before and twenty one during the same period the previous year.[38]

Mississauga's population was still very young, mobile, and largely middle class. There was an ample road network relative to the population, not highly congested as it often now is. There were still few cultural or linguistic barriers that could have hampered communication between emergency workers and citizens. The derailment took place late on a Saturday evening when most families were together and when businesses and schools were closed.

Only about thirty thousand people actually needed the shelters; others stayed with family or friends or booked themselves into hotels. In a central-city disaster, many more would probably have relied on public services. Gord Bentley concedes that colleagues in other jurisdictions sometimes reminded him of this. After day 3, McCallion managed to browbeat Canadian Pacific into arranging hotels for many of the remaining evacuees.

Some talking heads proclaimed this deferential, smooth response as characteristic of 'the Canadian way.'[39] Others surmised that the nature of the disaster had led people to obey. Many folks would have tried to wait out a hurricane or flood, but poison gas? *Globe and Mail* columnist Hugh Winsor claimed that the city was easy to evacuate 'because Mississauga really is as bland and boring as we had always imagined.'[40]

But for good fortune to redound on a leader it must be seized, Machiavelli reminds us. McCallion had seized it. She was the very image of resolute determination, of decisiveness, of a spirited advocate for her city.

It did take some posturing. There exist transcripts of the Central Control Group meetings held after the third day. They show McMurtry taking a consensus-building approach. They show McCallion determined that the coordinating group be kept small, with others brought in as needed. She was determined as well that the people would not hear overly optimistic promises, but was also making it clear that she would be the main conduit between the decision-makers and the people. 'I, as mayor' was a typical phrase. She even referred to the others in the room as her advisers. Had it not been for McMurtry's unassuming manner, a personality clash might have occurred.

On 15 November she insisted that she would tell the remaining stranded residents to be prepared to stay out at least two more nights ('I don't think we can go on with this night-by-night deal') despite officials' optimism that the requisite chemical containment would be completed before the second night.

'Well, leave it up to me to do a selling job, but I've got to do it. I can't let, unfortunately, the Attorney General do it, or Dr. Parrott [Ontario minister of the environment]. I've got to appeal to my people as their leader. Look, you've had confidence in me to date. I ask you to have confidence in that I have sought the best advice. I have to listen to it, and they know I'm not easy to convince.'[41]

McMurtry tried gently to remind the mayor that the government officials were collectively responsible, but he did not allow the meeting to get sidetracked and simply went on to other business. It was, indeed, McCallion who would do the explaining on this point in public.

McMurtry was taken aback at least once, however. At one of the meetings of the Central Control Group, those officials who had been deemed second rung were kept outside. They later were admitted in to be briefed on what had been happening. McMurtry did most of the talking. McCallion was not heard from; she had slipped away. Finally, one of the police commissioners (also a Mississauga councillor) made an interjection that caused the meeting to end abruptly:

> Mr. [Fred] Hooper: The commentary that is going on downstairs, Mr. Minister, we have not been informed of.
> Mr. McMurtry: There is nothing going on downstairs now.
> Mr. [Bill] Appleton [Police Commission chair]: The cameras are running and the Mayor is there.
> Deputy [Police] Chief [Bill] Teggart: Well, she's probably giving the citizens, making an appeal to the citizens.
> Mr. McMurtry: I hope the press conference hasn't been going on without us. Well, we better find out.[42]

Although McCallion, even during the crisis, had shown no qualms in taking the federal and provincial governments and the railways to task, she warned their officials and the railway and chemical companies not to launch into defences in public: 'Keep it quiet right now. Don't even discuss it because if it's brought up and I have to answer, I'm afraid I'll answer. And I don't want to. I would prefer not to right now.'[43]

Local officials acknowledged that there had been some problems with their response. Regional chair Frank Bean wrote to McMurtry noting that the Regional Emergency Plan had never been invoked – the police plan was simply used. 'Communication between what the media quaintly dubbed the "think tank" and the line departments (Social Services, Transit, C.A.O., City Manager, etc., etc.) suffered and for a variety of reasons.'[44] A report submitted to the chief of police by a Carleton University professor showed some communication problems in the early stages: it was hard to track people down; adequate records were not being kept on who was coming and going.[45] To Bean's consternation – he said he was worried about exposing the city and regional governments to attempts by the insurance companies to limit their liabilities – McCallion actually went to the press with her frustrations that not everything had worked perfectly.[46]

Was this smart pre-emptive politics on McCallion's part? She was heaping praises on municipal officials and volunteers; but if any concerns stuck, let it be known that she had been the first of the politicians to raise them. She insisted that the mandate of the future inquiry should cover any and all concerns about the actual response. The impression that would stick, however, was that this crisis had been very well managed.

The media clearly thought so. Their letters after the fact – many managers of media outlets did send letters to local officials – made clear that they had been impressed with the way their personnel had been treated and kept informed on the scene.

Large billboard messages from Her Worship started to appear. 'The Fire Fighters, the Police, the Volunteer workers. All those who helped. Bless and thank you, everyone.'[47]

Many constituents were thankful, too – to their mayor, above all. The letters were almost universally glowing. They were letters of which most politicians could only dream.

'I especially appreciate your dedication to the safety and interests of the citizens of Mississauga. You are right to demand an accounting of the costs involved in the evacuation crisis and in insisting that the taxpayers of Mississauga not foot the bill.'[48]

Or another: 'The tirelessly long, unselfish hours which you contributed over the past week will, I'm sure, not go unnoticed by the people of Mississauga.'[49]

Or yet another: 'In the past we have had a lot of mayors, but you are the only one who seemed to care for your people here in Mississauga no matter what color skin they have. We are indeed grateful for your concern.'[50]

Why reverse the good impressions? During the federal inquiry that followed, McCallion would resist requests to give direct testimony, noticing that liability-conscious lawyers for the corporate parties were, as Bean had predicted, trying to show that authorities may have overreacted. Mr Justice Samuel Grange spared her: 'I accept the submission of Mrs. Lax, Counsel for the Mayor, that the adversarial nature of this Inquiry simply does not lend itself to bringing forth the kind of information needed to deal with Term 6 [handling of emergencies]. Every witness who was present at any meeting of the Command Team and who has testified has been subject to detailed and vigorous cross-examination with regard to the proceedings. It has proved exceedingly difficult to separate the wheat of relevancy from the chaff of discovery.'[51]

But in public statements, McCallion would continue to be sure of herself and sure of what the city and the country needed to prevent potential dangerous-goods catastrophes. Already on 19 November 1979 transport minister Don Mazankowski rose in the House of Commons to introduce Bill C-25, An Act to Promote Public Safety in the Transportation of Dangerous Goods. It could be characterized as a direct response to the concerns that were being raised in the media, most prominently by the mayor of Mississauga.

The Grange Commission would echo many of the city's concerns, and many of its recommendations would be implemented. These included requiring detailed chemical clean-up plans, more sophisticated methods for measuring the amount of chlorine remaining in a box car, and that "all cars, whether dangerous-goods cars or not, should have roller bearings."[52]

After several years of fractious councils and interminable squabbling, it seemed to many that Mississauga now, finally, had a leader.

Consolidation

And so the voters seemed to think. McCallion was re-elected by acclamation in 1980.

The complexion of council did change, however. This worried the *Mississauga Times*. 'What has disappeared in the cleaning out of Fred Hooper and Ken Dear – and to a lesser extent Ron Starr – is the critical examination of Mayor McCallion's performance that supplies checks and balances to the political system.'[53]

The *Mississauga Times* would not be around to worry much longer. Six months later the progressive weekly was gone – purchased by Metroland, parent company of the *Mississauga News*. Now there would be only one media outlet regularly observing the local politicians. This was of some concern to the more observant citizens. Unsuccessful attempts were made to get the federal Kent Commission on newspaper ownership to look into this. The *News* assured its readers that local coverage would not suffer. Here is how the newspaper itself reported it:

John Baxter, president of Metroland Printing and Publishing Ltd., said the news and editorial policies of The Mississauga News and all other Metroland papers were determined without interference or guidelines from The Toronto Star [the flagship paper of Torstar, owner of Metroland]. Metroland's objective is to continue to improve its level of service to Mississauga and all other areas in which it publishes newspapers. As an illustration of this, he pointed to the recent invitation extended by the publisher of The Mississauga News to Regional Chairman Frank Bean, Mayor McCallion and all Mississauga councillors to write a weekly column each in The Mississauga News, for publication in the appropriate zone pages starting in the new year, if not earlier.[54]

So the political columnists, more often than not, would be the politicians themselves.

And now even fewer private citizens would henceforth be involved directly in the governance of Mississauga. Again the question concerned citizen appointments. Following what appeared to be a private caucus meeting of the mayor and councillors, the politicians emerged for their public meeting fifty seven minutes late. The discussion seemed headed in one direction. 'As time ticked by,' one reporter wrote, 'I had the impression that the image of the citizens was growing very small as the image of the mayor was growing very tall.'

There would still be citizen input, McCallion assured, but she promised to review the items on future committee agendas 'to determine what subjects we should have citizen input on.'[55]

She was more confident than ever – but also more intrusive. She would continue to protect municipal staff against at least some forms of political interference, but this did not include mayoral interference in minutiae. When some merchants complained about new, previously approved roadside potted plants in Port Credit, McCallion simply ordered the workers to halt. She was unfazed by the stern telegram from the president and vice-president of the Port Credit Business Improvement Association: 'Your action in reversing the decision made at the October 28 meeting at City Hall is incredible and totally unacceptable to the board of management of the business improvement area.'[56]

Councillors also – if they showed themselves to be deferential – would be allowed to give direction on small matters: a backed-up sewer here, a sidewalk there. Although McCallion was never reluctant to take action directly, she would sometimes hand a file to a councillor and let him or her deal with it and get some credit.[57]

A no-nonsense style of leadership had the effect of preserving discipline in the bureaucracy – there were no more high-profile leaks or resignations as there had been during the Dobkin mayoralty. But there were not many independent oversight mechanisms. There was therefore not the embarrassment that an auditor general or an ombudsman can bring. When some anonymous letters surfaced suggesting that Mississauga Transit managers and workers had been receiving gas, car washes, and repairs for their private vehicles with the bills being charged to Mississauga Transit, Peel Regional Police concluded not only that the accusations were groundless (although they acknowledged that some members of management had practised the 'informal policy' of putting gas in their vehicles at public expense instead of submitting expense claims for mileage used to perform city business), but that they would try to find the anonymous letter writer(s) to lay charges of mischief.[58]

The mayor's room to manoeuvre and to define the agenda without distracting questions being asked and without annoying revelations surfacing would soon be converted into what would surely stand as Mississauga's most significant public policy initiative, before or since.

It was time once and for all to abandon the idea of phasing, which had been championed by the reformers and by McCallion herself. This did not mean, however, capitulation to the developers. They would have to dig deeply into their pockets.

Before and after her 1978 election as mayor, McCallion had been making many speeches promising that the developers would be made 'to pay full freight' so as not to burden the local taxpayers.[59] As president of the Association of Municipalities of Ontario, she was demanding full legal authority for municipal councils to do this.[60]

In March 1980 the developers were put on notice. Council decided to release no new districts for development, saying it could simply not afford to do so (lands already zoned for development could still proceed). But the staff sensed that this was just posturing to get a good deal. Council was going in a different direction – it wanted, ultimately, to abandon phasing and to release almost all the remaining districts, provided the developers paid current and future costs. The advice from the senior bureaucrats at the city and the region was consistent: Don't do it! Don't go for this sort of sprawl! They were not suggesting that the city slow down development. But they were saying that existing neighbourhoods should be mostly built out before new neighbourhoods were opened up, and that those new neighbourhoods should be contiguous with the existing ones. Department heads prepared reams of information – financial data, engineering information, housing projections from the Canada Mortgage and Housing Corporation, all of it claiming to show that it made no sense to release new districts when the existing ones were not built out. The region's medical officer of health warned of the impact of scattered sprawl: it is conducive neither to pedestrians nor to the development of social networks.[61]

In October 1980 McCallion set up an eleven–member committee of city managers and development-industry representatives to try to come to some agreement. No consensus was reached.[62]

Finally in November 1981, following closed-door sessions that were deemed 'informal gatherings' rather than *in camera* meetings authorized by resolution,[63] city council passed the landmark resolutions 594 and 595. These stipulated that development levies should reflect all growth-related improvements and new infrastructure, including libraries, parks, roads, transit, watercourses, community centres, and other engineering and recreational expenses. It was further required that the Big Three be treated like any other developer (meaning that their obligations would increase) and that agreements with the Big Three be renegotiated accordingly.

McCallion censured the one opposing councillor, Larry Taylor, for raising objections at the public meeting, and she cut off discussion. 'I'm proud of this exercise,' she said in her defence. This very public enthusiasm, as we shall see, would make the mayor the subject of an unwanted court proceeding.[64]

Each department of the city was asked to list its needs based on ultimate populations in every district. Very detailed formulae were devised to determine the service standards the development charges would cover with respect to new development, everything from one new bus for every two thousand residents to an emergency vehicle's average response time not exceeding four minutes.[65]

The staff also gave council a warning: the city did not have the legislative authority to impose development charges for the soft services such as libraries and community centres.[66] If you wanted to do this, then special legislation would be needed. Or would it be? McCallion was convinced that, although the developers would be reluctant, they would pay. They would not want to put in jeopardy the prospect of developing their land.

Other public bodies thought that the municipal *bureaucrats* had been right all along, and they now said so publicly. Peel Board of Education chairman William Kent and all his fellow trustees denounced council's decision, charging that it would lead to monumental problems providing schools and transportation for scattered sites.[67] Hydro Mississauga and the *Mississauga News* joined the chorus of concern, citing the prospects for haphazard development.[68]

Even a few activists took notice. APPEAL (Association of Peel People Evaluating Agricultural Land), a small Mississauga-based group advocating for the preservation of farmland, saw this as the end of the 'hole in the doughnut,' the agricultural lands in north-central Mississauga that the reformist majority on the 1974–6 council had wanted to see preserved.[69]

But what about the ratepayers' groups, at least those that had not sunk into dormancy? This decision did not directly affect their neighbourhoods, did it? In fact, it relieved the pressure on infill – the very kind of development, the 'my backyard' kind, that could turn many a suburban homeowner into an environmentalist. Would it result in increased taxes? It might, if the new development charges could not be collected. But that was still an abstract debate; there was really nothing yet to which to react.

A month after the landmark resolutions, city manager Ed Halliday wrote an *in camera* memorandum to council explaining that the new marching orders had created some confusion among staff members because there were existing agreements in place with the Big Three.[70] It would be impossible to negotiate new agreements, he argued, because the council had required specifically that the Big Three be treated like all other developers. In other words, there was no room for negotiation. It would appear that council dismissed these concerns, because we learn from the solicitors of Cadillac Fairview (Erin Mills) that there had been a meeting with the Big Three on 15 February 1982, at which time Halliday, on council's orders, had issued a stern ultimatum. His statement to the developers is summarized in a letter to the city manager from developers' lawyer H.H. Solway:

You [Halliday] advised the 'Big Three' developers that there would be no development in the Municipality after March 31st unless:

(1) The Municipality obtains special legislation from the Province;

and (2) Special Agreements were entered into by each of the members of the 'Big Three', wherein they would agree to pay for all works and services in advance in cash whether directly related to their lands or not directly related, such as the Eglinton Avenue bridge;

and (3) We agreed to terminate our existing Development Agreement with the Municipality on the understanding that all our obligations would remain and all yours would be at an end;

and (4) We agreed to pay the new John Doe levies [the levies that apply to all the developers, large and small].

Solway went on to state that his client would not accede to these requests and would continue to be bound by the existing agreement.[71] 'The developers were threatening to take us to court,' recalls former councillor Dave Cook.[72]

Although the threat to halt development was not carried out, negotiations continued. The results, presented to council on 31 August 1982, were virtually the same as what council had called for unilaterally. As Halliday reported to his political masters: 'The figures included in each Draft Agreement are those figures Council reviewed some time ago prior to Resolution 595. The agreements reflect those costs.'[73]

The agreements, registered as easements on title, exceeded the powers that the municipality could legally have imposed by bylaw (the special legislation was not introduced at Queen's Park) and far exceeded standard lot levies. Council had 'proposed but not as yet funded' the capital works in the new neighbourhoods covered by the Big Three. Although council had already opened most of the remaining land in Mississauga to secondary planning, the agreements contained the statement that 'the City has determined that the development which is the subject of this agreement is premature in terms of the City's ability to finance the said capital works which will be made necessary by this development.' To try to close any escape hatches, there was also a clause that the developer 'acknowledges and agrees' that each of the statements about the city's needs 'is true in substance.'[74]

Although the Big Three controlled about 15 per cent of Mississauga's landmass, the city was not desperate for the development that the Big Three could bring. On the contrary, the politicians and the mayor in particular appeared assertive and independent. There was no danger of a major slump in the local economy should the Big Three balk, as there was still a sufficient number of the so-called John Doe developers. By contrast, the large developers were extremely anxious about the enormous, fixed investments that they had made in the municipality.[75] By making development contingent upon paying development charges not sanctioned by provincial legislation, McCallion admitted then – and recalls now – that the city was taking a 'gamble.'[76]

It was a gamble that almost backfired on the mayor. On Friday, 11 December 1981, McCallion was waiting to see attorney general Roy McMurtry on a different matter when a 'cheerful fellow' suddenly appeared, handed her a document, and wished her a Merry Christmas. It was a writ to appear before a judge.[77]

Lou Parsons had been taking a very keen interest in the development-charges debate. His McLaughlin-affiliated Traders Corporation had ownership or controlling interest in much of north-central Mississauga. Some of this land had been picked up after 1980 from Bruce McLaughlin, who had overextended himself and was now floundering.

McCallion had actually tried to appear friendly enough to Parsons, whom she had railed against ceaselessly when he was regional chairman and she was a councillor. She had even made him president of – wait for it – her new Mississauga Clean City Committee, which would tackle the litter problem. He took the position, but he remained convinced that McCallion was against him. Certainly he remained against her.

There was little doubt that Parsons was furious when he read resolutions 594 and 595. Much of the city was being opened up for development, but much of the Traders holdings were still being held back. What was the meaning of this?

McCallion made her way to the Peel Board of Education to defend city council's move. School board meetings can drone on endlessly over mundane subjects – professional development days, awards, bussing routes, tenders for new buildings, and the like. Reporters are there sometimes – but all too often they skip. Lou Parsons wanted to make sure that the press would hear McCallion. He called a local reporter. He did not say it, but he was building a case.[78]

That *case* would actually be presented by Jack Graham, the same Jack Graham who had been mayor of Streetsville and who had fallen out with McCallion. Now he had something that he thought could bring her down. McCallion owned five acres of land in one of the large districts that had been released for secondary planning (in other words, for anticipated development). By taking a direct part in the discussions on these watershed resolutions, McCallion had violated the Municipal Conflict of Interest Act.

The case proceeded quite quickly – pre-hearings in December, hearings by Judge Ernest West in the spring of 1982, a ruling in July. The media followed this one closely. The stakes had never been higher for a political leader in Mississauga. Councillors attended in numbers, ostensibly in solidarity with McCallion. (It was a sign of how things had changed in Mississauga. One can scarcely imagine a full force of councillors and staff showing up for Dobkin or Searle.) She even collected an undisclosed amount in donations from sympathizers. Local limousine drivers set up a fund to support her.

McCallion's lawyer, Douglas Laidlaw, argued that Her Worship had not in fact influenced the decision because by the time she clumsily decided to intervene in debate 'the decision had already been made,' an acknowledgment that some of the important council work had been going on behind closed doors. The result for McCallion was decidedly mixed. She had indeed violated the Municipal Conflict of Interest Act on four separate occasions – including when she reined in Taylor and when she attended the school board meeting – but it had been a bona fide error in judgment, His Honour said. Under the act at the time, without the error-in-judgment finding, West would have had to declare the mayor's seat vacant. He deemed it best that voters be left to make any such decision.[79] McCallion walked out and confidently proclaimed this a vindication. Graham was more sombre; he said he would appeal.

There lay Graham's mistake. Had he walked out and declared victory – after all, the court had found that the act had been violated – he would have left McCallion in a squeeze. (Indeed, he now tells everyone that his case was successful.) The *Mississauga News* was incredulous at her 'tunnel vision behaviour.'[80] But she never apologized. One suspects that had she been in an old central city – rather than a suburban city – with a full array of television, radio, and print media, not to mention 'gotcha' reporters, she might have been hounded to the point of contrition.

Re-enter Ron Searle. He thought that McCallion should not be allowed to get away with this. The municipal elections were scheduled for later that year. He proclaimed that another acclamation would be unthinkable. He would offer his own name as a challenger and run on a platform of integrity.

This would be the last serious challenge to McCallion's hold on the mayor's office. Searle, it seemed, decided to continue the 1978 campaign. He was the 'good mayor' who had completed his penalty and would pick up where he left off – with solid, calm leadership (at least that is how he saw his approach). He should have offered a more substantive platform.

McCallion was confident. Even with the looming election she publicly supported for the first time pay increases for the mayor and councillors, and would be quite happy to defend them. She did not have much of a platform: 'The only promise I will make is to be as visible and to work as hard as I have in the past – I don't think I could work any harder, and to lead this dynamic city to even greater heights.'[81]

Need she have said more? McCallion captured 71 per cent of the vote, contrasted with Searle's 24 per cent, with the remainder going to a little-known third candidate. For that she would certainly not apologize.

6 The Mayor-Builder

Hazel McCallion emerged from that 1982 election with an extremely strong hand. The old establishment had opposed her. Her old enemies had resurfaced to oppose her. One candidate for the Ward 2 council seat expressed alarm at the 'Drapeau-like council,'[1] a reference to the domineering Montreal mayor, but that candidate's vote had been marginal. The only regularly publishing local newspaper had opposed her. A judge had admonished her. And still she cruised to victory. If everyone were against her, it was, to paraphrase John Diefenbaker, everyone except the people.

On city council there was now but one problem child: Larry Taylor. While the conflict-of-interest proceedings had been going on, he had been allowed to snipe from the sidelines. He had even been calling up citizens in all parts of the city to try to set up a Mississauga-wide federation of ratepayers' organizations. Now, with McCallion presuming herself to be vindicated, he could be taught a lesson. Returning in February 1983 from a stint out of the country, he headed for what he thought would be a regular city council meeting. To his astonishment, the mayor and the other councillors had prepared a most unexpected greeting.

Taylor had helped to start a non-profit newspaper in his ward, a laudable objective in a media-barren environment. He and the volunteers arranged to print it on a city press in exchange for free advertisements for the municipality.

This now was portrayed as a major scandal. It was 'theft' of city resources. Other groups wanting city support had to apply to council for funding. Senior city staff did not use the word 'theft,' but they gravely confirmed that Taylor had been following a rather irregular procedure.[2] The newspaper stopped printing. The city-wide ratepayers' association concept was also fatally attacked. By trying to set one up, Taylor had supposedly been interfering inappropriately in the business of other wards.[3] The embattled councillor would henceforth be contained.

The *Mississauga News* for its part was not much of a threat to the mayor now. If sometimes it would report some controversial comments, these were always offset by the numerous feel-good photographs of the mayor at one function or another. When McCallion released only a partial list of her campaign donors from the 1982 campaign despite promising full disclosure, it merited only a blip.[4] When an inquest into a fatal fire revealed the city to be short of bylaw staff, none of the discussion redounded onto the mayor's penny-pinching.[7] When social service agencies complained that not enough was being done to build healthy and cohesive neighbourhoods, they were but voices in the wilderness. Indeed, David Raterman, a former Roman Catholic priest who headed Distress Centre Peel, lamented the fact that so many suburbanites did not see the social decay that he saw, or notice the extent to which family breakdown and addictions were affecting even the middle class. Mississauga and Peel were barely discussing the role they should play, even through land-use planning, to address these quality-of-life issues.[6]

Except for the occasional clashes with Taylor, council meetings were now dry. Gone were the days, *Mississauga News* publisher Ron Lenyk would tell me years later, when some councillor would show up with a sack of manure to illustrate his dissatisfaction, or would pound his fist on the table. If there was controversy, as Lenyk himself said, it was often being settled behind closed doors.[7]

And digging below the surface takes resources. It's not easy when you have but one city hall beat reporter who has to deal with the municipal government on the full range of issues and cannot easily afford to be ostracized. True, McCallion got some unwelcome publicity in 1983 when she returned from a trip to the Middle East, proclaimed her support for Palestinian independence, and awkwardly compared the Palestinian plight to the English in Quebec. She was rebuked by several Jewish organizations.[8] But no one took the time to ask questions about who was paying for this and the several other foreign trips she would take during this term, funded by ethnic organizations. When local member of Parliament Don Blenkarn took a similar trip, he, on the other hand, received decidedly negative publicity.[9]

Hazel McCallion, you see, was building. And she was not only *allowing* building to take place. She was doing some building herself.

She was starting to build a downtown.

People who study urban politics cannot get enough of downtown planning. They find in downtown cores raucous politics, all sorts of complex machinations between politicians and developers, active residents' and business groups, and lots of conflict. A local government – in visioning, in approving high rises, in agreeing to the demolition of existing buildings, in building a parking lot or in allowing a building to be put on a parking lot, even in trying to design a new park – can scarcely do anything without affecting someone's bottom line or offending someone's sensitivities. Even in Mississauga during the 1960s and early 1970s the very location of the downtown had been in dispute. Recall that Martin Dobkin had been talking about moving the city centre back to old Cooksville instead of allowing it to spring up in the middle of nowhere.

For years McCallion would say that her heart remained with the doctor. The city centre 'was started by a developer who decided he was going to build Square One [the major shopping centre, opened in 1973] in the middle of a farmer's field.'[10]

'But the die has been cast,' McCallion would say many times as mayor. And she is probably right. Even the consultants who had been sympathetic to the 1974–6 council could not countenance a move back to Cooksville.[11] By the time McCallion became mayor there was no push to shift the downtown back.

But wait. This was Bruce McLaughlin land, and the outspoken developer had shown himself to be no pushover. Could it be that McCallion would have to accommodate herself to him, or else take her chances in a great showdown? It seemed that when she first became mayor she was girding for battle. Over McLaughlin's protests, council acquired land for a new city hall. The municipality would not be McLaughlin's tenant.

Again good fortune smiled on the mayor. McLaughlin was teetering financially. Yes, he had been bruised by the reform movement. But he had overstretched himself – making some very bad investments in Montreal and in British Columbia's Grouse Mountain. (He would claim that he had been forced to look far afield because the reformers had been 'telling the big lie about developers' and had been thwarting him at every turn.)[12]

Already in the summer of 1978, the press had been reporting that 'McLaughlin plans to sell, sell, sell.'[13] The following year, he did indeed sell 385 acres in central Mississauga to Matthews Corporation, and some of his other holdings were being divested to the nascent Traders Corporation. In 1980 he was pleading with his shareholders for mercy.[14]

Soon, even the Ontario Securities Commission was in pursuit of the flamboyant developer for trying to resuscitate his flagging corporation by arranging unauthorized share transfers with other companies he controlled.[15] His board of directors temporarily removed him as president and renamed the company Mascan. The *coup de grâce* came in December 1983, when Canada Trust took over McLaughlin's crown jewel, Square One Shopping Centre, after Mascan defaulted on a mortgage.[16] The flagship of McLaughlin's empire was then sold to British-based Hammerson Corporation.

The dispersal of ownership made it more difficult for anyone to implement a grand vision for the city centre, but it weakened those who could exert influence on city hall. It appeared to give the mayor a strong hand at least to resist pressure from any corporation or interest group. It also created a vacuum that could be filled by a technocratic core at city hall.

The demise of McLaughlin did bring some other developers to the fore, including Shipp Corporation and Matthews Corporation. Harold Shipp constructed the Mississauga Executive Centre, three prominent glass office towers in the core. He partnered with Matthews on the Novotel Hotel, completed in 1986 and to this day the only hotel in the civic centre.[17] Matthews meanwhile built the shopping concourse known as the Sussex Centre. The city did little to interfere with these designs and appears not to have participated in their genesis. But it refused to relax the demanding development charges and the parking standards.[18] Shipp was also apparently seeking to have the city construct the new city hall within one of his developments, but this immediately was refused by the mayor.[19] His threats to cut densities where the city wanted high densities, ostensibly because the city would not give him a desired access road, were shrugged off by city officials.[20]

McCallion herself never really had a vision for the city centre, although promising that it would be 'dynamic' – an adjective she constantly applied to all sorts of activities. But even here she wanted to be seen as a rigid disciplinarian. In 1981 the *Mississauga News* published an insert trying to imagine how the city centre might look in the future. The introduction waxed eloquent, or tried to:

Dateline: January 1, 1999

This is the city where reflective pools mirror the architectural artistry of distinguished buildings and fountains silver the air around them to the rhythm of the old song: Downtown! Here, weather-protected resting areas, adorned with sculptures, shrubbery and flower beds, punctuate the network of open and covered walkways forming the pedestrian-dominated circulation system in and about the City's heart.[21]

Contrast that with McCallion's message in the same publication:

The day will come when the downtown area of Mississauga will be the dynamic centre of one of Canada's major cities. My primary duty, and Council's, is to ensure the application of business-like efficiency to public-sector activities directly related to the growth of the city as a whole and the development in the downtown area in particular. I want to see that our urban development is well planned and controlled. Growth should not be encouraged beyond the municipality's ability to provide services at reasonable cost to our taxpayers. We must maintain orderly, controlled growth.[22]

Although McCallion's words did little to conjure up images of a spectacular district, she did see the area being anchored by a prominent municipal building. Liberated from McLaughlin, Mississauga began planning the new civic centre (city hall). Despite her reputation for frugality, McCallion insisted that this building should be grand – marble and all[23] – and that it should be subject to an international architectural competition.

The ground was broken in 1984. McCallion boasted that the money was in the bank to pay for it. The development-charges policies were paying dividends.

The exact form of the city hall was not conceived by the mayor. The competition committee of the Ontario Association of Architects oversaw the process. She did, however, promote the need for something absolutely distinctive.

The design criteria, approved in advance by council and devised with no participation from outside interest groups, focused on two themes: distinctiveness and functionality for the delivery of services. It was thought that making a statement with the city hall would spur the development of a world-class downtown. But none of the criteria spoke to the need for an organic city centre. In other words, the city hall was *intended by the mayor and council* to make a stark impression rather than complement and facilitate urban vibrancy and civic democracy.

A stark impression is what they would get. The controversial post-modernist city hall that emerged from an international competition – won by the Toronto firm Jones and Kirkland, beating out 245 other submissions – was described in a review by University of British Columbia architect Trevor Boddy as a building that 'will rise above a suburban setting, standing as a harbinger of a new way of thinking about public architecture in Canada. This bewildering, witty, erudite building will serve to focus criticism and debate on public architecture in Canada more than any building since Viljo Revell's Toronto City Hall (1958–1965).'[24]

Although postmodern institutional architecture can be human-scale and soft and accommodating,[25] this city hall was anything but. Unlike the (modernist) Toronto city hall, it did not beckon people to enter or provide them with places to gather that would be integrated with an urban web, or make the politicians' offices literally and intentionally transparent to anyone in the square.[26] It is instead surrounded by opaque brick walls. The civic 'square' is almost wholly shrouded from the surrounding roads. Its many obscure ramps and stairs made it a haven for skateboarders, not events, and the skateboarders were constantly chased away by bylaw-enforcement officials.[27]

The council offices are segregated from the rest of the building. The council chamber is a vast room arranged theatre style with the first row of seats situated far from the mayor and councillors. The council table faces the audience and curves only slightly. The mayor and councillors cannot face each other when deliberating. This may contribute to giving council meetings the air of a scripted and stilted performance rather than a dynamic exchange of ideas.

McCallion concedes now to having had some misgivings about the design and appearance of the building. And she has often recalled that Prince Andrew, guest of honour at the grand opening, even called it 'the gas works.'[28] Others conjure up different images. A common joke in Mississauga is that the skeletal clock tower, which is meant to resemble a windmill but which strikes many as unfinished and cold, must be 'Hazel's sniper tower,' keeping would-be critics at quite a distance.

But the people of Mississauga did not need to see the distinctive city hall, whether or not they actually liked it, to see that the mayor was doing something. There she was all over the city – at ribbon cuttings and posing at grin-and-grip cheque presentations. The money was seldom hers, of course. It might be some school group's bake-sale money going to a good cause. She never regarded this endless succession of greetings and cake-cuttings as a waste of time. She even conceded that her job does not require specialized knowledge: 'As mayor, I don't design the sewers.'[29] But more than most mayors in Canada, McCallion realized the 'soft power' of the office. It is not the Municipal Act that gives a mayor authority. It is the stature that comes with being the one person elected city wide; it is the ability to command attention when gracing some group with the presence of the head of the city – the *mayor* has taken time out of her busy schedule to be with us! It is the power to summon people to a meeting.

The power of a mayor is often in the pedestal. A feisty and shrewd individual can exploit that power. 'My people know me,' McCallion had said in brushing off the conflict-of-interest case. She had indeed consolidated her office by developing a personal connection with her constituents.

The ubiquitous mayor was now even being regarded as a kind of landmark in her own right. In 1985 the *Mississauga News* published a 'Happy Birthday, Hazel' spread; it was a good draw for advertisers and a feature that would often be repeated in future years. Rick Drennan, the young sports editor for the paper who would run for office later that year against the mayor herself, acknowledged the leader's drawing power. She was

> a living relic, the world's oldest cheerleader. These are only some of the words to describe Mississauga's dynamic little mayor, 'Hurricane' Hazel McCallion. Like travelling to Rome and not seeing the Pope or visiting London and missing the Queen, a trip to Mississauga without seeing Hazel is a waste of time. Hear her shout 'M-I-S-S-I-S-S-A-U-G-A' like a 16-year-old cheerleader. Watch her cut ribbons to open stores, industrial malls, or housing complexes or get out to a local hockey arena as she drops the first puck. Hazel is everywhere.[30]

And not much, it seemed, would stop her from such cheerleading. She brushed off a death threat from some unknown crank,[31] and she made it a practice to shop at a different grocery store every week so as to be seen by as many constituents as possible.

The personal connection would easily survive a long 1985 transit lockout. Although most Mississaugans did not rely on buses, it would have worried other mayors, occurring as it did the two months before election day. Drennan thought her handling of it had been 'pig-headed.'[32] But no one was paying him much attention.

The personal connection would survive even instances of obvious misbehaviour. Again just two months before election day, and by her own admission, McCallion lost her temper when addressing a concerned caller to her live biweekly cable television program. She later conceded that she had consumed too much alcohol at earlier functions and even that she had been the one driving her car that evening.[33] It was reported in two articles, nothing more came of it, and she cruised easily to victory, gathering almost three times the votes of her two opponents combined.[34]

During the 1980s Albert Atkins was an occasional guest columnist for the *Mississauga News*. Watching several issues play out before city council, he became alarmed about how decisions were made and how debates were conducted. 'Nobody defies the mulish will of Hazel McCallion and escapes unscathed,' he would conclude.

> Mississauga council meetings are prim, proper, tightly controlled. They resemble stage scripts acted out as dull drama with a predictable climax. 'Democratic' at these gatherings means that criticism of elected officials is taboo. (You are supposed to do that in their private chambers.) It means tactful, circumspect speech. It means beating around the bush to avoid offending anyone on council, Mayor McCallion in particular.[35]

Indeed, in some respects McCallion's city hall had come to resemble a royal court from the days of yore – but with important differences. This reigning monarch did not remain mysteriously esconced in the Forbidden City relying on scheming eunuchs to interpret what was happening in the outside world. In fact, much of the intelligence that was being brought to Fort Hazel (aka city hall) was being brought by the head herself.

The Waterfront

And the building continued. But not all of it was stark, and not all of it would take form immediately.

In Toronto by the mid-1980s, waterfront redevelopment was all the rage. McCallion decided that Mississauga would not get left behind.

Until the 1970s policy and planning for harbours and waterfront land uses on Mississauga's twenty-two-kilometre-long Lake Ontario shore-

The Four Corners. The intersection of Hurontario Street and Dundas Street in the 1890s and in 1999. The crossroads at Cooksville were the main point of convergence in the rural Township of Toronto and site of the township hall. The Town of Mississauga decided in 1969 to move its municipal headquarters north to an empty 'greenfield' site on developer's land. Over time, ever-wider thoroughfares and strip plazas have removed most traces of old Cooksville. Photographs reprinted with the permission of the Mississauga Heritage Foundation.

A Gaspé Childhood. A very young Hazel Mary Muriel Journeaux, the 'baby of the family,' at home in Port-Daniel, Quebec. Photograph courtesy of Hazel McCallion.

Willing to Lead. The future mayor was president of the Anglican Young People's Association of Canada and later a district commander for the Girl Guides of Canada. She is shown here (at left) in the early 1960s. Photograph courtesy of Hazel McCallion.

From Rural to Suburban. Mary Fix (second from left) was the outspoken, high-profile reeve of the Township of Toronto in 1955 and 1957–9. She faced strident opposition from developers and from some of the township's old families. She was defeated by Robert Speck (second from right). Both are shown in this 1967 photograph with flamboyant developer Bruce McLaughlin, who proposed Square One and the 'City Centre.' Photograph reprinted with the permission of the Mississauga Library System.

The South Fills In. By 1972, southeast Mississauga had several established neighbourhoods, including Lakeview and Orchard Heights. The Lakeview Generating Station ('Four Sisters') is shown on the waterfront. As an employee of the engineering firm Canadian Kellogg, Hazel McCallion participated in the station's development. As mayor, she would preside over its demolition and over planning for waterfront recreational land. Photograph reprinted with the permission of the Mississauga Library System.

Her Worship the Mayor of Streetsville. Hazel McCallion was the deputy reeve of the Town of Streetsville in 1968, reeve in 1968–9, and mayor in 1970–3. This town council photograph of 1973 would be the final official portrait before Streetsville's forced amalgamation with the Town of Mississauga and the Town of Port Credit. Seated, left to right: Reeve Robert Weylie, Mayor Hazel McCallion, Deputy Reeve Jim Graham. Standing, left to right: Councillors Fred Dineley, Ted Rea, Doug Spencer, Jim Watkins, Graydon Petty, and Fred Kingsford. Photograph courtesy of Al Betts.

Honouring a Rival. Mayor Ron Searle unveils a portrait of his defeated predecessor, the young reformer Martin Dobkin, 1977. Searle himself would be defeated the following year by Councillor Hazel McCallion. Photograph courtesy of the Museums of Mississauga.

'The city is closed until further notice.' About 200,000 people had to evacuate Mississauga in November 1979 following the derailment of a Canadian Pacific train carrying highly toxic and flammable substances. McCallion's national, even international, profile on this occasion – and her unflinching, self-assured demeanour – did much to establish her reputation as a strong leader. Photograph courtesy of the Region of Peel Archives.

The Instant Nucleus. Burnhamthorpe Road, looking west toward the City Centre, c. 1987. As a member of the reformist faction on the 1974–6 city council, McCallion was critical of Mississauga's 'artificial heart,' arguing that the downtown should be at the Four Corners in Cooksville or even in Port Credit. But she soon came to accept that 'the die had been cast.' Photograph reprinted with permission of the Mississauga Library System.

Hockey Mayor. Hazel Journeaux played for the Montreal Kik Cola women's hockey team. Hazel McCallion, shown here in 1979, still often laces up her skates to take to the ice. Photograph reprinted with the permission of the Museums of Mississauga.

Crossing Jurisdictions. Municipalities may be 'creatures of the province,' but jurisdictional boundaries are often easily crossed by high-profile mayors as they press for projects, demand money, or promote their cities internationally. Shown at the 1994 sod turning for the Mississauga Living Arts Centre – whose performance as a facility would fall short of the mayor's promises – are, from left, McCallion, Mississauga West MP Carolyn Parrish, federal infrastructure minister Art Eggleton, Mississauga South MP Paul Szabo, Bramalea-Gore-Malton MP Gurbax Singh Malhi, Peel Regional Chairman Emil Kolb, and Mississauga East MPP John Sola. Photograph reprinted with the permission of the Museums of Mississauga.

A Fortress Rising. The design of the Mississauga City Hall, which opened in 1987, was controversial – McCallion remembers Prince Andrew calling it the 'gas works' – but it is widely considered to be the leading Canadian example of architectural post-modernism. The design takes its inspiration from a farm. The Council Chamber is in the silo. Photograph reprinted with the permission of the Museums of Mississauga.

Shop Till You Drop. The heart of the City Centre remains Square One, one of Ontario's largest indoor malls. It is shown here under expansion in 1985. In the 1990s, campus-style big-box retail outlets, with individual stores accessed from the parking lots, supplanted the indoor malls as centres of multi-purpose shopping. Square One remade itself with high-end fashion outlets, specialized shops, and big-screen theatres. Photograph reprinted with the permission of the Mississauga Library System.

Clean and Sterile. Most of the residential subdivisions of the 1980s and 1990s were not infill and provoked little opposition. Well-engineered and neatly designed, they lacked the colour and excitement of older urban neighbour-hoods. Typical plans included a great deal of empty park space, protruding garages, no frontage onto thoroughfares, and an assortment of crescents and cul-de-sacs. Most of the century farmhouses were lost to fire or demolition before they could be incorporated into the new developments. Some of the more recent developments, however, have come to embrace new-urbanist prin-ciples, including narrower streets, grid patterns, and less conspicuous garages. Photograph reprinted with the permission of the Museums of Mississauga.

On the Move. Hazel McCallion has not owned a motorcycle and is not often seen in this pose, but she has devoted much of her time to attending all manner of community events, using the occasions to gather intelligence and to get moral reinforcement from her constituents ('my people'). Photograph reprinted with the permission of Jeff Chevrier.

line had gone largely uncoordinated among the many public bodies that had a stake and ownership. The federal government owned Port Credit Harbour and had leased parcels of it to private parties without prior consultations with the municipality. The government of Canada also retained a thirty-acre, largely derelict site in southeastern Mississauga, which had served as a military training area during World War II – the undeveloped part of Mary Fix's coveted 'Rifle Ranges.' The provincial government owned a large tract of waterfront land, acquired years earlier in anticipation of the South Peel Water and Sewage System, although some of it was leased to the municipality for park purposes. Ontario Hydro, a provincial Crown corporation, owned and operated the massive Lakeview Generating Station. And in the late 1960s the Credit Valley Conservation Authority began leasing or acquiring its own land parcels as part of initial steps towards a scheme for regeneration.[36]

When one public body acted, it did so usually without much consultation with the other public bodies, unless agreement with another was a legal necessity (because of a leasing arrangement, for example). No one was surprised when the federal government, in the early 1950s, built with little warning a huge $4.5-million structure on its harbour lands in Port Credit to accommodate industrial marine vessels, mainly those of Canada Steamship Lines.[37] When the federal government became convinced that a breakwater was needed just offshore near Port Credit, it decided in 1974 to partially sink a rusty, large surplus freighter, the Ridgetown. Some residents objected at the time to what they deemed an eyesore.[38]

In 1974 the federal government's industrial harbour building lost all its tenants as large-vessel traffic ceased completely around Port Credit. A long-term lease (in effect for fifty years) with a private entrepreneur, who agreed to convert the terminal into a recreational docking facility, was then negotiated. Again, there appears to have been no serious consultation with other levels of government.[39]

Local visioning and planning were also happening largely in isolation from other governments, but some of these processes would eventually give momentum to a different vision of waterfront uses, a vision that would entice the senior levels of government, and ultimately encourage all parties, under municipal leadership, to pursue a plethora of opportunities for regeneration.

Cooperation between local and federal officials finally started to become more common in the late 1970s and early 1980s, when the city and the CVCA got the federal government to construct a $1.5-million breakwater in order to create dozens of new docking opportunities at the CVCA's new park, adjacent to the Lakeview Generating Station.[40] The federal government was also persuaded by the municipality to clean up the serious silt problem in Port Credit Harbour, a problem that was obstructing pleasure craft.[41] This was no small matter: Port Credit Harbour, with its one thousand berths and twenty-one hectares, had in recent years become one of North America's largest freshwater recreational harbours.[42] It was also home to the Port Credit Yacht Club.

But it would be 1984 before McCallion really levelled her gaze on the water. The federal government's lease with the yacht club (one of the major tenants) was set to expire in five years. The yacht club was eyeing new facilities at the future Lakefront Promenade Park, beside the generating station. And the city learned that the private entrepreneur who was leasing the former Canada Steamship facility was developing a proposal to purchase the site outright and to redevelop it. This had the mayor worried. If this private party could get his act together soon, he might pre-empt the city's future planning. It was therefore time for the city to get a plan.[43]

The Port Credit Harbour Study was promoted by the city as a formula for recreational and economic expansion. It became a multiyear, increasingly more expansive, planning and implementation process involving the city, the provincial government, the federal government, the Region of Peel, and the CVCA. In fact, the City at first was inclined to leave Ottawa out entirely because, as the minutes of one of the early meetings put it,

> the Federal Government represents an agency with a major vested interest in the Study area, similar to that of Texaco and St. Lawrence Starch. Since the majority of Federal lands are under leasehold to non-altruistic, corporate organizations [Centre City Capital, Dr William James], direct Federal involvement in the study may limit a creative and open-minded approach to an examination of land-use alternatives.

The city was finally persuaded by its consultant that federal involvement would be 'essential to implementation of the recommendations of the study.'[44] It was not much of a compromise. The City of Mississauga was always the leading – indeed, the dominant – public body in this multilevel, multilateral process. The steering committee for the Port Credit Harbour Study, which concerned itself mostly with federal land, was made up primarily of *city* staff, with only one person representing the federal government.

All the officials at the table were at liberty to comment on any aspect of the matters at hand, even if those lay outside their jurisdiction.[45] This appears to have been possible because all acknowledged the city's leadership, as the one municipality that would be affected directly. It was also understood from the early stages that the city would shoulder most of the costs and had more expertise in land-use planning than any of the other public bodies.[46]

Ottawa was not grovelling for more control. This was a new era for the bureaucrats. As of the mid-1980s, federal policy has called for the divestiture of all small-craft harbours.[47] By then, the government of Canada had fewer than a dozen staff overseeing its more than four hundred small harbours in Ontario, western Canada, and northern Canada. Sighing as they stared at their huge wall maps, they did not have the resources to take a detailed interest. 'We tried to operate in a non-confrontational way with the municipalities,' explains the federal government's Duane Blanchard, manager of small-craft harbours. 'We recognized [the municipalities] as partners. It made sense. We weren't trying to build a federal empire. We were trying to get this stuff managed as well as we could for as little as we could ... We let them be the lead.' He adds that the province has been involved in these municipal–federal relations only where it has a contractual interest in particular properties, although the federal government tried, without much luck, to divest all the small-craft harbours to the provincial government and to let the latter deal with the municipalities or other interested parties.[48]

There was no organized public movement pushing for waterfront revitalization.[49] The impetus seemed to come from within the bureaucracy, and was quickly endorsed by the mayor. Although McCallion involved herself only at strategic moments, she remained abreast of developments to the point that the chief federal official involved attests that he constantly 'felt' her presence.[50]

Once the process started, the interest and enthusiasm of local neighbourhoods and groups were piqued. Recreational groups and local small businesses saw the potential for a national sport-fishing hall of fame,[51] a project being promoted enthusiastically by the mayor, for whom this had become a favourite hobby.

The 1987 final report of the Port Credit Harbour Study recommended that the city try to secure all the federal land in the harbour at a very low purchase or long-term-lease rate and proceed to develop a modern marina, a restaurant, a mixture of shops and residences, a gallery and museum, and the sport-fishing hall of fame. On 9 July 1987 the mayor wrote to Fisheries and Oceans Canada insisting on a favourable long-term lease for the city.[52]

But there was still Dr William James. The president of Centre City Capital, the private entrepreneur leasing for recreational purposes the former Canada Steamship Lines Terminal (a lease that does not expire until 2023), was still drawing up his own proposal for all the federal lands. James's lawyer, John Keyser (also the long-time chair of the city's Committee of Adjustment), wrote to McCallion in March 1988: 'It has been a distinct pleasure to have received such a warm and favourable response from your staff and Dr. James asked that you look favorably upon this request.'[53]

McCallion was unmoved, despite Keyser's insistence that James would, in effect, be implementing the city's vision as expressed in the Port Credit Harbour Study. In a February 1989 report to city council, planning commissioner Russell Edmunds still argued that James's proposals are 'ideally suited and timely.' But he was soon sharing the mayor's concerns: 'Will control by one developer over a major share of lands on the east side of Port Credit harbour be beneficial or detrimental to implementation of the Port Credit Harbour Study Master Plan?'[54] Edmunds recommended that, at least for the time being, the city exercise its right of first refusal to prevent James from entering into new purchase or lease agreements with the federal government.

This issue with James convinced McCallion that the city needed to start planning for the *entire* waterfront. The Vision 2020 process was launched to take the exercise beyond Port Credit. One had to take the long view here. McCallion would have known that some of the plans would be twenty years or more (Vision 2020 refers to the year 2020) from being realized. She was convinced, however, that a waterfront could be part of her 'dynamic' city.

Land Development as a Political Asset

Land development can be a political hot potato. Massive land development can be politically fatal. Mary Fix's predecessors were lambasted for driving the municipality to the verge of bankruptcy by approving scattered subdivisions and then trying desperately to service them. Mary Fix herself raised the ire of suburban neighbourhoods by allowing industrial development too close to established areas. Robert Speck and Chic Murray had a good and comprehensive relationship with the large developers. For a time this seemed to bring order to major growth – for a time only. When too many slapdash developments started happening close to people's homes – and when post-war prosperity finally gave way to 'quality-of-life' agendas, even if some economic growth had to be sacrificed – the old guard was in trouble.

The unshakeable job security that by the mid-1980s had come to characterize Hazel McCallion's mayoralty is therefore quite intriguing. More than six thousand building permits a year were being issued, valued at more than one billion dollars. Were there not vested interests that found this change intolerable? Even McCallion herself mused in 1986 that 'a municipality with a billion dollars [in new assessment] should have the citizens upset.' She credited herself with keeping them happy. Mississauga had been growing in 'a very responsible way.'[55]

But does that give us the full picture?

In nearby municipalities, high-profile mayors who rode into office as tough-minded administrators had faced interminable political difficulties. True Davidson, for example, the 'ruler of all East York,' had been plagued with constant political opposition.[56] McCallion's contemporary counterparts in neighbouring Oakville, Etobicoke (and Toronto), and Brampton were all eventually defeated or nearly defeated in large part because of disenchantment with growth.[57]

There was, to be sure, some resistance here and there. Early in McCallion's mayoralty, for example, five hundred residents showed up at a public meeting to oppose an affordable-housing development, and cheered wildly when the mayor proclaimed her support for their position.[58] Council resisted what the ward councillor called a 'barbaric' subdivision in the exclusive Mississauga Road and Kane Road area.[59] And the Credit Reserve Association, in another affluent neighbourhood just north of Port Credit, never relaxed its vigilance. As one frustrated dentist wrote in 1981:

> I had previously in 1975 tried to rezone my property for commercial, so that I could practice dentistry in the house and not have to reside there.
>
> I was flatly refused together by council and the ratepayers 'Credit Valley Reserve.' I was told not to expect any commercial rezoning in my lifetime.[60]

Or consider the local councillor's reassuring letter, on another matter, to the association president:

For your information and files I am pleased to advise that the City Council passed a by-law on Sept. 14, 1981, restricting heavy truck traffic on Stavebank Road.

This came about as a result of a Credit Reserve Member calling me with respect to an abnormal amount of heavy trucks on Stavebank Road.[61]

Sometimes, the sheer pace of the boom brought calls to the mayor from prospective new homeowners. They were feeling cheated by vendors who were not honouring their agreements. Hearing these complaints, McCallion got city council to stop the sale of houses before formal registration, especially after disgruntled buyers were told they could not move in on schedule because of delays in receiving city permits. Other new residents were seeing their contracts lapse and being told by the seller that the home, once finished, would cost more. McCallion called the builders to her office and insisted on, and apparently got, public letters of apology because they had blamed the city. Indeed, she went further and blamed the developers for not being transparent with their customers. She insisted that the province require a standard contract. Even in audiences with many developers present, she publicly lambasted the bad apples. 'You'll notice it's a *he*,' the mayor said of the stereotypical unresponsive developer. 'I'm sure if it was a *she*, she'd respond!'[62]

And at times she had to anticipate trouble from future residents. The Region of Peel had a contract with the city to operate the Britannia landfill site in northern Mississauga until 1992. But what then? What if it just kept getting expanded to handle all the region's garbage? Not many people were residing around it, but development was coming. By the time additional capacity was added to the site, there could be angry residents blocking roads. Through the 1980s McCallion was pressing hard to have a site found in Brampton. We know that Peel bureaucrats would have been happy to see Britannia continue, at least for Mississauga garbage, but they were careful not to alienate McCallion on this. By August 1988 the mayor's office was contacting the provincial minister of the environment every week to make sure there would be no delays in getting the Brampton site approved.[63] (Thanks to the next provincial government, however, Britannia stayed open until 2002, and there would be no Brampton site. But Britannia's land coverage did not expand, and McCallion made life miserable for Queen's Park, publicly and constantly confronting the NDP ministers and probably thus contributing to the total degeneration of waste-management planning for the Greater Toronto Area. And even while garbage was still going into Britannia, the city put a golf course on a portion of it, just to be sure. Waste would soon have to go to Michigan.)

All said, however, animated, organized opposition from residents (or busy developers and builders, whose problems with labour shortages seemed to be of more immediate concern) was an exception. Localized flare-ups did not evolve into something bigger.

Why did the massive growth prompt so little protest? Perhaps McCallion was simply riding the economic crest caused by the transition of many North American residential suburbs to industrially powerful and extremely prosperous 'edge cities.' But Mississauga, let us recall, had been able to attract significant industrial development very early in its growth.[64] Suburban industrial development is not some sort of McCallion innovation.

As we have already seen, the activism that had flared in 1973 was largely extinguished because of dissatisfaction with or exhaustion among the reformers. As with so many reform movements, this one had discredited an old guard – in this case, a regime linked tightly to the developers – but overextended itself. Both the old guard and the reformers were lying bruised. The result, in the ensuing 'post-reform' era, appears to have been a leadership vacuum.

During the McCallion mayoralty extensive industrial growth, and even major residential developments, could be accommodated without significantly affecting the established residential neighbourhoods – those potentially politically volatile places where, in McCallion's own words, people 'want to know practically the colour of the building that's going next to them.'[65] This stands in sharp contrast with the reeveship of the feisty and sophisticated Mary Fix. Because of the limited basic infrastructure during Fix's time – in other words, the absence of a 'large suburban canvas' – new development had to be contiguous with, or situated within, the old.

It might be argued, of course, that the different reactions to industrial development during the Fix and McCallion periods can be attributed to the fact that, by the 1980s, industries had become cleaner. Many gleaming head offices were moving in. Some were attracted by the airport. Some had sought to move from Montreal following the election of a sovereigntist Parti Québécois provincial government in 1976. But many of the modern industries *are* disruptive. What about the proliferation of massive warehouse distribution centres that require the almost continuous comings and goings of tractor trailers? Conversely, many of the industries of the 1950s were not heavy, dirty polluters. The new Dixie industrial parks, including companies such as Dover Elevator and Samuel and Son, were not home to belching, dusty behemoths.

By taking a good look at planning, subdivision, and industrial maps from the 1950s to the 1980s, we get a better sense of the circumstances faced by the local leaderships with respect to land development. Although the Township of Toronto had virtually the same land base as today's City of Mississauga, most of it was not serviced with water and sewage infrastructure until the late 1960s. Map 6.1 shows the areas that, according to a 1960 assessment by senior staff of the municipality, could accommodate development without a major investment in new infrastructure. The existing conditions thus required growth to be received in close proximity to existing neighbourhoods.

Map 6.2 shows the active subdivision applications during Mary Fix's final year as reeve. Notice that they were mostly infill; they had to be. Most of the 'greenfields' were still not serviced for development. Such circumstances potentially lead to controversy and can be politically dangerous. It was only after 1976, after a development regime and an upstart slow-growth reform movement had both lost their credibility, and several years after the basic infrastructure had been put in place to facilitate major greenfield development, that the political path was cleared to take advantage of the prospect of growth without actually infringing on residents' backyards.

Map 6.3 shows the expansion of the built-up area between 1975 and 1985. Much of the new growth was now non-contiguous. This was confirmed in a 1987 city staff report on population and housing, which seemed to acknowledge that the negative side-effects of growth were not of immediate concern to the established neighbourhoods. It is worth quoting at some length:

> More than 70% of the net increment in residential units in the City between 1982 and 1985 occurred in six districts – Creditview, Erin Mills South, Meadowvale West, Mississauga Meadows, Mississauga Valleys, and North-North Dixie [all of which had been virtually empty ten years earlier] ... As these districts are now almost entirely built, residential construction activity will shift in the next few years. The bulk of future development is expected to occur in Central Erin Mills, East Credit, Erin Mills West, Hurontario, and Lisgar [also all virtually empty, with the exception of Central Erin Mills, which was under active development].

When viewing residential development activity in Mississauga, it is

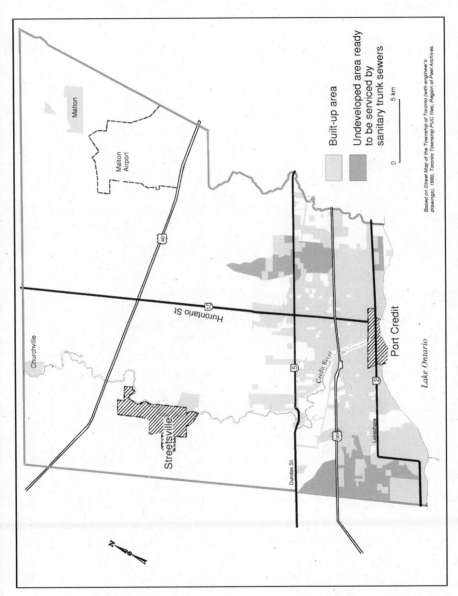

Map 6.1. Undeveloped Areas within the Township of Toronto Ready to Be Serviced by Sanitary Trunk Sewers, 1960

Built-up area

Undeveloped area ready to be serviced by sanitary trunk sewers

0   5 km

Based on Street Map of the Township of Toronto (with engineer's drawings), 1960, Toronto Township PUC files, Region of Peel Archives.

Malton

Malton Airport

Churchville

Streetsville

Hurontario St

Dundas St

Credit River

Port Credit

Lakeshore

Lake Ontario

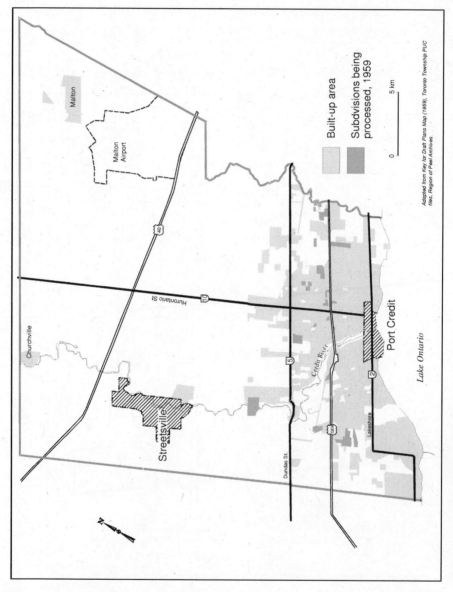

Adapted from Key for Draft Plans Map (1959), Toronto Township PUC files, Region of Peel Archives.

Built-up area

Subdivisions being
processed, 1959

0   5 km

Churchville

Malton

Malton
Airport

Streetsville

Credit River

Hurontario St.

Dundas St.

Lakeshore

Port Credit

Lake Ontario

Map 6.2. Subdivisions Being Processed, 1959

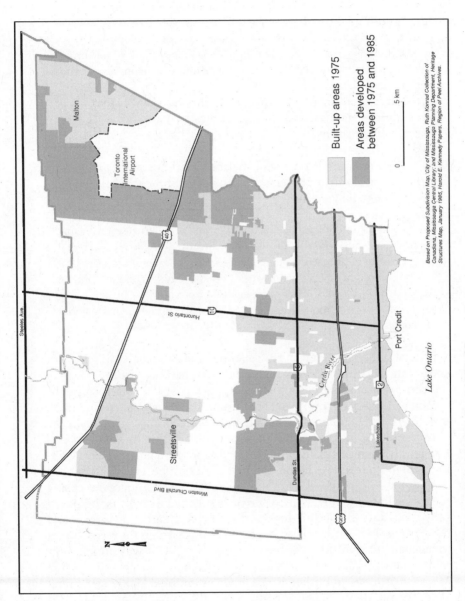

Built-up areas 1975

Areas developed
between 1975 and 1985

0   5 km

Based on Proposed Subdivision Map, City of Mississauga, Ruth Konrad Collection of
Canadiana, Mississauga Central Library; and Mississauga Planning Department, Heritage
Structures Map, January 1985, Harold E. Kennedy Papers, Region of Peel Archives.

Map 6.3. Development, Mississauga, 1975–85

useful to divide the city into three general areas. The first area is south of
Dundas Street, which has several well established residential communities. As such little new development is occurring in this area. Between
Dundas Street and Highway 403 is the second area of development. Much
of this area has recently been developed. Some opportunities for further
development still exist, but most of the City's future development will not
be concentrated here.

The third area is north of Highway 403 and this is where the bulk of
future development will occur. Large tracts of land are now in the early
stages of development.[66]

One councillor himself observed that he was having trouble getting
people excited about anything, unless the development happened to be
in their immediate vicinity.

I will continue to hold public meetings but one of the frustrations is that
people come out when it affects them directly and their backyard. I
would like to hold meetings to explain to the community the legal processes involved in development issues. Perhaps seminars on the Planning
Act and how it could affect your community would be of interest to
some, but I suspect [they] would draw a big yawn from the vast majority
of people.[67]

In 1984, when the mayor's own property was rezoned to allow for
single-family homes (the same property that had been at the centre of
the conflict-of-interest case), no one appeared at the statutory public
meeting in order to complain. That property was still surrounded by
open fields. (This time, McCallion declared her conflict of interest.)[68]
As a sign that visible opposition seemed to be draining away, McCallion finally even calculated that she could move on Larry Taylor. Waiting until just a few days before the 1988 election, she sent a letter at city
expense and on mayoral letterhead to Taylor's constituents, accusing
the councillor of telling 'a lie' when he blamed council for being politically motivated in rejecting his request for a stop sign. The furious and
now imperilled councillor charged that this last-minute missive was
'calculated' to prevent him from responding, that it was an inappropriate use of public money, and that McCallion had prevailed upon
Mississauga News publisher Ron Lenyk to endorse challenger Frank
Dale. (Lenyk denied being pressured by the mayor.) Taylor charged
that McCallion was supporting Dale 'because she wants to get rid of the

only council member who stands up to her and the developers, and replace me with a puppet.'[69]

Dale, who took Taylor's place and has been on council ever since, may not be a puppet. But he proved to be an unassuming person who has not made many waves and who says very little during council meetings.

Activists Stir

Would it stay quiet? The 1988 election, in which the mayor was acclaimed, resulted in not a single McCallion critic being found on the council or anywhere near it. Yet there were now some fresh murmur-ings. The city hall beat reporter for the *Mississauga News* was stirred to write his own opinion piece: 'It's very hard as you drive around Mississauga and see natural landmarks fall in succession to the developers' bulldozers not to agree that the city is changing too fast, and we're losing too much of our heritage in the stampede to jack up the population to 700,000 people as quickly as we can.'[70]

McCallion had been in politics long enough to know that a popular local politician could become an old-guard ogre. Witness what had happened to Chic Murray. Things could explode. On the other hand, rushing desperately to please the first activists who appear might only embolden them, encourage others, and allow things to spin out of control. McCallion must be a friend of the environment, she must keep her stature intact, she must shrewdly keep her credibility in place, and she must make success seem laborious.

In the late summer of 1987, University of Toronto botanists were introduced to a little-known, seventeen-hectare wetland in the vicinity of Creditview Road and Eglinton Avenue, a place that was then not contiguous with any existing development.[71] After a few months of tests, they deemed the 'Creditview Wetland' to be one of the most impressive inland eco-systems in the Greater Toronto Area; the shallow depression had been created twelve thousand years ago at the time of glacial retreat. The botanists were concerned to learn that the city had given draft subdivision approval for the site. A cursory environmental review had been conducted by two summer students working for the Credit Valley Conservation Authority.[72] The students had given the wetland a score of 7 (or low) on the provincial rating system. The botanists believed the rating should be 4 or better, making the wetland regionally, if not provincially, significant. It was home to the swamp rose, which had not been seen elsewhere in the area since 1901, and the Virginia chain fern, which was not found elsewhere in Peel. The tamarack trees were also considered rare in the region. These, they said, were but a few of its claims to distinction.[73]

The botanists' findings were shared with the normally politically inactive South Peel Naturalists Club, and a delegation was assembled to appear before city council. At that meeting, the mayor complained that the information was surfacing very late, perhaps too late. 'I only wish someone had taken the time to phone last summer. Now we're in the last strokes of development and we're in a bad situation ... You should understand it's way down the pipe unfortunately.'[74]

But she urged council to hire its own experts to do a review. She also insisted that the plan of subdivision not be registered until the review was completed.[75] The developers, Sherwood (later Wintor) and East Credit, mid-size corporations by Mississauga standards, predictably were not impressed. Harry Petschar, who had been Mississauga's planning commissioner in the 1960s and early 1970s and was now an agent for Sherwood, said that the wetland would be a breeding ground for encephalitis-carrying mosquitoes. 'If there's a chance a human life may be in danger, to hell with the grass and frogs.'[76]

The mayor could have argued that it was simply too late, and she could, perhaps, have dismissed the still-small delegation. Her early-morning calls to at least one of the botanists were apparently very forceful and gruff, as if hoping that some mayoral shock therapy would dissipate things.[77] But her political instincts in holding up the development seem to have been well placed. To be sure, the mayor's correspondence on the matter would always insist that 'the City had conducted studies on the wetland' and that there had been no concerns prior to draft approval.[78] But she knew that there was another version of events. Indeed, the concerned citizens had information that could embarrass the city. The summer students who had done the initial assessment would complete an affidavit saying that even they had had concerns. The flawed rating system has a 'social component,' one would write. But what could be said of the value to the public if the public did not know? Their superior was asked if there should be more assessment, and if anything could be done to stop development. No and no were the responses: don't worry about it![79]

Jocelyn Webber, University of Toronto doctoral student and author of a widely consulted book on Peel's vascular plant flora,[80] was making statements of her own. She insisted that she had come forward in time.

Eva Berlin of the Erin Mills Residents' Association and others were noticing: 'Why did the City of Mississauga, through planning (Dirk Blyleven), Council (David Culham) and the C.V.C.A. (Senior Planner) not act on the findings of Jocelyn Webber prior to draft plan approval?'[81]

And why were local environmental assessments carried out by summer students? 'This method of operating seems to have served its purposes in the past,' botany professor Paul Maycock would write to the mayor, 'but this whole nasty business of the Creditview Wetland seems to have sounded the death knell of this method of operating.'[82]

And the initial complaints about what was happening here seemed to have aroused a sleeping bear. The *Mississauga News* and even the *Toronto Star* editorial pages were filled with letters and statements by citizens complaining that too much of the city was being paved over too quickly. Provincial organizations, like the Field Botanists of Ontario, entered the fray.[83] The *Mississauga News'* editors themselves joined the chorus, calling on the council to do the right thing.[84] New local organizations, such as the Mississauga Citizens' Environmental Protection Association, suddenly appeared. The Creditview Wetland was a lightning rod for those concerns – and, for the mayor, potentially an opportunity to channel unfocused, latent grievances about development into a manageable issue.

Jocelyn Webber, who became one of the leading citizens in the campaign to protect the wetland, was surprised that the cause enjoyed such popularity. 'I thought people were really apathetic about the environment, but they aren't. They are anxious to sign our petitions. People are saying that this symbolizes their whole frustration with losing natural areas.'[85] Webber was not alone in her surprise. *Toronto Star* columnist Frank Jones also was perplexed that this Mississauga issue had garnered so much interest.[86]

Residents from parts of the city that were nowhere near the wetland actually became involved. The naturalists released a survey of property owners abutting the Rattray Marsh, which had been rescued in 1975 following a fifteen-year battle, showing that property values were higher for those who neighboured an ecological protection area.[87]

The report by the city-appointed consultant, Cameron Kitchen, was released in June 1988. It confirmed that the site was ecologically precious; although it raised questions about the validity of the provincial ranking system, which the Ministry of Natural Resources was now also beginning to doubt. Kitchen assigned the wetland a score of 6, but said that heavy rains could take the score to 3. He stopped short, however, of an outright recommendation to purchase, noting that this would be a political decision in light of a cost of seven to ten million dollars.[88]

In August city manager Doug Lychak submitted a report to council recommending against the purchase of the wetland in view of the 'administrative, legal, and financial' obstacles.[89] No surprise there. Developer John Switzer (East Credit) was saying that if council wanted to buy the wetland then he would 'fight them.'[90] Lychak suggested that the cost to the municipality would be thirty million dollars, including compensation to the developers. An astounded Webber wrote to members of the South Peel Naturalists Club that she had been told in private discussions that the cost would actually be about four million dollars.[91] Meanwhile, planning commissioner Russell Edmunds argued that the value of the bog 'is somewhat esoteric' because it 'is of interest primarily to scientists and educators who understand and appreciate its research and esoteric values.'[92]

McCallion did not endorse Lychak's report; she simply referenced it to show the environmentalists how monumental were the obstacles she was confronting. She now proposed an evening meeting at city hall to be devoted to the issue. She encouraged the naturalists to mobilize and to fill the council chamber with at least 600 people, which is 250 people over capacity. Meanwhile, she warned the developers against taking any precipitous action, such as paving over the wetland.[93] The mayor added that she would not be intimidated by threats to sue. The perplexed developers said they had never made such threats.[94]

The naturalists not only managed to fill the council chamber, they set up booths in local malls and ninety five people went door to door to gather ten thousand signatures for a petition calling for the preservation of the wetland.[95] And there was not much doubt that the provincial Ministry of Natural Resources was on the side of the citizens. At the public meeting, McCallion seized on a presentation by John Riley of that ministry, who urged the city to preserve the wetland in the interest of good planning. The mayor replied by charging that the province was shirking its duty. If the wetland was of provincial significance, she argued, then why was the province not buying it? Riley recalls that McCallion was successful in quelling a crowd that could have become hostile; she very effectively deflected the spotlight to the province. He grins as he recounts how, after the meeting, McCallion, who had denounced him sharply in public, approached him and initiated a pleasant conversation, as athletes might do after a well-fought match. She apparently explained that she wanted the wetland preserved but was intent on reducing to an absolute minimum the costs to the city.[96]

Following pressure from the mayor and a new report from the city showing that the wetland was rated Class 3 (high), the province and the developers began negotiating. Environment minister Jim Bradley indicated he would invoke the Environmental Assessment Act to review any development in the event that negotiations did not succeed. Negotiations dragged on through 1989, bolstered that fall by a report from the province's Environmental Assessment Advisory Committee recommending preservation.[97] In a verbal side comment, the chairman of that committee accused the city of playing 'a game of cat and mouse.'[98] But still the city sat out of the negotiations. The *Mississauga News* was critical of the city's non-participation and argued that if the wetland was lost the people at city hall would 'have no one to blame but themselves.'[99]

And still the city remained disengaged, continuing to send only observers.

As McCallion appeared to want, Bradley seized on all the publicity and on a realization that the province could, by putting up some money, present itself as a hero. In a letter to the chairman of the EAAC, the minister was emphatic in his conviction that something must be done and that the province would be part of the solution. He added that 97 per cent of the wetlands in Mississauga had been lost by 1982.[100]

Finally, in early 1990, with a deal about to crystallize, the city came to the table and agreed to pay four million dollars, with the province also contributing four million and the developers accepting some lost revenues.

This arrangement was not consummated, however. The Liberals lost the provincial election in September 1990. The new NDP government did not follow through, citing financial constraints, although environment minister Ruth Grier received two thousand letters from the naturalists and their supporters.

But as we shall see, McCallion now had other concerns. Development would hold off here on its own, at least for a while. Growth was slowing. Taxes and big government would be the targets of the 1990s.

7 The Mayor-Taxfighter

In politics, there are few iron laws. Hazel McCallion had nevertheless happened upon a formula for relatively easy governance and relatively easy popularity in a suburban context: be flamboyant and decisive, build new things, charge developers admission fees, and keep out of people's backyards.

Any formula, however, does not – cannot – include complacency.

By 1990 another sort of political restlessness was in the air. It was a general frustration with politicians. The federal Progressive Conservative government was reeling from record low polling numbers. Later that year, Ontario's David Peterson Liberals, popular for most of their mandate, suffered a stunning defeat, losing to the New Democratic Party.

As the economy showed signs of slowing, there was palpable exhaustion with taxes and with deficits. The NDP's 1991 budget, which had the effect of tripling the provincial deficit, confirmed that this would be a government without a honeymoon. The public mood was becoming crankier still.[1]

Hazel McCallion knew that the most pressing challenge of the next few years would not come from the Creditview Wetland types.

Tax increases and decreases in Mississauga have born a relationship to the general public's changing tolerance for footing the bills, as opposed to the strength of demands by the bureaucracy or any special interest. The Mississauga rate increase in 1990 was 7.7 per cent, after years of robust economic growth. In 1991, as a recession deepened and with signs of growing public sympathy for a neoliberal agenda, the increase was 0.6 per cent, falling to 0 per cent in 1992. Between 1994 and 2002, there would be no increases.[2]

Although McCallion had always presented herself as a consummate fiscal manager, by 1991 she was more strident than ever in criticizing other governments for their tax policies. She routinely castigated the boards of education for continuing to impose tax increases. She worried that citizens would blame the city for these increases, because the boards' property-tax *collection* was handled by the city.[3] She tried repeatedly to summon, by press release, the chairs of the two school boards to appear before council to justify themselves. They declined, but McCallion's grandstanding did receive considerable (and favourable) coverage in the local media.

Requests for money from the city were being deflected by pleading poverty – because of provincial downloading of costs, because of the NDP provincial government's public-service-retrenching 'social contract,' and because of other restrictions or difficulties created by the senior levels of government.[4] These arguments were used to cut snow clearing on many sidewalks, to significantly increase transit fares for seniors and increase them consistently for others, to dismiss the perennial demand that snowploughs have special equipment to remove the piles of snow that amass at the ends of private driveways,[5] and to replace snow-clearing grants to seniors with a loan program.[6] Less publicized were decisions in 1992 to cancel the annual New Year's Eve celebrations, which would not be revived, and to save two thousand dollars by scaling back the public consultation process for the official plan.[7] When the mayor complained about the city's promotions budget, arguing that more of the work should be done by volunteers, council dutifully referred the matter to the mayor to pare the budget down where she saw fit.[8]

Remarkably, this mindset carried over into organizations that receive city funding. McCallion insisted that all the funded groups – the Mississauga Arts Council, Mississauga Sports Council, Mississauga Heritage Foundation, Art Gallery of Mississauga, Mississauga Crime Prevention Association, and Mississauga Friendship Association (which manages Mississauga's twin-city relationship with Kariya, Japan) – should be working to wean themselves off city funding. In practice, the mayor was usually satisfied with no increases and evidence that city funding constitutes a diminishing percentage of the groups' operating funding.[9] It became highly unusual for an organization to request an increase in its grant.

More common were no increases or decreased requests, and certainly attempts by the groups to demonstrate the declining importance of city funding as a proportion of their budgets.[10] 'We're committed to reduce our requests until council says stop,' Harry Bryan, chair of the Mississauga Crime Prevention Association, told council.[11] This culture of restraint also affected junior city bureaucrats' relations with community groups. They were able to respond in the negative, and without hesitation or ambiguity, to any suggestions that the city consider extending its basic affiliate-group-insurance policy to cover the much-desired non-owned-automobile or directors'-and-officers'-liability categories.[12] Where on the odd occasion a funding increase has seemed reasonable to McCallion, she would volunteer to cover it from the proceeds of her Mayor's Charity Golf Tournament, which was raising close to two hundred thousand dollars per year. Those funds were almost always distributed at the sole discretion of the mayor.

Through most of the 1990s, McCallion boasted above all else about her tax policy. When the city announced a 1 per cent rate decrease in 1993, it earned McCallion national television appearances, and much praise, for running a debt-free city and reducing taxes when other governments were struggling.[13] Indeed, Mississauga was one of the first Canadian jurisdictions to introduce an across-the-board tax decrease – at least two years before this became a favoured policy for federal and provincial governments. This perception of outstanding fiscal management prevailed even though Mississauga's residential taxes were in fact generally higher than those in the old City of Toronto,[14] and even though Mississauga and Peel had managed to keep a much more substantial proportion of the tax burden on the residential ratepayers. The 1996 report of the Greater Toronto Area Task Force found that Toronto's ratio of residential to commercial/industrial rates was 0.42. Mississauga's ratio of 0.70 was the second highest in the Greater Toronto Area, just 0.01 basis points behind Caledon's.[15]

Members of the arts community always believed, although they expressed it in private, that McCallion was biased in favour of sports and was more willing to support sports funding than arts or heritage funding. Although she publicly favoured a major sports complex (and although one recently and cautiously took shape more than thirty years after it was first energetically proposed, before McCallion's mayoralty, by a group of fifty leading citizens),[16] the mayor forestalled any major grants.[17] She successfully championed user fees for baseball diamonds and other sports facilities, extending these to youth groups despite widespread disagreement. She even hazarded to ask for the Mississauga Sports Council's support on the user-fee issue, which she received, apparently in a unanimous vote.[18] The gesture did not bring the sports council any tangible rewards, except of course the mayor's rhetorical praise, which to some Mississauga organizations has been worth its weight in gold. She rejected a four thousand dollars grant request from the sports council to develop the Mississauga Sports Hall of Fame at city hall, telling the sports council members to focus their efforts on recruiting private benefactors.[19]

And she called for substantial user fees on fitness and recreation programs so that all operational costs (although not capital costs, which came primarily from development charges) could be recouped. She derided Toronto for its policy of offering many programs free of charge. When on one occasion the city's parks and recreation commissioner defended the notion that taxpayers should pick up an important part of the tab, McCallion snapped. 'I don't want to provide subsidized fitness. Do you get the message?'[20]

It would appear that he did get the message.

But McCallion still managed to advocate generous, full-time salaries for the mayor and councillors. She argued that, just as in a business, people get what they pay for. Although she appointed citizens' committees to make recommendations about how much the politicians should be remunerated, she did not hesitate to take responsibility for those decisions.[21] The fact that this never became a public controversy may be attributable in part to the image of personal frugality that the mayor herself managed to project. This was, after all, the mayor who eschewed a chauffeur and who was known to give rides to stranded pedestrians.[22]

Despite McCallion's tight control, it did happen occasionally that unwanted statements or descriptions slipped into the budget documents. In such instances, Her Worship did not hesitate to chastise the staff. One staff-prepared budget overview contained a statement implying that deferred maintenance was resulting in deterioration of facilities used by the public:

> Continuing funding pressures for capital reserve fund financing in the first six years resulted in significant deferrals of maintenance to the end of the forecast period (10 years). This results in continued deterioration of department facilities and is most noticeable where these facilities are heavily used by the public (eg. community centres, libraries, arenas, park trails and sports fields). Fire and emergency services is also severely impacted by this funding constraint as the training centre and station renovations cannot be funded within this plan.[23]

This brought a sharp rebuke from the mayor: the statement 'should either be retracted or adjusted. This is a very significant statement. It says to me that a roof is going to fall in on some of our buildings. Somebody's going to pick this up and say "yes, you're doing a great job on taxes but you've got significant deferrals. I think you should take that statement, redo it and tell it like it is."'

Community services commissioner Paul Mitcham tried at first to explain, but then conceded that 'it's probably not a good statement.' He promised it would be taken out.[24]

The Fish and the Peacock

Even on marquee projects, the mayor's hard-nosed business approach managed to filter down. So clear now was her 'run the city like a business' mantra that it seemed to act as a kind of invisible hand when city staff did its work.

Visit Hazel McCallion's office, and there you will find trophy fish prominently displayed. The mayor loves sport fishing. For years she headlined the *Toronto Star*'s Great Salmon Derby at Port Credit Harbour. So when it became clear that the Port Credit Yacht Club would be clearing out of that harbour and when all levels of government were willing to talk revitalization under the City's lead, McCallion embraced an idea for a new facility: a Canadian Sport Fishing Hall of Fame.

She devoted time to it, appointing in 1988 a steering committee of fishing magazine publishers, recreational leaders, and planners from across the province. A consultant's report was commissioned, and it included an examination of a similar facility in Wisconsin. A targeted opening date of 1994 was set.

The consultant and everyone else seemed excited by the idea. But some of the fine print was a little more disconcerting. The discussion of funding was imprecise. 'It is not possible for us to quantify other revenue sources [i.e., private sources] on the basis of the information available to us, but these sources could include the following.' A shopping list was then presented.[25]

If that did not alarm McCallion, then this would have: the city's acting director of economic development was suggesting that tax increases would be required to pay for the hall of fame.

In the 10-year budget and cash-flow analysis we should budget to have the City put a fixed sum per year into a reserve account that would gather interest. This sum could be earmarked by adding one or two mills to the tax rate for this purpose. It was also suggested that the City's total contribution including interest earned should be in the area of $3–3.5 million to be available by the start of construction.'[26]

By the end of 1990, the project had fizzled. The mayor's enthusiasm had waned significantly. The business case had not been made.

But business principles are not always in the public interest. They may clash with quality-of-life objectives. They may pre-empt proper research. That is what happened with the Peacock House.

'I don't have an artistic bone in my body,' McCallion conceded in a tribute video.[27] And indeed this self-described 'practical mayor' has not given much attention to the aesthetic realm.

So when waterfront revitalization – an admittedly progressive undertaking but one cast most often within the rubric of economic development and building a 'dynamic' new city – brushed up against a heritage issue, the principal players already had a sense of the general disposition of their leader, who was styling herself more and more as the dour fiscal disciplinarian.

And as a 'practical mayor.'

'I like to put myself in other people's shoes. I often wonder how we would feel if it was our house that was being preserved. We have to have some sympathy,' she said, referring to a private homeowner who wanted to replace historic millworkers' houses with a suburban residence.[28] In 1990, after the province's Conservation Review Board criticized the city for not taking steps to prevent the deterioration of the old Methodist parsonage in Streetsville, McCallion declared that the building 'should have been down years ago.'[29] It was demolished the following year, and the United Church parking lot was enlarged.

Even the old-guard, pro-development majority on the pre-1978 Mississauga city council had allocated fifty thousand dollars a year to purchase heritage-conservation easements (permanent, protective, contractual covenants).[30] By the late 1980s Mississauga had no budget for easements and no grants for rehabilitation of privately owned heritage buildings.

The Local Architectural Conservation Advisory Committee (LACAC) had been established in 1976 by the then slow-growth, reformer-dominated council, which acted almost immediately after the passage of the Ontario Heritage Act. (In fact, prior to the act, the reformist council had already established a Preservation of Historical Buildings Committee.)

Mayor Martin Dobkin was an active member of the predecessor committee and of the LACAC. Hazel McCallion showed much less interest
in the committee, and never served on it.

And so when an increasingly tight-fisted Mississauga, a Mississauga
whose mayor was certainly not a champion of heritage conservation,
had to decide what to do with the Adamson estate, a historically designated property it owned, the results were in some ways predictable.
This case merits a somewhat detailed exposition, as it provides a window on how a mayor who casts a long shadow can harbour a professional staff that feels it must operate within narrow, orthodox confines,
a staff that will restrain itself from engaging in creative imagination.

Recall that the estate had been purchased in 1975, thanks to the
Dobkin council, to prevent it from becoming a condominium development. Not much had been done with it in the decade that followed. But
in the late 1980s all levels of government were talking about beautify-
ing waterfronts. This property was on the waterfront.

In 1988 the city put out a proposal call to groups that might have a
use for the site. Said the city: We will let you move in, but you do the
upgrades and restoration – estimated cost about five hundred thousand
dollars. No one was willing to do that much, but the Royal Conservatory of Music wanted to use the main house and would cover two hundred thousand dollars in upgrades through annual rent payments (it
did not say in what amounts and instalments those payments would be
made).[31] The mayor and council had expected better; the matter was
deferred. Further enquiries did not reveal any white knights willing to
invest a half-million dollars, so in July 1989 council gave the go-ahead to
do some serious negotiating with the Royal Conservatory.[32]

Hardly anyone had been paying attention to this; there were no news
stories. But the president of the Mississauga Arts Council was aware,
and she was not very impressed. After all, letting in the Royal Conservatory would mean very limited access for the general public and for
all the small arts groups. She spoke to the ward councillor. As the councillor recorded it, the MAC president thought this was more 'a business
decision than an arts decision.'[33]

It was only after council was reasonably satisfied that there was a
group that would be willing to pay some bills that the development of
a master plan for the Adamson estate was commenced. The Royal Conservatory maintained its position that it would have no use for the
second home on the estate, the Peacock House, the only example in Mississauga of a period Frank Lloyd Wright–inspired Prairie style house.
So on 9 May 1990, in a report to the city's Administration and Finance

Committee, city staff recommended that the building – referred to erro-
neously and variously as 'the Gatehouse' and the 'Coachhouse' – be
removed from heritage designation and demolished.[34] 'Other than
occupying an historic piece of property, the Planning and Development
Department advises that the house has no unique architectural features,' said the submission from city clerk Terence Julian.

> The Building Services Division advises that a minimum expenditure of
> $7,900.00 is required to make the Coachhouse habitable to its present ten-
> ant, Mrs. Peacock, and that a cost of at least $60,000.00 is required to
> upgrade the facility to meet the various property codes which apply.
>   The Royal Conservatory of Music have also viewed the Coachhouse
> and their Consultant estimates that it would cost upwardly of $120,000 to
> make the facility suitable for the Conservatory's needs. Given the signifi-
> cant costs associated with upgrading the building, the Royal Conservatory
> advises that they do not wish to consider leasing the building.[35]

The report was forwarded to the LACAC, as required by the Ontario
Heritage Act.

In the meantime, Professor Anthony Adamson, the previous inhabit-
ant of the estate – the same Anthony Adamson who had been reeve of
the Township of Toronto (1953–4) – wrote to city clerk Julian arguing
that most of the city report 'contains some extraordinary misconcep-
tions, inaccuracies, and misnamings of buildings. This rather distresses
me.' Adamson enclosed a historical monograph he had written about
the site two years prior.[36]

Adamson disputed the city's claim that most of the home was built in
the 1930s. 'This house was built as it stands now except for a small rear
addition. This was built at one time [1905] and not as described. It is a
solid brick house with a full basement and, except for its septic tank, is
in good condition. As a shortage of affordable houses is the nation's
greatest social need, it seems to me that the City could find a "need."'

He observed that the city's priorities had changed since the period of
the reform-movement-dominated council (1974–6). 'The Conservation
Authority had no "need" for a park when they expropriated the land
from me [at the strong behest of city council]. I could have asked for an
OMB study to legitimize any expropriation on the grounds that a park
was needed.'

But he promised not to object if the city were now to sell off a small
acreage to subsidize the restoration of the house or to devote the house
to some commercial or social purpose:

I would have no qualms on moral, equitable, or legal grounds to object to a rational way of keeping a sound house suitable for sale, or for social housing, or for child care, or for other purposes. I think the action of the City in destroying a perfectly good house because a recreation department cannot think of a good use for it discredits the administration of the City.[37]

If reason failed, then perhaps humour would work. In a follow-up letter, the professor included an illustration of the building that was actually the gatehouse, but which the City called the folly: 'Whatever a building which looks like the above is, it is a building built for a road to go through. It may be a Folly, but it *is* a Gatehouse' (emphasis in original). The city risked being caught in a comedy of errors: 'Unless the city of Mississauga gets the names straight and stops calling the farmer's house a gatehouse some bylaw will end up doing the wrong thing to the right house or the right thing to the wrong house by mistake.'[38]

Toronto resident Kent Peacock, son of tenant Barbara Peacock, was also puzzled and frustrated. He insisted, in an eloquent letter to the LACAC, that the home was in good condition and that the city was acting out of bureaucratic convenience.

The only deterioration it yet shows is the almost total lack of ordinary exterior maintenance during the years that it has been administered by the Municipality; it is otherwise completely sound. (Much interior maintenance, including until recently regular furnace services, has been paid for by my parents.) The inference of the reported repair-cost estimates ... seems ambiguous – if not a good deal less than candid. Precisely what special 'property codes' are supposed to apply to a building such as this? And is some repair claim made beyond the ordinary range of responsible maintenance? It should be noted that full rent (approximately $6600 per year) has been paid to the Municipality since the property was expropriated [in 1975].... So far as funds for necessary maintenance repairs are concerned – what has happened to the rental income that has been paid over more than a decade of Municipal administration?

And finally there is the matter of custodial responsibility and the overriding duty to protect the public interest, versus bureaucratic authority and managerial convenience. How can the public interest possibly be served by the expedient demolition of a good house of unusual merit, when the rent paid to the public (Municipal) purse enormously exceeds any proper maintenance cost, and when the sole consequence of demolition is the destruction of a public asset – and the elimination of a bureaucratic embarrassment?[39]

Peacock, who went on to become a faculty member in philosophy at the University of Lethbridge, disputed almost the entire description of the architectural features. He kept up his correspondence: 'I lived in this building for several years and have been intimately familiar with it for 20 years, and I can assure you that this statement [that much of the house was built in the 1930s, not 1905] is pure fantasy.'[40]

These letters made a dent, but only a dent. Ian Scott, commissioner of recreation and parks, was willing to entertain only a modest reprieve. He advised a fellow bureaucrat that the bottom line must be maintained:

> While I sympathize with Mrs. Peacock's plight, it still doesn't change the long term situation in terms of the City's need to establish a parking lot in that location and also the repairs that need to be made to the house. Obviously it is not cost effective for the City to carry out these repairs.
>
> My suggestion, as long as it does not set any precedent for the Adamson Estate, is that we give Mrs. Peacock an extended notice period (suggestion 12 to 18 months) which would then give her sufficient time to find alternate accommodations. I don't think this will interfere with our need to develop the parking lot and it will provide some additional time and understanding of Mrs. Peacock's situation.[41]

Develop the parking lot! The argument for demolishing the house was not being put in quite these terms when the listeners were members of the LACAC. It was just an expensive-to-maintain house with no heritage value.

What about the public and the neighbours? Rest assured, they would be consulted – but only in due course. Early that summer, there was a public open house to discuss the draft Adamson estate master plan. Approximately twenty-five residents, most of whom lived in the immediate area, attended. The Minutes of the meeting indicate that there were some comments by the neighbours about the importance of the heritage buildings on the site, although there is no specific recorded reference to the Peacock House. However, Commissioner Scott was able to assume the moral high ground when Anthony Adamson stood up to suggest that the Peacock House be saved by selling off a small portion of the vacant public property and by using the proceeds to maintain the house. Scott brushed this off. City staff is opposed to disposing of parkland, the administrator declared solemnly.[42]

Things went into abeyance for awhile, as everyone tended to more pressing matters. Finally, on 15 November 1990, Scott wrote to Councillor Kennedy stating that a firm decision on the future of the Peacock House would have to be made soon to fit with the Royal Conservatory's move-in schedule for the main house and the access road that would have to be built. They met on 4 December, and decided to give Barbara Peacock eighteen months to leave and to help her find a new place. They did not even wait for this to go to LACAC. They simply communicated it to Kent Peacock.[43]

The news came as a relief, but something still bothered Kent Peacock about this whole business. He continued to 'have very strong disagreements with the overall policy, and indeed even the ethics, of the City's conduct as a landlord of the heritage properties it controls.' He promised to retain an interest in this issue even after his mother was relocated:

> It seems very clear to me that this decision has most definitely not been 'thoroughly investigated' (as you put it); I think it is high time that the whole policy and conduct of the City of Mississauga as a landlord receive a full airing. I'm sure that the community will in the long run benefit from this process, as acrimonious as it may become at times.[44]

The question of the future of the Peacock House appeared on the LACAC agenda for the final time on 26 February 1991. It was presented not as a separate item (removal of designation from the Peacock House) but together with the full master plan, allowing staff to spend considerable time discussing the conservation of the main house and the intention 'to investigate all means by which to restore and preserve [the adjoining building, which Adamson called the gatehouse and the city called the folly].'

With regard to the Peacock House, Scott rejected suggestions that the parking lot be built around it, saying that this would result in the removal of trees. One of Scott's subordinates suggested that, following demolition, a plaque be erected to recognize the building.

Councillor Maja Prentice, a member of the LACAC, was recorded in the minutes as arguing that 'it is not financially feasible to retain all buildings on this site and therefore, priorities must be set.' Councillor Ted Southorn opined that recent residential development near the Peacock House had already tended 'to diminish the property.' He moved that the LACAC endorse the Adamson estate master plan.

The motion was defeated, however. The LACAC then passed a resolution opposing the Peacock House's removal from designation.[45]

At the following city council meeting, council did defer the matter but there was no subsequent public debate before the heritage designation on the Peacock House was removed. The city's director of realty argued that there was not a business case to continue renting the house as a residence, as 'single-family housing does not carry itself as a rental form of investment.'[46] It was demolished in 1992. A seldom-used parking lot is now situated there. The plaque was never put up.

The specific notion that the entire Adamson estate had to be subject to lucrative tenancy, and maintained at the tenant's expense, probably did not originate with the mayor. It was, however, entirely consistent with the business philosophy she espoused, a philosophy that was common knowledge to city officials at all levels of the administration. When the most promising of the proponents had no use for the Peacock House and needed more parking space, the heritage home's fate was close to sealed, as revealed in part by the highly inadequate and superficial research on the heritage aspects. There was never any consideration given to simply paying out of general revenues for the necessary upkeep and renovation. Even the city's estimate of sixty thousand dollars to rehabilitate it for 'property code' purposes – deemed by Kent Peacock to be an exaggeration – would not have been a punishing expenditure for a municipality of 450,000 residents. But that option was off the agenda from the very beginning.

Although some heritage demolitions were reported in the local media, the city's heritage efforts – or lack thereof – received virtually no critical scrutiny. In September 1990, just as the plans for demolition of the Peacock House were being finalized at city hall, a *Mississauga News* editorial actually lauded the municipality for its heritage initiatives: 'The City is so far ahead in the field [of recycling] it is now trying to recycle its own past.' The editorial was referring not to the conservation of buildings but to a city storage facility ('the morgue,' as it is commonly known) where some salvaged bits and pieces from demolished heritage homes (banisters, floorboards, fireplace mantles, and the like) were stored, awaiting unspecified future use.[47]

Hazel McCallion had repeatedly instructed city staff to not be swayed by 'vocal minorities.' Here the LACAC had been uncomfortably intransigent. And not only on this issue. While this was happening, the LACAC was making the case – again unsuccessfully – for the conservation of a distinctive, century-old Gothic Revival home that was in the path of a road-widening.[48]

It was acting too independently. That would soon change.

In 1994 the LACAC was renamed the Heritage Advisory Committee

– although its mandate was made no broader. The privilege given to organizations like the Mississauga Heritage Foundation and the Streetsville Historical Society to nominate members was discontinued. All members would henceforth be appointed directly by city council. Since this restructuring a councillor, and not a citizen, has always been in the chair.

Between 1994 and 2005, Mississauga would pursue not a single designation under the Ontario Heritage Act that was not assented to by the owner. In fact, almost all of the small handful of designation bylaws that were passed in that period were *requested* by the owner.[49] The written protocol requiring city staff to consult with the Heritage Advisory Committee when a request for a demolition is received on any heritage-inventory building ceased to be followed, without notice to the committee.[50] Councillor Katie Mahoney, who chaired the committee between 1994 and 2003, defended her own lack of energy or initiative with respect to protecting heritage buildings by insisting that the fault is not hers but should be attributed to the fact that 'there doesn't seem to be any leadership for [heritage conservation] coming from anywhere,' obviously a reference to the mayor's apparent uninterest.[51] Apparently, Mahoney had determined that her position as chair of the committee did not give her a platform from which *she* could be proactive or fill the role of a 'leader' with respect to heritage conservation.

Taking Control of the Library Board

The LACAC was not the only brightening ember that had to be identified and extinguished.

In 1990 the city began trying to have the library board eliminated. The problem was this: any collective agreements between that board and the union representing library workers could complicate city council's own labour negotiations. If the library workers got too much, then the others might demand like treatment. In fact, a provincial pay-equity ruling seemed to suggest that the library workers and the city workers were indeed apples and apples.

Seeing the writing on the wall, the chief librarian supported the city position that the board should be eliminated and the library administration be put under the direct jurisdiction of city council.

But the board itself got a legal opinion opposing the city. A report from the city manager 'does not suggest a situation unique to Mississauga which would justify dissolution of the Library Board,'[52] the lawyers advised. Nevertheless, the board voted 6–3 to accept the city's position and to join in the petition for its own demise.[53]

The Canadian Union of Public Employees, which represented the library workers, opposed the city move, and the provincial NDP government delayed the introduction of a bill. The mayor took to writing to other municipalities to demand comprehensive, not just Mississauga-specific, legislation to allow municipalities – which already had the power to appoint most of the library board members – to dissolve the library boards outright.

While this was happening, McCallion made a mistake. In late 1991 it was time again to appoint a library board. In keeping, it would seem, with the mantra that the council – which was paying more than 90 per cent of the library costs – should control the library board, council appointed the maximum number of councillors (three) and the minimum number of citizens (three). But these two citizens were joined by three others – two appointed by the Peel Board of Education and one appointed by the Dufferin-Peel Roman Catholic Separate School Board, as was required in the legislation.

One of the Peel Board appointees, Michael Crawley, a writer of some renown, became a thorn in the city's side. 'I'm philosophically opposed to politicians controlling libraries,' he said, charging that the city had an even larger agenda than trying to gain a handle on the union: 'City Hall is quietly campaigning toward user fees.'[54]

In March 1994 Crawley presented a motion to repeal the library board's earlier support for dissolution. The motion carried 5–4, with all councillors on the board voting on the losing side.[55] Crawley knew there would be consequences for this. He predicted that, upon expiration of the board members' terms later that year, council would punish the library trustees who voted for retention. Only 'those who are malleable' would be picked.[56]

Although the mayor and council were now resigned to the continuation of the library board, significant changes were, indeed, implemented at the end of 1994. All but one of the citizen members were new; the board was expanded to eleven members, a move that was within the legal authority of the city, to allow council to appoint additional members to dilute the school boards' representation; council insisted that the school boards submit three names from which council would choose the school board representatives or request a new slate; and the new board quickly approved a city recommendation to make the City's commissioner of community services the chief executive officer of the library.

It worked. In 1996, a board resolution formally gave virtually all control to the city:

> The Library Board's Chief Executive Officer and management group are expected to operate the library in a sound financial manner that is consistent with the requirements and practices of the City. Where such practices contravene the Public Libraries Act and/or collective agreement, departures will be discussed with the City, documented, and brought forward to the Board for approval.[57]

Thus, taken literally, the board reserved for itself only the dubious authority to approve extralegal activities. All *intra vires* decision-making was delegated to the city.

Library board meetings have since consisted almost entirely of routine updates. There has seemingly been little opportunity for real decision-making.[58] Even the budget has often gone to council before its *pro forma* approval by the library board.

Keeping an Eye on the Neighbourhood Activists

The neighbourhood movement had been lying largely dormant since before McCallion became mayor, and the Creditview Wetland issue was in abeyance for the time being, but a few articulate activists could cause headaches. They could not always be dismissed out of hand. They might require some deftness. If handled well, their presence, such as it was, could advance, rather than detract from, the fiscal agenda, an agenda that was being greeted especially warmly by the casual observers of city hall in the early 1990s.

On 17 June 1991 a small group of citizens who were worried about the future of Streetsville came to see McCallion in her office. At that meeting, the mayor apparently brought up the Region of Peel's impending plans to widen the two-lane Britannia Road to four lanes through Streetsville, necessitating the demolition of houses fronting onto the road. McCallion also encouraged the formation of an organization to channel the residents' concerns. The Streetsville Preservation Association was born, growing to 123 members by the following year.[59]

The group became fixated on the Britannia widening, which was being promoted by regional bureaucrats who believed it would cure the rush-hour traffic bottlenecks (outside Streetsville, Britannia Road was four lanes wide). McCallion said she would tolerate a centre turning lane being added, but not widening to four lanes where the houses fronted the road. At two emotional public meetings, the Streetsville Preservation Association took the same position.

The views of McCallion and the SPA prevailed, and only the one additional lane was constructed. But during this process McCallion ignored the views of the Britannia Road Residents' Association, whose members (from some forty homes) would be affected most directly by any decision. They insisted that in the event of any expansion of Britannia, including the new turning lane, the region should offer to buy them out. They argued that their property values were already in decline. As one couple put it:

> One need only witness the present traffic conditions, both morning and evening, which make it near impossible to exit or enter our driveway, and which create a build-up of noxious fumes from idling cars and trucks, to envision the horrendous increase in these conditions when the proposed changes are completed.[60]

Perhaps by siding so quickly with the concerned Streetsville residents, McCallion was paying homage to a core of neighbourhood interests to whom she felt bound or who had helped to sustain her. Perhaps she was even defying the silent mass opinion, which might have favoured the four lanes to eliminate the bottlenecks. It should be remembered, however, that the neighbourhood and preservation interests were not being represented by any organization, until McCallion suggested that one be formed and until she proposed the issue.

The cost of three lanes was considerably lower than the four-lane option – three million dollars as opposed to twenty-four million.[61] Cost may thus have been a decisive factor in McCallion's calculations because she did not oppose widening to four lanes the Streetsville stretch of Britannia Road west of Queen Street, where no houses had to be purchased to be demolished. (Putting in four lanes in the eastern leg would have required buying the houses, which would have been in the way of the road.)

The issue was managed by the mayor in such a way that only a small group of homeowners was left disgruntled. The Streetsville preservationists went away persuaded that, with the mayor's sympathy from the very first day, a very bad project had been made much less bad. Any public angst about threats to Streetsville could be answered by pointing to a solution that had the blessing of a citizens' organization. Motorists fuming privately under their breath could rest assured that some action, albeit a half measure, was being taken. The mayor could take comfort that the price tag was much lower than it might have been.

Ethnic and Religious Politics

Unlike the Streetsville road widening, some planning issues were starting to take on cultural overtones. Mississauga's cultural face had been changing almost as quickly as its landscape. Although already home to many European immigrants when McCallion became mayor, the city had still been overwhelmingly white in 1978. By the mid-1990s approximately one-third of the population consisted of members of visible minority groups, a figure that was increasing rapidly. Almost 45 per cent of the population was born outside Canada, and almost 40 per cent had a language other than English or French as mother tongue.[62]

It has been very common in the past generation for new immigrants to make Canadian suburbs their new home, more so even than central cities. In the edge cities, new neighbourhoods were taking shape. Many single-family homes were modest enough to allow an extended family with some savings and with one or two breadwinners to make a purchase after meeting relatively permissive down-payment requirements. The property values in Mississauga have been high by Canadian standards, especially in the older, more exclusive southern neighbourhoods, which continued to be dominated by white, Canadian-born residents. But property values have generally not been nearly as high as in the established Toronto neighbourhoods. In some of the districts close to the Toronto core, it was hard for upwardly mobile immigrants and minorities to break through, in part because of long-term ownership stability, and in part perhaps because of a certain blue-blooded fear of those with a different colour of skin and different traditions.

In the early 1970s even jazz great Oscar Peterson had settled in Mississauga – and in a fairly typical suburban house. He had apparently been snubbed by a landlord in Toronto's Forest Hill who refused to rent to him because he was black. Mississauga, where almost everyone seemed to be just beginning to put down roots, in a new community if not in a new country, was a more comfortable place to live for the Canadian-born Peterson. 'I think it was a case of not being rejected,' Peterson's niece Sylvie Sweeney told the *Globe and Mail* in 2007 following the death of the world-renowned pianist. 'In Mississauga he got a chance to know his neighbours and build a history together.'[63] (Peterson and

McCallion became friends, even off the stages that they often shared. 'I always say you're my girlfriend, and my wife approves!' Peterson quipped at an event at which a rose was actually named after the mayor.)[64]

McCallion was not oblivious, at least at a superficial level, to the changing face of her city. She was, after all, ubiquitous, and her omnipresence included events hosted by ethnic organizations. But the multicultural reality of the city, a some-time topic of conversation at regional budget meetings when the politicians vented about the lack of federal support for settlement services, was virtually absent from policy and programming decisions at city hall.

McCallion did understand, it is true, that in rejecting or deferring demands emanating from minority communities, she had to show somewhat more nuance and subtlety than she showed to others with whom she disagreed. 'When McCallion goes on a tear, the object of her vitriol is usually caught mouth agape, like an animal in the headlights of an onrushing 18-wheeler,' the *Mississauga News* once felt compelled to editorialize, after the mayor kept cutting off an affordable-housing advocate who showed up at a city council meeting to support accessory units (or 'basement apartments,' as McCallion preferred to say) as a right. The city must not appear divided in opposing the province, she boomed. 'While [aggressive admonition] can be an effective tactic, it relies on fear. McCallion may be Mississauga's leading citizen, but she isn't a dictator.'[65] (She got her way on that issue when the next government, Mike Harris's, repealed the legislation.)

The mayor may not have read Machiavelli, but she knew that the prince could not always be a lion.

In 1993 city staff proposed that Second Line West, a major future arterial road, should have a new name south of Highway 401. Most of the numbered 'lines' had already been renamed as the city urbanized. Subdivisions were now planned along Second Line West, almost as far north as Meadowvale Village.

Years earlier, McCallion had deferred a request to name a street in central Mississauga after Mahatma Gandhi, arguing that his name should be attached to a major arterial road. The National Association of Indo-Canadians reminded the mayor of her earlier promise, and local councillor David Culham supported 'Gandhi' for the Second Line renaming. But just before ratification, several citizens who did not live in the notification area objected on the grounds that the name 'has no bearing on our Canadian background' and that it would change the character of the area.[66] The mayor promptly intervened, declaring that she would seek a negotiated solution. The following week, she announced that Second Line West would not be renamed after Gandhi, but that a future street in the city centre would be.[67]

Remarkably, the president of the National Association of Indo-Canadians said he was satisfied. '[The mayor] was trying to do her best to please everyone, and I respect her for it,' Nakul Jerath said. The organization's secretary, Vijay Kalhan, was less content, arguing in a presentation to council that McCallion had probably created 'synthetic opposition'[68] and charging that 'there was an agenda.' Although usually highly confrontational when faced with direct and public criticism, McCallion now donned the guise of a peacemaker: 'Let us deal with this in a non-confrontational manner,' she exhorted. 'Please, let's go in peace, not in conflict. You're certainly not demonstrating Gandhi's way of life,' she told the sceptical deputant.[69]

Second Line West was renamed Terry Fox Way south of Britannia Road and Silken Laumann Way north of Britannia Road. In the ensuing ten years, several new streets appeared in the city centre. None was named after Gandhi. Only in the past five years has a small residential crescent in a new subdivision south of the city centre appeared bearing the name of Gandhi. Indeed, although the city has named several streets after foreigners (Wallenberg and Walesa, for example), no other street in Mississauga was named after someone who was not of European or Aboriginal background.

Symbolic recognition could be politically perilous in other respects. For years, McCallion was happy to declare national and ethnic days (as well as days dedicated to finding various cures or honouring professions and sports) and to have the appropriate flag raised at city hall. However, in 1995 Hamilton mayor Robert Morrow was fined by the Ontario Human Rights Tribunal for refusing to declare Gay and Lesbian Pride Day. McCallion had never been asked to declare such a day. As another indication of the weak media coverage in Mississauga, no one pressed her on whether or not she would. To avoid controversy she promptly urged city council to pass a motion, which it did unanimously, ending all flag-raisings and declarations.[70]

It was not that she was determined to shun all national controversy. Just as she was putting a stop to the flag-raisings, she was saying that Quebec's separatist leaders should be put on trial for treason.[71] But McCallion obviously calculated that an argument on a gay-rights issue would be much more divisive within the city.[72] On the other hand,

hyperbole against the separatists, if not embraced as frank and courageous, would be received, at least outside Quebec, with a grin and a
chuckle. It was a safe way to reinforce the image of the mayor as outspoken and fearless and bold.

On occasion, the questions of identity and recognition were more
than symbolic, involving land-use planning issues in which considerable investments were at stake. As she was dealing with the flag-
raisings, McCallion was already hearing about a proposal to build a
mosque on South Sheridan Way. The Canadian Islamic Trust Foundation's requested rezoning would allow for the construction of a place of
worship with a prayer-hall capacity of 1,100, plus ancillary uses, the
principal one being a private secondary school for 100–125 pupils.

South Sheridan Way was an arterial road running parallel to – and
immediately south of – the Queen Elizabeth Way (expressway), just
west of Southdown Road in southwestern Mississauga. The site was in
an industrial area, with the nearest residential dwellings about 150
metres away, separated by a narrow green belt. The existing zoning's
failure to allow a place of religious assembly was an anomaly dating to
the 1950s, the rationale for which could not be determined by the city
staff members who searched the old records. In 1959 the council of the
Township of Toronto added more uses to most industrial zones, including banks, motels, and places of religious assembly. The provisions of
this amended zoning bylaw did not apply, however, to some of the
lands within sight of the Queen Elizabeth Way.[73] The existing zoning
did, nevertheless, allow such intensive uses as conference centres.

This rezoning proposal generated opposition from the nearby neighbourhood. Two meetings of the Planning and Development Committee
lasted well past midnight as a stream of deputants made their case for
and against the mosque. The stated reasons for opposition related to a
fear that the congregants would resort to on-street parking in the residential areas and would access the mosque via pedestrian walkways.
Also envisaged were traffic problems, especially during Friday rush
hours, in and around the antiquated interchange (since modernized) at
the QEW and Southdown Road, and in the vicinity of Iona Catholic
Secondary School, the occupant of the neighbouring property that was
also close to that interchange.

The mayor's opposition to the application was expressed before the
neighbouring residents became vocal and before city staff made any formal recommendation. In November 1996 McCallion convened a meeting of top city officials and ordered them to search for alternative sites.

Several were presented, all of them far removed from residential areas, and one of them in Oakville. By March 1997, all of these sites were rejected by the applicants because the mosque should be easily accessible to worshippers and because securing the alternative sites might prove complicated and expensive.[74] But the mayor continually cited these initial efforts as proof that she was not being hostile to the congregation. She also pointed out that a mosque in Vaughan was in the middle of an agricultural area, suggesting that this was the most appropriate place.[75] In handling the file in this manner, the mayor appears not to have been swayed by the fact that John Rogers, a ubiquitous consultant who represents many development applicants, was the agent for the mosque applicants. Rogers was also a past chair of the Mayor's Charity Golf Tournament.

The staff recommendation, prepared after the first public meeting and well after McCallion's search for alternative sites, opposed the application on the basis of traffic, arguing in part that some of the prayers would conflict with rush hours and that parking might spill outside the parking lot. McCallion was deft in limiting the debate to these technical issues, even though the provincial Ministry of Transportation released its own traffic study not anticipating any significant difficulties. Predictably, the applicant's own consultants concluded that the traffic impact would not be significant.

The city staff conceded that the Clarkson–Lorne Park Secondary Plan (now called the district plan) envisaged this type of development in this area, but the staff opposition was based upon the much broader and more vague statements on transportation in the Official Plan:

3.6 Goals and Objectives – Transportation
3.6.1 GOAL – To plan a transportation system for the rapid, safe, energy-efficient, economical, convenient, and comfortable movement of people and goods.
3.6.2 OBJECTIVES To keep trip times to a minimum.[76]

The staff did not entertain the possibility that integrating a mosque into the urban fabric, in a location close to transit, rather than situating it far from any other development, might actually uphold this goal and these objectives.

When one non-Muslim resident spoke in support of the application on the grounds that Muslims, like many Christians, should have places of worship close by, Councillor Maja Prentice, the councillor who tended to be the most vocally deferential to the mayor on a wide range of issues, rejected this argument. Council was dealing with planning issues, not cultural issues, she insisted.[77] Prentice had used a similar argument on a different issue to reject concerns by some residents of Chinese origin about having a funeral home in a residential area, in apparent violation of *feng shui* principles.[78] McCallion also again rejected the proposed siting of the mosque. She added now that 'it must be in the right place in order to build the bridge between communities.'[79]

Councillor David Culham, who by this time had developed a frosty relationship with the mayor,* was the one councillor to support the application. If need be, he maintained, spillover parking could use the school and a neighbouring industrial site during off-peak periods.[80] In his own correspondence with the applicants, Culham argued that a mosque at this location, next to a Catholic school, could lead to cultural sharing. A highly visible landmark such as this one could also help the Muslim community become part of the Canadian mainstream. Culham warned that the Ontario Municipal Board would not look favourably upon the fact that the city was imposing a still-unapproved parking standard on this application.[82]

Culham did not sway anyone on council. But his predictions about the OMB proved to be accurate. The provincial oversight body did indeed overturn the city decision.

Despite that ultimate reversal, the debate about the mosque could have unfolded very differently on a more fractious and weakly led council. Councillors who represented other wards might have made the rational calculation that they had little to lose siding with the applicants rather than those residential neighbours who opposed the mosque. They might have calculated that it was to their political advantage to present themselves as champions of inclusiveness. But this was

---

* The relationship took a turn for the worse in the early 1990s. Culham was a hard-working councillor who leaned to the right but who was progressive on environmental and child-welfare issues. He had mayoral ambitions, and it is widely speculated that he had been under the impression that McCallion would retire in 1991. As he began to publicly disagree with McCallion, Culham would find his own work in the ward increasingly difficult, believing that he had to be on guard almost around the clock lest the mayor take an action or decision that would have the effect of upsetting something on which he was working. An exhausted Culham resigned suddenly in 2000, before the end of his term, when he was offered a seat on the Ontario Municipal Board.

Mississauga – and supporting the proposal would have meant opposing the mayor. That would give any rational actor some reason to pause.

The Great Airport Juggle

The well-heeled, in-for-the-long-haul citizens' interest groups were hard to find in most planning debates. But what if neighbourhood activists, businesspeople, other levels of government, and the media were all taking an ongoing interest in the same file? That has not been common in Mississauga.

We have already seen that McCallion had the good fortune of being the mayor who was in the right place at the right time. But that is certainly not to suggest that just anyone would have been electorally successful or would have been able to exercise pre-emptive, overriding leadership. Even the mishandling of one or two complex, high-profile issues could seriously damage credibility on other issues, and could lead to a domino effect. Other malcontents or interests could be emboldened and start to emerge. *Fortuna* can never be the only precondition, Machiavelli reminds us. *Virtù* (skill) always factors in.

Having a major international airport within your boundaries can be a blessing, a potential blessing, and a curse. It brings industry. Hazel McCallion herself has stated that more than sixty of the Fortune 500 companies have their Canadian head offices in Mississauga primarily because of the proximity to Pearson International Airport. (The second reason, she has claimed, is Mississauga's sound management.) It is a potential blessing because if airport operations and expansions are tailored in the right way, the creation of high-quality jobs can be accelerated – and senior levels of government may be willing to make lucrative investments in the local infrastructure. But it can be a curse because airports have side effects: noise and traffic. If these be serious, then vast tracts of the municipality can end up sterilized. What's more, airports give other governments – the federal government, the provincial government, other municipalities even – excuses, sometimes good reasons, to interfere. Everyone is trying to capture the benefits and pass the side effects off elsewhere.

And so although Pearson International Airport falls under federal jurisdiction, airport politics can be of tremendous importance to the mayor of Mississauga. The former Town of Mississauga had been opposed to airport expansion, purely and simply (and indeed so had been Hazel McCallion as mayor of Streetsville). It made sense: until the mid-1970s most residents of Mississauga actually lived under existing or proposed flight paths.

By the 1980s the situation was more complicated. The mayor was conscious of the need to ensure that industrial/commercial development kept up with residential, so as not to put a heavy burden on residential ratepayers. And not everyone would be under the noise cones.

But simply letting the federal government run the show all by itself at the airport was not an option for McCallion. In 1987 Ottawa released a new airports policy. Generally, it fit the mould of the New Public Management paradigm: governments should steer and not row. Bureaucrats need not run airports. The federal government could devolve the airports to special authorities or private corporations, perhaps collect some royalties, and lay out the conditions for their operations. The policy did not state, however, what was to be done with *each* airport. A specific critical path for the largest airport, Pearson, was not laid out.

Toronto's business elite actually did not like privatization. No private company or consortium, it was feared, would have enough money to fix everything – and a great deal of fixing was required.

But this was not McCallion's position. It is not that she was a privatization ideologue. She has not, for example, called for the privatization of Mississauga's transit services. She was furious when the province demanded the privatization of hydro. Nor did she disagree that the airport needed expensive fixing. In fact, she was calling Terminal 1 'a slum' and was threatening to send in the Peel Health Department.[82] She would later tell a Senate committee that 'here we sit with Canada's most important airport and no action [on expansion].' And she would continue:

> We have 101 Japanese companies in our city. We have 86 German companies, and we consult with each company as they move in as to why they chose Mississauga. I would say that eight times out of 10 it is the airport. Others are because our taxes are the lowest. I am sure you know that we are a debt-free city. I thought that Ottawa might like to know that especially.[83]

But if the airport was to be privatized it would have to pay not only property taxes (which were largely being compensated for anyway by payments in lieu) but also development charges. In fact, in 1987 McCallion had threatened Huang and Danczkay, the outfit contracted by Ottawa to build Terminal 3, that she would cut off municipal services if they did not pay development charges. They relented.[84]

And then there was the noise issue. Yes, by the late 1980s aircraft were
of the 'Chapter 3' variety, quieter than the 'Chapter 2' planes of the
1970s. But it was still risky to have a Metro-dominated airport authority
deciding, in effect, where the noise cones could go. That might sterilize
development in large swaths of Mississauga.

In 1989 the Board of Trade of Metropolitan Toronto formed a group of
businesspeople charged with creating an airport authority that would
then seek control of the operations of Pearson International. The province supported these plans, and Gardner Church, Ontario's deputy
minister for the Greater Toronto Area, became involved as a facilitator.
He chaired an inter-municipal task force that attempted to secure
endorsements from the municipalities. The province later tried to fund
the fledgling group's redevelopment proposal, which was to be an
alternative to the private-sector bids for Terminals 1 and 2. This was
rejected by Ottawa on the grounds of provincial interference.[85]

The federal government itself announced in 1989 that it intended to
proceed with three new runways. McCallion equivocated now. An
expanded airport is good for the local economy, but expansion with
side effects concentrated in Mississauga should be avoided, if possible.

And anti-expansion groups were starting to pop up again.

For a while they could be assuaged by the mayor's aggressiveness
towards the Toronto backers of the airport authority. With the federal
government's promised call for private-sector proposals having still
failed to emerge, there was growing concern in Mississauga that the airport might yet be taken over by such a Metro-dominated body.

By 1991 this seemed to be a real possibility.

McCallion decided now to stir things up by crashing a private meeting between the would-be airport authority and senior federal and provincial officials – including ministers. Once seated, she wasted no time
before blasting the process. At meetings and in front of microphones,
she took to calling the Metro body 'the illegal airport authority.' It did
not take long for another idea to occur to the Mississauga mayor. If
there was to be an 'illegal' body, why should there be but one? McCallion decided to launch a rival airport authority.[86]

That ensured a temporary stalemate on one front, but some of the residents were now starting to become a problem. The November 1991
municipal elections were approaching. This was not a concern for
McCallion herself; she would face only a few fringe candidates. She
bought a few advertisements (this would be the last election on which
she would spend any money), but otherwise she did not campaign.

Councillor Maja Prentice seemed to be in trouble, however. Most of the anti-runway residents were concentrated in her Ward 3. Prentice had proven herself to be an unflinching McCallion loyalist. Her challenger, Peter Ferreira, was not directly criticizing the mayor, but he was calling on her to be much tougher on the runways. His rhetoric was quite probably becoming a concern. Prentice had to be saved. With one week to go before the election, McCallion agreed that Prentice should move a resolution opposing the new north–south runway (but not the two proposed east–west runways).[87]

Two months after the election, with Prentice safely back in her seat, having actually done better than expected against Ferreira, council backtracked. It would now support the north–south runway provided eighteen conditions were met.[88]

When the city presented its position to the 1992 federal Environmental Assessment Review Panel, McCallion, although in attendance and although very deeply involved in the issue, was quite content to have the city's airport liaison officer make the presentation about the eighteen conditions – and to make it technical. McCallion, however, was available for questions, emphasizing that the staff member's detailed and objective presentation demonstrated that the city had done its homework on airport issues. Even the panel chairman congratulated the city for this.[89] However, when the panel took the city's conditions to heart and recommended that the federal government delay the construction, and that it redesign its entire plan,[90] the jubilant residents soon found that the city was at best lukewarm in pushing these points with Ottawa.[91] (The north–south runway was finally completed in 1999, in violation of the environmental panel's recommendation.)

Councillor Prentice was positioning herself now as being much more concerned about the runway than were her council colleagues.[92] She even appeared at the environmental hearings on her own behalf to take a position that differed from the city's.[93] When faced with such insubordination on issues other than the airport, the mayor has often reacted harshly. Prentice recalls, still with a shudder, that the mayor would not speak with her for three months following a vote in which the mayor supported and Prentice opposed the immediate closure of the region's Britannia landfill site in Mississauga. On the airport issue, however, Prentice is more at ease. She remembers the mayor assuring her that the councillor was doing what had to be done.[94]

It all became rather comedic. But at least the Mississauga mayor had ensured that the competing airport authorities, neither of which had

any formal authority, were bogged down through much of 1992 negotiating a *modus vivendi*. A task force of the chairs of the regional municipalities within the Greater Toronto Area had to be set up to break the
impasse. An arrangement giving Peel the right to appoint (not just nominate) two of fifteen members, and limiting Metropolitan Toronto to two
members, was finally concluded late that year,[95] soon after which Mississauga resident Sid Valo became the chair.[96] The new set-up was
endorsed by the Region of Peel council and Mississauga council.

There was a wrinkle, however. Mississauga's endorsement was con-
ditional – and Peel council later was persuaded by Mississauga to support the city's qualified position. The city called on the new airport
authority to oversee both Pearson and the Toronto Island airport, even
though Toronto Island was being operated under a tripartite arrangement involving the City of Toronto, the Toronto Harbour Commissioners, and the federal government. This qualifier gave Ottawa the opening
it needed. The condition was cited by transport minister Jean Corbeil as
the reason for not negotiating with the local airport authority, but continuing instead with the privatization process.[97]

McCallion resisted Transport Canada's attempt in early 1993 to establish its own community advisory committee with representatives of
some of the vocal residents' groups.[98] When residents' angst over the
runways grew louder, and when some groups demanded not only city
support but also city funding to carry on their advocacy, McCallion
instead created her own residents' advisory committee (as well as a
business advisory committee) and tried to make it the focus for deliberations between the city and the residents on the positions that the city
should take to the federal government. It appears that she and her council colleagues controlled carefully the information that the committee
received. One preliminary city staff report about the results of the negotiations with Corbeil, which revealed that the city was willing to make
a deal accepting the runways, made it into the hands of the residents'
committee.[99] The city's airport liaison officer, from whose office the
report was mailed, left the employ of the city almost immediately afterwards, although the connection to this incident could not be verified.

But maybe McCallion could finally compel the feds to act in Mississauga's favour and please the anxious residents at the same time. To
force the issue, in June 1993 city council passed a resolution saying it
was now once again opposed to the new north–south runway, which
had been proposed by Ottawa along with two new east–west runways.
The stated motivation for Mississauga's resolution was the federal gov-

ernment's failure to meet the eighteen conditions laid down by the city in the January 1992 resolution.

This set the stage for negotiations between Mississauga and the federal government on an airport operating agreement. The federal government agreed to the establishment of a noise authority to monitor aircraft traffic and agreed that the runway would not be used at night, and not when the wind conditions were favourable for the use of the other runways. But the majority of the city's runway conditions were in fact infrastructure and financial matters, not noise issues. The minister agreed, for example, to construct new access roads, making it easier to get inside the airport from Mississauga.[100]

It all came together, almost literally, at five minutes to midnight. The day before the privatization deal was signed, the mayor and the transport minister were still in touch to ensure that the minister would honour his guarantee that Mississauga would not lose any federal revenue as a result of the privatization. The private consortium would pay property taxes, a significant portion of which would go to the school boards and the region. But, in the absence of property taxes, Mississauga had been receiving the full share of the federal payments in lieu of taxation. The switch to property taxes would mean an annual loss to Mississauga of approximately $3.2 million. The federal government acceded to Mississauga's demand to make up the difference.[101]

Any celebrating was short lived. An inconvenient obstacle got in the way – the federal election. In fact, the whole deal was announced in the middle of the campaign, prompting the opposition Liberals to cry foul. The influence that Mississauga had, or was about to have, came to an end in November 1993 with the new Liberal government. The Liberals had gravely promised to take a very different course on the Pearson file than had their predecessors. Even an attempt by Mississauga to appear conciliatory by dropping the Toronto Island condition did not so much as gain the mayor an audience with the minister.[102]

McCallion's airport descent was now irreversible. But although she would lose influence on this file, she had at least appeared active without managing to alienate to a significant degree any of her internal constituencies. Her political capital, in other words, was intact.

But LAC's Still On

The political capital acquired over the years could be translated into an actual capital project. Although the economic slowdown of the early

1990s seemed to put to rest ambitions for a Sport Fishing Hall of Fame, and seemed to put into suspended animation plans for other initiatives, like a large Mississauga Garden Park, it was during this period that the self-confessed unartistic McCallion decided to put her energy into getting a large Living Arts Centre built. This may have been a decision that was somewhat out of character.

Accounts differ on who came up with the idea. McCallion told me that it was her brainchild and that she had envisioned it from her first day as mayor.[103] Willson McTavish, a local lawyer and volunteer board member for various arts groups, says that the idea was his.[104] Regardless, in 1981 several citizens were invited by the mayor to form the Mississauga Arts Council. It would disburse small grants to the arts groups – to relieve the city of the grovelling for petty cash – and would raise some money from the private sector so that the city would not come to be seen as a cash cow. It was also mandated to study how to make the city centre the cultural nucleus for Mississauga.

Little was done for a few years on this last task. But in 1986 McTavish decided not to stand for re-election as chair of the arts council and agreed instead to head a committee that would hire a consultant to do a feasibility study for the centre. This sat well with the mayor, but there was little pressure from anywhere else. Even the councillors were not particularly enthusiastic. City staff sent a capital-budget survey to councillors in 1988. Seven responded. None saw the arts centre as a first or second priority for long-range capital planning. Two did not even list it.[105]

McCallion continued to insist that the centre would be built,[106] and in February 1988 city council agreed to provide $52,500 for the feasibility study with the same amount to be provided by the provincial Ministry of Culture.[107] Although the application for the city money came from McTavish's committee, a City staff member did most of the work on drafting the application. McCallion also now decided that the proceeds from her Mayor's Gala would go towards the arts centre.

The mayor was sending out mixed messages, however. And these arguably would contribute to making the centre a white elephant. This was supposed to be a 'world-class landmark,' even though the steering committee was to observe that

Much can be learned from arts and artist run centres across Canada. These centres, because they are developed from a grassroots level, have a good feeling of involvement and independence, providing a sympathetic environment for cultural activity. Often these centres, because of a notorious lack of funding are found in older buildings such as warehouses. These types of buildings, we have observed, despite their physical drawbacks often create a suitable, informal setting for cultural endeavours. They hum with activity day and night.[108]

At the same time, this was the mayor who prided herself constantly on 'running the city like a business.' The centre should thus be self-sufficient. And so to the committee McCallion often presented herself as sceptical and wanting to be convinced.

The committee dutifully took nothing from the consultant at face value. Its members 'must be adversaries [of the consultant] due to the strength and convictions of the mayor,' declared the secretary-treasurer in July 1990.[109]

But two months later McCallion suddenly decided to put the Living Arts Centre on the front burner. She supplied fresh statements to the media, made calls to senior federal and provincial politicians, and sent a letter to McTavish expressing impatience with the slow progress in bringing the feasibility study to a conclusion. It was reported at the time that McCallion had been taken aback by the apparent support the provincial and federal governments were about to offer to Toronto's proposed ballet opera house, and she was determined that Mississauga get its fair share of arts funding.[110] McTavish recalls that the mayor was visited by a scholar and arts promoter from the southern United States who persuaded her that a centre for the arts could be integral to creating a dynamic city.[111]

McTavish wrote back to McCallion urging patience – using, in fact, the mayor's own arguments about the need for cautious fiscal prudence. He enclosed in confidence one of his letters to the consultant, to try to demonstrate to the mayor that there were shortcomings in the report.[112] However, that spring McCallion travelled to London – without first informing McTavish or the Living Arts board, and to the surprise of the Mississauga Arts Council[113] – to press Hammerson, the parent company of Square One Shopping Centre (also in the city centre), to make a major contribution. A subsequent letter to McTavish from parks and recreation commissioner Ian Scott continued to make it clear that the city itself would not be the principal contributor, although there was no outright demand for self-sufficiency. Private funding would be critical. McTavish reiterated this to his successor on 10 September 1991, following his final presentation to city council. 'Mayor

McCallion, after the Presentation, advised me clearly that she supports the Living Arts Centre on the condition that every effort is made to make it as self-sufficient as possible.'[114]

Hammerson promised to make a major contribution, of an unspecified amount, and McCallion urged McTavish to step aside as chairman to make room for Hammerson Canada CEO Bruce Heyland, who had been chairing the Ballet Opera House Corporation in Toronto. As he passed the torch, we see McTavish expressing to Heyland the same caution that the mayor had once expressed:

> Once we have arrived at an optimum programme at a zero base, we should test, in my opinion, the marketplace by establishing the extent to which the public will use the Centre. We should test out the veracity of the figures that we now have. For example, if there are ten solo instrument rooms properly soundproofed so that a teacher and 'student' could interact, will there be a sufficient number of 'students' ready to pay through their parents or on their own the user fee so that each room is used 24 hours a day, 365 days a year? This represents 87,600 one-hour lessons over a year, or, in financial terms, at a rate of $10 per hour user fee, $876,000. We should be very careful to make sure that this will happen.[115]

These careful tests never were conducted – because the mayor wanted to proceed quickly. Shortly after the federal Liberals came to power in 1993, McCallion was determined that Mississauga would focus on funding for the Living Arts Centre under the new Canada-Ontario Infrastructure Program. Putting forth this position with neither opposition nor visible reluctance from councillors, who were forfeiting potential projects in their ward, must be deemed an achievement. The mayor made herself the chief lobbyist for funding and secured thirteen million dollars each from the federal and provincial governments, and five million from the regional government. Mississauga itself contributed twenty million from its development-charges reserve.[116]

Corporate, rather than mayoral, influence may have been responsible for the elimination of a much-touted money-raising component of the LAC: arts-related retail outlets, which would generate traffic and pay rent to the centre at commercial rates.[117] I could find no information on why this component was dropped. We do know, however, that it disappeared during the chairmanship of Hammerson's Bruce Heyland. It was during this period that Hammerson announced plans to expand the Square One Shopping Centre and to bring a walk-in entrance, leading to movie theatres, to a point immediately across the street from the centre.

With regard to the design of the centre, we see no mayoral direction with respect to the actual shape, massing, and artistry, but we do see the city remaining firmly attached to the apolitical professional international competition, a firmness the mayor had always demanded, even after the earlier city hall design that she had found somewhat questionable, and even after concerns were raised about the arts centre's appearance. These concerns surfaced not only after the fact – such as the stinging critique by the *Toronto Star*'s Christopher Hume, who charged that the campus-like design was a sign of slavish deference to the automobile culture.[118] Complaints, strong complaints, were being raised while the process was in train. Architect Stephen Irwin, who provided, for the centre's board, design-related comments for phase 2 of the Wolman study, was not at all impressed with the initial vision. 'We have yet another plaza,' he protested.[119]

Irwin's and Hume's misgivings were reinforced by the bleak, pedestrian-repelling design of the park, whose earth mounds and humps made the front door appear partially inaccessible, except through the drive-in lane. The city awarded the park design to the second-place finisher in a professional competition, after Community Services staff became concerned that the winner would not come in within budget.[120]

The hoped-for major private donations were not realized. Hammerson contributed approximately three million dollars,[121] and there were smaller donations from others, such as Rogers Cablesystems (one million dollars) and the Canadian Imperial Bank of Commerce (two hundred fifty thousand dollars).[122] The naming rights were not sold, as a generous enough sponsor (five million plus) could not be found.

The arts groups had remained marginalized throughout. Indeed, in 1991 the Mississauga Arts Council's board of directors, under which the Living Arts Centre board was nominally functioning, insisted on updates – it pleaded for them, in fact. It could not understand why the arts groups were not being kept informed.[123] It would get little more than updates.

The monument seemed impressive, but its operations, as we shall see later, were being set up to be more problematic.

The early to middle 1990s were a difficult time to be a politician. The cranky public was tired of taxes, tired of broken promises, tired of decisions being made behind closed doors, tired of 'special interests' draining resources at the expense of a 'hard-working' middle class, tired of politicians who seemed incapable of dealing with huge deficits while the economy seemed to be sputtering. In 1995 all the Mississauga provincial ridings would vote Conservative (three of the four had hitherto been Liberal), electing candidates who endorsed Mike Harris's decidedly right-wing 'Common Sense Revolution.'

The recession slowed, but certainly did not stop, the growth in Mississauga. The city had an advantage over much of the rest of the province, especially the communities that were hit hard by job losses in the traditional manufacturing sector. And yet, despite the more favourable economic conditions in her city, Hazel McCallion had to be careful – and she knew it. She still had to prove herself to be a mayor for all seasons.

However, a mayor for the seasons may not be a mayor for the ages. Legacies are not necessarily made by shrewdly minding the store, by cutting ribbons at subdivisions or even for a new city hall. Here was a leader, helped by circumstances, who had mastered the art of keeping interests subdued, in check, scattered, or immature. Yet for what purpose? Was there an inspired objective?

Mississauga would have developed with or without McCallion, perhaps with more friction, perhaps with differences on some of the particulars – but it would have developed nonetheless. Would it now take a better approach, a different approach, because of her stewardship?

8 The Mayor–Legacy-Maker

She lost Sam in 1997. The 'Husband of the Mayor' – as he had come often to call himself, almost like an official title – had been a calm and stable presence. He had long been active in the community himself. From 1974 until 1982, he was president of the Streetsville Founders' Bread and Honey Festival, a role he clearly enjoyed. He was a lay reader at Trinity Anglican Church. He was not a shy man; he enjoyed publicity. But it often appeared otherwise. He was always careful not to appear to be overshadowing his famous spouse.

The deterioration of his health was slow and painful to watch. It was Alzheimer's. In 1992 he went to pick up a *Booster* advertisement at a car dealership and inexplicably drove into the show room. No one was hurt, but it was clear that something was wrong.

As his health slowly declined, as he lost the movement of an arm, as his feet seemed to slide along the ground, as he forgot people's names, he still showed up every day to work at the *Booster* – still at the same little, rather run-down 'shop' at the corner of Falconer Drive and Alpha Mills Road. His part-time assistants kept the paper going, while still making him feel in charge. Finally, in the spring of 1996, son Paul took over. He redesigned and modernized the publication with the help of former *Mississauga News* editor Mike Toth, whom the mayor had personally recruited for the purpose and who agreed to do it for very little money.

Still Sam came to work. A personal assistant was hired for him, but she often ended up helping with the advertising, so Sam would sit in the front foyer greeting visitors. His wife would pop in when she could, but she was busy – very busy – on her normal fifteen-hour-per-day, seven-day-a-week schedule. She always tried to be home for the 11 o'clock news and would often be up the next day by 5:30, would do some housework, and return phone calls, often startling people out of their beds – and as a result gaining an upper hand in conversations.[1]

But as it became clear in May 1997 that Sam's latest hospitalization would be his last, Hazel McCallion made it to her husband's side and kept vigil. When he passed away, he was, as the obituaries would say, 'surrounded by his loving family.'

For two days before the funeral, his casket lay in Trinity's old sanctuary. Hazel McCallion, daughter Linda, sons Peter and Paul stood stoically, acknowledging those who came to pay respects. And they came: the lieutenant governor and the premier, politicians from near and far, heads of organization, religious leaders. The queues did not let up for hours on end.

The funeral itself saw a police honour guard. Roman Catholic bishop Pearce Lacey was given a seat on the altar as Trinity's rector, the Reverend Canon Harold Percy, officiated at the funeral, the crowds spilling onto the sidewalks. And for the only time that anyone could remember it happening in public, Hazel McCallion cried.

Indeed, one could tell that beneath her gritty, always-be-strong exterior, the death of her husband affected Hazel McCallion. In the years that followed, when talking about him publicly – something she has tried to avoid doing, probably so as not to show emotion – she has seemed on the verge of losing her composure.

And although Hazel McCallion has attended hundreds of funerals – and goes out of her way to attend funerals not only of political figures but anyone known to her because of civic work – it was her own husband's passing that seemed, on some level, to reinforce her own mortality. She was still in perfect health, but for how much longer?

It seemed now that Hazel McCallion may have started to give some thought to her place in history. For what would she be remembered? Yes, the city had grown tremendously. There was the city hall and the Living Arts Centre, the waterfront, the parks, the roads, the libraries, the recent tax cuts. The Hazel persona – the feisty little mayor – would always carry some resonance. But was this the stuff of a visionary and a statesperson? Could she become a statesperson, even if it would mean defying some of her instincts as a scrapper and as a shrewd calculator?

The Development Equation

The pattern of development was still, politically, highly favourable to McCallion. I examined the minutes of every statutory public meeting

Table 8.1
Statutory Public Meetings to Consider Planning Applications, 1994–2004

Concern expressed by any resident	Contiguous with a residential neighbourhood	Number of applications
Yes	Yes	214
No	Yes	54
Yes	No	19
No	No	220
–	–	507 Total

held between 1994 and 2004 on every application for a rezoning, official plan amendment, or plan of subdivision. In a slight majority of cases, no concern was expressed by any resident. And in most of the cases where there was public silence, the development was not contiguous (not within 250 metres) of a built-up area. Almost all of Churchill Meadows (future population sixty thousand, in the extreme west of Mississauga) was approved without a single public objection. Huge truck transfer facilities in the Heartland district (north-central Mississauga) were approved without a single public objection. The vast majority of the contentious issues were relatively easy to handle – resulting in minor modifications or merely explanations. There appear to have been fewer than thirty that threatened to become major public controversies. These were generally in affluent south Mississauga or the Mississauga Road corridor. In only one case was a social service agency involved. With the exception of one intervention by the Mississauga Cycling Advisory Committee and the involvement of the South Peel Naturalists Club in the Creditview Wetland development, there was no intervention by a city-wide organization on any of the 507 planning applications. We do not even see the embryo of a base or movement that could challenge the mayor on the way the city was being planned.

Very well, but perhaps we shall find more agonizing over competing visions when we turn to the more conceptual development of official plans. In its day, the Dobkin council had pulled out all the stops to encourage public participation. The centrepiece of that new official plan was to have been slow growth and phasing. That plan still sat unapproved when Dobkin was defeated by Searle, and it then was tossed around endlessly as the old guard and reformers continued to squabble during Searle's mayoralty. When an official plan finally was approved in 1981, its centrepieces were rapid growth and no phasing, but also a steep price of admission on the developers.

A review of this official plan took place between 1992 and 1997. It essentially confirmed the basic principles of the 1981 document. Although there were no dramatic changes, McCallion and city staff still thought they had reason to be proud. In 1996 they sought and received a Communications Award from the Ontario Professional Planners Institute. They deserved it, they claimed, because of a very progressive public participation process. In the past, they said, seemingly forgetting the outreach during the Dobkin mayoralty, a 'reactionary model' had been employed, whereby city staff prepared reports and recommendations and then submitted them for public feedback. But in this case a 'Varying Techniques Model' had been used. It was stated that there were efforts to receive public feedback before drafts were prepared, and if there were complex or controversial issues an advisory committee was formed for ongoing consultation.

Although an advisory committee was formed – in the Port Credit area, where four local ratepayers groups were determined to 'Say No to the Node' (major development) – it was actually the reactionary model that seemed to prevail this time. This becomes clear when we actually look at how the system played out in practice.

> Phase One: Preparation of twelve (12) background strategies. These papers examined the validity of the existing goals, objectives, and policies of each component of the Plan. This phase was completed in September 1992.
>
> Phase Two: The consolidation of the various background strategies into a Draft City Plan. This phase was completed with the 'launch' of the public participation process on January 18, 1993.
>
> Phase Three: A public participation program and the circulation of the Draft City Plan to the relevant agencies at all levels of government and neighbouring municipalities for review and comment. This phase was carried out over a six-month period, and was completed at the end of July 1993.
>
> Phase Four: Preparation of a series of reports dealing with issues raised during the public participation phase. Following Council consideration of these reports, a revised Plan will be prepared for approval by Council and forwarded to the Provincial Government for final approval. This phase is underway.[2]

So it was only at phase 3 that the public was given the opportunity to be engaged. City-wide groups were virtually silent in the process. Only two groups that could be considered city wide, the South Peel Naturalists Club and Environmentalists Plan Transportation (EPT), made any submissions. Only the latter, which was based in Toronto and had not been involved actively in other Mississauga issues, made more than one intervention. The group received no media attention. Six neighbourhood groups, all of them in Wards 1 and 2 (established areas in southern Mississauga), prepared written submissions, all focused on very localized matters, especially the possibility that Port Credit would be a major 'node.' This notion the groups opposed. Forty-four private citizens wrote in. In addition, there were nineteen submissions from builders or developers, or their agents.

The Planning and Building Department commented on all the submissions. There is no discernible pattern of favouring particular interest groups over others, such as the developers or the environmentalists. But there is a clear tendency to deflect issues that might trigger sustained debates, or conflict, at the municipal level. Take the following argument from the aforementioned and rather obscure group Environmentalists Plan Transportation (EPT):

> There is no commitment in the draft plan to take real action to reduce levels of greenhouse gas emissions and toxic emissions from automobiles in the official plan. The planned expansions to the public transportation system identified in the draft official plan are grossly inadequate, and would result in a 33 percent increase in auto traffic by 2021 AD, and likely only a small drop in vehicles emissions.
>
> This is in stark contrast to the need to reduce emissions of CO_2 by 80% in North America by 2010 AD if a global reduction in emissions of 20% is to be achieved.

Indeed, the issue of air pollution was barely mentioned in the draft plan. The staff responded to this by simply asserting that 'air pollution is beyond the jurisdiction of the City, however, the Plan encourages the provincial government to develop standards for analysis of impacts from development applications.'[3]

So development remained politically low key. On the fiscal side, however, things almost unravelled for McCallion.

She remains proud to this day that her city played a critical role in the drafting of the 1991 provincial Development Charges Act and that the legislation was based on the system already in place in Mississauga. She claims to be proudest, however, of the fact that the development charges and the discarding of phasing gave city hall control over the developers. 'We now had a membership fee, a price of admission,' she says. It was 'a gamble' that paid off.[4]

The creation of the Development Charges Act had been preceded by provincial negotiations with the developers. But the Urban Development Institute claimed to be a victim of the 'proverbial double cross,' when fifty-four amendments were suddenly introduced that were opposed by the development industry, including allowing municipalities wide scope to charge for 'soft' services.[5] McCallion, on the other hand, was extremely pleased with what she considered permissive legislation.

However, a new government would come to office with less permissive ideas.

McCallion at first seemed to welcome the 'Common Sense Revolution,' the crisp and unequivocal platform of the Ontario Progressive Conservative Party, which won a majority government in June 1995 on promises to reduce taxes, to force welfare recipients to work for their cheques, and to repeal the 'quota law,' among other standard neoconservative (neoliberal, to use the correct term) fare. McCallion herself had championed lower taxes and had vigorously opposed the NDP government's Employment Equity Act, mandating targets in some sectors for the hiring of women, visible minorities, Aboriginal Canadians, and persons with disabilities.[6]

But it soon became clear that the Conservatives were not too keen on the sensitivities of municipal governments. In late 1995, amid a flurry of provincially initiated restructuring, the new municipal affairs minister, Al Leach, was musing about prohibiting municipalities from collecting development charges for 'soft' services – libraries, community centres, civic centres, cultural centres, and other 'non-essential' facilities that, according to Leach, benefited the whole community and not only the growth areas. He argued that this would bring down the cost of housing and spur growth and development. The Conservatives had made such promises when responding to pre-election surveys circulated by the Greater Toronto Home Builders' Association and the Urban Development Institute. Thus, in November 1995 Leach began a formal review of the Development Charges Act.

An outraged McCallion reacted immediately to this process. It was a giveaway to the developers, she charged. She promised that Mississauga would halt all development if such amendments were proposed in the legislature. She even threatened (although did not go so far) to sue the Urban Development Institute after it issued a brochure showing Mississauga's city hall and stating that 'monumental town halls, luxurious recreation centres and expensive cultural facilities represent levels of service that municipalities have been able to give their residents seemingly "free of charge" because they have been financed largely by the development community and new homebuyers.[7] During the nearly twelve intervening months between the minister's public statements about soft services and the introduction of the Development Charges Act, 1996, there were attempts by the province and developers to engage McCallion and a few other municipal leaders in negotiations. McCallion refused.

The new legislation proposed that the municipalities would be permitted to charge for only 90 per cent of the cost of hard services (roads and sewers, for example) and 70 per cent of the soft services. The developers claimed that this was a concession. On McCallion's urging, Mississauga immediately passed a 'freeze on all building in the city.'[8]

In early 1997, in her capacity as chair of the Greater Toronto Mayors' Association, an organization she had formed a few years earlier, McCallion dispatched Oakville mayor Ann Mulvale to engage in discussions with representatives of the province and the developers. McCallion herself participated in some of these meetings.

When Bill 98 went to committee that March, the government introduced an amendment allowing municipalities to collect 100 per cent for the hard services but maintaining the 30 per cent 'co-payment' for soft services. In his appearance before the committee, Leach pointed out that only 10 per cent of Ontario's municipalities had development charges (Toronto had none at the time) and that, in Mississauga specifically, they were out of control.

Leach's exchange in committee with Liberal MPP Gerry Phillips focused in part on Mississauga. When Leach estimated that Mississauga might obtain $5,000 less for an average home, Phillips charged that Leach was transferring this burden from the developers to the taxpayers of Mississauga because the services would still be required. 'They're going to spend the money. Mississauga has to spend the money. The development charge drops by $5,000.'

'They haven't so far,' Leach replied. 'They've banked about $250 million so far in reserves, as they've charged for development charges and haven't spent the money.'[9]

When McCallion's turn came, she ripped into the provincial government and the developers, unfazed by the fact that large Mississauga developers, like Philip King of Orlando Corporation, had made strong statements on the side of the province. The developers had charged that communities like Mississauga were building 'gold-plated' facilities, far more opulent than required, and were forcing the developers, not the taxpayers, to pay for them. McCallion professed not to be impressed by the concessions that had been made by the province and the developers in the numerous meetings, stating that the unresolved issues were what concerned her most. The mayor also made clear how important the extraction of development charges had been to maintaining Mississauga residents' overall contentment.

> Can you imagine what the reaction there would be if we told a new community that was 80% built out that we could not build a community centre for their children because we could not afford it? New families move to these communities because of how we plan the community and integrate the amenities. The developers use these amenities to sell their homes – they do it in Mississauga, I can assure you – and now they want to take them away. The local councils are elected to make these decisions, not UDI.[10]

Before the end of the committee hearings, the provincial government relented further, and dropped the soft services co-payment minimum to 10 per cent. This was not a total victory for Mississauga, but city council now lifted its development freeze.

The mayor's tough-minded approach on development charges did not abate. In 1998, following a change in provincial policy, the city became the first jurisdiction in the province to make development contingent on there being enough land for schools and enough resources to build them. McCallion was not intimidated by one of the city's chief opponents on this, Marco Muzzo, head of Erin Mills Development Corporation and a man whose business scruples were not without blemish. In the late 1960s and early 1970s, he had owned Marel Contractors, a major concern in the drywall industry. His activities attracted considerable attention from the 1973 provincial Royal Commission on Certain Sectors of the Building Industry. Muzzo's attitude was summarized in the following exchange during the inquiry's hearings, quoted in the commissioner's final report:

> Mr. Humphrey [counsel]: So you were not opposed to the general practice of bribery; you were only concerned about whether it worked or not.
> Mr. Muzzo: That's right.[11]

The developers fought the school issue to the Ontario Municipal Board and then in the Divisional Court before the city prevailed.[12]

Realizing, as Mary Fix had realized, that the municipality needed industrial assessment to offset residential, McCallion would take a hard line on developers' proposed conversions from industrial to residential. In 1995 Jannock Inc. decommissioned its ninety-hectare Canada Brick former quarry site, northeast of downtown Streetsville. McCallion insisted that the land not be residential but remain industrial so as to protect 'employment lands,' which are much more lucrative to the tax base than residential areas. She maintained this position even though the company was adamant that 'in the current land market, residential lands are more valuable to landowners than employment lands.'[13]

The ward councillor, David Culham, and his successor, George Carlson, were equivocal. They insisted the city might need to compromise.[14] McCallion denounced this notion, despite the developer's assertion that government assistance would be required to detoxify the site.[15] The developer did eventually propose that fifteen hectares be retained for office/industrial uses, but McCallion was not satisfied. The case proceeded to the Ontario Municipal Board, where the city prevailed decisively.[16] The board agreed with the city that the question of whether continued industrial use would be economically viable to Jannock 'does not raise any authentic or genuine planning issue which requires adjudication by the Board.'[17]

The LAC Is Lacking

The fiscal underpinning of the McCallion legacy was being rescued, at least for the time being, but the Great Builder had reason to be deeply concerned about one of her legacy projects. The soon-to-be-opened, gleaming Living Arts Centre was not taking in much sponsorship. Big shows were not being booked.

McCallion thought she could fix it with a technocratic approach – by retaining hired experts. As the day of the grand opening neared, the city paid for executives and marketing men from outside Mississauga. These were confident characters, polished, dapper, even slick. But their magic did not work. All were promptly replaced. In June 1997 CEO Ian McCallum was dismissed. His successor, Jocelyn Robert, an outsider who had been appointed earlier that year to head the capital campaign, lasted only three months. Finally, with just three weeks remaining before the grand opening, and with no CEO in place, McCallion turned to city manager David O'Brien. It was left to him to step in as interim CEO.[18]

The management was in disarray, and there was no sign that this would be a buzzing 'twenty-four-hour-a-day' facility any time soon. However, at the official opening on 12 October 1997, McCallion still tried to put the best foot forward. Mississauga had its 'cultural heart,' she boasted. It would be a 'total experience.'[19] The local media sang the same tune. 'The world of arts and entertainment will never be the same again,' exclaimed the *Mississauga News*.[20] Letters to the editor urged that it be called the 'Hazel McCallion Centre,' a suggestion the mayor modestly declined.[21] Her humility was well placed. For years to come the 'twenty-four-hour-a-day centre' would sit idle for at least half the waking hours.

When the grand-opening guests had gone home, the board of the Living Arts Centre began to do some soul-searching. It now started to pay attention to what voices in the wilderness had been saying. Consultant Dory Vanderhoof, for example, had warned that the centre's only hope was to offer very low prices and be very community oriented. He had warned that Mississauga's market for high-end professional arts was limited to a small cohort – 11,000 'executive households and 6,000 urban elite households.'[22] Soccer moms apparently are not regular opera goers.

So the centre's mission statement was amended in the year following the grand opening. Words like 'world class' were taken out. Instead it would be a 'community place' for 'entertaining and enriching experiences in the living arts.'[23]

A permanent CEO was now also named. Once it became clear that Dan Donaldson would last longer than the ill-fated Jocelyn Robert, he tried to inoculate himself for the long term by insisting that the centre had been at a disadvantage from the start. Costs had been cut by reducing the size of the main theatre from two thousand seats to thirteen hundred. Do not be surprised, he said, if the big shows – the ones that bring in big money – fail to appear.

The only really viable alternative, it seemed, was to make some substantial investments in community programming, even if some were now wryly calling this 'Canada's most expensive community centre.' The city was already losing to the tune of one to two million dollars per year, not including staff secondments, and that seemed enough. A community access program was created in 2001 to give local groups low-cost trial packages for using the centre, but generally ticket prices and course enrolment fees have remained very high. For example, a two-hour writing or sketching class will set you back more than fifty dollars.[24]

The mayor began making very significant contributions from the proceeds of her charitable golf tournament and gala fund, whose disbursements she controlled entirely,[25] to one of the centre's major tenants (and therefore financial contributors) – the financially troubled Opera Mississauga. In 2002 and 2003 alone, $415,000 was pledged by the mayor.[26] These contributions continued even though the organization renamed itself Royal Opera Canada and shifted some of its performances to the Toronto Centre for the Performing Arts in North York. In late 2003 the city provided the opera with a $266,000 bail-out package and forgave its debts. The 2004 city grant to the Mississauga Arts Council stipulated that $100,000 of the money must be given to the opera. The arts groups were very perplexed by these bursts of generosity, although the contributions may indeed have been related to the fact that the opera hosted more shows (nineteen) annually at the Living Arts Centre than any other group and was therefore critical to maintaining a modicum of viability at the centre.[27] At the time of writing, however, the opera had entirely suspended its operations.

McCallion was lucky in one respect. As messy as the situation was, almost none of the criticism about the Living Arts Centre percolated into the media or the public, and it certainly did not spark any serious public debates at city council. The usually outspoken Mississauga MP Carolyn Parrish did, however, tell the *Toronto Star*'s Haroon Siddiqui in 2001 that the Living Arts Centre is 'the white elephant used by less than one percent of the [local] population.'[28] This is in contrast to her praise of the mayor at the grand opening for being an 'immovable object ... Chrétien is glad he doesn't have Hazel bothering him anymore [for money for the centre].'[29] The opera contributions generated some local media publicity, prompting the mayor to promise a full report detailing her golf-tournament investments to the arts, and the strategies and rationales underlying those contributions. But the publicity abated and the report never did materialize. The arts leaders, for their part, believe it is pointless, and potentially financially damaging to the Mississauga Arts Council, to try to spark a public debate while McCallion is in office.

Dan Donaldson extended the life expectancy of CEOs, but he too finally succumbed, resigning all of a sudden for undisclosed reasons in early 2003. McCallion now turned to Gerry Townsend (the same Gerry Townsend who had run for mayor in 1976). His résumé was impressive on the accounting side, and he had served on the board of governors of the University of Toronto and was seconded by the Canadian government to lead an effort in the colony of Montserrat to reform its finances. (Much of Montserrat was later buried by lava, and its capital city remains abandoned. Townsend must have been hoping that a better fate awaited the Living Arts Centre.) He had served on the LAC board but had very little arts experience. He has struggled, and by many accounts he has staunched much of the bleeding. But it is a struggle nonetheless; a struggle was likely inevitable.

So the LAC is floating – there are recent reports of a much improved financial situation – but still continuing to take on water. It may not have gone far enough on the accessibility continuum. 'The ordinary person can't afford it,' complains the now-relaxed Willson McTavish over a glass of lemonade. 'They have to learn to price it so that they can fill it. They started with a black-tie approach. They used the high-end approach.'[30]

The Living Arts Centre experience made the mayor very leery of other public developments in the city centre. She was against the construction in the centre of the city's largest arena complex, a concept pushed by staff and councillors as a potential magnet for the area. But the price for the land, specifically the plot north of the civic centre, was deemed by the mayor to be too high relative to the alternative, outlying site at Matheson Boulevard and Highway 403. McCallion's dogged reputation for frugality won this argument, and the Mississauga Icedogs, the city's provincial Junior A hockey team, led at the time by none other than Don Cherry, took up residence in its own far-off campus to which commuting is very difficult.[31] Although the discussions were in camera (as this was a property matter), I have been told by a councillor that Bruce Heyland, the CEO of Hammerson Canada, the largest property owner in the city centre at the time, was determined to have the sports facility in the city centre. His company owned the land and apparently lowered the price significantly. But this did not persuade the mayor because the remote site was city owned and therefore did not require an expenditure of any public funds for land acquisition.

The mayor was emphatic that virtually all new private-sector buildings in the city centre must be high-rise landmarks. Although McCallion was probably not directly familiar with the ideas of Le Corbusier – and his advocacy of singular, high 'machines for living,' each on its own pod – she has stated that the city centre will not be 'an urban area but a City Core.'[32] Townhouses and row dwellings must be rejected, and have been. It is better to have high buildings on the small footprints than integrated (and urbane) low- and medium-rise street-fronting edifices that attain the same densities through larger ground coverage.

Because of varying market conditions, developers have not always found it most profitable to build upscale high-rises, especially outside older urban centres. In addition to rejecting low-rise, McCallion has insisted that the city centre is not the place for 'affordable housing.' The mayor opposed vigorously the former NDP government's attempts to require 25 per cent affordable housing in the core, and sent city staff back-pedalling after she noticed they had reflected the provincial policy in an early draft of the new secondary plan for the city centre.[33] It must be noted that there were no established neighbouring residents to object to affordable housing, and the developers at the time perceived a depressed market for upscale condominiums. The consistent pressure for upscale appeared not to come from residents or developers or the province, but from the mayor.[34] This municipal-provincial struggle was decided in favour of Mississauga when a new Conservative government abandoned attempts to prescribe to municipalities any affordable housing targets. All residential construction has been upscale, although the city has been helped since the mid-1990s by better market conditions.

Frank Dale, the area councillor since 1988, insists that he has been certain to keep McCallion apprised of everything that is happening in the core. 'You don't want her to be blindsided when she's out and about.'[35]

In one area she was forced to relent, however. During the early 1990s McCallion was opposed to a plan by Hammerson to put up temporary restaurants, a Chapters bookstore, and amusement facilities to the north of the Square One Shopping Centre, south of Highway 403. She insisted on prestige office commercial being put there immediately, rather than in 2015. Dale and Hammerson took the position that the market was not yet ready for office commercial. McCallion manoeuvred relentlessly to get her way, Dale recalls, even calling a public meeting on a Saturday morning without his knowledge. In the end, she did sustain a rare defeat in a council vote.[36] However, after McCallion took this position, and even though there were no public objections, 'the [staff] Planning report was the most negative [against the Hammerson proposal] that I've ever seen.' Dale insists that within a few years the mayor experienced a change of heart and congratulated him for his foresight.[37]

But foresight involves articulating a vision for what should be: for a humane, liveable, green, and vibrant place. Although some new private projects – a 'Marilyn Monroe' hourglass-shaped building, for example – have prompted approving gasps and applause, only recently has the city begun 'place making,' looking at how the city centre can be a district where the pedestrian and the resident want to mill about and where an automobile is not obligatory. City staff had been talking for some time about taking some practical measures, such as knocking down the opaque walls around the city hall and luring the local Lions Club's farmers' market away from a Square One parking lot to the civic square. Such talk was deferred indefinitely by council,[38] but was finally allowed to re-emerge in 2005 when the New York–based Project for Public Spaces was brought in to try to facilitate a redesign process.

Grounded at the Airport

The airport, too, required a major transformation. But here McCallion was being shut out. The Greater Toronto Airports Authority's sixty–year ground lease, which began in December 1996, proved to be nothing but a headache for the mayor. (The rather pretentious GTAA uses the plural 'airports,' although it manages only Pearson. It is trying to revive dreams of another spectacular facility, east of Toronto.)[39] True, three of the board's fifteen members are nominees of the Region of Peel, two of whom are supposed to be suggested by the City of Mississauga. But these directors, business executives almost to the last person, must be appointed formally by the GTAA board itself, which is a different arrangement than the one McCallion thought she had secured. They are required by the GTAA's bylaws to concern themselves solely with the airport's interests. This is not an obscure clause; it is top of mind for GTAA officials. In 1998 the GTAA board flexed its muscles and rejected Peel nominee Lou Parsons* on the grounds that he would be more loyal to Mississauga than to the airport.[40] (This rejection was later overturned by the courts.) The board had earlier declined another nominee of the city and picked instead someone suggested by the Mississauga Board of Trade.

And then there was Louis Turpen. In this brash, ruthless man McCal-

---

* This is the same Lou Parsons who, as chair of the Region of Peel and later as president of the development firm Traders Associates, was considered by McCallion to be an adversary. But after he retired from municipal and land-development work, the mayor seemed to warm to him, sensing perhaps that his skills could be an asset now that his loyalties would not be conflicted. McCallion supported Parsons in his various new community/public-service roles, including chair of GO Transit, chair of the arms-length foundation for the Credit Valley Conservation Authority and of course as nominee to the airport authority.

lion may have, for a short time at least, met her match. Outspoken, yet apt to surface in public only at moments of his choosing, usually to scorch enemies, he landed in Mississauga in 1996 to take over as the first CEO of the airport authority. He had made more than a few enemies in his former job as head of the San Francisco Airport, where he had never shied away from confrontations with mayor and later United States senator Dianne Feinstein. Bringing Turpen down had become almost an obsession for another California politician, state senator Quentin Kopp. Typical of most Mississauga observers, the head of the Mississauga Board of Trade saw Turpen as a 'gunslinger' and compared him to New York's legendary but unaccountable master-builder, Robert Moses.[41] During his eight years running the airport, Turpen was one of the only people in a position of power who dared to publicly scorn the mayor of Mississauga. (Not only did he mock McCallion's oft-repeated declarations that the airport should be called 'Mississauga International,' he decided to reinstate part of its old name. 'Pearson' became 'Toronto-Pearson.')

Concerned perhaps that McCallion might still somehow get her loyalists onto the GTAA board, the sitting directors proceeded to rewrite the authority's bylaws to state that the regions *collectively* would nominate several candidates, and that the GTAA board would 'consider' whether to appoint any of these. These changes were approved by transport minister David Collenette, an action that McCallion attributes to Collenette having been 'a weak minister.'[42]

So McCallion took to the courts. The city insisted that the GTAA must pay development charges to the municipality on the planned $4.4-billion expansion. The airport should not be a 'city within a city,' McCallion insisted. The city finally lost in 2001 at the Supreme Court of Canada, despite an intervention on Mississauga's side by the Federation of Canadian Municipalities.

The court case had some appeal within the city, but another messy dispute with the GTAA had to be handled more delicately. In this case, the GTAA took the city to the Ontario Municipal Board in an unsuccessful attempt to stop it from converting land around Meadowvale Village (lands situated five to eight kilometres west of the airport) from industrial to residential to accommodate some twenty two thousand people, even though the new homes would be in an area of high-noise impact (30–35 NEF). The GTAA feared that these new residents would try to obstruct the airport's operations.

On the surface, the city's decision was a defeat for the mayor. She had spoken against the plan both because of the noise impact on the future residents and because of the loss of land that would otherwise have been used for industrial purposes, and which therefore could have optimized the city's assessment balance. The city, after all, had been trying hard to ensure that at least 40 per cent of its assessment comes from industrial/commercial ratepayers, a figure it had not yet attained.[43] On closer analysis, however, the mayor was rather more subdued on this issue than on many others in which she has taken an interest. She did not mount a strong effort to convince her fellow councillors. Indeed, Councillor Maja Prentice cannot recall for certain whether the mayor actually voted with her to oppose the (residential) Meadowvale Village Secondary Plan (she did).[44] GTAA vice-president Steve Shaw suspects that McCallion really favoured it: 'You and I both know that very little happens in Mississauga without Hazel's approval!'[45]

It seems that the mayor may have made a very rational *political* calculation in this instance. There was actually a citizens' movement in favour of the secondary plan. It comprised much of the city's Greek community, which had long wanted the construction of a major church complex, plus a surrounding neighbourhood with services for residents of Greek descent. Prentice remembers that leaders of the local Greek community were threatening to run candidates against councillors who opposed the plan. Moreover, much of the land was already owned by firms specializing in home-building (not in industrial development), such as Clergy Properties, Monarch Construction, and Valemont Homes. Therefore, unlike all the other greenfield planning issues in Mississauga, this one saw a convergence of interests between developers and an ethnic community. The usual room for mayoral discretion and pre-emption may not have been present. The mayor appears to have decided to maintain a low profile and conserve her leadership resources for those planning issues (the majority of cases) that did not present such constraints. Yet by *formally* opposing the application she could preserve her credibility for future debates on planning issues.

None of this did anything to improve relations with the airport. Even the coordination of routine functions was being affected by the political wrangling between Mississauga and the GTAA. According to the former city manager, the GTAA refused to submit to the municipal fire department any structural blueprints or information on the location of hazardous materials, even after pledges by the city to designate key officials who would undergo the strictest security clearances. The GTAA likewise refused to submit its projects to the city for building permits, a practice that the federal government followed when it had direct charge over the airport.[46]

But even during the darkest weeks of the Turpen era, McCallion maintained some residual confidence. His days are numbered, she speculated to me confidently in April 2003, claiming to know so on good authority. The projects were too ambitious, too expensive. He was fighting on too many fronts.[47]

On 26 August 2004 the GTAA suddenly announced that Turpen would be leaving on 30 September. There was hope now that city–airport relations would turn for the better. At very least, the public confrontations would subside almost entirely.

Mayor Green

With the city centre not developing as well as had been hoped, and with nothing at the airport redounding yet to the city's credit, maybe Hazel McCallion – the mayor that some media outlets would soon be calling the 'Queen of Sprawl' – could fashion a legacy as a green mayor.

After 1998 she started again to champion the Mississauga Garden Park concept, an idea that seemed to be moving forward in the late 1980s. But the environmental assessment process was not completed until 1992, at which point McCallion was eschewing most major capital projects.

This sixty–hectare garden was no longer to be sold as part of some vision for a city monumental, but as part of a 'city green.' Sensing that environmental concerns were again starting to lurk below the surface of public discourse, the mayor has promoted the garden park as an example of the city's commitment to the environment. This is somewhat ironic considering that in 1992 the Riverwood Conservation Association was opposing the garden park on the grounds that it would disrupt or destroy wildlife habitat, including the area's deer population. At the time, McCallion did not counter the protests by arguing that the garden would be an environmental gem, but that it was a facility required by a modern city.

It was now the need for green space that received top billing. This ethos would be reflected unmistakably in the *Master Plan and Implementation Strategy*'s call for adaptive, ecological gardens. The theme would be 'Time and Change.'[48] My review of archival documents and interviews with some of the principals have revealed no intensified campaign or mobilization for the public garden during this period. In fact, the garden council had started to diversify its activities after having been focused for many years solely on a central public-garden facility, which now seemed a distant dream.

At a March 1998 retreat meeting, comprising city officials and representatives of the garden council, the city broke the news that the garden-park project would be revived, but very cautiously. The minutes of that meeting reported commissioner of community services Paul Mitcham as telling the group that he

> would not go to Council [with a business plan] unless confident that money is in place and the project does not create a tax increase [and] recommends that we go to Council with a sound business plan which demonstrates teamwork to share fund raising responsibilities. The Mayor at a recent Council meeting indicated that we need to move ahead cautiously.[49]

Knowing that the Mississauga Board of Trade was looking for larger quarters, the mayor sought to have the board use the city-owned Chappell Estate residence, on the future garden site. The board would enjoy free rent in exchange for raising $3.5 million over the next five years to be applied to the capital costs of the new garden park. The board would also be the major organization on the new Riverwood Fundraising Cabinet.

This was a curious decision for the board. In moving to this relatively isolated house, the organization abandoned a prime city centre location. Fundraising for the garden became the MBOT's most significant project. Nevertheless, the board's managing director told me that the mayor was constantly complaining that the board was not doing enough to raise funds.[50]

But at least the Board of Trade would be kept meaningfully busy, citizens' desire for amenities – potentially beautiful amenities, in this case – would be satisfied, and the project would not break the bank.

The total, eventual cost in 2003 dollars was estimated at thirty-nine million dollars, most of which the city hopes will come from donors and sponsors.[51] Although this is by no means Mississauga's most expensive capital project (the Burnhamthorpe Road bridge over the Credit River, the Mississauga Civic Centre, and the Living Arts Centre were all more expensive), garden boosters believe that it will one day be Mississauga's pre-eminent and most popular public facility.

The Riverwood site opened in late 2005 as a basic public park. Four phases are to be undertaken successively to introduce the gardens. These will cover only 20.2 hectares of the total area; the rest will remain in its natural state, and even the gardens themselves are supposed to consist primarily of native plants that will blend with the natural surroundings. There is no established time line for the four garden phases

– the implementation has been made contingent on the success of fund-raising efforts. It is predicted that it will take about thirty years for the gardens to reach a state of maturity.

Property for Public Benefit

At the same time, McCallion was even showing willingness to purchase new properties for the public benefit. In 2000 the city bought the Port Credit Harbour land from the federal government for seven hundred thousand dollars,[52] which was market value minus clean-up costs. The city could probably have had it more cheaply had it been willing to sign a 'public covenant,' promising to keep the entire site in public hands for the long term.[53] It has been beautifully redone with paths and benches; Memorial Park across the street was then refurbished in part through federal-provincial infrastructure funding. But the bells and whistles – the tourist facilities, interpretive centres, and the like – have been specifically avoided.

With the pace of development accelerating and property values increasing in conjunction with an improving economy, it was time to act as well on the Creditview Wetland. For a time the issue had sat in abeyance, in part because the slumping economy had made the developers less anxious to proceed.[54] In 1993, as a result of new provincial planning regulations, the city decided to designate the area as a green belt in the new official plan.[55] The developers opposed this. 'It's fine to sit tight; but there's been a lot of sitting tight,' complained Gerald Swinkin, one of the developers' lawyers.[56] The city manager dismissed a letter from Swinkin claiming his clients would begin their bulldozing in fifteen days 'to comply with' the city's property standards bylaw, which prohibited owners from allowing water to accumulate on their properties.[57]

In 1994 city officials instructed the developers to redesign their subdivision to not include the wetland. Development around the wetland was then finally allowed to proceed. By 1997 McCallion was musing privately about a possible purchase of the ecological site. The recovering real-estate market was starting to result in increased property values, potentially renewing the danger to the site and making any public purchase more expensive.[58]

But the city did not present its purchase offer immediately. Instead, its public strategy was to finalize the green-belt redesignation in the official plan, which the developers were challenging at the Ontario Municipal Board. Still insisting that it was willing to proceed via this route, the city finally came to the negotiating table. The developers offered to sell the wetland to the municipality for four million dollars (the province was by now not involved), which is the same the city would have paid in 1990 for *its share* of the cost.

Indeed, even though council approved this purchase price *in camera*, the mayor ordered the matter brought back to council five months later, in October 1998, without the transaction having been made. In the meantime, preparations had begun for the OMB hearing. The local councillor wrote to the city's chief counsel on this issue, sensing that the staff was now being told by the mayor's office to play down the significance of the wetland so as to minimize any fee that the OMB might ask the city to expend on purchasing the wetland.[59]

The naturalists became alarmed at the continued absence of a purchase agreement. They believed the wetland was again threatened, and again they urged a letter-writing campaign. Cutting through the confusion, Jocelyn Webber argued that one person held the cards:

> How can we best use our time and energies to get the Creditview Wetland bought and saved in perpetuity? The key player to save the Creditview Wetland is Mayor Hazel McCallion. To get her support and to justify the purchase of the wetland before an expensive OMB hearing gets underway, it is necessary again to circulate petitions, to write letters to her and the newspapers and to get the media interested in this again.[60]

That October, McCallion finally urged an immediate purchase – the asking price having now been lowered by the developers to three million. In a subsequent letter to the president of the South Peel Naturalists, McCallion stated that her strategy had always been to protect the wetland but to withstand pressure from all sides and hold out for the best possible deal.

> It has been a long process but I think you will agree that we have saved the taxpayers of Mississauga some money due to the fact that years ago, when we decided to purchase the Creditview Wetland, it would have cost at least $4 million as that was the arrangement that was on the table. One third to be paid by the City, one third to be paid by the province and one third to be paid by the developers, for a total of $12 million.
>
> After intense negotiations with the developers, they have agreed to accept $3 million.[61]

The Creditview Wetland issue shows that the mayor was, indeed,

guided by her perception of the public mood, and her ability to anticipate public reaction. But she had also amassed enough political capital
and immunity from direct attack that she could plot a strategy that
involved biding her time and holding out for a solution that would
minimize the city's financial contribution. A weaker or more nervous
leader might have succumbed quickly to pressure from the developers
or, after the public onslaught, might have sought a hasty solution –
even an expensive one – to demonstrate her environmental credentials.
Hazel McCallion felt much less constrained.

Smart Growth

In the late 1990s McCallion began calling forcefully on the provincial
government to take 'swift action' to end uncontrolled urban sprawl.
And Mississauga has been a culprit, she has confessed. The confessions
have not been sombre. In fact, they have been loud and aggressive –
impossible to overlook. The 'Queen of Sprawl,' as some editorials have
wryly called her *after* she embraced the cause, had seen the light.

Why was she, a municipal leader, now championing provincial intervention? Although McCallion had argued in previous years that provincial policies should be favourable to the City of Toronto, even to the
point of giving Toronto special treatment relative to other municipalities
in the Toronto region,[62] she had not always been committed to a strong
provincial role in land-use planning. Just ask John Sewell. Following the
report of his Commission on Planning (1993), and the provincial government's move to implement some of those recommendations, McCallion had complained that it was an attempt to 'threaten local autonomy
even further.'[63] She had objected to changing the language in the Planning Act so that municipal planning decisions 'must be consistent with'
– rather than simply 'have regard to' – provincial growth-management
and other planning policies.[64]

The mayor had insisted that the only reason there was any reference
to intensification in *City Plan* (the official plan, developed in 1992–7)
was because the province had wanted it.[65] She had expressed frustration that members of the public were not rising up *against intensification*
– although she was certain they would grumble when individual
projects surfaced in their backyards.[66] In 1995 she had pressed successfully for the deletion of references to higher densities in the Revised
Streetsville District Plan.[67]

Before her conversion to Smart Growth, McCallion had demanded,
for example, no more than four storeys along the lakefront in Port

Credit. Later, as a champion of Smart Growth, she would defy the residents, the local councillor, and the developer (who actually wanted to downzone) and demand high-rises just north of Lakeshore Road in Port Credit, within one hundred metres of the GO commuter-rail station. Although McCallion conceded defeat on that issue, the developer has changed its mind and is now proposing high-rise condominiums.[68]

Former city manager David O'Brien attributed McCallion's conversion to Smart Growth to his own gentle persuasion.[69] But McCallion has hinted that her new cause was prompted by her perception, in the late 1990s, of a subtle shift in the public mood. In the summer of 2001, after hosting an international conference on 'healthy cities,' McCallion explained that she saw the seeds of a new 'urban reform movement' in the Greater Toronto Area. The general mood was shifting in favour of managing growth, providing better public transportation, and protecting agricultural and natural areas.[70] The *Globe and Mail*, which seldom reports on Mississauga politics, was now seeking out retirees who were isolated in their homes because there was nowhere to walk. 'There is only "there" there,' the *Globe* quoted one Mississauga writer. 'There are no attractive betwixt and betweens ... only isolated islands of activity.'[71]

Jim Faught, former executive director of the Federation of Ontario Naturalists, who would come to work closely with the Mississauga mayor, recalls that McCallion's growing interest in growth management led her to review some of the available research and projections by the Neptis Foundation and others.[72] She was struck that Mississauga's current pattern of development was not economically sustainable. When Mississauga is built out, as it now almost is, revenues from development charges will decline precipitously, but the physical infrastructure, much of which was put in place in a compressed time frame, will come due suddenly for rehabilitation and replacement. Noticing this, McCallion apparently exclaimed, 'We are creating a monster!'[73]

In 2002 Queen's Park called on McCallion to head the new Central Ontario Smart Growth Panel. Sitting with her would be a number of lesser worthies, or at least persons less well known: eight municipal leaders, the chair of GO Transit, two developers, two environmentalists, one academic, one municipal bureaucrat, and the director of the Toronto Waterfront Revitalization Corporation. Some critics saw the whole exercise as a smokescreen. When the panel was appointed, one *Toronto Star* columnist wrote that McCallion was left looking like a 'stooge' of the then premier, Mike Harris, for accepting such a role.[74]

McCallion moved quickly to require that all newspaper-interview requests directed to members of the panel be forwarded to the panel secretary, effectively ensuring that Chair McCallion alone would speak for the panel or decide who else would.[75] At an early meeting the members agreed to give McCallion alone the authority to name the subpanels and their chairs.[76]

On the task force itself, McCallion held approximately fifty 'sidebar' meetings with two environmentalist representatives and two development representatives, who, with McCallion, constituted the *de facto* core group of the panel. She was an effective mediator but also a 'pit bull' who was able to use her enormous stature to broker a consensus that was considered environmentally progressive.[77]

It took them a year, until April 2003, to release their final report, focusing on four priorities: 'Balanced growth; transit as the first priority of an integrated transportation network; protection for the environment; and a need for a more collaborative approach to waste management.'[78] There were calls for growth boundaries and a permanent body to regulate it all.

The media deemed the report progressive and credible. That was certainly an improvement on the coverage from the panel's early days.

Jim Faught, who was also on the panel, credits McCallion with prompting the Conservative government to take seriously the problems of planning and growth management for the Golden Horseshoe area.[79] McCallion entered the process without a specific blueprint in mind, he says, but she was determined that the work of the panel would result in some tangible antidotes to urban sprawl.

McCallion had come to be regarded as 'the senior statesperson of the 905 area,' Faught observes. He perhaps should know, as he was dealing almost daily with senior provincial officials in Municipal Affairs and Environment in his capacity as executive director of the Federation of Ontario Naturalists. He argues that McCallion's role and persistence were instrumental in the former Conservative cabinet's decision to set up the 'G9' multi-ministry committee to coordinate the implementation of the Smart Growth Panel's recommendations.

But the respect was not mutual. Not long after the 1999 provincial election, McCallion started to predict at regular intervals that the Conservative government would be hard-pressed to survive another election. By 2003 she had become a fierce opponent, raising at every turn her concerns about provincial downloading and pooling (forcing the suburban regions to contribute through their property taxes to Toronto's social costs instead of having it all come from the more progressive provincial income tax).

After the Conservatives' final budget, by which time Ernie Eves had replaced Mike Harris as party leader and premier, she put aside all restraint. Eves was proposing to force municipalities to hold referenda on any tax increases, something McCallion deemed outrageous. The Toronto media gave major coverage to McCallion's dramatic confrontation with cabinet ministers attending the 2003 meetings of the Association of Municipalities of Ontario. During the provincial election campaign that fall she made devastating statements against what she judged to be an incompetent and irresponsible government.[80]

Indeed, she would become convinced that she had been instrumental in swinging the tide in favour of a Liberal victory.

The Smart Growth process was continued by the Liberals, although the name fell out of favour. It was used to develop a plan for a major green belt in the Golden Horseshoe and a new, binding provincial policy statement on intensification. In 2004 McCallion was assertive in endorsing the provincial government's Bill 26, the centrepiece of which was the requirement that municipal decisions be 'consistent with' and not simply 'have regard to' provincial planning policy statements.[81] This of course was the exact opposite of the position she had taken on the 1993 Sewell report.

McCallion has continued to publicly support the Queen's Park planning initiatives, complimenting the province for finally having its own 'official plan.' And as we shall see, she believed her help in defeating the previous government and her support of the new government's initiatives could be converted into provincial backing of another project – a project that was not on the provincial agenda, but the implementation of which could cause Queen's Park considerable political angst.

9 Missed Opportunities

For years, Roy Willis was seen as an annoying gadfly. A perennial losing candidate for the Ward 5 council seat, he showed up frequently at council meetings criticizing the politicians for one thing or another. The mayor would spar with him, but after he left the microphone his input was largely ignored.

Longtime Ward 5 councillor Frank McKechnie died in 1997 and was succeeded by former Peel Board of Education trustee Cliff Gyles, who caused little disturbance on council and was re-elected handily in 2000. Willis would often strongly imply that Gyles was corrupt. This too was summarily dismissed by the mayor. Indeed, the common view was that corruption at city hall was impossible because the mayor meant business. In the words of former city manager David O'Brien, the unspoken injunction was supposedly, 'Don't break the rules because, man, if you break the rules in our City, Hazel's going to pick you up by the scruff of your neck and give you a kick you know where.'[1]

Many of those around city hall who knew Willis dismissed him as over the top, unfocused, without much of a following, and out to get the mayor and council. But was he right about Gyles?

In March 2000 businessperson Rick Benisasia arranged to purchase for five hundred thousand dollars the Malton hall of the Royal Canadian Legion. He wanted to turn it into a funeral home to serve the large local South Asian population. Gyles insisted that he would oppose the rezoning but eventually suggested, at a meeting in a local doughnut shop, that a payment of one hundred thousand dollars might persuade him to change his mind. Benisasia scratched out the figure and wrote on a napkin '50,000.' That is what they agreed to.

Benisasia now went to the police, who furnished him with fifteen thousand dollars in marked bills and with monitoring equipment. This first installment was paid, and Gyles proceeded to allay concerns at the community meeting, to the point that no one showed up at city hall for the statutory public meeting, although Gyles seems to have arranged for it to be held during the afternoon session, instead of the evening. Gyles moved that the recommendation be endorsed in principle.

Gyles also accepted bribes for the rezoning of a truck-driving school, taking advantage of the fact that early in the process planning staff had directed this small-time applicant to the councillor for advice on handling the matter. It seems that the professional planners wanted to devote most of their time to the big developers.[2]

Following Gyles's arrest in an arena parking lot in 2001, the mayor suddenly became very friendly with Roy Willis. She even met with him privately (she had been refusing to meet him without witnesses present). Willis, it seemed, emerged a changed man. He did not shout out to the media, 'I told you so.' In fact, he would have had a rare opportunity to do just that, as the Toronto media were taking an interest in this case. He was not issuing statements demanding a full inquiry into the affairs of Mississauga council. He was not making other allegations of corruption. Instead, he was more gracious and deferential to the mayor than ever he had been.

Gyles was finally convicted and removed from office shortly before the 2003 municipal election. His conduct – it was rumoured that he had a gambling problem – did not reveal a widespread pattern of corruption at city hall, but it should have led to some soul-searching. Why was there not more critical scrutiny of these 'minor' development applications? Why was it customary for a councillor to be involved so extensively and so early in a planning application, despite frequent statements by McCallion and senior management that Mississauga's politicians allow administrators to administer? Why had there not been a single residents' association, civic league, or non-governmental planning council in a watchdog role with respect to these issues? Why was there not a neighbourhood newspaper or newsletter that could have followed the files and perhaps learned through the grapevine that Gyles was up to funny business? Why was the only opposition coming from one man who had come to be regarded as marginal and could thus be safely ignored? Even after Willis had been assuaged, should there not have been an assertive organization – or an assertive councillor – to ask some of the tough questions?

And should the mayor not have used some of her own political capital to try to cultivate what the political scientist Douglas Rae calls 'the civic fauna'[3] – the civic organizations, watchdogs, visionaries, and capacity builders – even if some of the headaches they cause would be hers? Had McCallion missed opportunities to advance from a strong and feared leader to a statesperson?

McCallion has had an ambivalent, or shifting, disposition towards intellectuals. Renowned Canadian historian Desmond Morton worked on her campaigns in the 1970s. Some reporters visiting her office would notice that she had been leafing through some books on planning theory. But she would also often dismiss scholars as being out of touch with reality.

In recent years, she has certainly been making attempts to associate herself with the academy. Universities, after all, have a certain cachet, a certain respectability. Most members of the young generation know little about John P. Robarts. But if they go to the University of Toronto then they know that there is a massive library named after the former premier. He must have been a man of substance.

After years of barely noticing that Mississauga had a university campus, McCallion in the late 1990s became a champion of the University of Toronto's Erindale College, renamed in 1998 the University of Toronto at Mississauga (UTM).

Despite the absence of a standard application process, the city granted the university more than three million dollars for capital projects.

Paul Donoghue, UTM's current chief administrative officer, attributes the mayor's support to her unshakeable desire to create 'a great city.' The unambiguous mayoral support for the university has made it very easy for the institution to deal with municipal officials even on relatively minor but potentially protracted matters, such as building permits and the myriad of zoning and Committee of Adjustment applications, says Donoghue, although he does concede that a small but vocal group of affluent neighbours on the scenic Mississauga Road used legal and environmental challenges to delay (but not stop) a road widening that the university was seeking and which the mayor supported. All told, however, the mayor is 'supportive of anything the university needs,' the CAO says. 'As a result of her interest and her support we've never had any difficulty establishing good relationships with the bureaucracies of the City, which is critically important.'[4]

The grateful university decided to name after McCallion a thirty-four-million-dollar academic-learning centre, the largest facility on the

Mississauga campus and home to its main library. ('Meet me at The Hazel' became a favoured expression around campus soon after the 2007 opening.) It was the first and only time the University of Toronto named anything after a sitting politician. 'It was named for Hazel because of her contributions to us,' said UTM former principal Ian Orchard. 'She is our biggest cheerleader and talks about UTM globally and how important we are to the city.'[5]

In September 1999 Dr Yuji Kawaguchi, head of the World Health Organization's Kobe Centre, visited Mississauga. He spoke about healthy cities, about how cities in the first world could be models, and about how his centre wanted to work with such places. McCallion was clearly intrigued. She announced immediately that Mississauga wanted to be such a model city. She pledged to be Kawaguchi's best friend.[6]

And Kawaguchi would see a lot more of the Mississauga mayor. Shortly after his visit, she approached UTM. Its principal at the time, Bob McNutt, embraced the idea. Why could not faculty members feed the city with health-related best practices and be available for consultation? The municipality and the university had not really had much of a relationship. That should change. It was dubbed the 'Mississauga Model.' Nice diagrams emerged showing arrows running back and forth between the city and the university. McCallion was soon appearing at conferences – in Shanghai, in Kobe, in Mississauga itself – proudly presenting those diagrams. Here was a mayor who 'gets it.'

But it seemed to be more smoke than fire. The city did launch an anti-idling campaign, citing some of its consultations with the university, for which it got some funding from Natural Resources Canada. University academics are notoriously independent, however. Unless their partnership with the municipality is somehow embedded into a major multi-year research grant, then even tracking those academics down may be a problem.

This partnership did, however, have tremendous potential to evolve into something bigger. It still has that potential. In 2004 the city and the university brought some other partners to the table and started the Healthy City Stewardship Centre. These were heavy hitters: the city manager, the directors of the two school boards, the medical officer of health for the region, the head of the United Way, the president of one of the hospitals, and two presidents of multinational corporations. McCallion was made honorary chair. She named Michael Bator, director of education for the Catholic school board, as chair.

Two years later, this group tabled a credible plan for work to be done by 2010: it called for a review of the planning process to promote healthier urban form, to link UTM's new Centre for Emerging Energy Technologies with city and regional projects, and to develop a youth strategy. There has been some progress on implementation. The YMCA launched a 'Get Active' program, focused largely on events and marketing. The youth strategy development process got underway in late 2007. But the plan was vague on some of its priorities, including more sensitivity to the health needs of immigrants and the revitalization of volunteer programs. No specific champions or clear tasks were identified for those.[7]

The Healthy City Stewardship Centre was not given a dedicated staff, and it did not get the prominence it probably merited. Its identified priorities could easily have become the centrepiece of the mayor's political agenda. But only small pieces have made it to the top of her mind. Challenged in 2006 by a fringe candidate for mayor to state what is her platform, the mayor replied: 'My platform is to continue to build a city for the 21st century with all the challenges we face. We will concentrate on transit, developing the City Centre and the waterfront, and I'm going to fight for the elimination of the $44 million we send to Toronto every year for social service costs.'[8] These are elements of a healthy-city agenda but certainly not a bold vision.

It is not at all clear that McCallion realized that if Mississauga wanted to be truly a leader among the world's healthy cities then it would have to do things much differently. Yes, she had embraced Smart Growth and now realized that the city had a responsibility to provide good public transit, but she still continued to call for the provincial government to widen highways, arguing, for example, that Highway 401 should be widened from six to twelve lanes through Mississauga. The 'induced traffic' theory – it's 'like curing obesity by loosening your belt' (the more you widen the highways the more the city will sprawl and the less likely residents will be to get out of their cars)[9] – did not make much of an impression on her.

Nor did it dawn on the champion of healthy cities that parks and recreation services should be priced at low rates to encourage fitness. She continued to mock Toronto for offering many of its recreation services for free. No wonder they were crying poor!

'We lead the country in user fees, and that's a great credit to this council,' acting city manager Janice Baker told the December 2004 budget meeting. She was echoing the mayor's comment that 'Those who use something should pay. When people pay for something they appreciate it more.' McCallion even mused that emergency wards in hospitals would be used 'more responsibly' if the Mississauga principles (the user-fee principles, that is, not the healthy-city principles) were applied there. She suggested opportunities for new user fees, such as charging for Internet use in libraries. The city's manager of information technology responded that system upgrades would soon give council this option. There was no mention of the authority of the library board, nor did anyone argue that free Internet access in libraries provides information to some people who cannot afford Internet access at home.[10]

Overlooked entirely in the discussion were the issues summarized by the consultants who had prepared the *Future Directions for Recreation and Parks* report, released in June 2004. The authors noted that 'throughout the public meeting process concerns were raised about the financial accessibility to programs by many of Mississauga's residents.' The city's only existing subsidy program was the Jerry Love Fund, the revenues for which had been contributed *voluntarily* (as donations) by Parks and Recreation staff. It was available only to low-income youths under the age of sixteen.

The consultants therefore recommended that the city 'undertake the development of a thoughtful, fair, equitable and sensitive financial assistance policy that would subsidize individuals and groups who may not otherwise be able to access programs or facilities due to an inability to pay.'[11] Thoughtful and fair perhaps, but the notion was not getting much thought from the mayor.

And a healthy city should have attractive, pedestrian-friendly neighbourhoods with therapeutically designed green spaces and popular recreation areas. Some city planners certainly thought so, and they wanted to launch 'place-making' exercises in Mississauga neighbourhoods. But McCallion, at that important 2004 meeting, took the new planning commissioner to task for a proposal to hold 'community visioning' exercises for the Clarkson and Malton neighbourhoods. She was disturbed that a report had not come before council detailing what these exercises would entail and why those two communities were selected. 'Is it just because a few people complained, or are there technical reasons?' she queried. She became even more emphatic when explaining that such consultation processes might arouse public expectations that could not be fulfilled, especially considering that the city would not allocate funds for any new schemes. She ordered the matter sent back for further study.

Poverty is a visible problem in Malton and Cooksville; it is less visible but present nonetheless in other parts of Mississauga. The waiting list for the Region of Peel's non-profit housing corporation has stood at almost twenty thousand for the past several years. In 2000 the Region opened a forty-bed homeless shelter in Mississauga – and it immediately became filled to capacity. The vacancy rate for rental units stood at 0.5 per cent. Between 1995 and 2002 only seventy nine new rental spaces were created in the otherwise rapidly growing region, sixty of which were considered high end. In 1999 21.3 per cent of children under fourteen were living in poverty in Mississauga.[12]

'Never one to shrink from a fight, Mayor McCallion has launched offensive measures on three fronts,' observed Jack Layton in his first book on homelessness.

> She delivered blistering and very public criticisms of the federal government's abandonment of its affordable-housing mandate; she worked with her communities to establish emergency shelters; and she dispatched Peel Region housing agency head Keith Ward to help create the National Housing Policy Options Strategy of the FCM. A McCallion unleashed is a force that few voluntarily contend with. After all, as *Toronto Life* put it, 'Her Town, Her Rules.'

But in the very next paragraph, Layton presents a somewhat more subdued picture:

> Not that an explosion of affordable housing has begun in Peel Region. A summer 2000 policy and planning document put together for Peel Regional Council sets aside some modest funds for small affordable housing projects and supportive initiatives for the homeless, but, as so many other communities, Peel is waiting for Ottawa.[13]

Which scenario has best described the local stance: assertive, proactive, progressive; or reluctant, not particularly assertive, and waiting but not pushing too hard? A casual observer might say that McCallion became a tireless crusader for affordable housing. In the late 1990s seldom did a few days go by without a stirring speech by the mayor urging Ottawa to do more. And the regional non-profit housing corporation, the first in the GTA after Metropolitan Toronto's (1977), is regarded as one of the most innovative in the country.

But take a closer look: Mississauga council, over the years, has passed several resolutions that have specifically shunned an active role in promoting affordable housing. In 1995 the new Progressive Conservative provincial government pushed through legislation repealing the previous government's targets for ensuring affordable housing as part of the land-use planning process. After Bill 20 received royal assent, Mississauga council deleted the following statement in the draft updated official plan: 'The City will provide opportunities to ensure that on a City-wide basis a minimum of 30% of new housing units will be affordable.'[14]

The homelessness and affordability problems have figured prominently in the headlines in the Greater Toronto Area, especially since 1998 when Canada's Big-City Mayors' Caucus, which includes Mississauga, declared the problem to be a 'national emergency.' Toronto mayor Mel Lastman promptly appointed a Mayor's Task Force on Homelessness. The reverberations were felt in Peel, where housing is addressed at the regional level.

In 1999, following Toronto's report, the Region of Peel appointed its own Task Force on Homelessness, although this one consisted primarily of regional staff. Its recommendations called for a much-expanded role for the region and both senior levels of government, including re-engagement by the federal government in housing at least to the extent of the 1980s.[15]

Although new emergency shelters were established, and although the region's housing staff was respected by professional colleagues and by many advocates, most of the task force's recommendations for local initiatives were not implemented. In fact, in the summer of 2002 Mississauga council specifically decided against fast-tracking zoning and building approvals for private affordable rental accommodations. The region did not revise its strategic directions to place more emphasis on housing. Staff reports recommending new measures must therefore be justified by referring to the rather vague 'goal 3' in the strategic directions, which states that there will 'be a strong and effective regional government,' or the strategic direction calling on the region 'to act as a leader and advocate on issues of Regional concern.'[16]

In late 1999 federal labour minister Claudette Bradshaw announced $753 million over three years to assist homeless Canadians and to prevent homelessness. On 30 March 2000 regional staff were reporting to their political superiors that 'a number of preliminary decisions may have already taken place regarding the allocation of $250 million. It also appears to staff [that] funding may be directed towards 10 cities identified as facing acute homelessness. Peel Region was not included.'[17]

Staff urged councillors to demand federal support. Although council concurred, very little behind-the-scenes lobbying appears to have taken place prior to the regional public servants urging their political superiors to take up the mantle – and not a great deal more happened afterwards.

This apparent sluggishness does not characterize local advocacy on all social programs. There were some files on which the local politicians were more assertive. Regional chair Emil Kolb pushed hard, and successfully, to launch a federal-municipal pilot project, the 'Sponsorship Breakdown Program.' Under this plan, the federal government and the region have agreed jointly to be assertive in recouping social-service costs from sponsors of immigrants whose sponsoree becomes a burden on the welfare system.[18] At McCallion's urging, the region has also been sending a bill, with accumulating interest, to the federal government for all social service costs incurred by refugees.[19] It goes unpaid, but it gets some publicity.

Regional staff were working on ideas for pilot projects related to social housing,[20] but there is no evidence that the politicians were really prepared to take up the cause. When asked in 2003 by the author on which issue she spends more time, housing or immigration, the mayor replied without hesitation that it is the latter.[21]

And the city seems to have missed opportunities to work even with its own local organizations on poverty and quality-of-life issues. When the social-services sector and the federal and provincial governments began talking about 'early years' (services for young children), the city was at best a minor player. When several organizations, including the two English-language school boards, got together to do a 'community mapping' exercise of Dixie-Bloor, a district in east Misssissauga that contains two 'high-risk' neighbourhoods, the city was not one of the partners. The report talked about city services – including the proximity to transit routes but the less than consistently reliable transit service, and the fees for recreational services – but there were no details on access, affordability, and extent of usage.[22] Some good liaisons with the city would surely have helped.

'Native Costumes'

Not only could it be said that Hazel McCallion, for all her rhetoric, could not quite transcend a superficial understanding of – or at least a superficial commitment to – healthy cities and the alleviation of housing shortages and poverty. She also seemed to have not fully come to terms with the multicultural reality of the city.

News reports in the local media over the years have depicted McCallion as a champion of multiculturalism. On 14 February 2001 the *Mississauga News* published a special section on McCallion, to 'celebrate' her eightieth birthday. The newspaper pullout included articles by staff reporters and freelancers, none of whom offered a balanced account.

One writer touted the mayor's steadfast commitment to diversity, noting that the city's semi-annual parks and recreation guide is printed in multiple languages. Readers were also informed that 'McCallion's Mississauga offers culturally oriented Recreation and Parks programs and the public library has a Heritage Language Section with books in 26 different languages.'[23] In fact, Mississauga's recreation and parks booklets have never been issued in multiple languages. They include one page with a two-sentence notice in multiple languages informing non-English-speaking residents of the names and telephone numbers of agencies, such as the Dixie-Bloor Neighbourhood Centre and Catholic Cross-Cultural Community Services, that can provide interpretation of the booklet in various languages. These agencies do not receive funding from the city. Residents who do not speak one of the listed languages are advised in English to contact not the city but the Peel Multicultural Council, which also receives no funding from the city. As for the 'culturally oriented' programs – well, they have been very hard to find. The typical parks and recreation booklet would list making Ukrainian Easter eggs, perhaps a course in feng shui, but little else. The public library system does have a heritage language section, but none of these books is purchased with public funds. The non-English-language literature is donated by the various ethnic/linguistic communities.

McCallion does tend to bestow exuberant praise when addressing ethnic audiences – and she seldom hesitates before accepting such invitations. Despite remarking at other times that immigration policies are overburdening public services, she frequently tells ethnocultural groups that 'there should be more of' that particular ethnic group in Canada. She says this to Europeans and visible-minority groups alike. At Carassauga – an annual festival with culinary and artistic pavilions – McCallion dutifully visits each site and revels in the celebrations. She never misses a Carassauga awards banquet. She has enjoyed the harmony and good feelings so much that she has for many years been hosting her own multicultural breakfast.

To these audiences she does not express disquiet; to others, she has.

Usually, the conflicting messages do not come to public attention. In May 2001, however, she gave an interview to *National Post* columnist Diane Francis in which she complained that public services were being overwhelmed with immigrants and refugees – she cited the growing need for English as a second language in schools. She then issued her most memorable line: 'If you go to the Credit Valley Hospital, the emergency is loaded with people in their native costumes.'[24]

The other major newspapers picked up on this. Peter Mansbridge even made brief mention of it on CBC Television's *The National*. For two weeks McCallion stubbornly refused to apologize, saying that she had been referring to illegal immigrants. When the executive director of the Peel Multicultural Council met with her about a week after the controversy broke, she apparently pointed to two piles of letters – the pile supporting the mayor's position was much higher than the one containing critical letters.[25] McCallion, obstinate in the face of direct challenges, thus thought she had good reason for her obstinacy.

Two small protests were held at city hall, a very rare occurrence and therefore noteworthy. But the matter remained generally low key in Mississauga. Some ethnic organizations and social-service agencies met collectively to decide what to do. The head of one of these organizations told me that although there was concern that McCallion's failure to apologize might serve to legitimize race-baiting, there was also concern about the risk of openly and aggressively challenging the mayor. If the popular populist managed to stare down her critics, inter-ethnic relations might suffer a permanent setback. They were relieved, therefore, when the mayor finally issued a grudging apology, two weeks after the incident.

As intriguing as this organizational self-restraint and self-censorship may be at first glance, this particular non-profit-sector leader is by no means the first to have observed it. Political scientist Kristin Good, who conducted interviews in Mississauga as part of a multicity study on urban multiculturalism, found that ethnic-group leaders were quick to defer to McCallion in part because they feared losing credibility with their own memberships were they to be seen opposing her, especially if the high-profile civic leader were henceforth to spurn the respective groups' invitations to attend functions. In a sense, then, the mayor's resounding popularity became self-perpetuating and somewhat stifling.[26]

To be sure, McCallion has operated to some degree from a position of ignorance. In 2005, at a banquet to mark the bicentennial of the signing of the First Purchase between representatives of the Mississauga First Nation and the British crown, she addressed an audience of senior representatives of the Mississaugas of the New Credit First Nation (based near Hagersville, where most of the Credit Valley Mississaugas moved in 1847) and non-profit-sector leaders from the city of Mississauga. She made extremely awkward references to her pride that a Mississauga hockey association is named 'Braves,' and to her observation on a trip to Mississauga's twin city, Kariya, Japan, that the people there looked like 'the Indians' of Canada. She confused the Mississaugas with the Six Nations. People grimaced, but the story made it no further, even though two reporters and the publisher of the *Mississauga News* were in the audience.[27]

The City of Mississauga is notable for the number of senior positions held by women. At the time of writing, three-quarters of the members of council, plus the city manager, the city treasurer, the city solicitor, and the city clerk, were women. The senior ranks are not, however, representative of the cultural or racial make-up of the community. No current councillors or senior staff are members of visible-minority groups, although former city clerk Arthur Grannum, who had earlier been the mayor's executive assistant, is of African-Caribbean origin.

Separation from the Region

Perhaps the issue that best demonstrates that the octogenarian McCallion is still determined to go on the offensive, still enjoys tremendous influence, but arguably lacks the imagination and inspiration that distinguishes a strong leader from a true statesperson, has been her recent crusade for Mississauga's 'independence' from the Region of Peel.

The Region of Peel hardly seems like a monster, with its soft-spoken chair, its low-profile bureaucrats, and the lack of controversy over day-to-day operations. But if it is not a monster, it could be portrayed as a monstrosity – a wasteful tier of local government on whose council Mississauga is grossly under-represented. Smaller cities like London, Guelph, and Barrie are 'separated' cities. They do not groan under an upper-tier government. Why should Mississauga?

The Regional Municipality of Peel, established in 1974, has boundaries similar to the former County of Peel, created in 1867. The region, which oversees some roads, runs a non-profit-housing corporation, delivers some social services, decides on the fiscal allocation for policing, and oversees garbage disposal, among other functions, was governed until 2006 by twenty one councillors plus a regional chair selected by the councillors. Mississauga's mayor and all of its city councillors have also been regional councillors.

Although McCallion has been a long-time critic of regional government, and although the city recommended the elimination of all the regions in its 1995 submission to the Task Force on the Future of the Greater Toronto Area (the Anne Golden Task Force), and although McCallion has flirted in the past with a separation campaign[28] and has protested vigorously the system of weighted assessment (Mississauga has paid into regional coffers its share of the assessed value of property in the region rather than its share of services and infrastructure provided by the region),[29] it was 2001 when she calculated the time to be ripe to make her move.

In her inaugural address on 1 December 2000, just after she was sworn in for her ninth term as mayor, McCallion promised to create a Citizens' Task Force on the Future of Mississauga to determine if Mississaugans agreed with her that the city should not be amalgamated with any neighbouring municipality. The provincial push for municipal amalgamations, launched in 1997, had not yet abated.[30] There was serious concern that the province would force the '905' regional municipalities to become one-tier entities.

This could be the death knell for Mississauga. True, its mayor revelled in her influence, but the ideologically driven Mike Harris government seemed to be bulldozing over everyone. It was not uncommon to hear speculation about a future 'City of Peel.' Maybe, however, this all was being overblown. Perhaps McCallion struck more fear in the hearts of Harris et al. than even she realized. One former city employee with many years of intergovernmental connections told me she is convinced that the province would 'not touch' the suburban regions within the Greater Toronto Area as long as 'Hurricane Hazel' remained mayor of Mississauga. Whether true or not, the GTA '905' zone, as it is commonly called with reference to the telephone area code, was the only part of the province left completely untouched by amalgamations.

The author served on the Citizens' Task Force, which began its work in early 2001. It was appointed by the mayor, who selected two people from each ward, drawing from a list of five names submitted by each councillor. Two additional persons were selected as the 'mayor's appointees.'[31]

After the members of the task force had been appointed, but before their first meeting, the province ran out of steam. It announced that the era of forced amalgamations was over. The amalgamations might have made it easier for the province to download costs – a bigger local government might not crumble immediately under the weight – but there seemed to be an ideological inconsistency in all this. If the objective is 'smaller government,' then should you really be creating bigger governments? If the private sector is to be the model for all good things, then why is competition among municipalities so bad? Even government ministers were now talking about political scientist Andrew Sancton's study *Merger Mania: The Assault on Local Government*, which made precisely those arguments. A well-read copy of that book was sitting on McCallion's desk.[32]

So what now should be done with this new Citizens' Task Force? The city would have little to lose stirring up some trouble of its own. McCallion thus gave the task force a new *raison d'être*: to recommend whether or not the City of Mississauga should remain within the Region of Peel. She also encouraged it to consider what governance structures should be in place for the Greater Toronto Area. But the first assignment she deemed to be the more important one. At the task force's inaugural meeting on 18 February 2001, the mayor spoke for more than an hour. Most of her arguments were dedicated to cataloguing the alleged ills of regional government.

She then retreated and waited. City manager David O'Brien was in attendance at most of the task force's biweekly meetings during its first three months. Although he, too, did not try to influence the deliberations overtly, he ceased attending after it seemed clear that the task force would advocate the abolition of regional government.

In its interim and final reports (November 2001 and May 2002, respectively), the task force recommended that the Region of Peel be dissolved in five years. Its arguments were tied to the need for an indirectly elected Greater Toronto Area–wide coordinating body, which would cover an area large enough to deal with issues affecting most of the Toronto city-region. This would be effectively a reconstitution of the Greater Toronto Services Board (disbanded at the end of 2001), but with expanded powers for growth management and transportation planning. The task force argued that having three tiers of local government would compromise accountability, erode grass-roots democracy, and make influencing politicians the preserve of paid lobbyists and experts, who had the time and resources to navigate such a labyrinth. Also, the task force was concerned that the legitimacy of the region was impaired by the absence of representation by population in Peel (Mississauga, with 62 per cent of Peel's population, had fewer than half of the seats on regional council).[33]

When the task force presented its final report, McCallion, though effusive in her praise of the members, abruptly dismissed a suggestion by a councillor that city council should, then and there, endorse the report. Instead, on McCallion's recommendation, council referred the report to staff for review.[34]

The staff report, presented four months later, concentrated only on one of the task force's recommendations: that Mississauga should leave the Region of Peel. Virtually nothing was said of the Greater Toronto Area–wide coordinating body. The task force's recommendation that Mississauga's ward boundaries be adjusted (the largest ward had 115,000 people, while the smallest had only 44,000) was not accepted on the grounds that it would not be productive to make changes for the 2003 election if the region were to cease to exist in 2006. The staff pointed out that the dissolution of the Region would necessitate a further ward-boundary adjustment if Mississauga's council was to expand beyond ten members. On the other hand, once the Regional Municipality of Peel Act was repealed Mississauga could easily expand beyond the then ten-seat council.

Judging from the debate at council, the 'staff report' had received prior endorsement from the mayor. Every part of it was defended by McCallion. The week after the endorsement of the staff report, McCallion held a press conference to announce that Mississauga was beginning a 'campaign' to become an 'independent city' (separate from the region). In the months that followed, McCallion issued a newsletter to every household in Mississauga with a form to send in endorsing the city's position. Just over twenty thousand were reportedly returned, and the City announced that 99 per cent of respondents favoured the mayor's position.[35]

Although McCallion repeated constantly that the city acted 'on the recommendation of the Citizens' Task Force,' her arguments for separation from the region differed from the task force's. That body specifically rejected the fiscal argument, and in fact acknowledged that regional services had been provided well and at a reasonable cost. McCallion, however, made 'savings to the taxpayers' one of the centrepieces of her case.

Following the October 2003 provincial election, the mayor submitted the residents' postcards to the new Liberal provincial government and asked council to again request provincial action. Was she overplaying this issue? The *Mississauga News* now thought she might be.[36] The *Toronto Star* came out with a rare editorial criticizing McCallion, comparing her to former Quebec separatist premier Lucien Bouchard.[37] One columnist even accused McCallion of trying on the 'mayoral clown costume' worn so frequently by outgoing Toronto mayor Mel Lastman.[38] But municipal affairs minister John Gerretsen said he was willing to listen,[39] prompting one reporter to observe that 'if it was anyone but Hurricane Hazel McCallion, the threat might be ignored.'[40]

McCallion, meanwhile, was receiving a report that the city had commissioned from Day and Day Chartered Accountants to review the financial impact of separation. Using very limited data, it projected that separation would result in property tax savings of 5.97 per cent for a Mississauga residential property assessed at $250,000. The report conceded that similarly assessed properties in Brampton and Caledon would experience 6.94 per cent and 13.3 per cent increases, respectively. The consultants explained as follows:

> The tax shift generally occurs due to changes in the basis of sharing municipal costs and municipal property assessment. Those municipalities projected to experience tax increases will often oppose the restructuring plan based on unfair and inequitable tax increases. Their opposition stems from their assumption that the current distribution of taxes is not always fair. Where the method of funding upper tier municipal services is not reflective of service levels, needs or levels of usage of the lower tier municipality the current distribution of taxes is probably unfair and inequitable. In our opinion, restructuring will assist in correcting these inequities.[41]

The Region of Peel was funded on the basis of weighted assessment, meaning that Mississauga pays for regional services according to its share of the regional assessment. This amounted to 65.68 per cent. Mississauga had 61.98 per cent of Peel's population and 45 per cent of the seats on the regional council. The savings would presumably be realized because, with the exception of the services of conservation authorities, Mississauga received a smaller share of regional or regionally funded programs than its contribution. For example, it had 32.31 per cent of the regional road network but paid 65.68 per cent of the cost. Brampton had 38.27 per cent of the regional road network but paid only 28.63 per cent of the cost.[42]

There were some dubious assumptions, however. It was assumed, for example, that there would be no 'levelling up' of salaries for comparable positions when regional staff joined the staff of the separated lower-tier municipalities. (Some of the regional planning staff, for instance, would come to work for Mississauga's Planning and Building Department.) Most previous municipal-restructuring exercises in Ontario do not bear out the assumption that differential salaries can be maintained for those carrying out similar duties within the same municipality or that the higher-paid colleagues will take a decrease in remuneration.

At a meeting in January 2004 with members of the by-then-disbanded Citizens' Task Force, at which the consultants' financial report was presented, McCallion was perplexed by questions about the levelling-up issue. She insisted that this concern applies only to municipal amalgamations, not de-amalgamations. She did not appreciate that, though the region would be broken apart, there would still be fusions of staff from departments previously under separate administrations.[43]

The consultants also assumed that 'one-time transitional costs incurred by each municipality will be funded by Provincial grants, existing Region of Peel reserves/reserve funds and proceeds from the sale of redundant Region of Peel assets will not negatively effect [sic] annualized financial impacts and their effect on property taxation.'[44] These are quite the assumptions to make. It is little wonder, then, that the consultants thought fit to caution that 'property tax impacts reflect projected annual restructuring costs at maturity.'[45]

The overly optimistic conclusions about cost savings only fed the mayor's enthusiasm. The ever-compliant city council passed a resolution unanimously endorsing this consultant's report and calling again for Mississauga's separation from the region in time for the 2006 municipal elections. McCallion now convened a press conference and began lobbying Premier Dalton McGuinty directly through meetings, correspondence, and telephone calls.

After its sceptical December editorial, the *Mississauga News* remained silent on the issue all winter, but on 12 May 2004 it suddenly printed an unprecedented *front-page* editorial wholeheartedly endorsing McCallion's campaign.[46] Publisher Ron Lenyk says that initially he did not think this campaign was serious; he perceived at first that it was merely a personal hobby horse of the mayor. But the *Mississauga News* came to the realization that the issue would not go away; that the mayor would persist relentlessly and that a clear editorial position would have to be taken. Lenyk insists that the newspaper reached its position after an objective analysis and consultations with both city and regional officials, but he does concede that the mayor was angry with him because the paper had not earlier been voicing strong support.[47]

The mayors of Brampton and Caledon, predictably, were opposed to all these Mississauga machinations. They called on the provincial government to renounce McCallion's plans – to close the file and put a stop to this nuisance. Her Worship 'must be smoking something,' quipped one Brampton councillor.[48] By all accounts, Hazel Journeaux's youth had been anything but risky or countercultural, unless we count playing hockey and her business acumen. Was the octogenarian Hazel McCallion making up for it now?

Of course, the issue was causing great concern for regional chair Emil Kolb and chief administrative officer Roger Maloney.[49] But did they hold press conferences? They did not. Did they send out newsletters or purchase advertisements countering Mississauga's arguments? They did not consider it. Did either of them publicly challenge McCallion? Kolb made only occasional statements saying the region is serving citizens well. Some challenge.[50]

What was McCallion's endgame? Could she really have been absolutely convinced that the province would simply implement everything that was being demanded? She knew better. Outright and immediate separation could set a precedent, throwing wide open the debates across the province on all sorts of municipal grievances, separatist aspirations, de-amalgamations, annexationist proposals, and maybe even schemes not hitherto contemplated. At that January 2004 meeting with the task force members, McCallion had revealed that she indeed had a 'Plan B' – increasing Mississauga's representation on the regional council rather than outright separation, and devolving to the lower tier control over roads and all planning matters.

So in May, with the government finally signalling that separation was too dramatic a step and might open up a controversy involving all the regions, but that some reforms might be considered,[51] Plan B was unveiled. Mississauga would insist on a majority of seats on the regional council and a funding model that tied contributions more closely to benefits received. This was approved by city council unanimously and was described as 'a first step to separation.' McCallion instructed the acting city manager to draw up a new ward map showing eleven wards, instead of nine, insisting that this was necessary because the two largest wards had populations more than double the size of the two smallest ones. All eleven councillors plus the mayor would have to double up as regional councillors, meaning that Mississauga must have twelve seats on the regional council. The *Mississauga News* reported it from the city's angle, rather than pointing out that Mississauga was, in effect, climbing down from its initial position.[52]

On 30 June McCallion had a personal meeting with Premier Mc-Guinty at which she presented various studies prepared over the years on various subjects, which she insisted substantiated Mississauga's case. McGuinty deferred more detailed consideration to deputy premier and finance minister Greg Sorbara.

Later that week, McCallion was stunned that regional chair Kolb had sent a memorandum to members of regional council stating that McGuinty's office had just conveyed to him that there would be no restructuring. She noted that Kolb had departed from his habit of consulting with her on an almost daily basis on major decisions or actions emanating from his office. McCallion insisted that she had received no such notification, although the government was continuing to signal that restructuring would not include separation.[53]

The mayor's surprise that Kolb would take a position different from hers in correspondence with regional councillors is perhaps a reflection of some attempts by the region over the years to appease McCallion, despite her opposition to its very existence. In 1998, for example, it was agreed that the region would cover the costs of making the new provincially enforced transfer payments to Toronto to assist with that city's social-services burden resulting from provincial downloading. The new financial burden would be assigned to the region's constituent municipalities on the basis not of weighted assessment but of population.[54] Furthermore, Peel is the only regional municipality in the Greater Toronto Area with no budget for economic development and marketing.[55] As we have seen, McCallion had some role in this change in the early days of her mayoralty. The region had not tried to inch back into these endeavours.

The mayor was adamant that her Plan B proposals would not be rejected by the government. She confidently told councillors and task force members that the Liberals had not dismissed her – and would not – because she had played a crucial role in securing their victory in October 2003.

Finally, in August 2004, McCallion declared partial victory when the government agreed to name a mediator to try to find a solution. The mayor was even more satisfied when that mediator was described as a 'facilitator' in Minister John Gerretsen's statement of 7 October 2004 appointing retired judge George Adams.[56] He was invited to make recommendations even if the municipalities could not come to a consensus.

But Adams was no white knight. In December 2004 he recommended that Mississauga be assigned two more seats on the regional council. But he also recommended five more seats for Brampton. Granted, there would be a formula giving each Brampton representative slightly less weight than a Mississauga councillor. But there would be gradual increases in Brampton's weight to reflect its growing population, and at no point would the formula give Mississauga the majority on the regional council. McCallion greeted the report with scorn and promptly scheduled a meeting with McGuinty.[57] She then fell silent.

McCallion's Brampton and Caledon counterparts should have deduced that the Hurricane was not raging because a Mississauga-friendly arrangement was in the works. It was announced in April 2005. Mississauga would get its twelve seats, and Brampton would get one more, and one vote would be worth exactly one vote. With the chair to hold an additional seat, there was now a very good chance that Mississauga would control the regional council. McCallion declared victory. This was virtually Plan B.

She declared victory – but did not immediately give up. She was actively strategizing about how to make Mississauga's independence from the region an election issue in the 2007 provincial campaign. But the enthusiasm she had generated in her campaign was very hard to sustain – this was simply not a top-of-mind issue for citizens – and she held her fire during the election.

Although McCallion, still an avowed separatist, is unlikely to achieve Mississauga's 'independence' from Peel, the separation campaign does tend to reveal a pre-emptive, overriding mayoral role. She kept an issue on the political agenda that would almost certainly not have been taken seriously had it been advanced by another mayor. She enjoyed unanimous support from her council. And she put the region on the defensive, even managing to derail for a time discussions of a new headquarters building by pulling all the Mississauga representatives out of the meeting, thereby denying quorum.[58] She enjoyed complete cooperation from the city's senior bureaucrats, and she managed to secure the enthusiastic support of the initially reluctant local newspaper. Weaknesses in the city's case remained largely hidden from public view, and the response from the regional chair and regional senior staff was very muted, despite the region's extreme concern about McCallion's intentions and machinations.

This fight took time and energy, however. It was therefore not without cost. McCallion's championing of Smart Growth, for example, was relegated to the second tier at a time when a new provincial government was sympathetic to the concept and when she could have further developed and consolidated a reputation as a mayor who has taken the lead on provincial growth-management policy and on responsible land stewardship.

When Brampton and Peel regional councils decided that the north-west of Brampton would be developed, McCallion was too busy to raise concerns forcefully. Regional staff are even hoping that the province will put a 400-series expressway in that area, which would certainly not encourage an efficient use of land. McCallion has barely noticed. Caledon mayor Marilyn Morrison has been talking about exempting equestrian facilities from development charges: 'If we kill that industry, we will have fields of nothing.'[59] What about agriculture on what is generally highly fertile soil? Why can that not be a viable industry, supplying such a huge Greater Toronto Area market?

Could it be that McCallion, the 'senior statesperson,' would have gained more traction had she used her position on the regional council – and her influence with the province – to intelligently and more forcefully address these important planning, ecological, and economic issues?

10 New Potholes and More Perilous Politics

McCallion's partial success on the Region of Peel file, and in particular the expanded regional representation for the city, ensured that Mississauga would have at least two new faces on council as of December 2006. One of these newcomers would owe nothing to the mayor.

In recent years, Carolyn Parrish has come to rival Hazel McCallion for the unofficial title of best-known Mississauga politician. Now, it must be said that Parrish has never enjoyed the public adulation that has been accorded to McCallion, but she has always had a penchant for getting attention.

Born in 1946, and a high-school teacher by profession, she was first elected as a public school trustee in 1985. She would not try to hide her exuberant personality. 'I've always been outspoken and extremely opinionated ... some would even say I'm outrageous.'[1]

The style did distinguish Parrish from her fellow trustees, and they elected her board chair in December 1988. Then began a period of almost non-stop turbulence, with Parrish having to defend double-digit-percentage tax increases. She captured headlines by calling the Catholic school system 'the most wasteful, excessive duplication of service ever witnessed by this province.'[2] She fought unsuccessfully – and very publicly – to have kirpans (Sikh ceremonial daggers) banned outright from schools, losing at the Ontario Human Rights Tribunal and in the courts at a cost of more than two hundred thousand dollars.[3]

The exhausted board sidelined Parrish as chair in December 1990, returning past chair Bill Kent. She then decided not to seek re-election as trustee, instead challenging Mississauga Ward 7 councillor and long-time rival Nando Iannicca, taking some time off from that losing campaign to muse that school boards should be abolished.[4]

In 1993 she was elected the Liberal member of Parliament for Mississauga West (later Mississauga-Erindale). She had made no secret of the fact that she wanted to be in the federal cabinet, but she would be passed over, again and again. She soon gained some notoriety on home turf by declaring her support for new airport runways, after having said in the 1993 election campaign that they would be built 'over my dead body.'[5]

By 2004 many national political pundits assumed that Carolyn Parrish's federal political career was over. Even she had been hinting for some time that she had come as far as she could in federal politics and that her ambition was to become mayor of Mississauga after Hazel McCallion retires (it would appear that not even someone as brash and self-confident as Parrish would contemplate actually taking on McCallion directly). She had made several inappropriate – some would say immature – remarks. She had gained more notoriety (but tremendous publicity) for her 'Damn Americans! I hate those bastards.'[6] When another long-time politician, also a sitting MP, Steve Mahoney, challenged her for the Liberal nomination in Mississauga-Erindale (which, because of redistribution, contained parts of the ridings of both politicians), her prospects indeed seemed grim.

But Parrish had a formidable political machine and was a tireless campaigner without equal. Many of her active volunteers were members of local Muslim communities, impressed not only by Parrish's steadfast opposition to the war in Iraq but by her outspoken defence of the Palestinian cause and her willingness to strongly challenge Israeli policy.

Mahoney was the one sent into retirement.

Despite wavering Liberal prospects in the 2004 federal election, Parrish easily held on to her seat. And she continued to throw caution to the wind. The act that would finally cause her ejection from the Liberal caucus was an appearance in November 2004 on the CBC comedy show *This Hour Has 22 Minutes*, stomping on a doll of George W. Bush. She followed that up with scathing remarks against her party leader, Paul Martin, and blunt assertions that she no longer felt loyalty to the Liberal Party. She would remain high profile as an independent MP. Indeed, the media eagerly sought her out prior to a May 2005 confidence vote in the House of Commons in which her vote could have defeated the government.

She knew, however, that winning an election as an independent is nearly impossible in Canada. So when the minority government finally

fell in November 2005, Parrish retired from federal politics and immediately announced that she would set her sights on one of the new
municipal council seats.

Ron Starr was determined to stop her. The former councillor had
become a close associate of the mayor's, worked for developers, and
was chairman of the Mississauga Hydro Commission and its successor,
the privatized Enersource, in which the city had the majority stake. He
was on many local boards, often in high-profile capacities. Many people were speculating that Starr was gearing up to run for mayor after
the McCallion era; it was even suggested that McCallion herself wanted
to see him as her successor, although she has never publicly endorsed
anyone and there is no strong evidence that she has ever tried seriously
to groom a successor.

However, Starr's reputation was tarnished in 1998, when he was
charged with misappropriating funds destined to support projects for
disadvantaged children run by the Optimist Club, an organization in
which he was active.[7] These charges were eventually dropped, but as
almost always happens when a public figure is charged, the cloud never
goes away, regardless of the outcome.

McCallion was apprehensive about Parrish, but by the summer of
2006 she thought that Parrish had the momentum in the local campaign. Starr was making a mistake, she believed: he was focusing his
entire campaign against Parrish, instead of articulating a positive
agenda.[8] Parrish's platform was sketchy, too, but she managed to portray herself as a folksy and progressive character, riding around in a
tiny Smart car with her name on it, to emphasize her commitment to
the environment. McCallion could only take some solace in Parrish's
assurances that she would be a constructive councillor and would not
try to undermine the mayor.

Parrish won 49 per cent of the vote, to Starr's 37 per cent. She was
helped quietly by Councillor George Carlson, who had been her campaign manager when she was a federal politician. And sure enough, it
was not long before she was behaving as a kind of leader of the opposition. She was more cautious than usual around the mayor – but she
started asking questions, lots of questions. Why are the local politicians
who serve on the Enersource board, including the mayor, getting additional honoraria, valued in the tens of thousands of dollars? (McCallion
quickly sided with Parrish and renounced her extra pay.) Are city staff
really being fair to bidders who respond to tenders? Why is the city
paying for opinion polls that gauge the popularity of the council?[9]

Parrish eagerly volunteered to serve on the Heritage Advisory Committee – the committee that most councillors have shunned – and went on the attack immediately. Why is so little being done to protect the character of neighbourhoods?

And in March 2007 when a developer swooped in with a bulldozer on Port Credit's historic Gray House, Parrish showed up for the media photographs.

That photo opportunity was a direct challenge to the mayor. McCallion had wanted the Port Credit library moved to the corner of Park and Hurontario Streets, the site of a planned high-density development, close to the GO station. That library was in need of repairs. Why not get someone else to pay for them? In exchange for building a new library that would incorporate the Gray House, the developer, Fram-Slokker, would get high density. McCallion had wanted high density there for some time, citing her Smart Growth principles and the proximity to transit.

The circa-1908 Gray House, built in the Queen Anne style, was one of the last properties associated with the St. Lawrence Starch operation, most of which had been demolished in the early 1990s (though it surely could have been a spectacular example of adaptive reuse, Mississauga's version of Toronto's Distillery District). At that time, the city agreed not to retain a heritage designation on the Gray House in exchange for the conservation of two other buildings. The deal was broken, and only one of those other buildings remained standing. In July 2005 the City's Heritage Advisory Committee recommended that the Gray House be redesignated. This was deferred indefinitely by council.

The residents' movement in Port Credit has in recent years become far more active than those in other neighbourhoods. Yes, the Credit Reserve Association had always been looking out for its members. But there had been signs that there were more edgy elements that wanted to be heard. In 1998 Joan Kallis managed to get arrested for trespassing after climbing up one of Port Credit's most majestic 200-year-old trees, in an unsuccessful attempt to protect it from Legend Homes, a developer that has demolished a number of heritage homes in Mississauga. She was no more successful with two nearby 250-year-old maples with diameters of more than three hundred centimetres.[10] Often using poetry – even witty essays with reference to Henry David Thoreau – she got good publicity in the Toronto media. She and a small group of committed supporters (the support was more widespread, she insisted – 'she's got guts,' one bystander said – but many people did not themselves want to be seen doing anything countercultural) pressed the city to actually get a tree bylaw. A modest one was finally put in place, requiring a permit for cutting more than five large trees in a calendar year.[11]

Kallis's movement did not have permanence, but some long-time residents of Port Credit, for the most part now with grown children and some time on their hands, were coming to believe that spirited activism (without necessarily the civil disobedience) could be married with sophisticated policy analysis – the briefs, the visioning workshops with progressive architects, the sniffing around city hall, and the like. They were actually following local politics. And so they now easily deciphered the mayor's game insofar as it concerned the library. When the library move came up for discussion (as a separate item from the development application, which had not yet been considered), city staff showed up at public meetings with gleaming images of what could be and depressing photos of what was. Hundreds packed a high-school gymnasium, and most would hear nothing of it. McCallion even lost her temper when one resident insinuated that secret deals were being made with developers.[12]

And the majority of council, Parrish the most prominent among them, defied the mayor on this – voting to keep the library in place and to refurbish it in place. If that is what you want, then you will lose the Gray House, the mayor warned. But why must its fate be tied specifically to the library? some of the councillors wondered.

Its fate was tied to the library. Sure enough, the next day the developer received a demolition permit and was on the site almost immediately to begin the operation. The demolition seemed to be an act of spite. The developer would not hold on to the Gray House to see if it could still be leveraged for high density. Whereas before some residents had some sympathy for the mayor's perspective, the result now was rage and a widely held view that McCallion was hostile to Port Credit. Just a year earlier, a local artist who painted an unflattering piece showing a dour and angry McCallion for display in a shop window (the owner was asked to take it down by the Port Credit Business Asssociation) had been seen as a kind of fringe character, even though he claimed to want to draw attention to McCallion's neglect of the arts. Now, it was starting to seem that this artist was very much a part of the Port Credit mainstream.

Carolyn Parrish's political style has been undisciplined and sometimes excessive and opportunistic. She is quotable, *certes*, but the comments can be bizarre. 'I think when she finally goes we should embalm her,' the councillor said of the mayor. 'How are we going to know she's dead? Drive a steak knife through her heart. At the last moment, she'll reach out and grab it.'[13]

Can Parrish sustain a sharp and effective opposition, or will she discredit herself before that happens? Can she build a coalition with a vision of a different kind of city or at least a loose amalgam of the disenchanted? Or is Hazel McCallion, even in her old age, unshakeable?

Not since Larry Taylor – McCallion herself recalled him when talking to me about Parrish – has there been consistent opposition on the council. 'Debate is healthy, but controversy should not play a part,' the mayor insists, not explaining how controversy can be avoided if there is to be public debate. 'I had hoped [Parrish] would look at local government in a different light.'[14] In other words, raucous, entertaining politics is for the federal and provincial levels of government. Here we run things like a business. The public likes it that way, the mayor says. Why else are the city's approval ratings so high?

Certainly McCallion seems in some respects to be outflanking the scattered Parrish. When the latter thought she would put up some obstacles in the December 2007 budget debate by insisting that more savings could be found so that the tax increase would not have to be so high, McCallion pounced immediately. Which public services is Councillor Parrish proposing to cut? The public is tired of neglected services! It is the federal and provincial governments that should take the blame for any local tax increases.

The federal government especially. McCallion's relations with Ontario premier Dalton McGuinty are reasonably good: 'He is moving in the right direction.' But with Ottawa it is a different story. When finance minister Jim Flaherty's economic statement (mini-budget) of November 2007 contained no new funds for urban infrastructure, McCallion trotted out a Federation of Canadian Municipalities report showing a national municipal infrastructure deficit of $123.6 billion.[15]

And she did more. The idea came to city manager Janice Baker at 5 o'clock one Thursday morning: Why not adopt in principle a 5 per cent local 'infrastructure levy' to take effect if there is still no good news in the February budget? Baker spoke with McCallion later that morning. The mayor immediately endorsed the idea, announced it the following Monday, and had it approved on the Wednesday.

What was adopted in principle in the fall was not adopted in practice in the winter. Flaherty had some good news for cities in the 2008 budget, including a guaranteed share of the federal gas tax for the foreseeable future. Meanwhile the Board of Trade and some ratepayers' groups came out of hibernation to say they opposed the levy. Five per cent became one per cent, a result that clearly made the mayor bitter.

Still, by taking the initial action, McCallion made herself the darling of municipalities across the country, even more so when Flaherty replied with silly statements like 'The federal government is not in the pothole business.' (In response, McCallion started rhyming off every service imaginable – hospitals and universities, even – calling them all 'infrastructure.' The implication? The federal government is doing nothing for citizens, except cutting taxes.)[16]

And despite her loosening grip on the public discourse, McCallion could take solace that she was containing Parrish. Sitting at her kitchen table in December 2007, beside a large pile of papers and dozens upon dozens of pens and markers, McCallion shows that Parrish is very much on her mind, and we know that the mayor can be reactive when provoked in public. But Parrish has not become an obsession for her. It's like a school principal pondering what to do with a pupil who has been making trouble. When I asked McCallion to identify her own objectives for the rest of this term, what is the first thing she said? The development of a strategy for arts, culture, and heritage – this from the mayor with 'no artistic bone in my body.' To date, we haven't had a strategy, she complained, sounding almost like the leader of the opposition herself. Not only is the city budgeting for this – $463,000 in the 2008 budget – but McCallion says that the Mississauga Community Foundation will be supporting it as well, thanks to the fact that she has been depositing the Mayor's Gala proceeds with that new body.

She turns from arts and culture to public transit. She had feared that the Stephen Harper government would cut the annual share of the federal gas tax that the previous government had decided to funnel to municipalities. Those funds are going to transit infrastructure. In Mississauga, a bus rapid transit system along Highway 403, which has been talked about for years, is finally expected to be partially ready in 2009. McCallion, who is the one Peel representative on the board of Metrolinx (formerly the Greater Toronto Transit Authority), is talking more and more about light rail along Dundas and Hurontario streets.

And the mayor who once steadfastly opposed the provincial Employment Equity Act, who had no time for any formal protocols to deliver services in languages other than English, is now saying that she has asked council's nominating committee to make sure there are more members of the city's many cultural communities on boards and committees. The city will soon have to start advertising in multiple languages, she notes. (But she worries about this. Once the city starts advertising in a few ethnic newspapers, will it have to advertise in all of them?)[17]

She has, it would seem, come to anticipate and maybe even accept that the budding citizens' movement will only get stronger. In February 2008, when hundreds of Lakeview residents, supported by their increasingly well organized Port Credit brethren, showed up at a council meeting to present images of mixed-use medium-density residential neighbourhoods that they had developed with the help of local academics, McCallion embraced their cause wholeheartedly and called it a historic day for the city. Their scheme was not only better than a possible gas-fire generator, she assured, but she revealed that she had for some time been having quiet discussions with other owners of brownfield sites along the waterfront. She has been in talks with Imperial Oil so that something could be done – perhaps even the development of a new university campus! – on the fallow lands in western Port Credit. The residents were dumbfounded. The local councillor confessed that she had never heard of such discussions. But, alas, when the residents did some probing they found that it was all true.

So change would have been on the horizon without the prodding of a Carolyn Parrish. Major greenfield development in Mississauga is nearing a conclusion. The 'large suburban canvas' has been almost exhausted. Revenues from development charges are slipping, and much of the city's infrastructure, which was put in place in a very compressed time frame, is coming due for repair or replacement. Soon, any new development will be of the politically contentious infill variety. Mississauga will become more difficult to govern. McCallion herself concedes it. It's happening already: 'The development has stirred up the people in a major way.'

'Mississauga has grown from the outside in,' a councillor has observed.[18] The inside holes have become small and are now in established areas. As developers now set their sights on, for example, major condominium development in the city centre, they are starting to meet with hitherto unseen resistance. In the city centre case, a group of residents of a twenty-year-old condominium, who until now have enjoyed views of a mature hedgerow and even Lake Ontario, are aghast at a thirty-building development plan, with one to rise as high as fifty storeys, which will block the lake and even much of the sunlight. 'Those clowns' is how the most vocal residents' spokesperson referred to city council for promoting very high densities for the city centre.[19] Unlike those few anomic, intemperate gadflies who had gone largely ignored, these malcontents are getting media attention and are promising to use all available channels at the Ontario Municipal Board and in the courts.

In 1999 just under 50 per cent of Mississauga's capital costs were covered by property taxes. The rest came from development charges. Already in 2004 it was 63 per cent and 37 per cent, respectively. Tax increases of at least 5 per cent a year are expected for the foreseeable future, despite the federal Goods and Services Tax rebate, announced in 2004, and the restoration of previously cut provincial funds for public transit. For both capital and operating purposes, Mississauga had once intended to tap into only the interest on its $325-million Hydro Reserve Fund, but is now depleting the principal at a rate of at least $5 million a year.[20]

'Hazel can't help you this time,' McCallion told a lone senior who showed up at a recent General Committee meeting to protest the doubling of seniors' fares for Mississauga Transit. 'We're debt free. But for how much longer, I don't know,' the mayor conceded to a *Toronto Star* columnist.[21]

As stable as Mississauga has been during the McCallion era, local politics would become extremely fractious and incoherent were McCallion suddenly to depart from the scene. How have other cities adjusted following the death or retirement of a dominant leader, the only one most residents in the community have ever known? Perhaps the case of Jean Drapeau is instructive. But for about fifteen years before his departure, an increasingly sophisticated and visible opposition had been gaining momentum in Montreal. It had formulated policies, become familiar with city hall (some of its members were on council), and had some experience in building coalitions. In Mississauga, however, the *de facto* Hazel McCallion Party has held virtually every seat on council. Even if its members had grievances against the mayor, they almost never raised them in public. This is what has made Carolyn Parrish's advent as a municipal councillor so interesting to watch.

Stephen Juba often faced a hostile council in Winnipeg,[22] as did Ottawa's Charlotte Whitton[23] and 'Ruler of All East York' True Davidson.[24] Chicago's Mayor Richard Daley (Senior) stands as an example of what could happen after a towering leader dies. He was succeeded by inept mayors like Jane Byrne, and a chaotic political situation ensued. Eventually, a rather unstable but somewhat promising progressive coalition was established under Mayor Harold Washington.[25] It was cut short, however, by Washington's sudden death. After another few years of unstable, conflict-ridden local leadership, Chicagoans turned to another potentially dominant figure, Richard Daley (Junior).

The best result for Mississauga may therefore not be a sudden end to the McCallion era, but its whittling away by increasingly bold, better organized, confident, and broad coalitions. The 1973 reform movement overthrew the old guard within months of the movement surfacing. It was therefore immature, lacked political know-how, and was unprepared to govern. A sophisticated civil society, much less a 'parallel state,' had not been established. Analogous in some respects to the decade-long growth of the Solidarity movement in Poland, any urbane and progressive movement in Mississauga would require some time to mature within the shell of a gradually weakening old order.

It may now be happening. Taken aback by her Port Credit reception, and beginning to hear grumbling elsewhere in the city, but also looking at Mississauga's worsening financial situation, McCallion agreed in 2007 that it may be time to launch a conversation on the kind of city Mississaugans want.

Thus ensued the city's most wide-ranging public participation exercise to date. Thinkers, futurists, urbanists, and celebrities – people like Stephen Lewis ('Mississauga could become known as the centrepiece for the development of global citizens') and urbanist Ken Greenberg ('There is enormous potential here, but this potential speaks to a completely different way of looking at the world') – were invited to sessions to generate excitement. There were 110 community meetings and round tables. A special website averaged three thousand hits per day. Some of the feedback at the sessions was blunt: one representative comment envisioned a city 'that is more than just a place to put people. [It would be] a place that doesn't require a car to get anywhere. A place of art, not logos.'

Said another resident: 'Other than Square One, there's no reason to come to Mississauga.'

Even middle-class professionals were finding housing unaffordable. Students said they found Toronto more attractive. Mississauga should have 'lots of stores on the street and lots of people on the street.'[26]

The consultants organizing the exercise collapsed the thousands of ideas into eighteen planks that would represent for Mississauga a change of priorities. Neighbourhoods need 'personalities.' Density is good, if done right. Focus on small and 'creative' businesses. Make the needs of immigrants a local policy priority. Make transit an overarching priority – even if it hurts and even to the point of reducing the available automobile lanes. Redesign existing subdivisions to make it easy to walk from place to place.

'There is a stronger appetite for change than the politicians may realize,' consultant Jennifer Keesmaat told council's general committee.[27] But Mayor McCallion was not sure. True, the recommendations validated her support in recent years for densification (although, in contrast to the consultants, the mayor has tended to support the concept of high-rises surrounded by lawns, instead of the more eclectic and busy, not to mention interesting, low-rise but still-dense developments).

This is all good in principle, McCallion said, but when you start reconfiguring the city the protestors will come out. Yes, the reconfiguration may make economic sense in the long run. But in the short run it would cost the city money. That means tax increases.

With the consultants still at the microphone, McCallion launched into a rambling and somewhat confusing fifteen-minute address. It was a Hazel McCallion seldom seen in public – unsure of herself, vacillating in the same speech between one approach and another.

'We have to have courage,' she told her council colleagues. But would she have the courage herself? Perhaps the people would not be persuaded. She lamented how difficult it had been to get citizens engaged on other issues, like the former provincial government's property-tax pooling regime to force the suburban municipalities to support Toronto.

But pooling can be mundane. Its impact on the property tax is indirect. The 'Our Future Mississauga' process showed that people can get excited about designing a livable city. Perhaps we need to have a plebiscite on some of these issues, including tax increases, said the mayor. Her usual position – Streetsville excepted – had been that the politicians are elected to lead and should be permitted to do so. Now she speculated that maybe the silent majority would support paying more to bring about change and would help her ensure that the councillors do not become captive to 'vocal minorities.'

However, plebiscites can themselves be captured by shrill minorities. Perhaps the leadership required is a kind of deep 'animation,' leaders who are themselves long-term visionaries regardless of political cost, leaders who are patient educators, and leaders who are subtle cultivators of a new generation of visionaries at the neighbourhood and city-wide levels. Maybe such a leader could be McCallion herself. As Carolyn Parrish put it: 'Hazel McCallion is an icon. If anyone can convince the people, it's her.'[28]

Or maybe it is no longer up to Hazel McCallion. Maybe an aging icon who, for once, cannot bring herself to appear decisive is what Mississauga needs. Maybe this ambivalence, this gradual letting go, will provide both the breathing space and the relative stability to dream. Maybe it will provide the conditions that will allow citizens to come to understand the consequences of those dreams. The impetus and the responsibility for change could come from below.

But which politicians or groups will have the discipline and the methodical approach necessary to get the parallel structures off the ground? That is not yet clear.

11 Leadership Lessons

Like so many provincial cabinet ministers before and since, Gilles Pouliot thought he knew Hazel McCallion. She was the mayor who always seemed to be calling, demanding, and lecturing. If he had sometimes to hold the telephone receiver away from his ear, then he would not have been the first. Back in opposition after 1995, the New Democrat tried to sum up this municipal leader. The description: 'honestly dishonest.'[1]

This is harsh. Had it been applied to another honourable member in the legislature, it might have been ruled unparliamentary. It is also an ambiguous expression. How can one be honest and dishonest at the same time? Hazel McCallion would almost certainly never have *said* that she was dishonest.

Perhaps the honesty is a function of consistency. Perhaps she has been consistently dishonest. And yet dishonesty implies lying, as in advocating principles that you do not really espouse. To be sure, McCallion has not always championed the same causes or emphasized the same things. When the anti-developer reform movement was in ascendancy, she was a crusading reformer. When the public became cranky with politicians and taxes and wasteful spending, she gave voice to the disgruntlement. She could be so harsh talking about politicians that one would think she had forgotten that she was one herself. For a time, she could sound very much like a neoconservative. But she dramatically turned against this breed of federal and provincial politicians. She would revert to her posture of a generation ago, styling herself as an environmentalist and a champion of public transit and public services.

Pouliot had noticed the shifts and perhaps also the absence of a coherent, enduring, well-developed ideology.[2] McCallion's constituents had not made the same observation. They saw a principled and courageous mayor, the one authentic politician in Canada. Maybe, then, McCallion has been honestly dishonest in the sense that the people themselves have not been consistent. They have had mood swings. And 'they' have not always been the same breathing beings. Generations have come and gone. Newcomers have overwhelmed the old-timers. The seasons have changed.

And Hazel McCallion had decided to be a mayor for all seasons. She has been honest in grasping the moods and sentiments of her people, and in giving voice to those moods and sentiments even before many of the people have figured out how to give voice themselves, or collected themselves sufficiently to do so. She has gotten in front of the parades even before anyone came out for the event.

It has often been said that calculating politicians can play on fears. To describe McCallion as a fear-monger would be somewhat misleading. By the time fear has been instilled and installed, it may be too late to master a situation in a way that does not involve overreaching or unleashing forces beyond the leader's control. But the mayor of Mississauga has been remarkably adept at sensing unease and nagging insecurities, and their degrees, depths, and proportions at different times: about taxes, about community safety, about developers, about immigrants even. When other politicians would show up just for the photo, or sit on the stage, McCallion would mingle. A comment here, a snippet there – the more unvarnished the better – would register with her. It would somehow be processed with the hundreds, even thousands, of others she might have heard and received that week. This endless process of almost subconscious registration has been far more effective than would have been the most scientific of opinion polls. The polls might not be asking the right questions. They might not get a sense of the nuances or the ambivalence insofar as they concern the nagging and emerging insecurities.

Before the early 1970s many Canadians had seen the suburbs as 'utopia in the making,' the Canadian urbanist Pierre Filion tells us. 'The suburb was depicted as orderly, tidy, and safe by contrast to the central city, which was portrayed as chaotic, grimy, dangerous and poorly adapted to emerging realities such as growing reliance on the automobile.'[3]

But as much as Mississauga under McCallion has seemed politically sedate (even with a mayor who has been quite the character), as much as that orderliness and tidiness have seemed to characterize this upstart city's municipal decision-making, it has also been a place of nagging and emerging insecurities. At one time, it was making common cause with Toronto downtown reformers. At another time, it was embracing hard-edged tax-fighting provincial politicians, before rejecting them *en masse*. There should be dynamic leadership, yes, but do not disturb my peace and quiet. Show me a city on the move, but not in my backyard. Below the surface, there was always some malaise.

McCallion's very persona has been a kind of balm: the fighting matriarch, the grandmother to a young city (demographically young, too) going through childhood and adolescence, a city that had not yet found itself. She would be the soul of a city that seemed to lack one. She would be its historical landmark.

And here was a matriarch one could find and speak with – directly. Almost everyone in Mississauga seems to have a Hazel story: they claim to have run into her at a supermarket, at their church, at the hockey arena. They marvel at her incredible energy. Here is a celebrity who seems so real. And although conspicuous warmth and compassion are not part of her personal traits, she has inspired more than her people's respect and admiration. It would not be an exaggeration to describe the sentiment as love, the kind of love grounded in trust, familiarity, and security. Foibles and faux pas can therefore be forgiven or laughed off: 'Oh, that's our Hazel.' 'Say what you want about Mississauga, but we have Hazel!'

Like many parents, however, she has had emotional needs of her own. Some of her critics say that she is addicted to power. Why else would she stay on so long? Notice, however, that she has not often overreached. Her demands have not been so excessive as to seem dangerous to too many disparate interests at the same time. She has not sought higher office. True, she could easily have calculated that the office of mayor is one office where the incumbent is not hemmed in by advisers and media and opposition parties and powerful interest groups. But power-addicted politicians do not always make good calculations. For them, there seems to be more power in some other pasture.

And as abrasive as she has been in confronting other politicians, she has actually been a conservative crusader, not fighting on too many fronts at the same time and never really positioning herself outside the mainstream in what she is fighting for. Nor has she shown a desire to dominate the headlines every day. She has had the patience to wait and watch, to pounce, and then to consolidate. 'I am like a cat,' the master politician Franklin Delano Roosevelt once said. 'I make a quick stroke and then I relax.'[4] McCallion has not relaxed much in the sense of hibernating, nor was this what Roosevelt meant. Over a long political career, there have been many battles, to be sure. But she has picked them.

Although she is often able to rhyme off an endless succession of grievances, the actual running battles being waged at any given time have
been relatively few, and the mayor's own interventions quite calculated
and deliberate.

Perhaps McCallion's undeniable skills as a manager have been combined not with the insatiable needs of a power-hungry autocrat but
with a craving for affirmation, the kind of affirmation one gets when
being patted on the back at the Legion hall in the evening, and being
cheered the next morning by children at a Malton school when regaling
them with stories of her trips to India, the country of origin of many
members of her audience. She is by no means a spell-binding speaker
or the model of eloquence. But she is loud and confident as she delivers
a succession of one-liners on the subjects of the day. She is more humor-
ous in her speeches than she is in person. She'll refer to Toronto as Mississauga's suburb. She'll ask for forgiveness from certificate recipients
who have to be content with a folder rather than a frame: 'After all, we
run this city like a business!' She doesn't try to master phrases in other
languages to impress ethnic audiences. But she'll begin her speeches in
a way that would seem ridiculous coming from anyone else: 'As the
Polish mayor of Mississauga, I'm very happy to be here!' The crowd
laughs as it applauds heartily.

There is that intriguing relationship with 'my people.' On more than
a few occasions, I have seen McCallion arrive at an event looking and
sounding very tired, groggy even, only to be almost instantly trans-
formed, to come to life, when launching herself into the crowd of her
people. They sustain her not only politically but, it seems, emotionally
as well.

There has been at least one consistent McCallion refrain. 'I'm blessed
to lead a life filled with purpose,' she told a magazine writer in 2007.[5]
Unremarkable, standard political fare? Perhaps. But let us rewind
almost sixty years to Hazel Journeaux's AYPA presidency, to words we
have already encountered: 'Our lives can be wasted so easily if we allow ourselves to drift through life without an aim or purpose. We
become as drifting boats without helmsmen and there is every possibility that we will end up as driftwood on the shores of life's stream.'

It is impossible to know how much she reflected on those words
before putting them on record, but they tend to reveal something about
what she regards as a life well lived. Being a spectator on the shore is
the worst fate; helping on board a steady ship is better. But being the
helmsman is perhaps the greatest form of self-actualization.

What kind of helmsman? Some would say that a life of purpose means going against the current, even to the point of crashing onto shore in defence of a noble cause. For Hazel Journeaux, and arguably also for the politically seasoned Hazel McCallion, the stream continues regardless. The helmsman must stay afloat, steady the boat, keep it moving forward, make sure it is not beached. The helmsman is decisive but not reckless. If the stream starts to change course, the helmsman must take note, must be prepared also to change course.

If the helmsman is harsh and sometimes abrasive with crew and sub-ordinates, it is to ensure that, despite the delegation of tasks, there is ultimately only the one helmsman. The latter will invite comments from time to time, will venture frequently among the passengers, will personally ascertain the conditions on board. But once a decision is taken it must be efficiently carried out.

Hazel McCallion would have appreciated the bemused and im-pressed analogies of Toronto councillors after she managed in the space of days to get her council, without controversy, to give approval in prin-ciple in 2007 to the new 5 per cent infrastructure levy. 'Hazel can do it because she runs a tight ship,' said Denzil Minnan Wong of the Big T-O. '[Toronto mayor] David Miller's ship is leaking all over the place.'[6]

The boat is not drifting. It has a helmsman.

Hazel McCallion has known it to be true because her people remind her every day. They remind her, even if they do not use the actual words, that she is leading a life of purpose.

A Leadership Model?

The mayor of Mississauga will probably not be asked to teach a course on political leadership at the new Hazel McCallion Academic Learning Centre at the University of Toronto at Mississauga. Were such an oppor-tunity to present itself, however, she might say what she often says when she muses briefly on the subject. She might cite her mother's folk wisdom: 'If you tell the truth, you don't have to remember' or the more questionable 'Hard work never killed anyone.' She might point favour-ably to the unflappability and steely resolve of her idols, Charlotte Whitton and Margaret Thatcher. She might say – as she often has said – that her motto has been 'Think like a man, act like a lady, work like a dog.' She might even add that her only regret is that she did not enter public life sooner. If her mood on this occasion is somewhat introspec-tive, then she may acknowledge a fear that she has mentioned on occa-sion – that if she stops now she might not be able to get going again.

All this is thin gruel, however, in describing what is without question a sharp and shrewd political personality. Indeed, it is not easy to place McCallion neatly into a leadership typology. Although her ways tend to be spartan and her love of luxury limited (despite her zest for world travel, sparked by that trip to Oslo more than sixty years ago), her often bombastic demeanour would tend to disqualify her from the ranks of Benedictine ascetic servant-leadership. Nor has she been the crusader for a single cause. And unlike political scientist James MacGregor Burns's 'transformative' leader,[7] she has often tried to satisfy populist undercurrents without the painstaking cultivation of a higher level of public enlightenment.

Although we have observed that she has shown an instinctive understanding of the ways of Machiavelli's prince, it would not be wholly accurate simply to characterize McCallion as the stereotypical Machiavellian – the cynical and scheming leader willing to sacrifice all morality for the promise of power-wielding and an earthly immortality gained by impressive but not necessarily noble exploits. There has at times been a genuine streak of social consciousness. She returned from a trip to Tanzania moved by how HIV/AIDS was ravaging the country. Is there something we can do? she asked members of her parish, not insisting on putting herself at the front of this parade. They told her she should insist that every Mississauga resident donate at least a toonie. Call it 'Hazel's Hope.' About six hundred thousand dollars have been raised, and the money was handed over to World Vision.

McCallion really does appear to have drawn from a smorgasbord of leadership typologies. She has been highly visible and has spoken like a populist, but has not tried *constantly* to organize or inflame the masses. Populist crusades can take on lives of their own and run ahead of the leader. She has been almost fanatical in her desire to ensure that she will not be surrounded by a constant group of advisers, but instead gets tidbits of advice from multiple sources, including (indeed especially) citizens with no formal role or title.

Despite being well known for sometimes taking too many drinks, McCallion's lifestyle has usually been highly regimented. She knows that she must always appear decisive and sure of herself. At city hall and in government circles she has constantly admonished, but when addressing public audiences she has had nothing but praise for her listeners. Many a cleric has been dubbed 'my favourite priest,' many a youth leader labelled 'a future mayor' or 'future prime minister,' many a school given the moniker 'the best school in Mississauga.' The populism and the praise sometimes mask the lack of tangibles. The mayoral visits may come with a special treat – a small donation from the Mayor's Charity Golf Tournament. But city funds, or major changes in city operations, are quite a different matter.

But here again we must invoke the 'personality'of the people – even if the people be a poorly organized mass. The case of Hazel McCallion demonstrates the applicability to the political world of Thomas Kuhn's thesis on scientific revolutions. Kuhn, philosopher and historian, argues that scientific progress is not a steady, linear process. Instead, scientists in their various subdisciplines alternate between quakes and long periods of mere puzzle-solving. In other words, there usually is a basic consensus about organizing principles and certain theories or notions (even if they be groundless), and the subsequent intellectual energies are applied to particular issues that are not ground-breaking at all. This continues until the paradigm is unseated, which usually happens with great difficulty and after persistent attempts to subsume contradictory evidence into the old paradigm or overlook it altogether. The successful challenges appear to be sudden and generally come from outside the subdiscipline.

Of course, there will always be some who disagree with the prevailing paradigm or 'those who cling to one or another of the older views.' However, 'they are simply read out of the profession, which thereafter ignores their work. The new paradigm implies a new and more rigid definition of the field. Those unwilling or unable to accommodate their work to it must proceed in isolation or attach themselves to some other group.'[8]

In the case of Mississauga, a municipality that had previously been home to chaotic local politics and a sharply divided council, a self-assured, business-like leader gave rise to a new paradigm, which crystallized soon after McCallion's election and certainly after the 1979 train disaster. This paradigm can be summarized as follows: Hazel McCallion is an exceptional leader, wholly devoted to the city. The overwhelming mass opinion became self-perpetuating because anyone who thought otherwise was seen as neither credible nor rational. This was exacerbated by the dynamics of a large suburb, too large and scattered for an alternate view to be shaped by word of mouth but too poorly developed for extensive media scrutiny or powerful organizations with their own long-standing bases of power.

In the absence of a strong civil society, the McCallion paradigm gave dissenters no place for comfortable shelter if they wanted to remain active on civic matters. This, in turn, arrested the maturation of the local civil society, a maturation that might have progressed more quickly in the face of weak leadership and conflict. The obstacles are analogous to those described by Alexis de Tocqueville:

> The sovereign can no longer say, 'You shall think as I do on pain of death'; but he says, 'You are free to think differently from me, and to retain your life, your property, and all that you possess; but if such be your determination, you are henceforth an alien among your people ... you will never be chosen by your fellow citizens, if you solicit their suffrages; and they will affect to scorn you, if you solicit their esteem ... and those who are mostly persuaded of your innocence will abandon you too, lest they should be shunned in their turn.[9]

A variation of this observation may have been at play in Mississauga. Because local politics is limited politics, local civic activism is not often seen as fundamental to one's sense of well-being, efficacy, and identity unless one's own immediate surroundings come under serious threat. It is tempting, therefore, for a dissenter or concerned activist who senses that the mayor is very well entrenched to simply apply his or her talents and concerns to some noble cause that does not involve the mayor or the local government. The alternative is the monumental task of trying to persuade a scattered local public that has settled so cohesively on its approval, indeed its immense respect, for the mayor. This might explain why the few opponents of McCallion who have emerged into the open before now have tended to be extremely volatile in their approach, prone to the most intemperate statements. Their interventions, to the extent they are noticed, in fact reinforced the mayor's popularity by drawing sympathy to her.

Notice that an *individual* has been able to fill this pre-emptive role. Urban regime theorists, this merits your consideration. Regime theorists, who have come to dominate the urban politics literature of late, see stable local governance as the product of a coalition of organized groups with resources – usually money or votes. In the most-cited case, the Atlanta of political scientist Clarence Stone, it was hard to move anything forward if you were not in with the downtown business elite or the leaders of the African American middle class. They were the coalition. They had fixed resources; they needed each other.[10] But what if the resources are scattered? What if there is no downtown worthy of the designation? What if the voters are in disparate communities and

poorly organized and relatively new to the city? What if the city is in
the path of development anyway, without requiring grinding efforts to
attract it? What if it already has the 'empty' space in which to put that
development? This is not an uncommon suburban dynamic.

American social scientists have recently coined the term 'boomburb'[11]
to describe places like Mississauga, places that have seen major urban
sprawl in a short time, places that are large canvases and not tiny incorporated enclaves. But it might have been harder for McCallion to dominate an American boomburb. Although Canadian suburbs bear many
physical resemblances to their American counterparts, and although in
both cases political attitudes tend to be more conservative and municipal deliberations less overtly conflict ridden than in the old urban centres, the allergy to politicians has not been as strong in the Canadian
suburban context. If Mississauga were in the United States, or at least in
one of many states, it would probably still have a part-time council and
a part-time mayor. The city manager would be more publicly prominent. Its residents would not be consistently supporting a centrist political party. Referenda on tax increases or bond issues would themselves
be catalysts for interest groups, some of them no doubt rabidly reactionary, more reactionary than Hazel McCallion has ever been.

Perhaps the pre-emptive, overriding leadership of a Hazel McCallion
is what a large suburb requires at a critical point in its history. It is possible to imagine a more problem-plagued Mississauga: one where
developers ran rampant, where favouritism resulted in significant dis-
counts on development charges, where builders paved over all significant natural areas like the lands that have become the Mississauga
Garden Park and the Creditview Wetland, and where waterfront revitalization would be in its infancy. It could also be a place where reactionary ratepayers thwarted every perfectly reasonable development.[12]

But various leaders in the relatively weak business, arts, heritage,
and neighbourhood organizations have quietly expressed to the author
considerable displeasure about the city's direction. They have been
critical of the stagnation in culture and the arts, of the mayor's high-
handed and insulting tone when faced with the slightest public
criticism, of the lack of concern for the conservation of architectural heritage. I have been told, off the record, by more than a few civically
aware Mississaugans that the mayor's campaign to lead Mississauga
out of the Region of Peel was a wasteful diversion. McCallion's boast
that 'we have eliminated confrontation on council'[13] was seen as unfortunate, if not eerie, in a democratic polity. In how many large cities was

there almost no confrontation on council for more than a quarter of a century?

The otherwise articulate critics almost never raised their concerns in public. Here again we might probe more deeply the formidable rational and psychological disincentives to standing on the outside of a public consensus or to challenging a leader who has been described as 'an icon' and 'a legend.' Most dissenters have made the calculated decision to remain quiet and bide their time.

It was, of course, possible that McCallion's leadership could have unravelled in the face of some galvanizing event that caused latent concerns to rise almost spontaneously to the surface. The Creditview Wetland issue demonstrated that there was latent concern about the paving over of green space, a concern that was not finding its place in the public discourse. Had the mayor simply dismissed the complainants and allowed the bulldozers to proceed, the issue might have become a symbolic or watershed event. It might have unleashed accumulated frustration.

The downward spiral of New York's legendary but unaccountable 'master builder' Robert Moses began when he proposed to give over a small part of Central Park for a private development. The subterranean murmuring over massive dislocation because of freeways and other public works finally crashed into the public realm – over a seemingly minor matter with symbolic and emotional resonance. The leader's previously acclaimed achievements were now being reinterpreted as examples of planning gone awry and of an arrogant abuse of power.[14]

But the probability of a sudden paradigm implosion in Mississauga was diminished because such implosions need to be fuelled by publicity. In compact communities, like Streetsville, where Mayor McCallion had to align herself with a dense network of civic and community organizations, this can often be achieved by word of mouth. In such communities informal communications, such as calls to rallies, newsletters, meetings, and telephone and e-mail networks, can serve this purpose. Barring these networks, an aggressive and effective media would be indispensable in following up day by day and in generating new revelations and new investigations.

For this to have happened in Mississauga, the Toronto media would have had to have been animated and motivated to remain latched on to a controversial Mississauga story, something that has seldom happened. Thus far, as McCallion herself puts it, 'The Toronto media is not very interested in Mississauga – unless there's a murder.'[15]

Lessons for the Province

Without a large suburban canvas that could accommodate major new development on scattered sites, there almost certainly could not have been a Hazel McCallion in the dominant role that she has assumed as mayor of Mississauga. In the small suburban municipality of Streetsville – which had grown up around a historic old town – McCallion was forced to govern in coalition with the well-established progressive middle-class interests in that community.

But do small suburban municipalities necessarily harbour responsible municipal leadership? The worst elements of reactionary, insular suburban politics could probably be overcome in the Canadian environment, where even small suburban neighbourhoods can be ethnically diverse and where the traditionally strong provincial role can mitigate excesses. Perhaps smaller is better, although an optimal size probably is impossible to pin down.

How, then, aside from advocating unlikely de-amalgamations, should citizens concerned with the pursuit of equity deal with a municipal environment dominated by a generally tight-fisted mayor who is seen to have massive public support?

Provincial growth boundaries or land-banking forcing more intensification much earlier in Mississauga's physical and political development might have bred in it many of the challenges of mature urban areas. During the McCallion mayoralty, Mississauga was permitted to expand without facing the consequences. Developers were forced to pay their own way, the assessment base grew significantly, taxes were relatively stable, and intensification was very limited. This helped to allow the mayor to oversee what seemed to be an issue-less community and successfully to keep at bay those who would have brought new issues and grievances to the fore. Only recently, as the city runs out of room to grow, was it suggested – and McCallion herself was among the first to articulate it, after reviewing long-term fiscal projections – that 'we have created a monster.'[16]

Effective growth boundaries (and, potentially, the resulting higher price of land) *might* also force the designated growth areas to grapple with how to foster medium (rather than low) densities in a way that promotes vibrant and attractive neighbourhoods.[17] All too often the tendency has been to see density as bad; when suburban residents hear about increased densities they think of bulky towers. In the Mississauga context, few people realize that very attractive, pedestrian-friendly communities like Port Credit and Streetsville actually have higher densities than most of the other neighbourhoods in Mississauga. Forcing intensification before ecological or infrastructure breaking points are reached could also force communities to plan more intelligently and to compensate for higher densities by protecting natural and architectural heritage, allowing more mixed-use development, and placing a priority on public transit. It could, if implemented carefully, likewise force more creativity and sophistication in public-participation processes. Instead of the standard public meeting to react to proposals, charrette workshops using modern computer graphics and technology would allow residents to help design virtual-reality communities and see the consequences of low-density sprawl as well as the potential benefits of urbane, higher-density neighbourhoods.

Lessons for Local Activists

Organized citizen pressure can at least create some precise boundaries for a strong mayor, despite the enormous effort that is sometimes required. In a city whose leader is astute, efforts to alter the public pulse, or to cultivate a sophisticated web of public-interest groups to which even a strong mayor must be attentive, may bear results. After all, McCallion, as we have seen, has been publicly professing concern about the problem of homelessness, and this has helped to draw attention to the issue, even if she has not always been working vigorously on the file behind the scenes. It may be possible, therefore, to enlist strong, spirited, and persistent participation from the municipal government in support of a progressive urban agenda. Perhaps the mayor's stature and influence could be used as an asset. As the MP for Mississauga East said at a public meeting with the mayor present, 'Everyone who lives in Mississauga knows the prowess of Hazel McCallion. If she wanted to stop the runways and she put her mind to it, she could.'[18]

Maybe, then, concerned citizens should focus initially on long-term mobilization strategies and on convincing the municipal government to nurture the conditions that make constructive civic participation a natural part of living in the community. Under McCallion, at least until very recently, the municipality has been reluctant to do this. For example, it rejected in 1999 a recommendation from the Mississauga Crime Prevention Association that the words 'cultivate an ethos of civic engagement' be included in the city's revised strategic plan, arguing that this was already covered by a commitment to 'open and transparent government.'[19] Despite encouraging words, the city also decided against contributing any funds to the nascent Mississauga Community Foundation, which was very slow in getting started.

So the efforts will be difficult, but are there changes that would at once allow for the maturation of local civil society, ensure good government and competent administration, but also promote healthy and vigorous debates? Striking such a balance has been an enterprise that has bedevilled democratic governments for centuries. However, in large suburban municipalities such as Mississauga, the following may prove advantageous:

1. *Smaller wards*. None of Mississauga's wards encompasses one community of interest; large, arbitrarily drawn wards are the norm in Canadian suburbs, almost all of which have opted for small councils. There is no ward-wide consciousness, and the councillor and the mayor are the only people involved in civic affairs who can take a ward-wide view. This gives them a position of enormous strength relative to any community groups, which, if they exist at all, are organized on the basis of neighbourhoods.

In the case of Mississauga, smaller wards would also have the advantage of guaranteeing representation for some of Mississauga's relatively impoverished neighbourhoods, such as Cooksville, Dixie-Bloor, and Malton. This would increase the probability of electing progressive or left-leaning councillors who could help to generate different ideas about the basic principles on which the municipality is run. Historically vibrant, trendy, and pedestrian-friendly neighbourhoods like Port Credit and Streetsville might also have their own councillor, who would likely bring a progressive voice to council.

2. *Capacity-building for city-wide organizations*. Some of the few existing city-wide organizations have been helped by funding from the provincial Trillium Foundation and student-employment funding from Human Resources Development Canada. Funds should be allocated, however, specifically for civil-society building and advocacy. Community animation efforts – where local people are hired to help communities organize – should be targeted not only to inner-city neighbourhoods but also to assist in the political maturation process in outlying communities.

Western societies seem to have embraced narrow conceptions of activism: it is an all-consuming undertaking, or a reactionary outburst, or it is not done at all. Public and community engagement needs to be seen as part of a healthy, balanced lifestyle. Paul Rogat Loeb, in *The*

Impossible Will Take a Little While[20] and *Soul of a Citizen*, argues for such an approach, and has been credited with inspiring it in many communities. In a society fixated on instant results, wealth, and celebrity, the rediscovery of community as a positive force, rather than as a marketplace with the occasional 'not-in-my-backyard' flare-ups, will require considerable effort.[21]

A capacity for local research and the marshalling of intellectual expertise might make a difference. In observing first hand the mayor of Mississauga for almost two decades, I have noticed that she is impressed not so much with shows of force – she can usually sense the public mood on her own – but with firm, confident, well-researched arguments. She usually shows scorn for people who appear weak and, ironically, for those who seem to bend to her will. She actually relishes vigorous debate if it is based on facts and figures.

But she relishes it in private – and here lies the dilemma and also, no doubt, part of the reason why comprehensive local movements have had difficulty emerging. Cultivating participation and building cross-cutting interests almost certainly means the public airing of some grievances. But these risk attracting the scorn of Canada's most popular politician. The credibility and legitimacy of any movement would then be threatened.

3. *Elimination of the upper-tier level of government.* Although it has been suggested here that McCallion's crusade against the Region of Peel has caused some distraction and squandering of political capital, local advocacy for a provincial decision to dissolve the upper tier may produce some benefits. The elimination of the regional government would bring some debates about social services and childcare to the level of local government most recognized by citizens (in other words, the lower tier). It would force debates about progressive versus conservative priorities and would reinforce the political, as opposed to the administrative or 'business,' role of the municipality.

4. *Combining of organizational forces.* The existing civic organizations should come together in an Urban League of Mississauga, with the express purpose of functioning as a watchdog organization. The only precedent was the short-lived Mississauga Concerned Citizens, set up by resident Terry Harrison in 1979 after council voted itself a significant pay increase. But it never held formal meetings and fizzled out the same year.[22] It was a one-issue organization. As some citizens' groups in south Mississauga develop more sophistication, and as an aging population results in some retirees being able to devote themselves

almost full time to civic affairs, the prospects for a sophisticated citizens' think tank or advocacy group are probably now greater.

Nascent environmental and heritage groups could partner on a 'Walk Mississauga' campaign, whose starting goal could simply be to organize neighbourhood, historical, and nature walks on Sunday afternoons or on weekdays for school groups. This discovery and appreciation of the city up close, rather than from a windshield, would also expose some of the problems of urban planning and perhaps lead to a 'Pedestrians' and Cyclists' Charter' to govern development and redevelopment. This could help to ensure that amenities are within walking distance, that roads are designed to calm traffic and are not widened unnecessarily, that cherished landmarks and pleasant vistas are preserved.

5. *Neighbourhood renewal.* The decline of ratepayers' groups in the 1980s and 1990s was remarkable, and the remaining ones were serving mostly the wealthiest communities in the city. Gone were the likes of Albert Crookes, a citizen watchdog in the 1940s and 1950s for the working-class Lakeview community. His mission was not to run for public office or to embarrass the politicians but to keep the process honest. He appeared at almost every council and committee meeting. As late as 1982, Councillor Larry Taylor was able to encourage residents to join five active ratepayers' associations in his ward, all of them in areas that were not especially affluent: the Mississauga Valley Community Association, Meadows Community Association, Mississauga Core Community Association, Creditview Community Association, and North Cooksville Community Association. All of these now either are largely dormant or have been disbanded.[23]

Reviving neighbourhood stewardship, especially in less affluent areas, should be a priority for the Mississauga Community Foundation, which has hitherto been reluctant to undertake anything that could be construed as 'political.' The foundation could do what the city has been reluctant to do: pursue funding from the senior levels of government, the Cultural Spaces Canada Fund being a recent example of a source that could have been tapped, for neighbourhood-enrichment initiatives.

6. *Reappraisal of stringent, single-use zoning.* In recent years, as we have seen, some local planners have realized the value of multiple uses, of mixing commercial, residential, and institutional uses. The planning commissioner's 2004 recommendation for 'visioning studies' initially met with a cool reaction from the mayor. The recommendation seems to have been motivated by a desire to rethink orthodox suburban planning

practices. Of course, for more than forty years Jane Jacobs was advocating organic planning, narrow streets, short blocks, and a healthy mixture of the old and new. More recently, scholars like Pietro Nivola have advocated capturing the essence of London's 'high streets' or many of the Parisian *arrondissements* as a way of saving small businesses and ensuring the long-term viability of a local economy.[24]

The Port Credit and Lakeview groups seem now to understand these principles, and they have been able to keep the staff recommendation on the agenda and even, as we have seen, to get the mayor to realize that she had better not get left behind by an increasingly sophisticated planning discourse in some areas.

Lessons for Other Municipalities

There are other suburban municipalities that are entering development phases akin to what Mississauga was experiencing in the late 1960s and early 1970s. Vaughan and Pickering, for example, have been experiencing 5 to 10 per cent annual growth rates, and major conflicts are brewing over such issues as the Duffins Creek Agricultural Preserve and the ecological integrity of Boyd Conservation Area, which is threatened with a major road reconstruction. In one of his final public appearances before his death in November 2004, nationally renowned writer Pierre Berton (a resident of Kleinburg, a village in Vaughan recently overtaken by sprawl) told residents he was 'mad as hell' about the municipality's plan to push a road through an ecologically sensitive area to meet up with new subdivisions.[25]

In those municipalities, once dormant or boosterist local newspapers and groups are now on the trail of alleged corruption. Growth is becoming an issue. Slow growth or even no growth still appears as a viable option in these emerging edge cities. A more subtle indication of a brewing reaction to rapid suburban development is when the amateur local histories of villages or hamlets stop hailing 'progress' and start lamenting something that has been lost or seems destined to disappear. 'Nashville is fading,' writes Jim Maw in his history of a village in Vaughan on the edge of the suburban fringe. 'Gone is the general store, the post office, the railroad station, the church – meeting places where friendships and community spirit developed and grew. It has become the bedroom and labour pool for the commercial and industrial exploiters of the greater Toronto area.'[26]

But, like the pre-1973 old-guard politicians in Mississauga, the elected officials who are part of today's development regimes north and east of Toronto appear stubbornly unaware of the possibility that seemingly pesky and occasional protests can emerge to deal them a stunning surprise at election time. 'Once developments such as big box plazas come to town, other businesses perk up and take note,' the mayor of Whitchurch-Stouffville proudly told her local newspaper, describing not one but two massive commercial centres being planned just outside the town's quaint historic core. The rapidly growing town has not yet had a slow-growth reform council.[27] Meanwhile, the municipal denizens in York Region, including the regional chair and several of the mayors, were busy protesting the province's plans to establish a green belt that would constrain development in the northern parts of the region.[28]

For those suburban municipalities that have only recently been entering the reform phase, the Mississauga experience would appear to demonstrate that time and care must be taken to develop a sophisticated and pro-active coalition. A loose, upstart network of malcontents may hand the reformers a quick electoral victory but ultimately doom them and pave the way for pre-emptive, overriding mayoral leadership that is only mildly sympathetic to the conservation and aesthetic components of the reform agenda.

The reform movements in Markham and Oakville, which came to prominence before the municipal elections in November 2000, did not at that time win the majority of council seats or the mayor's office. In opposition, however, the reformers scored successes; the veteran mayors sought alliances with them on some issues. In Oakville, opposition councillors such as Allan Egar used the extra incubation time to rally neighbourhood groups to think beyond their parochial boundaries and about the development of the town as a whole. Neighbourhood groups, coalescing in 'Oakvillegreen,' have thus opposed vigorously proposals to develop greenfield areas north of Dundas Street, even while understanding that imposing such a growth boundary might encourage infill development.[29] By the time a reformist, Rob Burton, became mayor in 2006, the social-capital infrastructure seemed to be in place.

Although Mississauga is the largest of the Toronto-area suburban municipalities lying within the 905 area code, and although it is ahead of the others in terms of development, its experience of pre-emptive, overriding mayoral leadership may not be without precedent. There may be some food for thought for historians.

Unlike leaders of the Township of Toronto, Metropolitan Toronto's first chairman, Frederick Gardiner, was indirectly elected and may have derived some of his influence from a close friendship with Premier Leslie Frost. But like Hazel McCallion, he had a large suburban canvas, and indeed imposed subdivision charges over howls of futile protest from the developers. 'Gardiner built with order and stability in mind, even while claiming to give free enterprise the initiative,' writes Timothy Colton.[30] He was a post-reform leader in the sense that he governed in the period immediately following the establishment of Metropolitan Toronto. He had a new slate. This is analogous to the relatively clean slate inherited by Hazel McCallion after the old-guard development regime and the upstart reformers had both injured themselves seriously with their perceived excesses.

Like Hazel McCallion, Gardiner did not go radically against the current of either public opinion or the prevailing economic order. But by having a keen sense of both, and by exploiting the resources that were there for the taking, he was able not perhaps to go directly against the current but to widen the river and extend the valley. Thus, when he decided that Toronto must invest heavily in transit, and not only roads, so as to avoid the fate of Detroit and Los Angeles, he was able to foist this upon reluctant suburban councillors. Hazel McCallion's championing in recent years of Smart Growth and public transit, and her arguments that senior levels of government must pay special attention to *Toronto*, or else Mississauga will also fail, have been accepted by her suburban mayoral counterparts and her colleagues on the Mississauga and Peel councils. Likewise, Gardiner's 'arbitrary ceilings'[31] for expenditures, imposed to temper demands, deflect special interests, prevent excessive log-rolling on council, and avoid veering off course in the implementation of his agenda, worked because councillors saw minimal political advantage in being estranged from a business-like leader who seemed to have everything under control and who, despite his reputation for fiscal restraint, could still point with pride to a continuous stream of public works and amenities in the ever-growing municipality. The parallels with Hazel McCallion seem obvious.

The North York mayoralty of Mel Lastman (1972–97) also merits further study. There has been virtually no research, not even by amateur historians, on the recent history of North York or of Lastman's colourful and intriguing political career. It does appear, however, that the political phases experienced by North York during its rapid development parallel those of Mississauga. Between 1947 and 1967, North York's population mushroomed from 33,167 to 411,517.[32] In 1952 Reeve Nelson

Boylen, like Mary Fix's predecessors in the Township of Toronto, was blamed for huge tax increases caused by major growth. He was replaced by Fred J. McMahon, 'who put council meetings on a more business-like basis,' and Norman Goodhead, who forced the subdividers to pay extensive levies. With the large suburban canvas ensured (the basic infrastructure was in place) and with the developers bruised by the reputation for haphazard development and by Goodhead's policy, it may be that Vernon Singer was the first pre-emptive, overriding leader.[33]

After six years, however, the extremely popular reeve entered provincial politics and was succeeded by James Service, who appears to have tried to deal more collaboratively, rather than unilaterally, with the developers. The election of Lastman in 1972 may therefore represent the restoration of the strong mayoral leadership that is possible in a large, serviced, growing, post-reform suburb. And although not anti-development, Lastman was often seen as charting a course that was *independent from the developers*, first raising the ire of North York's many apartment developers and landlords when he advocated successfully, from 1973 to 1975, for provincial rent control.[34]

Towards a Setting Sun

When Mel Lastman announced in 2003 that he would not be seeking re-election as mayor of the amalgamated City of Toronto, no one was surprised. Indeed, many were relieved. Although he faced a level of scrutiny that no mayor of Mississauga will likely ever experience, his descent from glory followed a common pattern for veteran politicians. The descent was exacerbated in part by physical illness and a general sense that the mayor had become disoriented and had lost a sense of the city.

As this is written, Hazel McCallion remains energetic and alert at age eight-seven. She has a handle on the big issues. She remains a voracious world traveller, having never lost the appetite she developed on that 1947 overseas flight en route to Oslo. She is, however, showing some subtle signs of slowing down – losing her place more frequently on council agendas, sometimes straining to hear what is being said, no longer rushing to be in five places at once, occasionally seeming to doze off.

That said, a steady retreat while still firmly holding the office is by no means impossible for a mayor accustomed to being in control. Her persona looms so large over the city that the sophisticated public relations staff – of which there were very few until recently, their role having been more often than not played in person by the mayor – will pick up some of the slack. They know a great trademark when they see one, and for them McCallion is Mississauga's trademark. They have certainly been projecting her image of late. 'Together, we'll weather the storm!' say the bus-shelter posters of a shovel-wielding, parka-wearing mayor, appealing for cooperation after winter storms. Is it only about snow? 'Weather the storm.' 'A boat with a helmsman ...'

But as McCallion experiences more and more resistance on council, as those around her know that her era is years, not decades, away from its sunset, there are signs that she may not always be taking too well to the new friction. She has been alleging that 'backroom deals'[35] are being made to defy her. She is admittedly nostalgic for the old days of unanimity on council.

Her instinct here again is to be a scrapper – to take on directly the supposed authors of the intrigue – instead of a statesperson who gives the impression that she has long since outgrown such petty politics, an elder statesperson who prefers the national and international podium, an oracle for healthy and vibrant cities.

In many ways, such has been McCallion's whole political career: the statesperson instinct struggling to overtake the scrapper instinct.

The statesperson has not yet won. Perhaps there is yet time. 'The kindest of all God's dispensations is that individuals cannot predict the future in detail,' writes the Canadian political philosopher George Grant.[36]

Or as Hazel McCallion herself puts it: 'There isn't a road that doesn't have a bend in it.'[37]

Postscript: Writing Local Political History

If you have been to Mississauga, or even passed through it, then you probably have caught a glimpse of this property. On the north side of Highway 401, just west of the Hurontario Street interchange, you will have seen something that has almost disappeared from this suburban landscape. It's a farm. The large white barn, which in June 2008 burned to the ground in a suspicious fire, displayed prominently the name of the family Madill.

Almost hidden behind the mature trees, Ben and Marjory Madill hold forth, and hold out, in their fifty-year-old red-bricked farmhouse, built after fire destroyed the last one. The farm is surrounded by industrial development. If not for those trees, they would seem almost imprisoned behind eight-lane thoroughfares where there is never a lull in traffic. Their nearby Britannia United Church and its cemetery, barely spared by the merciless and ever-widening Hurontario, are often obscured by the tractor trailers that have pulled off the freeway for a double-double next door at Tim Horton's, a kind of contemporary, franchised, drive-through parish hall. The harried just-in-time suburbanites idling in those 'May I take your order?' lanes are probably too involved with their cell phones to notice the tombstones or to reflect on time and change and their own mortality.

The population of the small cemetery far outnumbers today's parishioners. In fact, regular services have ceased. But in a more reassuring example of the coming together of the old and the new, the trustees have been able to rent out the church to denominations that would have been unknown in these parts when the country shrine was built.

The Madills, mind you, were not able to hold out with everything. About ninety of the original two hundred acres were expropriated for the expressway in the 1950s. The 401 reached Hurontario Street in 1957 and was extended almost to Milton the following year. Land prices went up and the speculators soon showed up in droves. The Madills went into semi-retirement in the early 1970s when they finally sold all but six acres and used the proceeds to buy farms north of Guelph for their children.

At the time of writing, Ben, still in excellent health at age ninety-two, had given up his livestock but is still growing beans and making rope and helping with the Britannia schoolhouse, the one-room building that he attended in 1921–31. It is now run as a museum of sorts by the Peel District School Board.

And Ben Madill has been telling his life story to anyone who cares to listen. In recent years, more people have been listening. 'We have suddenly come alive,' he chuckles. They are being treated as rare specimens. They might be called 'living treasures' in those countries that have programs to designate *people* as well as buildings. But there is also a sense that their knowledge – analogous to the remaining native speakers of a dying language – could somehow prove useful as Mississauga settles down, as it looks for its soul, as it creates an identity that is based on more than dizzying growth, those ubiquitous drive-throughs, and its also ubiquitous and legendary matriarch.

Local history, as Ben Madill tells it, has many random anecdotes and reflections. Did you know that in 1912 this very farm hosted one of Ontario Hydro's first rural power demonstrations, and that the contraption brought to the site to perform the magic was called 'Adam Beck's circus'? Did you know that within living memory – Ben Madill's living memory – Hurontario Street was a dirt road that would simply close for most of the winter? Did you know that the place where Hurontario met Burnhamthorpe Road, where today the exquisite Marilyn Monroe tower is being built in Hazel McCallion's city centre, was called Payne's Corners and that you had to turn onto Burnhamthorpe in order to rejoin Hurontario?

Not surprisingly, Marjory and Ben Madill have met Hazel McCallion on several occasions. She showed up at their fiftieth wedding anniversary. Another time, they got a picture of her standing beside her car and its 'Mayor1' licence plate. But in their local history Hazel McCallion is not the dominant figure. They remember enough to put people in their place.[1]

Many historians would not give much credence to the perspective of Ben and Marjory Madill; their history is not the product of rigorous training; it is not scientific. Granted, history is not scientific in the sense of the 'exact sciences,' R.G. Collingwood concedes. But it is, he insists, nevertheless a science. A problem is to be identified, sceptical questions are to be posed, facts are to be discerned. The contextual and social underpinnings need not be excluded, of course, but there is a presumption that the trained historian will have identified the problem and will methodically attack it.[2] But is one 'problem statement' more legitimate than another? My problem may be 'to understand the McCallion phenomenon, to discern the historical-structural variables that made it possible, and to speculate on lessons learned for the governance of Mississauga and other municipalities.' The Madills' problem may be 'to retain memories and a sense of place as a way of coping serenely with astounding change.' Both histories have a place, both can be of service, one can learn from the other. Indeed, if more people had access to the Madill version of local history – if these living treasures and their physical imprint on the landscape were not hidden behind expressway on-ramps – maybe new residents would also find it easier to situate themselves in a larger and longer narrative of place. They might be less intimidated by the pace of change or the imposing public figures they encounter when settling in their new city. A group of concerned citizens could hold out in the face of immense pressure, to be eventually rediscovered and re-embraced, not unlike the Madills' experience. Maybe the development of civil society and enlightened political activism would come more easily.

The same can be said for the written record. Shortly after taking office in 1979 as the young CAO of the Region of Peel, Richard Frost became appalled that most records were being discarded when they were deemed no longer necessary for the conduct of business. He was dismayed to find virtually no papers in the regional archives from the office of the former regional chair. This makes everything vague and fleeting. 'The resulting anonymity undermines the whole idea of community,' Frost observed eloquently.[3]

Things have not become better since Frost made those observations. Local governments pride themselves on being closest to the people, but records from the federal and provincial governments are better kept and easier to access. By contrast, there are virtually no transcripts of local meetings (only relatively brief minutes). Committee meetings are not sound or video recorded. Council meetings are televised, but the local cable television station has discarded most of the tapes of those meetings and of the mayor's biweekly television program.

'Historians are prisoners of sources that can never be made fully reliable,' write Martha Howell and Walter Prevenier. 'But if they are skilled readers of sources and always mindful of their captivity, they can make their sources yield meaningful stories about a past and our relationship to it.'[4] It could be said that the uneven and often disappointing state of municipal records forces one out of complacency; it forces an attempt to be a 'skilled reader.' One must be patient in interviews and allow interviewees to meander into territory one may not have known about. One must be prepared to spend considerable time sifting through uncatalogued records that seem to be irrelevant, knowing that something very intriguing may turn up. One must stand back and try dispassionately to reflect on personal experiences in civic affairs. One must know that there will be a great deal of circumstantial evidence and that time must be invested to see if there is corroboration.

The process of developing historical accounts can be very subjective and impressionistic, as even Thucydides discovered in his famous *History of the Peloponnesian War*, the first known scholarly history. Why have certain facts been deemed germane and others not? What standards are employed to ascertain and verify evidence? Was corroboration sought where necessary? Is the evidence skewed because the writer interviewed some people and not others, or because certain primary documents were located and not others? Unassailable objectivity is probably impossible in this research.

As Clarence Stone has put it,

Judgement and subjectivity cannot be abolished [from history and social science]. In the cold light of experience, both theory and evidence are human constructs, inevitably imperfect and limited in their capacity to explain the world around us. No research technique can ignore that unyielding fact: even though judgement itself is sure to have shortcomings, no technique obviates its necessity.[5]

Or consider V.O. Key's landmark study of southern politics in the United States. 'Extensive interviews give the impression that these local potentates loom larger in Arkansas than in most southern states,' he writes.[6] It is very difficult, in some instances, to move beyond the 'impression,' but to render it inadmissible would be to dismiss some potentially promising scholarship.

Now consider the following impressionistic, anecdotal account by *Toronto Star* columnist Jim Coyle. It is difficult to quantify, but it is potentially of some value in understanding leadership and influence in the City of Mississauga:

The first clue that one is dealing with no ordinary mayor when dealing with Hazel McCallion occurs upon calling Mississauga City Hall to arrange an interview. A request to be put through to the media office to discuss same leaves the secretary baffled.

There is no media office, the woman explains. Requests for such audiences must be submitted by letter. In the fullness of time, there being no particular need for media exposure in these parts, no need to curry favour with journalists, no fear whatever of their wrath, a reply will be issued.

And who, asks an exasperated scrivener, still not getting it, makes the decision?

Oh, the mayor makes all the decisions here, sir,' the receptionist says.

Welcome to Mississauga, Hazel's world.[7]

A thoughtful writer would be ill advised to make sweeping conclusions based on random journalists' accounts, or on one survey of experts, or on an analysis of Planning Committee minutes. But recurring circumstantial evidence from these and other sources, especially primary sources, renders a 'conviction' more likely, and can initiate a healthy debate.

In general, in developing these historical narratives, I favoured primary records generated at the time of the events, followed by press accounts generated at the time, followed by post-event memoirs or personal letters, followed by interviews conducted by me. A fact reported by one interviewee and corroborated nowhere else was not dismissed summarily, but a subjective judgment was made about the closeness of the interviewee to the situation, any motives for bias on the part of the interviewee, and whether there may be indirect corroboration elsewhere.

I have had some immersion in the policy process in Mississauga, having served on various Mississauga and Peel task forces and boards, and as a part-time local journalist for eight years (1996–2004). Since 1990, when I became involved in civic volunteer work – my first direct exposure was as an executive member and later chair of the Mayor's Youth Advisory Committee – and long before I embarked on this project, I have been sitting through many council, committee, and neighbourhood meetings. I have interacted with local and regional officials on various projects, such as the governance of the Peel Children's Aid Society, whose board I chaired in 1999–2000; the restructuring of the Mississauga Crime Prevention Association; the conservation of historic buildings; and as a part-time journalist for the *Mississauga Booster*, where I worked while attending university.

Some political scientists are advocates of the immersion method, and thus favour according value to first-hand experiences.[8] To acquire additional insight, Robert Dahl's assistants found temporary jobs at city hall, helping him with his research for *Who Governs?*[9] Todd Swanstrom situated himself as an assistant in the Cleveland mayor's office for a year while researching Mayor Dennis Kucinich, and therefore had to gather observations as a scholar while maintaining professional loyalty to his superior.[10] Participant observation has formed the methodological centrepiece of Richard Fenno's career as a political scientist. Reporting on first-hand experiences, however, does require more care than, for example, citing an interview for which the interviewee has given permission to be on the record. Otherwise, the anonymity of subjects must be protected whenever information is gleaned outside of a public forum or without the source's knowledge and approval for the intended use.

Generally, my personal observations have aided in the formulation of hypotheses rather than conclusions. At most, the observations have served as evidence to corroborate or verify information and interpretations that surfaced in archival research, media reviews, and interviews. I hope that my own previous acquaintance with some of the Mississauga debates and personalities has not caused me to economize in the search for documentary research material and other data.

And I must remember that my acquaintance with the events, whether direct or acquired through sleuthing, is not the kind of acquaintance that Ben Madill on the one hand, or a recent immigrant to Canada on the other, has had with the events and with the public officials. If ever they were to undertake to sort through the evidence, or even to search for it, they might ask different questions, think to look elsewhere, or start with the premise that the characters are more or less imposing than their portrayal here.

One must therefore hope that a publication such as this one will serve as an appetizer rather than a last course, that it will prompt more digging, more questions, more critical examination of different notions of leadership and community, and that it will encourage more people to think of ways to get involved in their communities, however those communities are defined. Perhaps, then, in some small way, the political scientist and the historian can take satisfaction in having served the public good.

Notes

Introduction

1 The author was present at the meeting and recalls well the remark.
2 Hazel McCallion in Ron Duquette (producer), *Hurricane Warning: The Life and Times of Hazel McCallion* (Mississauga: Ad-Venture Sights and Sounds, 2001), video.
3 Jennifer Wells, 'Her Town, Her Rules,' *Toronto Life*, May 2000.
4 'Hazel McCallion: A Tough Act to Follow,' *The Seniors' Digest*, inaugural issue, Spring 2003, p. 35.
5 For a good account of the modern edge cities – with their head offices and industries but without old cores or downtowns – see Joel Garreau, *Edge City: Life on the New Frontier* (New York: Doubleday, 1991).
6 Frank Calleja, '2 opponents can't freeze tough "Hurricane Hazel,"' *Toronto Star*, 29 October 1985.
7 See, for example, 'Dobkin roasts development policies,' *Mississauga Times*, 12 September 1973.
8 Dave Cook, interview with author, 14 July 2004.
9 For a good discussion of regime theory, see Clarence N. Stone, 'Urban Regimes and the Capacity to Govern,' *Journal of Urban Affairs* 15:1 (1993).
10 Douglas Yates, *The Ungovernable City* (Cambridge, MA: MIT Press, 1977).

1 The Road to 327 Queen

1 John Westbrook, 'Seaside Stories: Remembering Port Daniel Summers' (unpublished manuscript, Port-Daniel-Gascons Library, 2004).
2 See, for example, Gabrielle Roy, *Le temps qui m'a manqué* (Montréal: Boréal, 1997), pp. 81, 87; and François Ricard, *Gabrielle Roy: Une vie* (Montréal: Boréal, 1996).

3 Register, 1886–1903, St. Paul's Shigawake, Leaf 87, Anglican Diocese of Quebec Archives, Bishop's University, Lennoxville.

4 Entries for 3 and 13 February 1885 in 1872–86 parish register, St. Paul's Shigawake, Anglican Diocese of Quebec Archives.

5 *A Century of Witness* (Centennial Committee booklet manuscript), chap. 1, pt. 1, in Port Daniel – Parish of Saint James fonds, Anglican Diocese of Quebec Archives.

6 Ken Annett, 'The Port Daniel–PEI Connection,' in *Gaspe of Yesterday,* vol. 8, 1994, Bishop's University, Lennoxville.

7 *Saint James Centennial News,* vol. 1, no. 6, p. 1, quoting the 'Macpherson Diaries,' Port Daniel – Parish of Saint James fonds, Anglican Diocese of Quebec Archives.

8 This is James Sweeny, with whom I conversed in December 2007 while researching the archives of the Anglican Diocese of Quebec.

9 *Saint James Centennial News,* vol. 1, no. 2, p. 2, Port Daniel – Parish of Saint James fonds, Anglican Diocese of Quebec Archives.

10 Index, Anglican Church Records, 1856–1909, p. 120, British Heritage Centre, New Richmond, Quebec.

11 *Report of the Incorporated Church Society for the Diocese of Quebec, 1908,* p. 121, Anglican Diocese of Quebec Archives.

12 Jo-ann Smith Gibson, 'Mayor says women should push ahead,' *Mississauga News,* 11 April 1984.

13 Margaret Grant Macwhirter, *Treasure Trove in Gaspe and the Baie des Chaleurs* (Quebec: Telegraph Printing Company, 1919), pp. 43–50.

14 Hazel McCallion, interview with author, 19 December 2005.

15 Macwhirter, *Treasure Trove,* p. 54.

16 Joan Dow, interview with the author, 31 July 2006.

17 Quoted in Ron Duquette (producer), *Hurricane Warning: The Life and Times of Hazel McCallion* (Mississauga: Ad-Venture Sights and Sounds, 2001), video.

18 Christa Brentnall, 'The Traveller: Margaret Best,' Alberta centennial oral histories, http://www.alberta2005.com/mbest.htm.

19 See Anglican Young People's Association papers, 1946–51, General Synod Archives, Anglican Church of Canada, Toronto.

20 Hazel McCallion, interview with author, 19 December 2005.

21 'Agreement – His Majesty the King in Right of Canada Acting Through Polymer Corporation Limited and the Canadian Kellogg Co. Ltd. and the M.W. Kellogg Company,' 1 October 1942, pp. 5–6, RG 28, Vol. 542, File 96–1, National Archives of Canada, Ottawa.

22 Matthew J. Bellamy, *Profiting the Crown: Canada's Polymer Corporation, 1942–1990* (Montreal: McGill-Queen's University Press, 2005), p. 55.

23 James Ferres, *The First Fifty Years: The Anglican Church of St. Michael and All Angels, Toronto, 1907–1957* (Toronto: Parish of Anglican Church of St. Michael and All Angels, 1957), Canadiana Collection, North York Central Library, Toronto, n.p. See chapter entitled 'The Fourth Decade.'

24 See, for example, *AYPA Monthly,* January 1947, in GS 75–104, Series 5, Box 46, General Synod Archives, Anglican Church of Canada, Toronto.

25 Arthur Murcott, chairman, Toronto Co-ordinating Committee of AYPA to the Dominion Executive, 2 February 1948, Correspondence, GS 75–104, General Synod Archives, Anglican Church of Canada.

26 'One of Our Staff – Hazel Journeaux, Assistant Business Manager,' *AYPA Monthly,* January 1947, op. cit. note 24.

27 Paul Griswold Macy, ed., *The Report of the Second World Conference of Christian Youth, Oslo, Norway, July 22 to 31, 1947,* first edition (Geneva: World Council of Churches, 1947), United Church of Canada Archives, Victoria University, Toronto.

28 William Wylie-Kellerman, 'Naming the Powers: William Stringfellow as Student and Theologian,' *Student World* 1, (2003), p. 28.

29 Hazel Journeaux to William Lyon Mackenzie King, 24 May 1947, King Papers, Primary Series Correspondence, Microfilm reel C-11038, MG 26–J1, National Archives of Canada.

30 'I Flew to Oslo,' *AYPA Monthly,* October 1947, op. cit. note 24.

31 Hazel McCallion, interview with author, 19 December 2005.

32 Hazel Journeaux, 'President's Message – Bible Study,' *AYPA Monthly,* April 1951, op. cit. note 24.

33 Hazel Journeaux to Mary Hill, chair, Leadership Training Committee, 24 July 1949. GS 75–104, Series 5, Box 48, General Synod Archives, Anglican Church of Canada, Toronto.

34 Hazel Journeaux to branch presidents, 9 February 1948, op. cit. note 24.

35 Hazel Journeaux, 'Farewell Message,' *AYPA Monthly,* May 1951. GS 75–104, Series 5, Box 51, General Synod Archives, Anglican Church of Canada, Toronto.

36 Hazel Journeaux, 'Aim,' *AYPA Monthly,* September 1950, op. cit. note 35.

37 Jack Guy to Hazel Journeaux, 13 November 1949, op. cit. note 24.

38 Hazel Journeaux to Jim MacLean, 28 January 1950, op. cit. note 24.

39 Hazel Journeaux, 'Dominion President Tells of Her Maritime Trip,' *AYPA Monthly,* January 1950, op. cit. note 35.

40 Hazel Journeaux, 'Let Your Light Shine,' *AYPA Monthly,* October 1949, op. cit. note 24.

41 Hazel Journeaux, 'Christian Citizenship,' *AYPA Monthly,* November 1949, op. cit. note 24.

42 'President's Message,' in Anglican Young People's Association, *AYPA Golden Jubilee* (Toronto: AYPA, 1952), National Library of Canada, p. 7.

43 Hazel Journeaux, 'Christian Citizenship,' *AYPA Monthly,* November 1949, op. cit. note 24.

44 Richard Ragg to Hazel Journeaux, 13 January 1950, GS 75–104, Series 5, Box 46, General Synod Archives, Anglican Church of Canada, Toronto.

45 Hazel Journeaux to Richard Ragg, 16 February 1950, GS 75–104, Series 5, Box 47, General Synod Archives, Anglican Church of Canada, Toronto.

46 S. Alexander, *Story of a Parish: A Jubilee History of the Church of the Good Shepherd, Mount Dennis, Anglican Diocese of Toronto, 1911–1962,* Canadiana Collection, North York Central Library, Toronto. The reference to the McCallion plaque is on p. 74. For an example of interaction with St Michael and All Angels, see p. 57.

47 See, for example, Jack Guy to Hazel Journeaux, 7 January 1950, op. cit. note 24.

48 Hazel Journeaux to Fraser Berry, Montreal Diocesan Council, 15 September 1949, op. cit. note 24.

49 Hazel Journeaux to Hazel Greenwood, international relations convenor, 12 May 1951, GS 75–104, Series 5, Box 48, General Synod Archives, Anglican Church of Canada, Toronto.

50 Mary Tasker, AYPA president, to Charles Piercey, VP, Ecc. Prov. of Canada, 7 October 1951, op. cit. note 24.

51 Mary Fix, Introduction, *A History of Peel County to Mark Its Centenary as a Separate County* (Brampton: County of Peel, 1967), p. 12.

52 Richard Harris, *Unplanned Suburbs: Toronto's American Tragedy, 1900 to 1950* (Baltimore: Johns Hopkins University Press, 1950).

53 For an excellent account of southern Ontario's cultural geography, see Thomas F. McIlwraith, *Looking for Old Ontario: Two Centuries of Landscape Change* (Toronto: University of Toronto Press, 1997).

54 See, for example, Robert M. Stamp, *Riding the Radials: Toronto's Electric Streetcar Lines* (Erin, ON: Boston Mills Press, 1989).

55 Donald B. Smith, *Sacred Feathers: The Reverend Peter Jones (Kahkewaquonaby) and the Mississauga Indians* (Lincoln: University of Nebraska Press, 1987).

56 In 2004 the Grange became the office for the Mississauga Heritage Foundation, which has amassed a considerable file on the building's history.

57 David Gagan, *Hopeful Travellers: Families, Land, and Social Change in Mid-Victorian Peel County, Canada West* (Toronto: University of Toronto Press, 1981).

58 See, for example, James Filby, *Credit Valley Railway: The Third Giant: A History* (Erin, ON: Boston Mills Press, 1974).

59 This is part of a longer poem called 'Pines Speak,' reprinted in Lorne Park Estates Historical Committee, *A Village within a City: The Story of Lorne Park Estates* (Cheltenham, ON: Boston Mills Press, 1980).

60 Dena Doroszenko, 'A Family's Legacy: The Benares Farmstead,' chap. 12 in *Mississauga: The First 10,000 Years*, ed. Frank Dieterman (Toronto: Eastendbooks/Mississauga Heritage Foundation, 2002); Daniel L. Bratton, *Thirty-Two Short Views of Mazo de la Roche: A Biographical Essay* (Toronto: ECW Press, 1996).

61 See, for example, David Somers et al., *Painted in Peel: The Peel Landscape by the Group of Seven and Their Contemporaries* (Brampton: Peel Heritage Complex, 2004).

62 Kathleen A. Hicks, *Cooksville: Country to City* (Mississauga, ON: Friends of the Library, 2005).

63 Tom Urbaniak, *Farewell, Town of Streetsville: The Year Before Amalgamation* (Belleville, ON: Epic Press, 2002), p. 163.

64 Thomas L. Kennedy, *Tom Kennedy's Story as Told to Ralph Hyman* (series of articles) (Toronto: *Globe and Mail*, 1960), p. 45.

65 The letter is dated 9 December 1952, file 1, MU 7111, F13, T.L. Kennedy fonds, Archives of Ontario, Toronto.

66 Introductory letter in *Suburban Life*, March 1946.

67 M.D. Lundy, *Memories of Early Days in Streetsville* (booklet issued by *The Streetsville Review*, 1957), p. 1, Mary Manning Collection, 1998.035, Series 4, File 5, Region of Peel Archives.

68 See, for example, Tom Urbaniak, 'Streetsville's grave robber(s): "Streetsville ghouls" haunted the village 65 years ago,' *The Booster*, 31 October 2001.

69 Streetsville Planning Board minutes, 26 April 1960, RG 1, 94.0063, Region of Peel Archives.

70 Streetsville Planning Board minutes, 28 August 1962, RG 1, 94.0063, Region of Peel Archives.

71 Planning Board minutes, 1965–6, 1996.065.025 AR, Box 5, Region of Peel Archives. For a good example of McCallion's frustration with the board, see the minutes for 13 September 1965.

72 Tom Urbaniak, *Farewell, Town of Streetsville*, p. 26.

73 See, for example, 'Editorial,' *Streetsville Booster*, 4 January 1966.

74 Ibid., pp. 32–3. See also *Building Program for Centennial Public Library in Streetsville*, 2nd draft, in 'Newsclippings and Correspondence' file, Streetsville Public Library Documents, Box 1, 1985.174 AR, Region of Peel Archives.

75 See, for example, Streetsville Planning Board minutes, 26 January 1965, 1996.065.025, Region of Peel Archives.

76 See, for example, 'Planning board recommends hold on apartment,' *Streets-ville Booster*, 10 January 1967.

77 Urbaniak, *Farewell, Town of Streetsville*, p. 27.

78 See, for example, Streetsville Town Council minutes, 4 March 1968; 3 June 1968; 15 July 1968; 1994.063, Box 3, Region of Peel Archives. See also '"Don't fence us in," say lawnbowlers,' *Streetsville Review*, 29 May 1968; 'Lawn-bowlers retain new lawyer,' *Streetsville Review*, 19 June 1968; Tom Urbaniak, 'A sport for everyone: Inside the Streetsville Lawn Bowling Club,' *The Booster*, 26 July 2001.

79 'Report study awaited,' *South Peel Weekly*, 5 October 1966.

80 'Regional government,' *Booster*, 3 July 1968.

81 Municipal Planning Consultants et al., *Town of Streetsville Boundary Study* (1968), Streetsville Historical Society Archives.

82 The boundary study was finally endorsed on 16 December 1968 (minutes, Box 3, 1994.063, Region of Peel Archives).

83 'Streetsville mayor to quit, assails amalgamation foes,' *Toronto Star*, 1 October 1969.

84 Urbaniak, *Farewell, Town of Streetsville*, p. 117.

2 'A Public – Not a Mass'

1 'Who or What?' *Booster*, 7 June 1966.

2 This is from a recording made by Bob Keeping and reprinted in Tom Urba-niak, *Farewell, Town of Streetsville: The Year Before Amalgamation* (Belleville, ON: Epic Press, 2002), p. 206.

3 E.L. Hoople, 'Town with a heart,' *Streetsville Review*, 31 October 1973.

4 Kilbourn uses this term in the article 'Reflections of a city hall clubman,' which appeared in the Toronto reformers' newspaper *City Hall* (April 1970). It is reprinted in *Inside City Hall: The Year of the Opposition* (Toronto: Hakkert, 1971).

5 See, for example, Kathleen Hicks, *Meadowvale: Mills to Millennium* (Missis-sauga: Friends of the Library, 2004), p. 232. See also Rob Roy, 'Old times on the dividing line between Peel and Halton,' *Streetsville Review and Port Credit Herald*, 29 May 1913.

6 Mary E. Manning, *Street: The Man, The Family, The Village* (Mississauga: Streetsville Historical Society, 1996), p. 96.

7 William Perkins Bull, *From Strachan to Owen: How the Church of England Was Planted and Tended in British North America* (Toronto: Perkins Bull Founda-tion, 1937), pp. 193–4.

8 See Mary E. Manning, *The Streetsville Cenotaph: A Village Memorial* (Missis-sauga: Streetsville Historical Society, 1992).

9 Hicks, *Meadowvale*, p. 113.

10 A ten-year perspective on the town's finances can be found in McGillivray and Co., *Corporation of the Town of Streetsville – Financial Papers for the Year Ended December 31, 1972*, in 'Streetsville Financial Statements' file, RG 1, · 1994.063.070 AR, Box 5, Region of Peel Archives.

11 Rudy Platiel, 'Streetsville fights for survival,' *Globe and Mail*, 21 April 1972.

12 Jim Robinson, 'Beehoo Industries faces shut-down, Streetsville economy debate builds,' *Mississauga News*, 10 February 1971.

13 These mayoral remarks (11 December 1972) are included in an appendix with the eleven-point Streetsville policy statement, included with the *Submission of the Town of Streetsville on Proposed Municipal Reorganization in Peel County*, 28 March 1973, TB 7, RG 19–131, Archives of Ontario.

14 This is discussed in the McGillivray Report, appended to Streetsville's official response to the provincial government, op. cit. note 13.

15 The eleven-point program was officially announced on 11 December 1972. It is included as an appendix to Streetsville's official response (28 March 1973) to the January 1973 provincial proposals for regional government (Streetsville Clerk's files, 1973, Region of Peel Archives, RG 1, 1994.063.070 AR, Box 5). See also Archives of Ontario, RG 19–131, TB 7.

16 'Streetsville helps itself,' *Mississauga Times*, 10 February 1973.

17 TB 8, RG 19–131, Archives of Ontario.

18 Letter from Darcy McKeough to H.H. Rutherford, clerk of Peel County, 6 November 1969, 'Regional Government 1969' file, Box 41, 1990.092 AR, Region of Peel Archives.

19 A.K. McDougall, *John P. Robarts: His Life and Government* (Toronto: University of Toronto Press, 1986), p. 229.

20 The formal application was dated 10 June 1970 (Archives of Ontario, RG 19–131, TB 7).

21 See, for example, 'Debate heats up over amalgamation in Mississauga,' *Toronto Star*, 6 April 1971.

22 See, for example, Mike Solomon, 'New region proposes Streetsville, Mississauga cities,' *Mississauga News*, 6 May 1970.

23 'Regional Government 1970' file, Box 42, 1990.092 AR, Box 41.

24 'Mississauga land "safe,"' *Toronto Star*, 13 May, 1970.

25 It was dated 4 January 1971 (TB 8, RG 19–131, Archives of Ontario).

26 Sam Clasky to Darcy McKeough, TB 8, RG 19–131, Archives of Ontario.

27 For a good summary of the SCORE campaign, see Rudy Platiel, 'Streetsville fights for survival,' *Globe and Mail*, 21 April 1972. See also Blake Goodings, 'SCORE,' *Booster*, 5 April 1972.

28 'Statement by the Honourable Darcy McKeough, Treasurer of Ontario, to the Founding Convention of the Association of Municipalities of Ontario,'

19 June 1972, in *Design for Development: Phase Three* (Toronto: Queen's Printer, 1972), p. 10.

29 Davis interview on CHIC Radio, 2 June 1972, Clare Westcott recordings, F 2093–8–0–40, Archives of Ontario.

30 Memorandum from J. Gardner Church, regional studies officer, to Ron Farrow, director, Local Government Organization Branch, 7 July 1972, TB 6, RG 19–131, Archives of Ontario. The list of alternatives is in TB 14, RG 19–131.

31 *Report on Local Government Reform East and West of Metro to Policy and Priorities Board*, 16 August 1972, p. 20, TB 14, RG 19–131, Archives of Ontario.

32 County of Peel, *Submission on Municipal Reorganization to the Ministry of Treasury, Economics and Intergovernmental Affairs*, 7 September 1972, Box 41, 1990.092 AR, Region of Peel Archives.

33 John Beaufoy, '2 towns don't want to be part of Mississauga's growth,' *Globe and Mail*, 30 November 1972.

34 Rudy Platiel, 'Plan for 3 regions west of Metro greeted with boos,' *Globe and Mail*, 24 January 1973.

35 'To all residents of Streetsville – From SPUR Citizen's [sic] Action Committee,' *Streetsville Booster*, 6 March 1973.

36 Urbaniak, *Farewell, Town of Streetsville*, p. 101.

37 Rudy Platiel, 'Plan for 3 regions west of Metro greeted with boos,' *Globe and Mail*, 24 January 1973.

38 See p. 3 of the Mississauga brief in 'Referendum re future status of town, 1973' file, Box 5, 1994.963.070 AR, Region of Peel Archives.

39 See, for example, John White to Ken Cameron, executive assistant, 17 August 1973, TB 81, F 4151, John White papers, Archives of Ontario. See also the text of White's speech to the Ontario Association of Rural Municipalities, 4 February 1974, TB 34, Range A, RG 3–49, Davis General Correspondence, Archives of Ontario.

40 *Comments Regarding the Submission of the Corporation of the Town of Streetsville on Proposed Municipal Reorganization in Peel*, 13 April 1973, TB 7, RG 19–131, Archives of Ontario.

41 This statement is in TB 9, RG 19–131, Archives of Ontario.

42 29 May 1973, TB 7, RG 19–131, Archives of Ontario.

43 For descriptions of Davis's appearance in Streetsville, see, for example, 'Premier loudly booed by Streetsville crowd, *Globe and Mail*, 15 June 1973; and 'Streetsville residents boo Davis over merger with Mississauga,' *Toronto Star*, 15 June 1973.

44 This letter is reprinted in the *Streetsville Booster*, 6 March 1973.

45 Elizabeth Colley to William G. Davis, 22 March 1972, RG 3–49, TB 9, Davis General Correspondence, Archives of Ontario.

46 Mary Manning to Premier Bill Davis, 1 March 1973, RG 19–131, TB 7, Archives of Ontario.
47 Desmond Morton, 'Politicians, powerful developers obstructed region,' *Mississauga Times*, 4 April 1973.
48 Tom Urbaniak, Farewell, *Town of Streetsville*, p. 179.
49 'Region to begin without fanfare,' *Toronto Star*, 27 December 1973.
50 This is from a recording of the meeting shared with the author by Bob Keeping.

3 Growing Pains

1 The reeve in question was E.D. Maguire, 1942. He is quoted in retrospect in 'People,' *Mississauga Times*, 4 April 1979.
2 Betty and Victor Pinchin, interview with author, 13 July 2004.
3 Pat McNenly, 'Toronto Twp sewer cost said $104 each for 20 years,' *Toronto Daily Star*, undated from August 1952, Mary Fix papers (uncatalogued), Ruth Konrad Collection of Canadiana, Mississauga Central Library. These documents were donated in 2003 to the library by Inge and Bill Cumberland and had not been catalogued at the time of writing. They probably eventually will be transferred to the Region of Peel Archives.
4 For example, Bill Bateman, interview with author, 15 August 2004. Bateman did note, however, that McCallion could be better-humoured at times.
5 This is from an unpublished, untitled political memoir written by Mary Fix in 1968. It is unknown whether the document was ever circulated. It is found in a blue binder labelled 'Miss M. McNulty's file' in the uncatalogued Mary Fix papers, Ruth Konrad Collection of Canadiana, Mississauga Central Library.
6 *Toronto Daily Star*, 28 November 1952.
7 See Fix's letter to Dunbar, 4 September 1952, Mary Fix papers.
8 Fix's correspondence with Graydon is in Vol. 1 of the Mary Fix scrapbooks, Ruth Konrad Collection of Canadiana, Mississauga Central Library. The scrapbooks are kept separately from the Mary Fix papers.
9 John S. Entwistle, *Provincial-Municipal Audit Report: Township of Toronto* (Toronto: John S. Entwistle and Co., 1952), p. 1.
10 Ibid., p. 78.
11 'Township's tax turmoil,' *South Peel Weekly*, 31 July 1952.
12 The result was a report, *The Development of a Canadian Municipality With Comments on the Assistance of Fellowship Studies*, United Nations/Technical Assistance Administration, 1953, Ruth Konrad Collection of Canadiana, Mississauga Central Library.
13 Adamson was often intriguingly contrarian. Although a noted landscape

architect and heritage conservationist, he could be cavalier about the aesthetic and social impact of suburban development. As he put it in one speech: 'The parking lot, the beastly parking lot of the supermarket is its supreme antithesis; the glitter and disorder of the "Kleenex" culture, the flash of neon and chrome ... These things should not cry out to us as the enemies of our achievement. We should not be guilt-ridden.' See Anthony Adamson, 'Improvement in Planning Procedure' (public lecture, 13 May 1964), in North York Planning Board and North York Community Council, *Public Lectures*, n.d., Moffat and Shore Architecture Library, University of Toronto.

14 Anthony Adamson, 'Wasps in the Attic,' unpublished memoir, 1987, Ruth Konrad Collection of Canadiana, Mississauga Central Library.

15 Brochure, 'The Planks of My Platform,' 1952, Mary Fix papers.

16 Cumberland, interview with author, 30 January 2004.

17 These remarks were made to me on a not-for-attribution basis.

18 Clarke Morrison, *The Growth of a City: Mississauga, 1930–1974*, p. 9, Ruth Konrad Collection of Canadiana, Mississauga Central Library. This short document was prepared for the Mississauga Judicial Inquiry in 1975.

19 Township of Toronto Building Report, 1965, in Mary Fix papers.

20 John S. Entwistle, *Provincial-Municipal Audit Report: Township of Toronto*, p. 18.

21 Fix papers.

22 The title of this section of the unpublished memoirs is '1954 – Industrial Promotion or Great Oaks from Little Acorns.'

23 Peggy MacKintosh, 'Public reaction shows industrial development, deputy reeve tells W.I.,' *South Peel Weekly*, 14 October 1954 – the quote is MacKintosh's paraphrase of Fix's statement.

24 Ibid., p. 25.

25 These statements are presented in an undated clipping in vol. 1 of the Mary Fix scrapbook, 1952, Ruth Konrad Collection of Canadiana, Mississauga Central Library.

26 See, for example, minutes, Development Committee, 10 November 1958, Fix papers.

27 *Globe and Mail*, 17 March 1959.

28 This section of Fix's unpublished memoirs, although without page numbers, is labelled 'Subdivision Control' (Mary Fix papers).

29 Ibid.

30 McNulty binder, op cit. note 5.

31 In Mary Fix papers.

32 Bill Bateman, interview with author, 15 August 2004.
33 'The Workable Unit of Government – What is It?' speech delivered by Mary Fix on CHWO Radio, 20 September 1958, Mary Fix papers.
34 1957 election pamphlet, Mary Fix papers; emphasis in original.
35 Unpublished memoirs, Mary Fix papers.
36 'Shipp corporation founder dies,' *Mississauga News*, 11 February 1981.
37 Kathleen Hicks, 'A VIP and Me,' *Mississauga News*, 3 July 1974.
38 See, for example, Harvey Molotch, 'The City as Growth Machine: Toward a Political Economy of Place,' *American Journal of Sociology* 82:2 (1976).
39 'Review of tax base' section, p. 3, Report on Development, 1960, by M.D. Henderson, treasurer; C.J. Madgett, assessment commissioner, W.J. Anderson, township engineer, M.J. Bacon, director of planning; D.J. Reddington, director of development; assisted by H.J.A. Brown, business administrator SPBE, A.P. Kennedy, manager PUC, in 'Subdivision Policy' file, PUC – Toronto Township papers, RG 3 90.0057, Region of Peel Archives.
40 Ibid., p. 1.
41 For an engineering report providing an overview of the municipality's capacity and plans, see Ontario Water Resources Commission, *Report on Water Resources Survey, County of Peel* (May 1963), Engineering Library, University of Toronto. See especially p. 165.
42 'Big Three' file, box 2, Harold Kennedy papers, 95.0015, Region of Peel Archives.
43 Peat, Marwick and Partners, *Mississauga Urban Development and Transportation Study: Development Controls* (Toronto, 1975) (available at the Toronto Urban Affairs Library), p. A-18.
44 See, for example, 'McLaughlin makes new offer: Town hall fire may lead to City Centre,' *South Peel Weekly*, 18 June 1969.
45 'Council looking at move to new city centre,' *Mississauga Times*, 24 August 1974.
46 See, for example, 'McLaughlin offer too good to miss,' *The Mississauga News*, 2 July 1969.
47 John Stewart, 'A City Hall in search of a site,' *Mississauga Times*, 12 February 1975.
48 Minutes, Mississauga Town Council, 23 February 1973 (Clerk's Office, City of Mississauga).
49 The often raucous debate is recorded in Ontario, Legislative Assembly, *Hansard*, 18 June 1973, pp. 3335–78; and 21 June 1973, pp. 3709–39.
50 Clarkson was also one of two councillors to vote against Mississauga's submission to oppose Streetsville's petition to the Ontario Municipal Board

to hold a referendum on the regional government scheme. See minutes, Mississauga Town Council, 21 March 1973, Clerk's Office, City of Mississauga.

51 Kathleen Hicks, *VIPs of Mississauga* (Mississauga: Mississauga Library System, 1998), p. 231.

4 'Big City Politics'

1 Tom Urbaniak, *Farewell, Town of Streetsville: The Year Before Amalgamation* (Belleville, ON: Epic Press, 2002), p. 168.

2 'Dobkin roasts development policies,' *Mississauga Times*, 12 September 1973.

3 'T'ain't so, says Chic,' *Mississauga Review*, 19 September 1973.

4 'Mayoralty race: Tense Dobkin versus Murray,' *Mississauga Times*, 19 September 1973.

5 Urbaniak, *Farewell, Town of Streetsville*, p. 172.

6 Ibid., p. 173.

7 'Population up 10 percent, high rise units triple,' *Mississauga Times*, 19 June 1974.

8 See, for example, Ruth Hussey and Judith M. Goulin, *Rattray Marsh, Then and Now: Articles on the Human Settlement and Natural History of the Rattray Marsh Conservation Area* (Mississauga: Rattray Marsh Conservation Association, 1990).

9 See, for example, 'Feeding frenzy,' *Mississauga Times*, 5 July 1972.

10 'Streetsville mayor "political warmonger," says conservationist,' *Toronto Star*, 8 February 1973.

11 The Mississauga Library System has compiled an excellent collection of articles on the 1973 election campaign. See *Mississauga Election Campaign of 1973 and Its Aftermath, July–December, 1973: A Collection of Newspaper and Magazine Articles* (compiled by Janet Morton), Mississauga Historical Anthology no. 18, Ruth Konrad Collection of Canadiana, Mississauga Central Library.

12 See 'Doctor's prescription for Mississauga – cut out high density,' *Globe and Mail*, 1 January 1974.

13 Ibid. See also Dobkin's advertisement in *The Mississauga News*, 19 September 1973. Not surprisingly, *The Mississauga News* put its editorial support behind incumbent mayor Murray.

14 Hubert Wolf, who went on to run for and win the Port Credit seat in the 1973 municipal election, wrote to MPP Doug Kennedy arguing that 'Port Credit is an example of rape of the environment, an example of financial bungling which caused a fiasco in our tax structure. Too many high rises, overpopu-

lation and wasteful, non-vital road construction got us deep into debts' 10 May 1973, copy in Davis General Correspondence, 1073, RG 3–49, TB 38, Archives of Ontario).

15 'Shipp backs Mississauga song,' *Mississauga Times*, 6 February 1974.

16 *City of Mississauga Socio-economic Review and Forecast: A Summary of Current Indicators*, June 1977, p. 30, Toronto Urban Affairs Library, Metro Hall.

17 Stevenson and Kellogg Limited, *City of Mississauga Management Review*, 1974, Ruth Konrad Collection of Canadiana, Mississauga Central Library.

18 'McLaughlin puts rap on gov't delays,' *Mississauga News*, 1 May 1974.

19 'Developer–Council rapport bad – McLaughlin,' *Mississauga Times*, 1 May 1974.

20 Dave Cook, interview with author, 14 July 2004.

21 Michael Solomon, 'New mayor for new city says high rise is development lunacy,' *Globe and Mail*, 1 January 1974.

22 Jim Robinson, 'Make way for development, Tories told at policy conference,' *Mississauga News*, 24 February 1974.

23 See, for example, Martin Dobkin, 'Why your taxes increased,' *Booster*, 8 October 1974.

24 'Resignations in Mississauga a concern at Queen's Park,' *Globe and Mail*, 11 November 1974.

25 Martin Dobkin, 'Mississauga staff exodus: Another side of story,' *Mississauga News*, 31 December 1974.

26 Martin Dobkin, 'Staff turnover – the numbers game,' *Mississauga News*, 29 January 1975.

27 'Dobkin charges "manoeuvring" in grant to region for study on city,' *Mississauga Times*, 3 November 1976.

28 Desmond Morton, 'Mississauga: The Story of a Municipal Investigation,' *City Magazine* 3:3 (February 1976).

29 Harold Greer to Stuart Smith, 6 December 1977, in 'Mississauga 1975–77' file, Research director's files, cont. 80, F-2093-1-3-7, David Peterson fonds, Archives of Ontario.

30 See, for example, 'Hydro Electric Commission of Mississauga v. City of Mississauga et al. Re Murray and City of Mississauga et al.,' *Ontario Reports* 13 O.R. (2d), 1977, pp. 511–27.

31 For an excellent collection of articles and commentaries describing the dramatic twists and turns of the ill-fated Mississauga judicial inquiry, see *Mississauga Judicial Inquiry: A Collection of Newspaper and Magazine Articles* (compiled by Janet Morton); Mississauga Historical Anthology no. 20, Ruth Konrad Collection of Canadiana, Mississauga Central Library.

32 This recognition was bestowed in 1978. See minutes, Mississauga City Council, 14 August 1978, p. 29–93.

33 The mayoral policy statement is contained in an appendix to Streetsville's *Brief on Local Government Restructuring West of Metro*, 30 March 1973, RG 19–131, Box 7, Archives of Ontario. The brief is also in the Streetsville clerk's files, 1973, 1994.063.070 AR, Box 5, Region of Peel Archives.

34 The CSMCA often worked with a few other residents' groups from south Mississauga, including the Meadow Wood Rattray Residents' Association and the Port Credit Residents' Association. See, for example, minutes, Mississauga City Council, 10 July 1978, p. 25.85, Office of the City Clerk, Mississauga City Hall.

35 This submission is in *Public Response*, Vol. 3, Ruth Konrad Collection of Canadiana, Mississauga Central Library.

36 Graham Fraser, 'Getting along with developers,' *Globe and Mail*, 3 March 1975.

37 Mississauga, Public Participation Office, Official Plan Task Force, *Interim Report on Public Participation in the Preparation of the Official Plan* (January 1976), p. 44, Canadiana Room, Mississauga Central Library.

38 Credit Reserve Association, 'Brief on Mississauga Official Plan Review,' in Mississauga, Official Plan Task Force, *Public Response*, Vol. 3, p. 72, Ruth Konrad Collection of Canadiana, Mississauga Central Library.

39 Ibid., Vol. 5, p. 162.

40 *Interim Report on Public Participation in the Preparation of the Official Plan*, p. 31.

41 John Rutherford, 'Mineola-Credit bridge proves unpopular,' *Mississauga News*, 3 June 1975.

42 Hazel McCallion, interview with author, 24 July 2004.

43 'Searle says Dobkin can't lead,' *Mississauga Times*, 3 November 1976.

44 Oral history interview with Nick Covelli of the Mississauga Heritage Foundation, 12 August 1997, Office of the Mississauga Heritage Foundation.

45 *1977 City of Mississauga Socio-economic Review and Forecast: A Summary of Current Indicators*, Policy Planning Unit, p. 37, Toronto Urban Affairs Library, Metro Hall.

46 Townsend advertisement, *Mississauga Times*, 6 October 1976.

47 'Election results still unofficial until Thursday,' *Mississauga Times*, 8 December 1976.

48 Larry Taylor, interview with author, 7 August 2007.

49 Mary Helen Spence, interview with author, 10 August 2007.

50 John Stewart, 'Let's sing, everyone!' *Mississauga Times*, 23 January 1978.

51 'Dobkin is the leader this city clearly needs,' *Mississauga Times*, 1 December 1976.

52 Mississauga Heritage Foundation interview.

53 Mississauga Heritage Foundation interview.
54 'SOTAS applauds bill on trees,' *Mississauga Times*, 23 November 1977.
55 See the list of committees in the advertisement (call for applications), *Mississauga Times*, 26 January 1977.
56 'Plan needs mayor's support,' *Mississauga Times*, 26 January 1977.
57 'Official Plan deadline urged,' *Mississauga Times*, 25 January 1978.
58 'Official Plan not set this year,' *Mississauga Times*, 15 June 1977.
59 'Flood plan protecting Cooksville is passed,' *Mississauga Times*, 2 February 1977.
60 'City to discuss more in private,' *Mississauga Times*, 15 March 1978.
61 'Press, but not public, will hear talks with developers on lot levies,' *Mississauga Times*, 9 February 1977.
62 'New talks begin with developers,' *Mississauga Times*, 18 January 1978.
63 See, for example, minutes, Mississauga City Council, 13 February 1978, p. 4.53, Office of the City Clerk, Mississauga City Hall.
64 'Councillors wary of man-made lake costs,' *Mississauga Times*, 9 February 1977.
65 'Council reaction is mixed to developer's housing plan,' *Mississauga News*, 2 March 1977.
66 'Development phasing proposals criticized,' *Mississauga Times*, 12 July 1977.
67 'Developer has plan to give city a new centre by 1979,' *Mississauga Times*, 3 August 1977.
68 'City adopts core plan report,' *Mississauga Times*, 17 August 1977.
69 John Stewart, 'The great challenge,' *Mississauga Times*, 17 August 1977.
70 'McCallion in race for mayor,' *Mississauga Times*, 18 January 1978.
71 John Stewart, 'Plan would mean 3.6% mill hike until '87,' *Mississauga Times*, 15 June, 1977.
72 'Budget talk time is now,' *Mississauga News*, 9 March 1977.
73 'Playground cutbacks,' *Mississauga Times*, 3 February 1978.
74 'Hazel slams grants,' *Mississauga Times*, 17 January 1977.
75 Indeed, planning commissioner Russell Edmunds asserted that phasing was the 'cornerstone' of the Official Plan. See, for example, John Stewart, 'Ministry won't meddle with decision on phasing,' *Mississauga Times*, 5 July 1978.
76 'Official plan "jeopardy" seen if phasing is dropped,' *Mississauga Times*, 18 May 1977.
77 Connie Rae, 'McCallion praises environmentalists,' *Mississauga Times*, 15 March 1978.
78 The vote at city council was 5–5 with Frank Bean siding with the reformers. See minutes, Mississauga City Council, 19 December 1977, p. 39.67, Office of the City Clerk, Mississauga City Hall.

79 Sid Rodaway, 'The Ron and Hazel show,' *Mississauga Times*, 1 March 1978.
80 John Stewart, 'New study urges road widenings,' *Mississauga Times*, 26 October 1978.
81 Willson McTavish, interview with author, 30 July 2004.
82 'Phasing debate sparks accusations,' *Mississauga Times*, 25 May 1977.
83 It is perhaps noteworthy, however, that McCallion was neither the mover nor the seconder of the resolution 'that the Phasing Policy as contained in the Draft Official Plan adopted by Council in December 1976 be reinstated, and the relevant text changes revised accordingly.' This resolution was defeated 6–4 along old-guard/reformist lines, with McCallion voting with the minority. See minutes, Mississauga City Council, 2 June 1978, p. 20.14, Office of the City Clerk, Mississauga City Hall.
84 See, for example, 'Hazel, mayor clash over lot levy issue,' *Mississauga Times*, 16 May 1977.
85 This can be found on p. 39.82 of the Mississauga City Council minutes, 19 December 1977 (Office of the City Clerk, Mississauga City Hall).
86 John Stewart, 'Searle fails to lift cloud over inquiry,' *Mississauga Times*, 21 December 1977.
87 Hazel McCallion, interview with author, 14 July 2004.
88 Ibid.

5 'My People ... Their Leader'

1 Jennifer Wells, 'Her Town, Her Rules,' *Toronto Life*, May 2000.
2 *1977 City of Mississauga Socio-economic Review and Forecast: A Summary of Current Indicators*, Policy Planning Unit, June 1977, Toronto Urban Affairs Library, Metro Hall.
3 John Stewart, 'Full-scale battle fails to develop,' *Mississauga Times*, 8 November 1978.
4 'Mayor says Searle left items off agenda,' *Mississauga Times*, 13 December 1978.
5 Frank Bean, address to Mississauga council, 26 May 1980, Records of the Regional Municipality of Peel, Office of the Chairman, 1990.061 AR, Box 4.
6 'Getting to know you,' *Mississauga Times*, 6 December 1978.
7 Penney Kome, 'Her Honor [sic] the Mayor,' *Homemaker*, June 1980. See also minutes, Mississauga City Council, 18 December 1978, p. 42.40, Office of the City Clerk, Mississauga City Hall.
8 'Little relief seen for the book budget,' *Mississauga Times*, 29 December 1978.
9 John Stewart, 'Hazel takes the grandstand,' *Mississauga Times*, 21 February 1979.

10 'What do you do with $1.35 million,' *Mississauga Times*, 7 March 1979.

11 Regional Council minutes, 13, 14 March 1979, Region of Peel Archives.

12 Debbie Irvine, 'Peel chairman resigns,' *Mississauga Times*, 25 April 1979.

13 Chris Zelkovich, 'The first lady's first man's first choice,' *Mississauga Times*, 28 February 1979.

14 See, for example, 'Curbs on chair posts,' *Mississauga Times*, 17 January 1979.

15 Sir Humphrey is the chief departmental bureaucrat and later the cabinet secretary (the most senior bureaucrat in Britain) in the fictional (but some would insist not entirely unrealistic) British sitcom series of the 1980s *Yes, Minister* and *Yes, Prime Minister*.

16 David Boesel and Peter H. Rossi, eds., *Cities under Siege: Anatomy of Ghetto Riots, 1964–68* (New York: Basic Books, 1971). Frost refers to this in the final bound volume of his correspondence, held at the Region of Peel Archives.

17 Hazel McCallion to city manager Ed Halliday, copied to CAO Richard Frost, 28 August 1979, CAO's Correspondence, 1979 bound volume, Region of Peel Archives.

18 R.L. Frost to R.F. Bean, 16 June 1981, CAO's Correspondence, 1981 bound volume, Region of Peel Archives.

19 R.L. Frost to R.A. Spence and J.A. Terrell, 18 December 1979, CAO's Correspondence, 1979 bound volume, Region of Peel Archives.

20 Legislative Assembly of Ontario, *Hansard*, 11 December 1979, p. 5407.

21 Ibid., p. 5408.

22 'Hazel' (editorial), *Mississauga Times*, 22 October 1980.

23 Address to Mississauga council, 26 May 1980, Records of the Regional Municipality of Peel, Office of the Chairman, 1990.061 AR, Box 4.

24 Ed Halliday to Hazel McCallion, 4 January 1979, 'Fritterfest' file, Box 2, Harold Kennedy papers, 95.0015, Region of Peel Archives.

25 '$45,000 lesson,' *Mississauga Times*, 29 November 1978.

26 Minutes of the Mississauga Community Festival meeting, 8 January 1979, in 'Fritterfest' file, op cit. note 24. This is consistent with McCallion's comments at the city council meeting of 13 February 1978, before she was elected mayor. She is recorded to have said that 'festivals are becoming a tax burden on citizens.' See minutes, Mississauga City Council, 13 February 1978, p. 4.4, Office of the City Clerk, Mississauga City Hall.

27 Harold Shipp to Dorothy McAnally, 12 January 1979, in 'Fritterfest' file, op. cit. note 24.

28 John Smithson to Dorothy McAnally, 12 January 1979, in 'Fritterfest' file, op. cit. note 24.

29 'Fitter Fritterfest favored,' *Mississauga Times*, 28 February 1979. See also 'Chappell to head festival,' *Mississauga Times*, 7 March 1979.

30 Mr Justice Samuel G.M. Grange, *Report of the Mississauga Railway Accident Inquiry* (Ottawa: Minister of Supply and Services, December 1980), pp. 147–8.

31 Regional Municipality of Peel, Department of Social Services, *The Mississauga Evacuation: Lessons for Emergency Planning*, August 1980, Mississauga Evacuation Internal Assessment, 1980 file, Records of the Regional Municipality of Peel, Office of the CAO, 1992.026 AR, Region of Peel Archives.

32 CAO's 1979 Correspondence, bound volume, Region of Peel Archives. Arthur Kennedy was the formally designated emergency officer.

33 John Yoannou, 590/CKEY, to Chief Doug Burrows, 19 November 1979, 'Thank you letters: Private industry' file, Box 2, Peel Regional Police, RG 13, Region of Peel Archives.

34 John Stewart, 'We get PCB reprieve,' *Mississauga Times*, 7 November 1979.

35 See, for example, 'Feds to test rail safety,' *Mississauga Times*, 7 November 1979.

36 Dave Cook, interview with author, 14 July 2004.

37 *Ontario Derailment: The Mississauga Miracle*, p. 43, 'Reports file,' Peel Regional Police, RG 13, Region of Peel Archives.

38 In 'Reported Offenses' document, General Correspondence, Box 1, Peel Regional Police, RG 13 1997.004, Region of Peel Archives.

39 See, for example, 'Exodus 1979 – the Canadian way,' *Toronto Star*, 13 November 1979.

40 'Great aspirations – MPP comes to our ade ... er ... aid.,' *Mississauga Times*, 28 November 1979.

41 The transcripts are in Emergency Mobile Command Unit meeting, Peel Regional Police, RG 13 1997.0064, Region of Peel Archives.

42 This is the 15 November meeting, p. 27, ibid.

43 7:40 p.m. meeting, 16 November, p. 3, ibid.

44 20 November 1979, General Correspondence, Box 1, Peel Regional Police, RG 13 1997.0064, Region of Peel Archives.

45 Joseph Scanlon, *Peel Regional Police and the Mississauga Evacuation*, Emergency Communications Research Unit, 1980, box 3, Peel Regional Police, RG 13 1997.004, Region of Peel Archives.

46 R.F. Bean to R. McMurtry, 22 November 1979, attaching article from *Mississauga News*, 20 November 1979, Box 1, Peel Regional Police, RG 13 1997.004, Region of Peel Archives.

47 Cal Millar, 'Dateline Mississauga,' *The Canadian Firefighter* 3:18, January/February 1980. On p. 7 is a photograph of McCallion with a crutch, pointing to the billboard.

48 Paul M. Moore, *Mississauga Times*, 28 November 1979.

49 Caroline E. Whitehead, ibid.

50 Dora Lucas, ibid.

51 P. 10,772 of the transcript in 'Mississauga Derailment, Mississauga Railway Accident Inquiry' file, Box 2, Region of Peel Police, RG 13 1997.0064, Region of Peel Archives.

52 Grange, *Report*, p. 87.

53 'A dangerous alliance' (editorial), *Mississauga Times*, 12 November 1980.

54 Publisher's note, 5 December 1981.

55 Mary Louise Birks, 'Off with their heads, the Queen cried,' *Mississauga News*, 19 December 1979.

56 President Wally Mach and vice-president Terry King, Port Credit Business Improvement Association, 29 October 1981, in 'Port Credit Business Improvement' file, Harold Kennedy papers, Box 5, Region of Peel Archives.

57 See, for example, Hazel McCallion to Harold Kennedy, 15 June 1981, 'Complaints' file, Harold Kennedy papers, Box 4, Region of Peel Archives.

58 'Mississauga Transit Investigation,' press release, 10 July 1981, 'Police' file, Harold Kennedy papers, Box 4, Region of Peel Archives.

59 'Developers say crisis near,' *Mississauga Times*, 19 September 1979. See also the fiscal-capacity amendments to the official plan moved by McCallion while still a councillor, in Minutes, Mississauga City Council, 2 June 1978.

60 Randall McQuaker, 'Hazel says Bennett best keep promise of election,' *Mississauga News*, 9 September 1981.

61 Regional Municipality of Peel, *Mississauga Residential Development Priorities: September 1980 Update*, Toronto Urban Affairs Library, Metro Hall.

62 '"Council must decide": Housing body advocates study of six key area,' *Mississauga News*, 17 October 1979.

63 Mary Louise Birks, 'Council did homework in secret session,' *Mississauga News*, 7 November 1981.

64 The judge's ruling is reprinted in full under the title 'Mayor Hazel McCallion has her day in court,' *Mississauga News*, 28 July 1982.

65 This is in Schedule A of the 1982 agreement, in 'Big Three Agreement' file, Box 5, Harold E. Kennedy papers, 95.0015, Region of Peel Archives.

66 Mary Louise Birks, 'Flood of homes expected in wake of land release,' *Mississauga News*, 4 November 1981.

67 John Stewart, 'Board chairman predicts "monumental problems" with city release decision,' *Mississauga News*, 4 November 1981; and John Stewart, 'Board ponders fight at OMB,' *Mississauga News*, 14 November 1981.

68 'Residents are the losers as city heads for sprawl' (editorial), *Mississauga News*, 4 November 1981.

69 'APPEAL vows to keep up fight,' *Mississauga News*, 7 November 1981.
70 16 December 1981, 'Big Three Agreement' file, Harold Kennedy papers, 95.0015, Region of Peel Archives.
71 Found in the 'Big Three Agreement' file, op cit. note 71.
72 Dave Cook, interview with author, 14 July 2004.
73 E. Halliday to Council, 10 September 1982, 'Big Three Agreement' file, op. cit. note 71.
74 Ibid.
75 Frank Calleja, 'Go-ahead given for residential areas,' *Toronto Star*, 6 November 1981.
76 Hazel McCallion, interview with author, 13 July 2004.
77 Mary Louise Birks, 'Mayor served with writ,' *Mississauga News*, 12 December 1981.
78 'Transcript of Cross-Examination of John J. Graham on his affidavit, 9 February 1982,' in 'Graham and McCallion' file, Box 4, Harold Kennedy papers, 95.0015, Region of Peel Archives.
79 The judge's ruling is reprinted in full under the title 'Mayor Hazel McCallion has her day in court,' *Mississauga News*, 28 July 1982.
80 'Conduct breach unacceptable,' *Mississauga News*, 28 July 1982.
81 Mary Louise Birks, 'Challengers are swept aside,' *Mississauga News*, 10 November 1982.

6 The Mayor-Builder

1 'Drapeau-like council sparks race,' *Mississauga News*, 20 October 1982.
2 '"Blatant" theft charges guide stormy session of council,' *Mississauga News*, 9 February 1983.
3 Mary Louise Birks, 'Storm sweeps council over "federation" idea for city ratepayers' groups,' *Mississauga News*, 16 November 1983.
4 Mary Louise Birks, 'Election expense list is incomplete,' *Mississauga News*, 6 June 1983.
5 'Jury calls for expansion of bylaw staff,' *Mississauga News*, 9 July 1980.
6 'The Raterman challenge' (editorial), *Mississauga Times*, 15 August 1979.
7 Ron Lenyk, interview with author, 16 August 2004.
8 Mary Louise Birks, 'World-saving role possible for Canada,' *Mississauga News*, 18 May 1983
9 'Blenkarn defends junket to Taiwan,' *Mississauga News*, 16 October 1985.
10 Royson James, 'McCallion sees error of her ways,' *Toronto Star*, 28 August 2002.
11 Zeidler Staples, planning consultants, *Mississauga City Centre: Summary*

Report, 1975, Ruth Konrad Collection of Canadiana, Mississauga Central Library.

12 Don Edwards, 'Bruce McLaughlin, "a frustrated developer,"' *Mississauga News*, 5 January 1974.

13 Sid Rodaway, 'McLaughlin plans to sell, sell, sell,' *Mississauga Times*, 5 July 1978.

14 'Be patient, McLaughlin tells critics,' *Mississauga News*, 2 July 1980.

15 See, for example, 'Ontario Securities Commission v. McLaughlin' (appeal, High Court of Justice), *Ontario Reports* 38 O.R. 2(d) 1983, pp. 390–403.

16 Pat Brennan, 'Square One Mall seized from Mascan,' *Toronto Star*, 20 December 1983.

17 See, for example, 'Luxury hotel planned for core,' *Mississauga News*, 7 July 1982.

18 See, for example, Brian Clark, 'Downtown plans give Mississauga new urban image,' *Toronto Star*, 23 November 1982.

19 Former councillor Dave Cook, interview with author, 14 July 2004.

20 John Stewart, 'Shipp's vow to cut density dismissed as "idle threat,"' *Mississauga News*, 8 September 1989.

21 'Downtown Mississauga' (insert), *Mississauga News*, 10 July 1981.

22 Ibid.

23 'Councillors vote to spend $76,000 on Italian marble,' *Mississauga News*, 20 October 1985.

24 City of Mississauga, *Mississauga City Hall: A Canadian Competition* (New York: Rizzoli, 1984), p. 152.

25 See, for example, Witold Rybczynski, *The Look of Architecture* (New York: Oxford University Press, 2001).

26 To acquire some formal training in the basics of urban architecture, I took a course ('Architecture in Toronto') with architect Paul Raff through the School of Continuing Studies, University of Toronto (May–June 2004).

27 'City Hall overrun with skateboards,' *Mississauga News*, 10 September 1995.

28 The mayor has made this comment in many speeches. Among them was the First Annual Mary Fix Memorial Lecture, hosted by the Mississauga Heritage Foundation on 18 November 2003. The recording is on file with the foundation. See also Joaquim Menzies, 'Mayor tells all at lecture series,' *Mississauga News*, 23 November 2003.

29 Jo-ann Smith Gibson, 'Mayor says women should push ahead,' *Mississauga News*, 11 April 1984.

30 Rick Drennan, 'Mississauga – The Place,' *Mississauga News*, 13 March 1985.

31 'Caller threatens to shoot mayor,' *Mississauga News*, 14 January 1981.
32 Frank Calleja, '2 opponents can't faze tough Hurricane Hazel,' *Toronto Star*, 29 October 1985.
33 John Stewart, 'Mayor says she drove car after "tipsy" TV show,' *Mississauga News*, 23 October 1985.
34 See, for example, John Stewart, 'No election surprises,' *Mississauga News*, 13 November 1985.
35 Albert Atkins, 'A question for electorate to ponder,' *Mississauga News*, 1 November 1989.
36 For brief overviews of the historical context, see chap. 1 of Credit Valley Conservation Authority, *Interim Watershed Plan*, vol. 8: *Mississauga Waterfront Program*, 1983; see also the introduction to Credit Valley Conservation Authority/Crysler and Lathem, Engineers and Planners, *Mississauga Waterfront: A Plan for the Development of the Mississauga Waterfront Sector of the Metro Toronto Planning Area*, 1972. The reports are available in the Ruth Konrad Collection, Mississauga Central Library. Some of the information was also gleaned from the author's interview with former long-time Mississauga councillor Harold E. Kennedy (11 April 2003).
37 There are differing accounts about the federal motives for proceeding with this particular project, although the author's interviewees who have first- or second-hand familiarity with this issue have suspected local favouritism of some kind. One version of events, articulated most assertively by former councillor Harold E. Kennedy, has it that the Liberal government of Louis Saint-Laurent believed that it could capture the Peel riding from the Conservatives, and that such an economic development project was part of the arsenal. Others, most notably former MP Don Blenkarn (a Conservative), assert that the then-Conservative MP, Gordon Graydon, was so well regarded on both sides of the House that he was successful in obtaining the project from a Liberal government.
38 City of Mississauga with Hough, Stansbury and Woodland Limited, *Port Credit Harbour Study and Waterfront Concept*, 1987.
39 Duane Blanchard, regional director, Small Craft Harbours, Fisheries and Oceans Canada, interview with author, 27 June 2003.
40 Harold Kennedy, interview with author, 11 April 2003.
41 Bruce Carr and Lorenzo Ruffini, Community Services Department, City of Mississauga, interviews with author, 21 March 2003, and interview with Harold Kennedy, 11 April 2003.
42 See, for example, City of Mississauga, *Vision 2020: A Draft Plan for the Mississauga Waterfront* (1990). For the status of the recreational harbour, see David Crombie's report *Regeneration: Report of the Royal Commission on the Future of*

the Toronto Waterfront (Toronto: Minister of Supply and Services, 1992), p. 279.

43 City of Mississauga, *Vision 2020*, p. 11.
44 Study Advisory Committee, minutes, 14 June 1985, p. 4, Port Credit Harbour file, Box 6, Kennedy papers, 95.0015, Region of Peel Archives.
45 Vicki Barron, former general manager, Credit Valley Conservation Authority, interview with author, 3 March 2003.
46 Carr, Ruffini, and McCallion (2003) interviews with author.
47 Don Blenkarn, 'M.P.'s update,' *Port Credit Beacon*, Spring 1987; Blanchard, interview with author.
48 Blanchard, interview with author.
49 McCallion, Carr, Ruffini, Kennedy interviews with author; also (current Ward 1 councillor) Carmen Corbasson, interview with author, 21 April 2003.
50 Blanchard, interview with author.
51 The feasibility plan is the Port Credit Harbour file, Box 6, Kennedy papers, 95.0015, Region of Peel Archives.
52 Box 7, Harold Kennedy papers, 95.0015, Region of Peel Archives.
53 Keyser has been the long-time chair of the city's Committee of Adjustment. The letter in question is dated 4 March 1988, 'Port Credit Harbour Study '89' file, Box 7, Harold Kennedy papers, 95.0015, Region of Peel Archives.
54 This is on p. 8n of planning commissioner Russell Edmunds' report, 'Federal Lands, Port Credit Harbour,' 6 February 1989, 'Port Credit Harbour' file, Box 7, Harold Kennedy papers, Region of Peel Archives.
55 McCallion's remarks are recorded on the tape *Trends in Real Estate and Urban Planning Legislation in Ontario*, Toronto Urban Affairs Library, Metro Hall. This is a recording of a 1986 conference. The host is not identified, but it may have been the Greater Toronto Homebuilders' Association.
56 For a good overview of Davidson's career, see Eleanor Darke, *Call Me True: A Biography of True Davidson* (Toronto: Natural Heritage/Natural History, 1997).
57 Darke, *Call Me True*.
58 Deborah Irvine, '500 oppose house plan,' *Mississauga Times*, 20 June 1979.
59 John Stewart, 'Sorokolit subdivision called "intrusion,"' *Mississauga News*, 7 October 1981.
60 Allan R. Hawryluk to Councillor Harold Kennedy, 1 December 1981, Box 4, Harold Kennedy papers, 95.0015, Region of Peel Archives.
61 Harold Kennedy to Fred Henderson, 4 November 1981, Box 4, Harold Kennedy papers, Region of Peel Archives.
62 *Trends in Real Estate and Urban Planning Legislation in Ontario* tape, op. cit. note 55.

63 Regional CAO R.L. Frost to regional chair R.F. Bean, 13 September 1988, CAO's 1988 Correspondence, bound volume, Region of Peel Archives.

64 'More!' (editorial), *Mississauga Times*, 12 September 1979.

65 *Trends in Real Estate and Urban Planning Legislation in Ontario* tape, op. cit. note 55.

66 Mississauga Planning and Building Department, *Population and Housing Study – 1985* (issued April 1997), Region of Peel fonds, RG 4, 94.047, Region of Peel Archives.

67 Steve Mahoney, 'Councillor's Corner' clipping, 13 August 1984, Box 5, Harold Kennedy papers, Region of Peel Archives.

68 'Mayor's property rezoned to allow single housing,' *Mississauga News*, 5 December 1984.

69 Gary Webb-Proctor, 'McCallion is accused of using smear tactic,' *Globe and Mail*, clipping from November 1988, LPC Scrapbook # 60, Local History Archives, Ruth Konrad Collection of Canadiana, Mississauga Central Library.

70 John Stewart, 'Erindale College botanist goes to bat for bog,' *Mississauga News*, 8 April 1988.

71 John Stewart, 'Naturalists go to battle to preserve ancient bog,' *Mississauga News*, 8 April 1988.

72 John Stewart, 'Swamp triggers call for experts,' *Mississauga News*, 21 November 1988.

73 'Council set to take new look at old bog's status,' *Mississauga News*, 13 April 1988.

74 Ibid.

75 Mike Funston, 'Mississauga hopes to stop destruction of ancient bog,' *Toronto Star*, 12 April 1988.

76 'Quotable quote,' *Mississauga News*, 18 April 1988.

77 Jocelyn Webber, interview with author, 3 January 2008.

78 Hazel McCallion, letter to residents, 15 September 1988, Eva Berlin personal papers.

79 The affidavits are included in *Report to the Ministry of the Environment* (compiled by the Erin Mills Residents' Association and others), 1988, Eva Berlin personal papers.

80 Jocelyn M. Webber, *The Vascular Plant Flora of Peel County, Ontario* (Toronto: Botany Press, 1984).

81 *Report to the Ministry of the Environment*, op. cit. note 79, no page number but first leaf.

82 The letter is dated 15 November 1988, and is included in the *Report to the Ministry of the Environment*, op. cit. note 79.

83 See, for example, letters, *Mississauga News*, 19 April 1988 and 8 June 1988.

84 'Battle for the bog,' *Mississauga News*, 13 April 1988.

85 John Stewart, 'Botanist elevates Creditview Swamp to much better class,' *Mississauga News*, 1 June 1988.

86 'Subdivision threatens historic bog,' *Toronto Star*, 7 June 1988.

87 John Stewart, 'Marshlands good for property values – survey,' *Mississauga News*, 17 June 1988.

88 Jo-Ann Smith Gibson and Vic MacBournie, 'Creditview bog supporters win the first round,' *Mississauga News*, 10 July 1988.

89 'Official rejects saving bog in Mississauga,' *Toronto Star*, 7 September 1988.

90 John Stewart, 'Creditview Swamp owner set to fight back,' *Mississauga News*, 15 June 1988.

91 Fall 1988 bulletin to members of the South Peel Naturalists Club, in South Peel Naturalists Club fonds, 2002.083, Region of Peel Archives.

92 John Stewart, 'Battle of the bog faces many hurdles,' *Mississauga News*, 22 June 1988.

93 'Mississauga delays decision on fate of bog,' *Mississauga News*, 8 September 1988.

94 John Stewart, 'Citizens get chance to have say on The Bog,' *Mississauga News*, 14 September 1988.

95 Mike Funston, 'Petition to save rare bog may be signed by 10,000,' *Toronto Star*, 21 June 1988.

96 John Riley, interview with author, 10 August 2004.

97 See Jim Bradley's letter to Philip H. Byer, chairman of the EAAC, 31 October 1989, in 'Creditview Wetland' file, Box 2, David Culham papers, 2000.061, Region of Peel Archives.

98 'Quotable Quote,' *Mississauga News*, 17 September 1989.

99 Editorial in *Mississauga News*, 21 June 1989.

100 See Jim Bradley's letter to Philip H. Byer, chairman of the EAAC, 31 October 1989, in 'Creditview Wetland' file, Box 2, David Culham papers, 2000.061, Region of Peel Archives.

7 The Mayor-Taxfighter

1 See, for example, Thomas Walkom, *Rae Days* (Toronto: Key Porter, 1994).

2 See, for example, 'It's official – mill rate frozen,' *Mississauga News*, 10 February 1994.

3 See, for example, 'Here's how much you'll pay in '92,' *Mississauga News*, 8 May 1992.

4 'We're going to get it,' *Mississauga News*, 14 December 1997.

5 'Councillors expect flurry of complaints over cutback on snow clearing,' *Mississauga News*, 16 September 1992.

6 'Loan replacing snow-shovelling grant,' *Mississauga News*, 17 December 1992.

7 John Stewart, '1.9 percent City tax hike on the table,' *Mississauga News*, 16 February 1992.

8 'City promotions budget under the gun,' *Mississauga News*, 4 March 1992. McCallion took a similar position as a councillor, moving in 1978 to cut the promotions budget. See minutes, Mississauga City Council, 24 April 1978, p. 14.53, Office of the City Clerk, Mississauga City Hall.

9 See, for example, 'Grants getting tougher,' *Mississauga News*, 28 June 1995.

10 'No surprises, few complaints as City doles out annual grants,' *Mississauga News*, 17 February 1993.

11 'Groups digging deep into their own pockets,' *Mississauga News*, 2 February 1997.

12 This has continued. The author attended a risk-management meeting for the 'affiliate' organizations on 16 February 2005 in the Mississauga Central Library. The groups (about forty were represented) expressed a strong desire for extended insurance coverage and a willingness to cover part of the cost. The affiliate groups are sports clubs, ratepayers' associations, arts groups, and other local organizations. Their affiliate status is gained by virtue of meeting some criteria, such as being non-denominational, not being primarily political, and having an annual general meeting. The decision to offer basic insurance coverage was made in 1978, before McCallion became mayor. See minutes, Mississauga City Council, 10 April 1978.

13 'City tax cut big news across Canada,' *Mississauga News*, 14 March 1993.

14 'Toronto blues not sung here by City Council,' *Mississauga News*, 1 March 1998.

15 Anne Golden et al., *Greater Toronto: Report of the GTA Task Force* (Toronto: Queen's Printer, 1996), p. 81.

16 Mississauga Sports Complex Foundation, *A Preliminary Concept for the Development of a Major Sports and Recreational Complex for the Residents of the City of Mississauga* (1977), Ruth Konrad Collection of Canadiana, Mississauga Central Library.

17 Indeed, in 1977 when the delegation appeared before council, McCallion, as councillor, was concerned about any sports complex's operating-cost implications for the city. She also opposed a motion to 'make a commitment in principle of financial support' to Mississauga's (eventually unsuccessful) bid to host the 1981 Canada Summer Games. See minutes, Mississauga City Council, August 15, 1977; Office of the City Clerk, Mississauga City Hall.

18 Diane Kalenchuk, past co-chair, Mississauga Sports Council, interview with author, 15 July 2004.
19 'Hall of fame request turned down,' *Mississauga News*, 13 February 1992.
20 John Stewart, 'City fitness centres under the gun,' *Mississauga News*, 29 January 1992.
21 See, for example, 'Pay hike now official,' *Toronto Star*, 30 May 1989.
22 See, for example, 'Mississauga best because of mayor,' letter to the editor, *Toronto Star*, 17 April 2004.
23 'City staff ordered on damage control mission,' *Mississauga News*, 14 December, 1994.
24 Ibid.
25 City of Mississauga, Economic Development Office, *Canadian Sport Fishing Hall of Fame: A Feasibility Study* (July 1989), Box 4, Harold Kennedy papers, Region of Peel Archives.
26 Jack Terrell to Michael Michalski, 20 April, 1989, Box 4, Harold Kennedy papers, Region of Peel Archives.
27 Ron Duquette (producer), *Hurricane Warning: The Life and Times of Hazel McCallion* (Mississauga: Ad-Venture Sights and Sounds, 2001).
28 Mike Funston, 'Mississauga councillor seeks protection for historic buildings,' *Toronto Star*, 21 February 1989.
29 'No funds for historic Streetsville church,' *Mississauga News*, 21 December 1990.
30 Minutes, Mississauga City Council, 13 March 1978, p. 9–20, Office of the City Clerk, Mississauga City Hall.
31 Gordon Kushner, scting principal, Royal Conservatory of Music, to Robert K. Johnston, director of realty services, City of Mississauga, 29 November 1988, in Adamson Estate '88 file, Box 7, Harold Kennedy papers, 95.0015, Region of Peel Archives.
32 Ian Scott, commissioner of Recreation and Parks, to Community Planning and Development Committee, 'Adamson Estate – Long-Term Use,' 10 July 1989, Clerk's Office, Committee Records, City of Mississauga.
33 See Harold Kennedy's notes in the margins of the above report, Adamson Estate file, Box 8, Harold Kennedy papers, 95.0015, Region of Peel Archives.
34 From 1975 to 2005, the Ontario Heritage Act gave only municipalities (not the province) authority to 'designate' properties for their architectural, historical, cultural, and contextual value and interest. Designation offered temporary protection (six to nine months). In 2005 new legislation gave the province authority to designate properties. Municipalities can now deny demolition, subject to appeal to the Ontario Municipal Board.
35 T. Julian, Report to Administration and Finance Committee, 9 May 1990,

pp. 1–2, in the Adamson Estate –1990 file, Box 8, Harold Kennedy papers, 95.0015, Region of Peel Archives.

36 The monograph mentions the Gatehouse on p. 13. See Anthony Adamson, *A Monograph on the Grove Farm, Port Credit: Prepared for the Regional Archives of Mississauga [sic] and Peel*, 1988, Ruth Konrad Collection of Canadiana, Mississauga Central Library.

37 A. Adamson to T. Julian, 15 June 1990, pp. 1–2, Adamson Estate – 1990 file, Box 8, Harold Kennedy papers, 95.0015, Region of Peel Archives.

38 Undated but date stamped by the Clerk's Office, 31 July 1990, Adamson Estate – 1990 file, Box 8, Harold Kennedy papers, 95.0015, Region of Peel Archives.

39 K. Peacock to T. Julian, 15 June 1990, Adamson Estate – 1990 file, Box 8, Harold Kennedy papers, 95.0015, Region of Peel Archives.

40 K. Peacock to T. Julian, 20 June 1990, Adamson Estate – 1990 file, Box 8, Harold Kennedy papers, 95.0015, Region of Peel Archives.

41 The letter is dated 22 June 1990 (in Adamson Estate – 1990 file, Box 8, Harold Kennedy papers, 95.0015, Region of Peel Archives).

42 Minutes of Public Open House Meeting, Adamson Estate Master Plan, 26 June 1990, Adamson Estate – 1990 file, Box 8, Harold Kennedy papers, 95.0015, Region of Peel Archives.

43 Both letters are in the Adamson Estate – 1990 file, ibid.

44 K. Peacock to R. Johnston, 27 December 1990, Adamson Estate – 1990 file, ibid.

45 P. 4 of the minutes, Adamson Estate (1991) file, Box 8, Harold Kennedy papers, 95.0015, Region of Peel Archives.

46 Robert Johnston, as recorded in the minutes of the Community Planning and Development Committee, 15 April 1991.

47 'Salvaging our history' (editorial), *Mississauga News*, 16 September 1990.

48 This was the Hepton-Sheard House, 7233 Airport Road (minutes, Community Planning and Development Committee, 4 May 1992, Clerk's Office, Mississauga City Hall).

49 The only post-1994 designation that appears not to have had the express consent of the owner was the one in 2001 for the Gold Medal Farm, at Lakeshore Road and Winston Churchill Boulevard. This property is owned by Hydro One, which apparently did not respond to the city's pre-designation letters.

50 This obvious gap in transparency finally became the subject of part of a report by the Mississauga Heritage Foundation to the city's Heritage Advisory Committee in July 2004. See the agenda package for the committee meeting of 6 July 2004, Office of the City Clerk, Mississauga City Hall. Fol-

lowing extensive meetings with the Heritage Advisory Committee, city staff, the mayor, and councillors, it was finally agreed to resume reporting to the Heritage Advisory Committee on threatened heritage inventory properties.

51 Tom Urbaniak, 'Historic landmark sacrificed,' *Streetsville/Meadowvale Booster*, 8 October 2003.

52 The opinion is contained in a letter from lawyer Scott Farley of Lang Michener Lawrence and Shaw to Library Board chairman Douglas Stanley, 10 May 1990. It is in the 1990 Library Board minutes binder, Ruth Konrad Collection of Canadiana, Mississauga Central Library.

53 Library Board minutes, 20 November 1990.

54 'Library board changes tune on City takeover,' *Mississauga News*, 9 March 1994.

55 See minutes, Mississauga Public Library Board, 29 March 1994, Ruth Konrad Collection of Canadiana, Mississauga Central Library.

56 John Stewart, 'Departing library board members decry City's power-play,' *Mississauga News*, 4 January 1995.

57 This resolution can be accessed by going to the 'Library–City relationship' link at www.mississauga.ca/portal/residents/libraryboard. The resolution was passed on 12 October 1996.

58 Staff's relations with the library board were described by Don Mills in his interview with the author and are contained on the library home page www.mississauga.ca/library. Proceed to the library-board link.

59 Helena Verveake (chair of the Streetsville Preservation Association) to Emil Kolb, 16 November 1993, 'Britannia Road widening' file, Box 3, David Culham papers, 2000.015, Region of Peel Archives.

60 Fred and Helen Rallings to Culham, 14 October 1993, 'Britannia Road widening' file, op. cit. note 57.

61 Minutes of meeting, Britannia Road Environmental Assessment, 14 February 1992, 'Britannia Road widening' file, op cit. note 57.

62 See 1996 statistics in Social Planning Council of Peel, *Portraits of Peel* (2003).

63 Peter Cheney, 'The humble legend,' *Globe and Mail*, 26 December 2007.

64 Joseph Chin, 'Hazel honoured with own rose,' *Mississauga News*, 14–15 April 2007.

65 The deputant was Mike Balkwill, executive director of the short-lived Affordable Housing Action Association. The editorial is in the *Mississauga News*, 18 April 1994.

66 John Stewart, 'Residents fight recommendation for a street re-named Gandhi,' *Mississauga News*, 22 April 1993.

67 Leslie Ferenc, 'How Hazel helped cool row over road,' *Toronto Star*, 6 May 1993.

68 Vijay Kalhan in *Mississauga News*, 22 April 1993.

69 'City council puts an end to Gandhi Rd.,' *Mississauga News*, 29 April 1993.

70 'Flag waving a lost cause for city councillors,' *Mississauga News*, 2 April 1995. See also 'No flags' (editorial) *Mississauga News*, 16 July 1995.

71 'Prosecute Bouchard for treason, mayor urges,' *Toronto Star*, 24 April 1995.

72 In 1978 McCallion supported a library board decision to keep the award-winning autobiographical film *The Naked Civil Servant* out of the libraries, despite objection by the since-disbanded advocacy group Gay Equality Mississauga. Minutes, Mississauga City Council, 27 February 1978, p. 6.7 and p. 6.52, Office of the City Clerk, Mississauga City Hall.

73 Thomas S. Mokrzycki, Commissioner of Planning and Building, Supplementary Report to the Planning and Development Committee, 16 June 1997, Office of the City Clerk, Mississauga City Hall. It is included with the agenda package for the Planning and Development Committee meeting held on 23 June 1997.

74 This sequence of events is outlined in a report from Commissioner Mokrzycki dated 29 April 1997 and appearing with the agenda package for the public meeting of the Planning and Development Committee for 20 May 1997 (Office of the City Clerk, Mississauga City Hall).

75 This comment is on p. 14 of the minutes of the Planning and Development Committee, 23 June 1997. For additional comments by the mayor see the minutes of the public meeting of the Planning and Development Committee held on 20 May 1997. Both documents are in the Office of the City Clerk, Mississauga City Hall.

76 Ibid., p. 6.

77 Minutes, Planning and Development Committee, 23 June 1997, Office of the City Clerk, Mississauga City Hall.

78 This funeral home was built in the area of Eglinton and Fallingbrook avenues (minutes, Planning and Development Committee, 15 June 1998).

79 This is on p. 19 of the minutes. The non-Muslim resident is Edward Joseph Barrington.

80 Culham's remarks are summarized on p. 10 of the 23 June minutes.

81 See, for example, David Culham to Sayed and Sabahat Huda, 9 July 1997, in 'Correspondence, 1997, May–August' file, Box 3, David J. Culham papers, 2000.061, Region of Peel Archives.

82 McCallion's dramatic language was even quoted prominently in the final

report of the Special Senate Committee on the Pearson Airport Agreements, 1995. At the start of chap. 2 (p. 21), she is cited as follows: 'I said if there is any delay in getting on with renovating terminals 1 and 2, then I would suggest you board it up.'

83 Special Senate Committee on the Pearson Airport Agreements, *Proceedings*, Issue 20, p. 10.

84 *Report of the Special Senate Committee on the Pearson Airport Agreements*, p. 111.

85 The group behind the early LAA testified on 25 July 1995. Their remarks are transcribed in the committee's Report 5.

86 McCallion's Senate testimony contains the reference frequently. It is also mentioned by the Conservative senators in their report (p. 44).

87 See, for example, John Stewart, 'Council says "no" to airport runways,' *Mississauga News*, 6 November 1991. Council claimed that its position was based on information from airport manager Chern Heed that aircraft would be flying one thousand feet over existing neighbourhoods. The same edition of the *News* had an editorial speculating that this 'turnabout' had everything to do with the upcoming election. 'Is this information really new or revealing?' the editorial asked with reference to Heed's letter.

88 Bruce Campion-Smith, 'City reverses itself: Pearson expansion will hurt east end, Prentice charges,' *Toronto Star*, 30 January 1992.

89 Airport liaison officer Marc Neeb presented on 27 January 1992. Canada, Environmental Assessment Panel Reviewing Air Transportation Proposals in the Toronto Area, *Public Hearings* (Toronto: International Reporting 1992).

90 See, for example, Bruce Campion Smith, 'Environmental panel in limbo at runway decision,' *Toronto Star*, 4 March 1992.

91 Raffaela Baratta, former co-chair, Council of Concerned Residents, interview with author, 6 December 2002.

92 Many residents were suspicious of how committed Prentice really was to their cause. She faced tough questions at some public meetings. When interviewing the councillor (10 February 2003), I asked why it was that the city of Etobicoke opposed the runways while Mississauga did not take such a strong stand. Prentice replied that Etobicoke based its position on 'politics,' while Mississauga had the interests of the whole city in mind.' However, her public position was essentially the same as Etobicoke's.

93 Prentice appeared on 27 January 1992 (*Hearings*, op. cit. note 86). See the panel's transcripts for that day.

94 Prentice, interview with author, 10 February 2003.

95 See Emil V. Kolb (Peel Regional Chair), 'Regional Chairman's Task Force

on Establishing a Local Airport Authority' (Memo to members of Peel Regional Council), 19 November 1992. Raffaela Barratta (past co-chair, Council of Concerned Residents), personal papers.

96 Valo lasted as chair until shortly after the 1996 ground lease took effect. He was then offered a job by Turpen as the airport's vice-president of legal services. He therefore resigned as chair to take the new position. Within a few months, he had suddenly departed without any explanation being offered by the GTAA.

97 See the Senate Committee's transcripts for 19 September 1995, when Corbeil testified at length.

98 See, for example, Leslie Ferenc, 'City won't name staff to residents' airport group,' *Toronto Star*, 25 February 1993.

99 John Stewart, 'Oops – Mail snafu delivers airport deal to expansion foes,' *Mississauga News*, 3 October 1993.

100 See, for example, Steve Pecar, 'City cuts deal on runways, opponents say it's a betrayal,' *Mississauga News*, 15 July 1993.

101 'Privatization won't cost Mississauga revenue, Corbeil vows,' *Mississauga News*, 19 October 1993. See also McCallion's testimony to the Senate Committee.

102 McCallion told the author that she could not recall why the city finally dropped the Toronto Island condition. But in her testimony to the Senate Committee, she stated that this was done 'only very reluctantly,' after it was clear that it would make no impression on the new government. Larry Petovello, the city's director of economic development, who was once very active on airport issues, believes that the cold shoulder from the federal government was the direct result of the Toronto business community's new-found influence and its determination not to allow Hazel McCallion to have much influence over the airport (interview, 10 January 2003).

103 Hazel McCallion, interview with author, 13 July 2004.

104 Willson McTavish, interview with author, 20 July 2004.

105 'City Manager' file, David J. Culham papers, 2000.061, Box 4, Region of Peel Archives.

106 See, for example, Eva Chui, 'New arts centre will be Mississauga's "coming of age,"' *Toronto Star*, 9 December 1986.

107 Mississauga Living Arts Centre minutes, 24 February 1988, Willson McTavish personal papers.

108 'Overview and Recommendations of the Board of Directors of the Mississauga Living Arts Centre concerning the Feasibility Study and Report of Frank Wolman and Associates Inc.,' (n.d.), p. 10, Willson McTavish personal papers.

109 Mississauga Living Arts Centre minutes, 25 July 1990, Willson McTavish personal papers.
110 See, for example, Hazel McCallion to Willson McTavish, 27 September 1990, Willson McTavish personal papers.
111 McTavish, interview with author, 20 July 2004.
112 McTavish to McCallion, 9 October 1990, Willson McTavish personal papers.
113 Steve Pecar, 'Mayor looks to England for City's arts centre,' *Mississauga News*, 15 April 1991.
114 McTavish to Bruce Heyland, 10 September 1991, Willson McTavish personal papers.
115 Ibid.
116 Living Arts Centre file, Ruth Konrad Collection of Canadiana, Mississauga Central Library.
117 See, for example, McTavish's letter to *Mississauga News* publisher Ron Lenyk and editor Mike Toth, 17 July 1991, Ruth Konrad Collection of Canadiana, Mississauga Central Library.
118 'Mississauga – A step forward and back,' *Toronto Star*, 4 October 1997.
119 Contained in the compendium of individual comments by members of the board of directors, Willson McTavish personal papers.
120 'Second place is better in this case,' *Mississauga News*, 24 November 1995.
121 'The Living Arts Centre – The Dream Comes True,' essay in 1997 inaugural program, pp. 8–9, Living Arts Centre file, Ruth Konrad Collection of Canadiana, Mississauga Central Library.
122 Alyssa Stuart, 'Bank backs arts centre,' *Mississauga News*, 7 April 1995.
123 Jean Sinclair, chair, Mississauga Arts Council, to Willson McTavish, 21 March 1989, Willson McTavish personal papers. (See also Willson McTavish's response, dated 5 April 1989.)

8 The Mayor–Legacy-Maker

1 In 1996 the author came to work part-time at *The Booster*, while attending university, and records these observations from his recollection.
2 Report on Participation, *Draft City Plan*, 1994, p. 2, City of Mississauga Planning and Development Department records, Mississauga City Hall.
3 Ibid., p. 4.
4 Ibid.
5 *The Land Economist*, Summer 1994, p. 5.
6 See, for example, 'Lower standards employment equity myth,' *Mississauga News*, 22 February 1994.

7 John Stewart, 'UDI not backing down in fight with McCallion,' *Mississauga News*, 18 December 1996.

8 The city's description of its reaction can be found at www.cityofmississauga .ca/CORPSVCS/COMMUNIC/HTML/press/Issues/debc hrgs.htm.

9 See *Hansard* for the Legislative Assembly of Ontario's Standing Committee for Resources Development, 24 March 1997, www.ontla.on.ca/hansard/ committee/debates/36_parl/session1/resdev /r041.htm; there are no page or line numbers in this document.

10 Ibid.

11 Mr Justice Harry Waisberg, *Report of the Royal Commission on Certain Sectors of the Building Industry* (Toronto: Queen's Printer, 1973), p. 113.

12 'Boards welcome city help,' *Mississauga News*, 22 July 1998; and John Stewart, 'Developers set to build schools,' *Mississauga News*, 19 August 1998.

13 Decision 0363 by OMB member P.K. Wyger, 19 February 2004, File PL970870, Ontario Municipal Board, p. 23.

14 I noted McCallion's uncompromising position, contrasted with Carlson's clumsy equivocation, at the meeting of the city's Planning and Development Committee on 26 February 2002. See also Tom Urbaniak, 'Councillors, residents concerned about Canada Brick plans,' *Streetsville/Meadowvale Booster*, 5 March 2002.

15 Minutes, Planning and Development Committee, 19 October 1998, Office of the City Clerk, Mississauga City Hall.

16 Thomas S. Mokrzycki, Commissioner of Planning and Building, City of Mississauga, *Report to the Planning and Development Committee – File OZ 97/ 014 W6*, 26 February 2002. See also 'Jannock Ltd.' file, Box 3, David Culham papers, 2000.061, Region of Peel Archives.

17 See p. 20 of the decision, op. cit. note 13.

18 'LAC CEO resigns, city manager takes over,' *Mississauga News*, 3 September 1997.

19 Living Arts Centre file, Ruth Konrad Collection of Canadiana, Mississauga Central Library.

20 Editorial, 8 October 1997.

21 'Thanks, but no thanks, Hazel says to LAC name,' *Mississauga News*, 24 July 1994.

22 Gerry Timbers, 'LAC faces tough sell for next 25 years,' *Mississauga News*, 29 May 1996.

23 John Stewart, 'LAC aspires to grassroots operation,' *Mississauga News*, 29 January 1988.

24 For a listing of courses and fees, see the Living Arts Centre's website, www.livingarts.on.ca.

25 Jim Murray, the perennial emcee for the Mayor's Gala, insists that plans are now afoot to create a more professional and standardized disbursement procedure (interview with author, 22 June 2004).

26 Jan Dean, 'Mayor gives $415,000 to save the opera,' *Mississauga News*, 8 October 2003.

27 For discussion of the opera saga, see Joseph Chin, 'Good news, bad news in LAC's budget,' *Mississauga News*, 8 December 2004; Jan Dean, 'No harmony at the opera; no response to calls,' *Mississauga News*, 14 November 2004; Chris Clay, 'Opera cancels again,' *Mississauga News*, 7 November 2004; 'Questions surround LAC opera season,' *Mississauga News*, 3 October 2004; 'Mayor defends opera payouts,' *Mississauga News*, 3 December 2003.

28 Haroon Siddiqui, 'Politicians – playing the game,' *Toronto Star* article quoted in *CRRF Perspectives* (Canadian Race Relations Foundation), Autumn/Winter 2001–2.

29 John Stewart, 'It's official – LAC is open,' *Mississauga News*, 15 October 1997.

30 McTavish, interview with author, 20 July 2004.

31 John Stewart, 'City seeks some help downtown,' *Mississauga News*, 27 August 1997.

32 This quote paraphrases McCallion's remarks in minutes, Planning and Development Committee, 3 December 2001, p. 24, Office of the City Clerk, Mississauga City Hall.

33 'Contradiction embarrasses politicians,' *Mississauga News*, 11 October 1992.

34 For a general description of the city's vision for the city centre, see, for example, Mike Funston, 'Downtown plan for Mississauga in 21st century,' *Toronto Star*, 31 May 1990.

35 Councillor Frank Dale, interview with author, 6 July 2004.

36 John Stewart, 'Plans set for city centre,' *Mississauga News*, 10 March 1996.

37 Dale, interview with author, 6 July 2004.

38 See report of Thomas J. Mokrzycki, Commissioner of Planning and Building, 11 September 2001. It was discussed at the Planning and Development Committee meeting of 1 October 2001, minutes, pp. 6–10, Office of the City Clerk, Mississauga City Hall.

39 The new Liberal government gave Mississauga a very cold shoulder. For more than a year, McCallion could not get a meeting with the new transport minister, Doug Young.

40 'Judge says Peel's nominee should be on GTAA board,' *Mississauga News*, 1 October 1999.

41 David A. Gordon, interview with author, 6 December 2002; Robert A. Caro, *The Power Broker: Robert Moses and the Fall of New York* (New York: Knopf, 1974).

42 Hazel McCallion, interview with author, 22 April 2003.

43 Councillor Carmen Corbasson, who supported the residential development, argued in an interview with the author that the municipality's economic interest was not being short-changed because there were willing residential developers but not necessarily willing industrial developers. But Mississauga has been in the path of major development of all kinds, which continued apace even during the recession of the early 1990s. The city can afford to be discriminating. Witness, for example, Mississauga's battle against Jannock Properties to ensure that a formerly industrial site near Streetsville would not be converted into residential. The city has been uncompromising with the developer. See, for example, Tom Urbaniak 'Councillors, residents concerned about Canada Brick plans,' *Streetsville/Meadowvale Booster*, 5 March 2002.

44 Prentice, interview with author, 10 February 2003.

45 Shaw, interview with author, 17 March 2003.

46 David O'Brien, interview with author, 15 February 2003.

47 Hazel McCallion, interview with author, 22 April 2003.

48 Landplan Collaborative Inc., *Mississauga Garden Park: Master Plan and Implementation Strategy*. February 2002, Ruth Konrad Collection of Canadiana, Mississauga Central Library.

49 Minutes, Retreat, 3 March 1998, 'Mississauga Garden Park' file, Box 1, David Culham papers, 2000.061, Region of Peel Archives.

50 David Gordon, interview with author, 6 December 2002.

51 Landplan Collaborative Inc., *Mississauga Garden Park: Master Plan and Implementation Strategy*, op. cit. note 48.

52 The figure was obtained from Julian Pattison, Realty Services, City of Mississauga. The improvements that the city had undertaken did not count against the municipality in setting the property value.

53 Blanchard, interview with author.

54 'No cash for bog, says Queen's Park,' *Mississauga News*, 13 July 1993.

55 John Stewart, 'Greenbelt rezoning of wetland doesn't guarantee it will be saved,' *Mississauga News*, 10 February 1993.

56 'Bog owners call for action, *Mississauga News*, 21 February 1993.

57 'Threat to bulldoze bog just a ploy,' *Mississauga News*, 6 June 1993; and John Stewart, 'Owners make veiled threat to bulldoze bog,' *Mississauga News*, 3 June 1993. See also the letter from Gerald Swinkin to Robert Johnston, Mississauga's director of realty, 10 May 1993, in 'Creditview Wetland' file, Box 2, David Culham papers, 2000.061, Region of Peel Archives.

58 See, for example, Councillor David Culham's internal memorandum to city manager David O'Brien, 3 February 1997, in 'Creditview Wetland' file, Box 2, David Culham papers, 2000.061, Region of Peel Archives.

59 David Culham to Mike Minkowski, 15 August 1998, in 'Creditview Wetland' file, Box 2, David Culham papers, Region of Peel Archives, 2000.061.

60 Jocelyn Webber, 'Creditview Wetland deserves protection,' *Mississauga News*, 30 September 1998.

61 Hazel McCallion to Mark Cranford, 25 November 1998, South Peel Nauralists Club files, Box 1, 2002.083, Region of Peel Archives.

62 See, for example, John Stewart, 'Mayor's State of the City address "music to the ears" of local business,' *Mississauga News*, 8 June 1994.

63 'City calls special meeting to discuss Sewell report,' *Mississauga News*, 2 September 1993.

64 'Bill 136 threatening local autonomy further,' *Mississauga News*, 15 June 1994.

65 John Stewart, 'Planning staff fear City's losing control to Queen's Park,' *Mississauga News*, 27 April 1994.

66 'Queen's Park intensification scheme far too excessive, city councillors complain,' *Mississauga News*, 14 January 1993.

67 Minutes, Planning and Development Committee, 13 November 1995, Office of the City Clerk, Mississauga City Hall.

68 Sandy McLean, 'Planning Department chided over revised Port Credit plan,' *Mississauga News*, 14 June 1995.

69 The author recalls O'Brien saying this on two occasions in the spring of 2001 to the Citizens' Task Force on the Future of Mississauga, on which the author served.

70 'Better life ahead in outer cities,' *Toronto Star*, 6 September 2001.

71 Wallace Immen, 'Mississauga searches for people space,' *Globe and Mail*, 29 January 2000.

72 See, for example, IBI Group and Dillon Consulting, *Toronto-Related Region Futures Study: Interim Report – Implications of Business-as-Usual Development* (Toronto: Neptis Foundation, 2002).

73 Jim Faught, interview with author, 27 July 2004.

74 Christopher Hume, 'McCallion left looking like Harris' stooge,' *Toronto Star*, 13 February 2002.

75 Minutes, Central Ontario Smart Growth Panel, 25 March 2002, Office of the Executive Director, Federation of Ontario Naturalists.

76 Minutes, Central Ontario Smart Growth Panel, 27 February 2002, Office of the Executive Director, Federation of Ontario Naturalists.

77 I was given permission to examine Faught's Smart Growth records, kept in two large boxes at the Toronto office of the Federation of Ontario Naturalists. They include minutes for the formal meetings of the task force, but not the sidebar meetings, for which minutes were not taken. The minutes and correspondence that do exist, however, give the impression that McCallion acted in a subtle fashion – and sought skilfully to mediate rather than to be overbearing, as she sometimes is at Mississauga council meetings.

78 Hazel McCallion, letter of transmittal to Municipal Affairs Minister David Young, 17 April 2003, in Central Ontario Smart Growth Panel, *Shape the Future: Final Report* (Toronto: Queen's Printer, April 2003).

79 Jim Faught, interview with author, 27 July 2004.

80 See, for example, Vanessa Lu, 'Tories get an earful over tax referendum,' *Toronto Star*, 20 August 2003. See also Royson James, 'Read between Hazel's lines,' *Toronto Star*, 27 August 2003.

81 City council's formal endorsement came in approving a report by planning commissioner Edward Sajecki dated 2 March 2004. See the agenda package for the Planning and Development Committee, 22 March 2004, Office of the City Clerk, Mississauga City Hall.

9 Missed Opportunities

1 O'Brien's comments during the 'Good Government' phase of the Toronto Computer Leasing inquiry, p. 71 of the transcript (www.torontoinquiry.com.ca/gg/index; scroll to O'Brien's testimony).

2 Madam Justice Wein's decision of 25 June 2003 in *R. v. Gyles* (Court File 60892/02) can be found at www.canlii.org.

3 Douglas Rae, *City: End of Urbanism* (New Haven: Yale University Press, 2004).

4 Paul Donoghue, interview with author, 6 August 2004.

5 Julie Tylos, 'Academic centre honours Mayor McCallion,' *The Medium*, University of Toronto at Mississauga, 8 November 2004.

6 The author was present at a community leaders' breakfast convened by McCallion to hear Kawaguchi. After his speech, she was brimming with enthusiasm and made her pledge.

7 *Healthy Mississauga 2010 Plan* (Mississauga: Healthy City Stewardship Centre, 2006).

8 John Stewart, 'Hopefuls take run at mayor,' *Mississauga News*, 4–5 November 2006.

9 Andres Duany, Elizabeth Plater-Zyberk, and Jeff Speck, *Suburban Nation* (New York: North Point Press, 2001).

10 The author was present at the Budget Committee meeting on 13 December 2004 at which this discussion took place.

11 Monteith Planning Consultants, *2004 Future Directions for Recreation and Parks, City of Mississauga,* June 2004, p. 102.

12 For statistics on the housing problem in Mississauga and Peel Region, see Jack Layton, *Homelessness: The Making and Unmaking of a Crisis* (Toronto: Penguin, 2000), pp. 89–92.

13 Layton, *Homelessness,* pp. 91–2.

14 This was section 4.2.2.3 (Planning and Building Department papers, Office of William Waite, Mississauga City Hall).

15 The recommendations can be viewed at www.region.peel.on.ca/housing/homeless/report/recom.htm.

16 Keith Ward, commissioner of housing, Paul Vezina, commissioner of social services, and Peter Graham, commissioner of health, 'Community Supports Plan to Address Homelessness in the Region of Peel,' Report to Regional Council, 1 March 2001, p. 2.

17 'Peel wants its share of new federal homeless program funds,' press release from the Commissioner of Housing, 30 March 2000 (www.region.peel.on.ca).

18 See, for example, the press release of 12 December 1997 (www.region.peel.on.ca).

19 Regional chair Emil Kolb and CAO Roger Maloney, interview with author, 18 July 2003. Kolb's office subsequently sent me a copy of this invoice, which appears just as any other invoice for monies owing.

20 Ward, interview with author, 30 June 2003.

21 McCallion, interview with author, 22 April 2003.

22 Paul Favaro, Kathleen Russell, and Elana Gray, *Understanding the Early Years: Early Childhood Develoopment in the Dixie-Bloor Community of Mississauga, Ontario* (Toronto: KSI Research International/Human Resources Deveopment Canada, 2003), available from Toronto Urban Affairs Library, Metro Hall.

23 Angela Blackburn, 'Ethnic community sees Hazel through rosey [sic] glasses' (special section entitled 'Happy Birthday, Hazel!'), *Mississauga News,* 14 February 2001.

24 Diane Francis, 'Cities fight for a fair refugee policy,' *National Post,* 15 May 2001.

25 Naveed Chaudhry, interview with author, 24 March 2003.

26 Kristin Good, *Explaining Municipal Responsiveness to Immigration: An Urban Regime Analysis of Toronto and Mississauga,* Research Paper 199 (Toronto: Centre for Urban and Community Studies, University of Toronto, January 2005), see esp. p. 19.

27 Author's observations at banquet.
28 Jim Robinson, 'Politicians ready for showdown at Peel Region,' *Mississauga News*, 15 June 1997.
29 John Stewart, 'Mississauga councillors threaten walkout after losing vote on equal tax share bid,' *Mississauga News*, 12 December 1993.
30 For a good account of the ruthless speed with which the amalgamations were brought about, and the fear they created among many municipal officials, see Andrew Sancton, *Merger Mania: The Assault on Local Government* (Montreal: McGill-Queen's University Press, 2000).
31 I was nominated by one of the councillors, Ward 3's Maja Prentice.
32 Op. cit. note 30. I gave McCallion her copy, which was observed on her desk by the *Globe and Mail's* John Barber.
33 See *Securing Our Future: Report of the Citizens' Task Force on the Future of Mississauga* (May 2002). This report is posted on the City of Mississauga's website (www.mississauga.ca). Proceed to the 'Separated City' link.
34 Author's recollection of the city council meeting on 11 May 2003.
35 See the 'Separated City' home page at www.mississauga.ca. Proceed to the 'City Hall' link and then to the 'Separated City' link.
36 'Convince us,' *Mississauga News*, 17 December 2003.
37 'Keep Mississauga part of Peel Region' (editorial), *Toronto Star*, 4 December 2003.
38 Jim Coyle, 'Hazel's giving us a splitting headache,' *Toronto Star*, 4 December 2003.
39 Mike Funston and Caroline Mallan, 'Politicians divided over an independent Mississauga,' *Toronto Star*, 3 December 2003.
40 Laurie Monsebraaten, 'Hazel could start "domino,"' *Toronto Star*, 13 December 2003.
41 Day and Day Chartered Accountants, *Financial Report to the City of Mississauga on the Transition to a Single Tier*, 2003, p. iii.
42 Ibid., p. 31.
43 The author was present at this meeting as a member of the now formally disbanded task force.
44 Day and Day, *Financial Report*, p. 30.
45 Similar results were outlined in a consultant's report commissioned by the City of Brampton. See Hemson Consulting, *Restructuring Analysis: Key Issues – Final Report*, January 2004.
46 'It's time to leave,' *Mississauga News*, 12 May 2004.
47 Ron Lenyk, interview with author, 16 August 2004.
48 'Dividing Peel costly: Report,' *Toronto Star*, 13 January 2004.
49 This was quite clear to me when I interviewed both of these officials on 14 July 2003.

50 Kolb was present at the inaugural meeting of the Mississauga city council on 1 December 2003. A significant part of McCallion's speech was devoted to stinging criticism of the region, including the dubious statement that Mississauga councillors often have to tell complaining constituents that they should instead be calling the region, even though all Mississauga councillors are also regional councillors. Kolb stood up with everyone else to give the mayor a standing ovation. In his speech, Kolb did not address any criticisms directly (author's notes and observations at inaugural meeting).

51 See, for example, 'Please lead us' (editorial) *Mississauga News*, 5 March 2004.

52 Declan Finucane, 'City tries new ploy; new plan gives greater control,' *Mississauga News*, 14 July 2004.

53 Author's notes at a meeting of task force convened by the mayor on 5 July 2004.

54 John Stewart, 'Peel plan saves city,' *Mississauga News*, 13 May 1998.

55 See, for example, Anne Golden et al., *Greater Toronto: Report of the GTA Task Force* (Toronto: Queen's Printer, 1996), p. 69.

56 Ministry of Municipal Affairs and Housing, 'Ontario government appoints facilitator for Peel Region,' press release, 7 October 2004, www.mah.gov .on.ca; proceed to 'Newsroom' link.

57 Honourable George W. Adams, *Facilitator's Report – Region of Peel* (2004), www.mah.gov.on.ca/userfiles/HTML/nts_1_22741_1.html.

58 Even if a majority of councillors are present, quorum requires that at least one councillor from each of the three municipalities be in attendance. See, for example, Joseph Chin and Declan Finucane, 'Peel fight heats up as Hazel, crew walk,' *Mississauga News*, 13 August 2004.

59 Remarks at regional council, 31 May 2007, at which meeting the author was present.

10 New Potholes and More Perilous Politics

1 'Sophomore chairman reflects,' *Mississauga News*, 7 February 1990.

2 'Bits and bites,' *Mississauga News*, 28 November 1990.

3 See, for example, 'Kirpan battle costly,' *Mississauga News*, 20 February 1991.

4 See, for example, Pierre Klein, 'Parrish has right idea, but solution is wrong' (letter to the editor), *Toronto Star*, 24 October 1991.

5 'Carolyn Parrish: What else is new?' *Mississauga News*, 5 June 1994.

6 See, for example, 'MP Parrish abdicates NATO chair,' *Mississauga News*, 2 April 2003.

7 See, for example, 'Judge wants Starrs in court,' *Mississauga News*, 26 December 2001.

8 McCallion made these remarks at a meeting of the officially disbanded Cit-

izens' Task Force on the Future of Mississauga at the Living Arts Centre on 14 June 2006.

9 Parrish made these comments at the meeting of Mississauga city council on 20 February 2007, which the author attended.

10 'Maple trees centuries old topple,' *Mississauga News*, 17 July 1998.

11 'Woman loses battle to save maple tree,' *Toronto Star*, 24 September 1998.

12 This meeting, held on 21 February 2007, was attended by the author.

13 Will Tremain, 'Parrish issues apology after McCallion joke,' *National Post*, 22 November 2007.

14 Hazel McCallion, interview with author, 17 December 2007.

15 Saeed Mirza, *Danger Ahead: The Coming Collapse of Canada's Municipal Infrastructure – A Report for the Federation of Canadian Municipalities*, November 2007.

16 McCallion, interview with author, 17 December 2007.

17 Ibid.

18 Frank Dale, interview with author, 6 July 2004.

19 Mike Funston, 'Council endorses 30-building plan,' *Toronto Star*, 10 March 2005.

20 Brenda Breault, acting commissioner of corporate services, presentation to Mississauga Budget Committee, 13 December 2004.

21 Royson James, 'Suburbs grapple with price of growth,' *Toronto Star*, 18 December 2004.

22 Allan Levine, 'Stephen Juba: The Great City Salesman,' in Levine, ed., *Your Worship: The Lives of Eight of Canada's Most Unforgettable Mayors* (Toronto: Lorimer, 1989).

23 See, for example, R.L. Schnell and P.T. Rooke, 'Queen Charlotte's Reign,' in Allan Levine, ed., *Your Worship*.

24 Eleanor Darke, *Call Me True: A Biography of True Davidson* (Toronto: Natural Heritage/Natural History, 1997).

25 Pierre Clavel and Wim Wiewel, eds., *Harold Washington and the Neighborhoods, 1983–1987* (New Brunswick, NJ: Rutgers University Press, 1991).

26 All the preceding comments generated in the visioning exercise can be found in Mississauga, *Community Engagement and Directions Report* (June 2008).

27 Author's notes at Mississauga General Committee, 11 June 2008.

28 Ibid.

11 Leadership Lessons

1 Transcript, Standing Committee on Regulations and Private Bills, Legisla-

tive Assembly of Ontario (22 November 1995), City of Mississauga Act, 1995.

2 The comments were made during a discussion on a minor piece of legislation before the Standing Committee on Regulations and Private Bills. The bill would renew existing authority enjoyed by the city to give low-income seniors minor property tax relief, by counting the relief as a loan to be registered as a lien against the property, recoverable when the property is sold. Pouliot expressed himself thus: 'I didn't know, I was not aware, not that I am a judge of character, that Hazel McCallion was the chairperson of the house of benevolence. I was all wrong, because she was in my office – I had four ministries with the previous administration, and she was in my office constantly making some presentation. In fact I once referred to the distinguished mayor as being so honestly dishonest. She didn't come bearing gifts, but when we parted she was bearing my gifts on the behalf of the province' (Transcript, Standing Committee on Regulations and Private Bills, 22 November 1995 – City of Mississauga Act, 1995).

3 Pierre Filion, *Planning in a Post-modern World: The Weight of Tradition and the Need for Innovation* (Waterloo: University of Waterloo, Faculty of Environmental Studies, 2000), p. 5.

4 James MacGregor Burns, *Leadership* (New York: Harper and Row, 1978), p. 281.

5 Archie D'Cruz, 'Hazel: In her own words,' *Confidence Bound*, June/July 2007.

6 'We do things quickly here: Hazel McCallion,' *National Post*, 8 November 2007.

7 George MacGregor Burns, *Leadership* (New York: Harper and Row, 1978).

8 Thomas S. Kuhn, *The Structure of Scientific Revolutions*, 2nd ed. (Chicago: University of Chicago Press, 1970), p. 19.

9 *Democracy in America*, chap. 15.

10 Clarence N. Stone, *Regime Politics: Governing Atlanta, 1946–1988* (Lawrence: University Press of Kansas, 1989).

11 Robert E. Lang and Jennifer B. Lefurgy, *Boomburbs: The Rise of America's Accidental Cities* (Washington: Brookings Institution Press, 2006).

12 See, for example, 'Public opposition not good enough,' *Mississauga News*, 29 April 1993.

13 Stephen Dale, 'In the path of Hurricane Hazel,' *Globe and Mail*, 5 March 1983.

14 For the best account of Robert Moses' career, see Robert Caro's magisterial *The Power Broker: Robert Moses and the Fall of New York* (New York: Knopf, 1974).

15 McCallion made this remark during the city's Budget Committee meeting

on 13 December 2004. It was noted by the author, who was in attendance. For coverage on Vaughan, see, for example, 'City councillors vote to screen calls from the news media,' *Toronto Star*, 30 March 2004; the *Toronto Star*'s 'dart' to Mayor Di Biase for blocking media access, 31 March 2004; Gail Swanson, 'Vaughan pushes to hire lobbyist,' *Toronto Star*, 15 April 2004; Gail Swanson, 'Road extension over park stalled,' 15 July 2004; Gail Swanson, 'Vaughan settles with former staffer,' *Toronto Star*, 10 August 2004; Leslie Papp, 'Politicians' club enjoys its perks,' *Toronto Star*, 25 September 2004.

16 Jim Faught, personal interview, 27 July 2004.

17 Some studies of the famous growth boundary in Portland, Oregon, in place now for more than a generation, have found that growth patterns and development behaviours within the boundary have not changed dramatically, perhaps in anticipation that the boundary would simply be extended upon being reached. See, for example, Andres Duany, Elizabeth Plater Zyberk, and Robert Alminana, *The New Civic Art: Elements of Town Planning* (New York: Rizzoli, 2003), p. 16.

18 Albina Guarnieri quoted in 'Mayor McCallion takes a licking from runway foes,' *Mississauga News*, 31 March 1993.

19 The author was chair of the Mississauga Crime Prevention Association at the time and was therefore involved in this issue.

20 Paul Rogat Loeb, *The Impossible Will Take a Little While* (New York: Basic Books, 2004).

21 There is a risk, of course, that cultivating civic engagement might actually exacerbate NIMBYism, a concern to which Hazel McCallion herself has alluded. But a more optimistic view, promoted by Robert Putnam and Amitai Etzioni among others, suggests that a culture of participation will result in traditionally disadvantaged groups having more influence and all groups articulating less simplistic critiques of problems and threats. Michael Hough, one of Canada's leading landscape architects, has catalogued some of the innovative urban projects resulting from a democratic commitment to urban revitalization – everything from urban agriculture to rooftop gardens to replacing lawn mowers with sheep in some parks. One of his case studies focuses on Mississauga, where a corporation (Petro Canada) in 1975 initiated a community-collaborative landscape-planning process to revitalize much of its 225–acre lakeshore oil refinery site. See Hough, *Cities and Natural Process* (London: Routledge, 1995), pp. 193–8.

One of the most promising current possibilities for developing and piloting mature community stewardship in Mississauga involves a unique educational property. The Peel District School Board has launched a planning process for the Britannia Farm, a two hundred-acre green space now surrounded by industrial and residential development. The former clergy reserve is under a covenant precluding private development.

22 John Stewart, 'They keep an eye on our city hall,' *Mississauga Times*, 22 March 1979; and 'Asleep' (editorial) *Mississauga Times*, 25 July 1979.

23 Larry Taylor, 'Get involved in community,' *Mississauga News*, 13 January 1982.

24 Pietro S. Nivola, *Laws of the Landscape: How Policies Shape Cities in Europe and America* (Washington: Brookings Institution Press, 1999), p. 32.

25 Jim Wilkes, 'Pierre Berton "mad as hell" about road,' *Toronto Star*, 20 September 2004.

26 Jim Maw, *History of Nashville*, n.d. (available from the Kleinburg Book Company), p. 81.

27 Hannelore Volpe, 'Town fifth most popular with new businesses,' *Stouffville Tribune*, 30 December 2004.

28 Mike Adler, 'Greenbelt plan too expensive for region,' *Stouffville Tribune*, 29 April 2004.

29 See, for example, the websites *oakvillegreen.ca* and *allanelgar.ca*.

30 Timothy J. Colton, *Big Daddy: Frederick G. Gardiner and the Building of Metropolitan Toronto* (Toronto: University of Toronto Press, 1980), p. 166.

31 Ibid., p. 114.

32 Patricia W. Hart, *Pioneering in North York: A History of the Borough* (Toronto: General Publishing, 1968), p. 258.

33 Dwight Duncan's remarks in *Hansard*, reflecting on the passing of Vernon Singer, 2 December 2003. See also Hart, *Pioneering in North York*, p. 258.

34 Margaret Daly, 'Rent controls: City wants them, province doesn't and tenants' complaints are rising,' *Toronto Star*, 26 April 1975.

35 Phinjo Gombu, 'Backroom dealers vie for Hazel's job,' *Toronto Star*, 14 May 2007.

36 George Grant, *Lament for a Nation: The Defeat of Canadian Nationalism* (Montreal: McGill-Queen's University Press, [1965], 2003), p. 97.

37 Gombu, 'Backroom dealers vie for Hazel's job.

Postscript: Writing Local Political History

1 Ben and Marjory Madill shared their memories with me in a lengthy interview on 2 August 2008. He also lent me a copy of his collection of personal and family memories, collected in a bound edition, *Family History and Memoirs of Benson A. Madill*, Vol. 1B, 1994.

2 R.G. Collingwood, *The Idea of History* (Oxford: Oxford University Press, 1946).

3 R.L. Frost to chairman F. Bean, 5 September 1979, CAO's Correspondence, 1979 bound volume, Region of Peel Archives.

4 Martha Howell and Walter Prevenier, *Reliable Sources: Introduction to Historical Methods* (Ithaca, NY: Cornell University Press, 2001), p. 3.

5 Clarence N. Stone, *Regime Politics: Governing Atlanta, 1946–88* (Lawrence: University Press of Kansas, 1989), pp. 254–5.

6 V.O. Key, *Southern Politics in State and Nation* (New York: Random House, 1949), p. 195.

7 Jim Coyle, 'Hazel's world reigns supreme,' *Toronto Star*, 17 October 2000.

8 In asserting the potential contribution of first-hand and participant observation, I am not making as emphatic an assertion as did Polybius, although the remarks of the Greek statesman and historian are duly noted. Polybius considers first-hand observation to be 'of prime importance and [to make] the greatest contribution of all to history' (*The Rise of the Roman Empire*, ed. Ian Scott Kilvert [London: Penguin, 1979], p. 448).

9 Robert Dahl, *Who Governs? Democracy and Power in an American City* (New Haven: Yale University Press, 1961).

10 Todd Swanstrom, *The Crisis of Growth Politics* (Philadelphia: Temple University Press, 1985).

Bibliography

Adams, Hon. George W. 'Facilitator's Report – Region of Peel.' Prepared for the Ontario Minister of Municipal Affairs and Housing, December 2004.

Adamson, Anthony. *The Development of a Canadian Municipality with Comments on the Assistance of Fellowship Studies*. New York: United Nations/Technical Assistance Administration, 1953.

– *Wasps in the Attic*. Mississauga: Author, 1987.

Ajzenstat, Janet, and Peter J. Smith. 'The "Tory Touch" Thesis: Bad History, Poor Political Science.' In *Crosscurrents: Contemporary Political Issues*, ed. Mark Charlton and Paul Barker. Toronto: Nelson, 2002.

Alexander, S. 'Story of a Parish: A Jubilee History of the Church of the Good Shepherd, Mount Dennis, Anglican Diocese of Toronto, 1911–1962.' Unpublished manuscript, Canadiana Collection, North York Central Library.

Aquinas, Thomas. *On Law, Morality and Politics*. Indianapolis: Hackett, 1988.

Arnell, Peter, and Ted Bickford. *Mississauga City Hall: A Canadian Competition*. New York: Rizzoli, 1984.

Bachrach, Peter, and Morton S. Baratz. 'Two Faces of Power.' *American Political Science Review* 57 (December 1962).

Bellamy, Matthew J. *Profiting the Crown: Canada's Polymer Corporation, 1942–1990*. Montreal: McGill-Queen's University Press, 2005.

Bratton, Daniel L. *Thirty-Two Short Views of Mazo de la Roche: A Biographical Essay*. Toronto: ECW Press, 1996.

Brehm, Robert. 'The City and the Neighborhoods: Was It Really a Two-Way Street?' In *Harold Washington and the Neighborhoods: Progressive City Government in Chicago, 1983–1987*, ed. Pierre Clavel and Wim Wiewel. New Brunswick, NJ: Rutgers University Press, 1991.

Bull, William Perkins. *From Macdonell to McGuigan: The History of the Growth of the Roman Catholic Church in Upper Canada*. Toronto: Perkins Bull Foundation, 1939.

– *From Strachan to Owen: How the Church of England Was Planted and Tended in British North America*. Toronto: Perkins Bull Foundation, 1937.

Burke, Edmund. *Reflections on the Revolution in France*, ed. Conor Cruise O'Brien. Harmondsworth: Penguin, [1790] 1969.

Burns, James MacGregor. *Leadership*. New York: Harper and Row, 1978.

– *Roosevelt: The Lion and the Fox*. New York: Harcourt Brace, 1956.

Canada, Department of Transport. *A New Policy Concerning a Future Management Framework for Airports in Canada*. Ottawa: Minister of Supply and Services, 1987.

Canada, Senate of Canada. Transcripts of Hearings of the Special Senate Committee on the Pearson Airport Agreements, 1995. www.parl.gc.ca/35/1/parlbus.

– *Report of the Special Senate Committee on the Pearson Airport Agreements*, December 1995.

Cannato, Vincent. *The Ungovernable City: John Lindsay and His Struggle to Save New York*. New York: Basic Books, 2001.

Caro, Robert. *The Power Broker: Robert Moses and the Fall of New York*. New York: Knopf, 1974.

Castells, Manuel. 'The Wild City.' In *The Internal Structure of the Cities: Readings on Urban Form, Growth, and Policy*, ed. Larry Bourne. 2nd ed. New York: Oxford University Press, 1982.

Caulfield, Jon. *The Tiny Perfect Mayor*. Toronto: James Lorimer, 1974.

Chipman, John George. *A Law unto Itself: How the Ontario Municipal Board Has Developed and Applied Land-Use Planning Policy*. Toronto: University of Toronto Press, 2002.

Clavel, Pierre. *The Progressive City: Planning and Participation, 1969–1984*. New Brunswick, NJ: Rutgers University Press, 1986.

Cohen, Adam, and Elizabeth Taylor. *American Pharaoh: Mayor Richard J. Daley – His Battle for Chicago and the Nation*. Boston: Little Brown, 2000.

Colton, Timothy J. *Big Daddy: Frederick G. Gardiner and the Building of Metropolitan Toronto*. Toronto: University of Toronto Press, 1980.

Cook, Dave. *Apple Blossoms and Satellite Dishes: Celebrating the Golden Jubilee of Applewood Acres*. Mississauga: Applewood Acres Residents' Association, 2004.

Cook, Terry. 'John Beverley Robinson and the Conservative Blueprint for the Upper Canadian Community.' *Ontario History* (1972).

Crawford, Pleasance, and Nicholas Holman, *Mississauga Garden Park: Basic Park Development – Cultural Resource Management Plan* (prepared for the City of Mississauga), 4 March 2003.

Crombie, David. *Regeneration: Report of the Royal Commission on the Future of the Toronto Waterfront*. Ottawa: Minister of Supply and Services, 1992.

Cruikshank, Tom, and John de Visser. *Old Toronto Houses*. Toronto: Firefly, 2003.

Crysler and Lathem (engineers and planners). *Mississauga Waterfront: A Plan for the Development of the Mississauga Waterfront Sector of the Metro Toronto Planning Area*, 1972.

Dahl, Robert A. *Who Governs? Democracy and Power in an American City*. New Haven: Yale University Press, 1961.

Dale, Stephen. *Lost in the Suburbs*. Toronto: Stoddart, 1999.

Davies, Jonathan S. 'Urban Regime Theory: A Normative-Empirical Critique.' *Journal of Urban Affairs* 24:1 (2002).

Day and Day (chartered accountants). *Financial Report to the City of Mississauga on Transition to a Single Tier*. December 2003.

Dean, William G. *Toronto Township: A Geographical Reconaissance*. Bachelor of arts thesis, University of Toronto, 1949.

DeLeon, Richard. *Left Coast City: Progressive Politics in San Franciso, 1975–1991*. Lawrence: University Press of Kansas, 1992.

Dexter, Lewis Anthony. *Elite and Specialized Interviewing*. Evanston, IL: Northwestern University Press, 1970.

Donaldson, Scott. *The Suburban Myth*. New York: Columbia University Press, 1969.

Doroszenko, Dena. 'A Family's Legacy: The Benares Farmstead.' Chap. 12 in *Mississauga: The First 10,000 Years*. Toronto: Eastendbooks/Mississauga Heritage Foundation, 2002.

Duquette, Ron (producer). *Hurricane Warning: The Life and Times of Hazel McCallion*. Mississauga: Ad-Venture Sights and Sounds, 2001.

Elkin, Stephen. *City and Regime in the American Republic*. Chicago: University of Chicago Press, 1996.

Farago, Anna. *The Patron Saint of Business Management: A New Management Style from a Wise Monk*. Toronto: Insomniac Press, 2002.

Favaro, Paul, Kathleen Russell, and Elana Gray. *Understanding the Early Years: Early Childhood Development in the Dixie-Bloor Community of Mississauga, Ontario* (Toronto KSI Research International/Human Resources Development Canada, 2003).

Federal Environmental Assessment Review Office. *Air Traffic Management in Southern Ontario: Report of the Environmental Assessment Review Panel*, November 1992.

Federation of Canadian Municipalities. 'Media Advisory – FCM: Open Letter From the Mayors of Canada's Largest Cities to Finance Minister Manley,' 13 February 2003. www2.cdn-news.com.

Feldman, Elliott J., and Jerome Milch. *The Politics of Canadian Airport Development: Lessons for Federalism*. Durham, NC: Duke University Press, 1983.

Fenno, Richard. *Senators on the Campaign Trail*. Stillwater, OK: University of Oklahoma Press, 1996.

Ferman, Barbara. *Challenging the Growth Machine: Neighborhood Politics in Chicago and Pittsburgh*. Lawrence: University Press of Kansas, 1996.

– *Governing the Ungovernable City: Political Skill, Leadership, and the Modern Mayor*. Philadelphia: Temple University Press, 1985.

Ferres, James. *The First Fifty Years: The Anglican Church of Saint Michael and All Angels, Toronto, 1907–1957*. Unpublished booklet, Canadiana Collection, North York Central Library.

Filby, James. *Credit Valley Railway – The Third Giant – A History*. Erin, ON: Boston Mills Press, 1974.

Foran, Max. 'Practising More than Preaching: Grant MacEwan and Calgary Civic Politics.' In *Your Worship: The Lives of Eight of Canada's Most Unforgettable Mayors*, ed. Allan Levine. Toronto: Lorimer, 1989.

Fram, Mark. *Well-Preserved: The Ontario Heritage Foundation's Manual of Principles and Practice for Architectural Conservation*. 3rd rev. ed. Erin, ON: Boston Mills Press, 2003.

Francis, Diane. 'Cities fight for a fair refugee policy.' *National Post*, 15 May 2001.

Franks, C.E.S. *The Parliament of Canada*. Toronto: University of Toronto Press, 1987.

Frisken, Frances, and Marcia Wallace. *The Response of the Municipal Public Service Sector to the Challenge of Immigrant Settlement*, October 2000 (rev. May 2002).

Fuchs, Ester R. *Mayors and Money: Fiscal Policy in Chicago and New York*. Chicago: University of Chicago Press, 1992.

Gagan, David. *Hopeful Travellers: Families, Land, and Social Change in mid-Victorian Peel County, Canada West*. Toronto: University of Toronto Press, 1981.

Garreau, Joel. *Edge City: Life and Times on the New Frontier*. New York: Doubleday, 1991.

George, Alexander L., and Juliet George. *Woodrow Wilson and Colonel House: A Personality Study*. New York: Dover, 1964.

Gibson, Eric. *Mississauga Moments: An Anthology of Local Fact, Fiction, Legend*. Mississauga: Onaway Associates, 1999.

Giuliani, Rudolph W. *Leadership*. New York: Hyperion, 2002.

Golden, Anne, et al. *Greater Toronto: Report of the GTA Task Force*. Toronto: Queen's Printer, January 1996.

Good, Kristin. *Explaining Municipal Responsiveness to Immigration: An Urban Regime Analysis of Toronto and Mississauga*. Research paper 199. Toronto: University of Toronto Centre for Urban and Community Studies, January 2005.

– 'Multiculturalism in the City: A Comparative Analysis of Municipal Responsiveness to Immigration in the Greater Toronto Area (GTA) and the Greater Vancouver Regional District (Some Preliminary Findings).' Paper presented at the Annual Meeting of the Canadian Political Science Association, Winnipeg, 3–6 June 2004.

Gordon, Richard E., Katherine K. Gordon, and Max Gunther. *The Split-Level Trap*. New York: Geis, 1960.

Grange, Mr Justice Samuel G.M. *Report of the Mississauga Railway Accident Inquiry*. Ottawa: Minister of Supply and Services, December 1980.

Grant, George. 'The Battle Between Teaching and Research.' In *The George Grant Reader*, ed. William Christian and Sheila Grant. Toronto: University of Toronto Press, 1998.

– *Lament for a Nation: The Defeat of Canadian Nationalism*. Montréal: McGill-Queen's University Press, [1965], 2003.

Green, Arthur. 'Memoirs of a Business Life.' Unpublished memoirs. Mississauga, 1997.

Harris, Richard. *Unplanned Suburbs: Toronto's American Tragedy, 1900 to 1950*. Baltimore: Johns Hopkins University Press, 1996.

Hart, Patricia W. *Pioneering in North York: A History of the Borough*. Toronto: General Publishing, 1968.

Hemson Consulting. *Growth in a Maturing Community* (prepared for the City of Mississauga), 2003.

Hicks, Kathleen. *Clarkson and Its Many Corners*. Mississauga: Mississauga Library System, 2003.

– *Cooksville: Country to City*. Mississauga: Friends of the Library, 2005.

– *Meadowvale: Mills to Millennium*. Mississauga: Friends of the Library, 2004.

– *VIPs of Mississauga*. Mississauga: Mississauga Library System, 1998.

Hodge, Gerald. *Planning Canadian Communities: An Introduction to the Principles, Practice, and Participants*. 2nd ed. Scarborough: Nelson, 1991.

Holli, Melvin. *The American Mayor: The Best and Worst Big-City Leaders*. University Park, PA: Pennsylvania State University Press, 1999.

Hook, Sidney. 'The Eventful Man and the Event-Making Man,' In *Political Leadership: A Source Book*, ed. Barbara Kellerman. Pittsburgh: University of Pittsburgh Press, 1986.

– *The Hero in History: A Study in Limitation and Possibility*. Boston: Beacon Press, 1943.

Howell, Martha, and Walter Prevenier. *Reliable Sources: Introduction to Historical Methods*. Ithaca: Cornell University Press, 2001.

Hunter, Floyd. *Community Power Structure*. Chapel Hill: University of North Carolina Press, 1953.

IBI Group and Dillon Consulting. *Toronto-Related Region Futures Study: Interim*

Report – Implications of Business as Usual Development. Toronto: Neptis Foundation, 2002.

Isaacson, Walter. *Benjamin Franklin: An American Life.* New York: Simon and Schuster, 2003.

Jacobs, Jane. *Dark Age Ahead.* Toronto: Random House Canada, 2004.

– *The Death and Life of Great American Cities.* New York: Random House, 1961.

Jenkins, Roy. *Churchill: A Biography.* New York: Penguin, 2002.

Jones, Bryan D., and Lynn W. Bachelor. *The Sustaining Hand: Community Leadership and Corporate Power.* Lawrence: University Press of Kansas, 1986.

Kahn, Melvin A., and Frances J. Majors. *The Winning Ticket: Daley, the Chicago Machine, and Illinois Politics.* New York: Praeger, 1984.

Kann, Mark E. *Middle Class Radicalism in Santa Monica.* Philadelphia: Temple University Press, 1986.

Kaplan, Harold. *Reform, Planning, and City Politics: Montreal, Winnipeg, Toronto.* Toronto: University of Toronto Press, 1982.

Keats, John. *The Crack in the Picture Window.* Boston: Houghton-Mifflin, 1956.

Kennedy, Thomas L. *Tom Kennedy's Story as Told to Ralph Hyman* (series of articles). Toronto: *Globe and Mail*, 1960.

Kessner, Thomas. *Fiorello H. La Guardia and the Making of Modern New York.* New York: McGraw-Hill, 1989.

Key, V.O. *Southern Politics in State and Nation.* New York: Random House, 1949.

Kilbourn, William. 'Reflections of a City Hall Clubman.' In *Hall: the Year of the Opposition,* ed. John Sewell et al. Toronto: Hakkert, 1971.

King, Gary, Robert O. Keohane, and Sidney Verba. *Designing Social Inquiry: Scientific Inference in Qualitative Research.* Princeton: Princeton University Press, 1994.

Kuhn, Thomas S. *The Structure of Scientific Revolutions.* 2nd ed. Chicago: University of Chicago Press, 1970.

Kunstler, James Howard. *The Geography of Nowhere: The Rise and Decline of America's Man-Made Landscape.* New York: Simon and Schuster, 1994.

Landplan Collaborative Inc. *Mississauga Garden Park: Master Plan and Implementation Strategy,* February 2002. Ruth Konrad Collection of Canadiana, Mississauga Central Library.

Layton, Jack. *Homelessness: The Making and Unmaking of a Crisis.* Toronto: Penguin, 2000.

Levine, Allan. 'Stephen Juba: The Great City Salesman.' In *Your Worship: The Lives of Eight of Canada's Most Unforgettable Mayors,* ed. Levine, Toronto: Lorimer, 1989.

Lewis, Eugene. 'The Political Leader as Entrepreneur.' In *Political Leadership: A*

Source Book, ed. Barbara Kellerman. Pittsburgh: University of Pittsburgh Press, 1986.

Lightbody, James. '"Wild Bill" Hawrelak: Let's Get Edmonton Rolling Again.' In *Your Worship: The Lives of Eight of Canada's Most Unforgettable Mayors*, ed. Allan Levine. Toronto: Lorimer, 1989.

Linteau, Paul-André. *Histoire de Montréal depuis la Confédération*. Montreal: Boreal, 1992.

Lo, Lucia. 'The Great Malls: Mississauga's Chinese Community.' In *Mississauga: The First 10,000 Years*, ed. Frank Dieterman. Mississauga: Mississauga Heritage Foundation, 2002.

Loeb, Paul Rogat. *The Impossible Will Take a Little While*. New York: Basic Books, 2004.

Longstreth, Richard. *City Center to Regional Mall: Architecture, the Automobile, and Retailing in Los Angeles, 1920–1950*. Cambridge, MA: MIT Press, 1997.

Lorimer, James. *The Developers*. Toronto: Lorimer, 1978.

Lorinc, John. 'The Story of Sprawl.' *Toronto Life*, May 2001.

Lorne Park Estates Historical Committee. *A Village within a City: The Story of Lorne Park Estates*. Cheltenham, ON: Boston Mills Press, 1980.

Lundy, M.D. *Memories of Early Days in Streetsville*. Streetsville, ON: *Streetsville Review*, 1957.

Machiavelli, Niccolo. *The Prince*. Ed. Harvey Mansfield. Chicago: University of Chicago Press, [1514] 1985.

MacInnis, Grace. *J.S. Woodsworth: A Man to Remember*. Toronto: Macmillan, 1953.

Macwhirter, Margaret Grant. *Treasure Trove in Gaspé and the Baie des Chaleurs*. Quebec: Telegraph Printing Company, 1919.

Macy, Paul Griswold, ed. *The Report of the Second World Conference of Christian Youth – Oslo, Norway – July 22 to 31, 1947*. Geneva: World Christian Congress, 1947.

Magnusson, Warren. 'The local state in Canada: Theoretical perspectives.' *Canadian Public Administration* 28:4 (Winter 1985).

Mancuso, Maureen et al. 'Preface.' In *Leaders and Leadership in Canada*, ed. Mancuso et al. Don Mills: Oxford University Press, 1994.

Manning, Mary E. *Street: The Man, The Family, The Village*. Mississauga: Streetsville Historical Society, 1996.

Manthorpe, Jonathan. *The Power and the Tories: Ontario Politics, 1943 to the Present*. Toronto: Macmillan, 1974.

Mattingly, Paul H. *Suburban Landscapes: Culture and Politics in a New York Metropolitan Community*. Baltimore: Johns Hopkins University Press, 2001.

Maxwell, John C. *The 21 Irrefutable Laws of Leadership*. New York: Nelson Books, 1998.

McCallion, Hazel. 'Needed: A New Deal.' *Mississauga Board of Trade Business Bulletin*, January 2003.

McIlwraith, Thomas F. *Looking for Old Ontario: Two Centuries of Landscape Change.* Toronto: University of Toronto Press, 1997.

McLaughlin, S.B. *40 Million Places to Stand: A Development Policy for Ontario.* Mississauga: S.B. McLaughlin, 1975.

– *100 Million Canadians: A Development Policy for Canada.* Mississauga: McLaughlin Planning and Research Institute, 1973.

Mississauga, City of. Community Services. *Vision 2020: A Draft Plan for the Mississauga Waterfront*, 1990.

Mississauga, City of. Planning and Building Department. *The Evolution of a City: Report to the Mayor and Members of Council*, February 2004.

– *Report on Participation, Draft City Plan*, 1994.

Mississauga, City of. Public Participation Office. *City Plan: Official Plan of the City of Mississauga*, 1997.

– *Interim Report on Public Participation in the Preparation of the Official Plan*, January 1976. Ruth Konrad Collection of Canadiana, Mississauga Central Library.

– *Mississauga Plan: Official Plan of the City of Mississauga*, 2003.

– *Official Plan of the City of Mississauga*, 1981.

Mississauga, City of. *Operating and Capital Budgets*, 1994–2004.

– *Running the GTA Like a Business: Report to the GTA Task Force*, July 1995.

Mississauga, City of, with Hough, Stansbury and Woodland Limited. *Port Credit Harbour Study and Waterfront Concept*, 1987.

Mississauga Sports Complex Foundation. *A Preliminary Concept for the Development of a Major Sports and Recreational Complex for the Residents of the City of Mississauga*, 1977. Ruth Konrad Collection of Canadiana, Mississauga Central Library.

Moe, Richard, and Carter Wilkie. *Changing Places: Rebuilding Community in the Age of Sprawl.* New York: Henry Holt, 1997.

Molotch, Harvey. 'The City as Growth Machine: Toward a Political Economy of Place.' *American Journal of Sociology* 82:2 (1976).

Morrison, Clarke. *The Growth of a City: Mississauga, 1930–1974.* Mississauga: Mississauga Judicial Inquiry, 1975.

Nelles, H.V. *The Politics of Development: Forests, Mines & Hydro-Electric Power in Ontario, 1849–1941.* Toronto: Macmillan, 1974.

Neustadt, Richard E. *Presidential Power and the Modern Presidents: The Politics of Leadership from Roosevelt to Reagan.* New York: Macmillan, 1990.

Nivola, Pietro S. *Laws of the Landscape: How Policies Shape Cities in Europe and America.* Washington: Brookings Institution Press, 1999.

O'Brien, David S. 'Testimony to the Toronto Computer-Leasing Judicial Inquiry,' 29 January 2004. www.torontoinquiry.com.

Ontario. Metropolitan Toronto and Region Transportation Study. *Choices for a Growing Region – A Study of the Emerging Development Pattern and Its Comparison with Alternative Concepts: Final Report No. 2.* Toronto: Queen's Printer, 1966.

– Department of Municipal Affairs. *Design for Development: The Toronto-Centred Region.* Toronto: Queen's Printer, 1970.

– Legislative Assembly. *Hansard,* June 1973 and 2 December 2003.

– Ministry of the Treasury, Economics and Intergovernmental Affairs. *The Parkway Belt West Plan: Multi-Purpose Utility Corridor, Urban Separator and Linked Open Space.* Toronto: Queen's Printer, 1978.

'Ontario Securities Commission v. McLaughlin.' *Ontario Reports* 38 O.R. (2d), 1983, pp. 390–403.

Ontario Water Resources Commission. *Report on Water Resources Survey, County of Peel,* May 1963. Engineering Library, University of Toronto.

Oraclepoll Research Limited. *Environmental Issues in Mississauga* (prepared for Ecosource Mississauga), March 2003.

Orr, Marion E., and Gerry Stoker. 'Urban Regimes and Leadership in Detroit.' *Urban Affairs Quarterly* 30:1 (September 1994).

Peat, Marwick and Partners. *Mississauga Urban Development and Transportation Study,* 1975. Toronto Urban Affairs Library, Metro Hall.

Peel, Region of. *Community Supports Plan to Address Homelessness in the Region of Peel: Report to Regional Council,* March 2001.

Peterson, Paul. *City Limits.* Chicago: University of Chicago Press, 1981.

Plato. 'The Philosopher King.' In *Political Leadership: A Source Book,* ed. Barbara Kellerman. Pittsburgh: University of Pittsburgh Press, 1986.

Plutarch. *Greek Lives.* Trans. Robin Waterfield. Oxford: Oxford University Press, 1998.

Polybius. *The Rise of the Roman Empire.* Trans. Ian Scott-Kilvert. London: Penguin, 1979.

Pressman, Jeffrey L. 'Preconditions of Mayoral Leadership.' *American Political Science Review* 66 (1972).

Preston, Valerie. 'A Community Enriched: Moving to Mississauga.' In *Mississauga: The First 10,000 Years,* ed. Frank Dieterman. Mississauga: Mississauga Heritage Foundation, 2002.

Price, Hugh Douglas. 'Review of *Who Governs?*' *Yale Law Journal* 71 (1962).

Putnam, Robert D. *Bowling Alone: The Collapse and Revival of American Community.* New York: Simon and Schuster, 2000.

– *Making Democracy Work: Civic Traditions in Modern Italy.* Princeton, NJ: Princeton University Press, 1993.

Rae, Douglas W. *City: The End of Urbanism*. New Haven: Yale University Press, 2003.

Raible, Chris. *Muddy York Mud: Scandal and Scurrility in Upper Canada*. Creemore, ON: Curiosity House, 2002.

Rakove, Milton. *Don't Make No Waves – Don't Back No Losers: An Insider's Analysis of the Daley Machine*. Bloomington: Indiana University Press, 1975.

Ricard, François. *Gabrielle Roy: Une vie*. Montreal: Boréal, 1996.

Riendeau, Roger E. *Mississauga: An Illustrated History*. Northridge, CA: Windsor, 1985.

Riordon, William L. *Plunkitt of Tammany Hall: A Series of Very Plain Talks on Very Practical Politics* (ed. Terrence J. McDonald). New York: St. Martin's, 1994.

Robinson, C.W. *Life of Sir John Beverley Robinson*. London: William Blackwood and Sons, 1904.

Robinson, John Beverley. *Canada and the Canada Bill: An Examination of the Proposed Measure for the Future Government of Canada*. London: J. Hatchard and Son, 1840.

Rohmer, Richard. *E.P. Taylor – The Biography of Edward Plunket Taylor*. Toronto: McClelland and Stewart, 1978.

Rolston, Bruce. 'Centre levy passes.' *The Bulletin* (University of Toronto). 8 December 1997.

Rooke, P.T., and R.L. Schnell. *No Bleeding Heart: Charlotte Whitton – A Feminist on the Right*. Vancouver: University of British Columbia Press, 1987.

Rousseau, Jean-Jacques. *On the Social Contract* (ed. Roger D. Masters). New York: St. Martin, 1978.

Roy, Gabrielle. *Le temps qui m'a manqué*. Montreal: Boréal, 1997.

Rubin, Herbert, and Irene Rubin. *Qualitative Interviewing: The Art of Hearing Data*. Thousand Oaks, CA: Sage, 1995.

Rybczynski, Witold. *The Look of Architecture*. New York: Oxford University Press, 2001.

Sancton, Andrew. 'Downtown Revitalization in London, Ontario: Implementing the City's Economic Interest or the Product of an Urban Regime?' Paper presented at the Annual Conference of the Canadian Political Science Association, 8 June 1993.

– 'Mayors as Political Leaders.' In *Leaders and Leadership in Canada*, ed. Maureen Mancuso et al. Don Mills, ON: Oxford University Press, 1994.

– *Merger Mania: The Assault on Local Government*. Montreal: McGill-Queen's University Press, 2000.

Seeley, John R., et al. *Crestwood Heights: A Study of the Culture of Suburban Life*. Toronto: University of Toronto Press, 1956.

Sewell, John. *Up Against City Hall*. Toronto: Hakkert, 1972.

– *Houses and Homes: Housing for Canadians.* Toronto: James Lorimer, 1994.
– *Mackenzie: A Political Biography of William Lyon Mackenzie.* Toronto: James Lorimer, 2002.
Shakespeare, William. *The Tragedy of King Richard III* (ed. John Jowett). Oxford: Oxford University Press, 2000.
Shively, W. Phillips. *The Craft of Political Research.* 4th ed. Upper Saddle River, NJ: Prentice Hall, 1998.
Skeoch, Alan. *Mississauga: Where the River Speaks.* Mississauga: Mississauga Library System, 2000.
Skocpol, Theda. *Boomerang: Clinton's Health Security Effort and the Turn against Government in United States Politics.* New York: W.W. Norton, 1986.
Slack, Enid. *Municipal Finance and Governance in the Greater Toronto Area: Can the GTA Meet the Challenges of the 21st Century?* Toronto: Neptis Foundation, January 2000.
Smith, Donald B. *Sacred Feathers: The Reverend Peter Jones (Kahkewaquonaby) and the Mississauga Indians.* Lincoln: University of Nebraska Press, 1987.
Somers, David, et al. *Painted in Peel: The Peel Landscape by the Group of Seven and their Contemporaries.* Brampton, ON: Peel Heritage Complex, 2004.
Stamp, Robert M. *Riding the Radials: Toronto's Electric Streetcar Lines.* Erin, ON: Boston Mills Press, 1989.
Statistics Canada. *Census Tract Bulletin – Toronto, 1971 Census of Canada.*
– *Census of Canada* – Community Profiles, 2001. Available at www.statscan.ca.
Stoker, Gerry. 'Regime Theory and Urban Politics.' In *Theories of Urban Politics,* ed. David Judge et al. London: Sage, 1995.
Stone, Clarence N. *Regime Politics: Governing Atlanta, 1946–1988.* Lawrence: University Press of Kansas, 1989.
– 'Regime Politics and the Capacity to Govern.' *Journal of Urban Affairs* 15:1 (1993).
– 'Political Leadership in Urban Politics.' In *Theories of Urban Politics,* ed. David Judge et al. London: Sage, 1995.
Svara, James H. 'Notes on Forms of Local Government.' In *Facilitative Leadership in Local Government,* ed. James Svara. San Francisco: Jossey-Bass, 1994.
– 'Redefining Leadership in Local Government: The Facilitative Model.' In *Facilitative Leadership in Local Government,* ed. James Svara. San Francisco: Jossey-Bass, 1994.
Swanstrom, Todd C. *The Crisis of Growth of Politics.* Philadelphia: Temple University Press, 1985.
Teaford, Jon C. *Post Suburbia: Government and Politics in the Edge Cities.* Baltimore: Johns Hopkins University Press, 1996.
Teixeira, Carlos. 'A Village of Dream Homes: The Portuguese in Mississauga.'

In *Mississauga: The First 10,000 Years*, ed. Frank Dieterman. Mississauga: Mississauga Heritage Foundation 2002.

Tindal, C. Richard, and Susan Nobes Tindal. *Local Government in Canada*. 5th ed. Scarborough, ON: Nelson, 2000.

Tocqueville, Alexis de. *Democracy in America* (ed. Harvey Mansfield and Debra Winthop). Chicago: University of Chicago Press, 2000.

Toronto, Township of. Planning Board. *Industrial Development Strategy*. Toronto Urban Affairs Library, Metro Hall, 1958.

– *The Cinderella Township* (film narrated by Joel Aldred). Toronto: 1958. Ruth Konrad Collection of Canadiana, Mississauga Central Library.

Tung, Anthony M. *Preserving the World's Great Cities: The Destruction and Renewal of the Historic Metropolis*. New York: Three Rivers Press, 2001.

Urbaniak, Tom. *Farewell, Town of Streetsville: The Year before Amalgamation*. Belleville, ON: Epic, 2002.

Valentich, Mary. 'A Striking Imbalance: Croatian Women in Cooksville.' In *Mississauga: The First 10,000 Years*, ed. Frank Dieterman. Mississauga: Mississauga Heritage Foundation, 2002.

Van Evera, Stephen. *Causes of War: Power and the Roots of Conflict*. Ithaca, NY: Cornell University Press, 1999.

Waisberg, Mr. Justice Harry. *Report of the Royal Commission on Certain Sectors of the Building Industry*. Toronto: Queen's Printer, 1973.

Weber, Max. *The Theory of Economic and Social Organization* (ed. A.M. Henderson and Talcott Parsons). Glencoe, IL: Free Press, 1947.

Wegemer, Gerald. *Thomas More on Statesmanship*. Washington, DC: Catholic University of America Press, 1996.

Weyeneth, Robert R. *Historic Preservation for a Living City: Historic Charleston Foundation, 1947–1997*. Columbia, SC: University of South Carolina Press, 2000.

Wildavsky, Aaron. *Leadership in a Small Town*. Totawa, NJ: Bedminster, 1964.

Wilson, James Q. 'Mayors vs. the Cities.' *Public Interest* 16 (Summer 1969).

Wilson, Woodrow. 'Leaders of Men.' In *Political Leadership: A Source Book*, ed. Barbara Kellerman. Pittsburgh: University of Pittsburgh Press, 1986.

Webber, Jocelyn M. *The Vascular Plant Flora of Peel County, Ontario*. Toronto: Botany Press, 1984.

Weeks, Verna Mae. *Cooksville: Village of the Past*. Mississauga: Verna Mae Weeks, 1996.

Wells, Jennifer. 'Her Town, Her Rules.' *Toronto Life*, May 2000.

Whyte, William H. *The Organization Man*. New York: Doubleday, 1956.

Wolman, Harold. 'Local Government Institutions and Democratic Governance.' In *Theories of Urban Politics*, ed. David Judge et al. London: Sage, 1995.

Wolpert, Stanley. *Gandhi's Passion: The Life and Legacy of Mahatma Gandhi*. New York: Oxford University Press, 2001.

Wylie-Kellerman, William. 'Naming the Powers: William Stringfellow as Student and Theologian.' *Student World* (2003/1).

Yates, Douglas. *The Ungovernable City*. Cambridge, MA: MIT Press, 1977.

Zeidler Staples (planning consultants). *Mississauga City Centre: Summary Report*, 1975. Ruth Konrad Collection of Canadiana, Mississauga Central Library.

Acknowledgments

This project relied heavily on the assistance and goodwill of many people. I am grateful to the staff of the Region of Peel Archives, especially Diane Kuster, Brian Gilchrist, and David Farrell. At the Mississauga Central Library's Ruth Konrad Collection, Dorothy Kew, Marian Kutarna, and Liz McQuaiq were willing to go beyond the call of duty, as were Matthew Wilkinson of the Mississauga Heritage Foundation and Tracy Oliveira and Stephanie Meeuwse in the Museums of Mississauga. The staff in the Mississauga Clerk's Office and the Planning and Development Department, as well as the Archives of Ontario, Library and Archives Canada, the General Synod Archives of the Anglican Church of Canada, and the Archives of the Anglican Diocese of Quebec, were likewise very welcoming and professional.

My interviewees were most generous with their time and, in some cases, with the access they granted to personal documents. The numerous other public officials and community volunteers, as well as Journeaux family members gathered in Port-Daniel, Quebec, during the summer of 2006, who guided me to prospective interviewees or potentially useful information, or who were willing to engage in informal exchanges about my research, likewise deserve acknowledgment. Cartographer Marie Puddister provided invaluable assistance with the creation of accurate maps based on complex and assorted records.

Significant parts of the research for my doctoral thesis, *Beyond Regime Theory: Mayoral Leadership, Suburban Development, and the Politics of Mississauga, Ontario*, were critical to this project. The 2001–2004 doctoral fellowship of the Social Sciences and Humanities Research Council of Canada sustained me during that work, leading to my defence in 2005. My thesis committee at the University of Western Ontario, consisting of professors Carol Agocs, Martin Westmacott, and Andrew Sancton, provided thorough and expeditious feedback. Andrew Sancton, as my principal supervisor, endured many meetings with patience and good humour, and reviewed chapter drafts and fragments in various states of preparation. His calm input and reflective questioning sharpened my thinking. Examiners William Code, Martin Horak, and David Siegel were helpful with their comments and encouraged me to write this book.

The anonymous reviewers for University of Toronto Press made detailed suggestions. Lionel Feldman and John Sewell provided constructive criticism of an earlier version that still seemed too much like a thesis. Virgil Duff, Daniel Quinlan, Anne Laughlin, and their colleagues at University of Toronto Press were models of efficiency and professional support. Copy editor Terry Teskey deserves much praise for a sharp eye and incisive queries.

My colleagues in the Political Science Department of Cape Breton University have given me constant encouragement and a work environment that simply could not be better for a young academic wishing to explore ideas, subdisciplines, and interdisciplinary opportunities. I thank them all: Lee-Anne Broadhead, Terry Gibbs, James Guy, Brian Howe, David Johnson, Garry Leech, and Andrew Molloy.

I acknowledge my parents, Irene and Joseph Urbaniak, not only for providing me with a place to stay in Mississauga but for affirming the value of time spent on academic pursuits. Their support means a great deal.

Any errors and all deficiencies should in no way reflect on those who so kindly provided assistance or guidance, but rather on my own shortcomings.

Index